PERGAMON GENERAL PSYCHOLOGY SERIES
EDITORS
Arnold P. Goldstein, *Syracuse University*
Leonard Krasner, *SUNY at Stony Brook*

YOUTH

VIOLENCE

PROGRAMS & PROSPECTS

edited by
Steven J. Apter
Arnold P. Goldstein
Syracuse University

Sponsored by
the Begun Institute and
the Society for the Prevention of Violence
Cleveland, Ohio

PERGAMON PRESS
New York   Oxford   Toronto   Sydney   Frankfurt

Pergamon Press Offices:

U.S.A.   Pergamon Press Inc., Maxwell House, Fairview Park,
            Elmsford, New York 10523, U.S.A.

U.K.   Pergamon Press Ltd., Headington Hill Hall,
            Oxford OX3 0BW, England

CANADA   Porgamon Press Canada Ltd., Suite 104, 150 Consumers Road,
            Willowdale, Ontario M2J 1P9, Canada

AUSTRALIA   Pergamon Press (Aust.) Pty. Ltd., P.O. Box 544,
            Potts Point, NSW 2011, Australia

**FEDERAL REPUBLIC   Pergamon Press GmbH, Hammerweg 6,
OF GERMANY**   D-6242 Kronberg-Taunus, Federal Republic of Germany

BRAZIL   Pergamon Editora Ltda., Rua Eça de Queiros, 346,
            CEP 04011, São Paulo, Brazil

JAPAN   Pergamon Press Ltd., 8th Floor, Matsuoka Central Building,
            1-7-1 Nishishinjuku, Shinjuku, Tokyo 160, Japan

**PEOPLE'S REPUBLIC   Pergamon Press, Qianmen Hotel, Beijing,
OF CHINA**   People's Republic of China

First printing 1986

Library of Congress Cataloging in Publication Data
Main entry under title:

Youth violence.

   (Pergamon general psychology series ; 135)
      1. Juvenile delinquency--United States--
Prevention. 2. School violence--United States--
Prevention. 3. Violence--United States--Prevention.
I. Apter, Steven J. (Steven Jeffrey), 1945-
II. Goldstein, Arnold P. III. Series. [DNLM:
1. Crisis Intervention. 2. Juvenile Deliquency.
3. Violence--in adolescence. WS 463 Y63]
HV9104.Y686   1985   303.6'2'088055   85-12296
ISBN 0-08-031922-X

Printed in Great Britain by A. Wheaton & Co. Ltd., Exeter

To Burton Blatt, who by his energy, humanity, and enor-
mous concern about the wrongs he saw showed us the
great difference one person can make.

Steve Apter died on September 1, 1985. He was 40 years old. He was for so many of his students a wise and beloved professor; and for so many of his colleagues a creative scholar and very special friend. We all will miss him deeply, but rejoice in what we each have learned from him. He taught us by what he wrote and said; he taught us by how he lived and how he cared. His mark is upon us, and we are all very much the better for it.

A.P.G.

Contents

Preface   xi

Acknowledgments   xiii

1 Special Education for Disturbed Adolescents   1
   Frank H. Wood

2 Social Learning Treatment within Juvenile Justice: A Meta-Analysis of Impact
   in the Natural Environment   24
   Jeffrey P. Mayer
   Leah K. Gensheimer
   William S. Davidson II
   Rand Gottschalk

3 Diverting Youth from the Juvenile Justice System: A Meta-Analysis of
   Intervention Efficacy   39
   Leah K. Gensheimer
   Jeffrey P. Mayer
   Rand Gottschalk
   William S. Davidson II

4 Neurological Bases of Youth Violence   58
   Lawrence J. Lewandowski
   Barbara Forsstrom-Cohen

5 Institutional Treatment Programs for the Violent Juvenile   75
   Vicki L. Agee

6 Psychological Skill Training and the Aggressive Adolescent   89
   Arnold P. Goldstein

7 School Violence and Vandalism   120
   Berj Harootunian

8 Ecological Perspectives on Youth Violence   140
   Steven J. Apter
   Cathy A. Propper

9 Social Competence, Coping Skills, and Youth Crime: A Pragmatic and
   Theory-Based Approach   160
   Richard J. Gable

10 Television and Film Violence   178
    George Comstock

11 Programming for Juvenile Delinquents: An Administrative Perspective   219
    Barry Glick

12 Legal Perspectives on Youth Violence   237
    Richard A. Ellison

13 Cross-Cultural Perspectives on Youth Violence   262
    Lea Pulkkinen
    Marketta Saastamoinen

   Author Index   283

   Subject Index   295

   About the Editors and Contributors   299

   Pergamon General Psychology Series   302

Preface

A variety of sources have repeatedly demonstrated that adolescents contribute to violent behavior in society well beyond and highly disproportionate to their actual numbers. School violence and vandalism, aggravated assault, gang fighting, rape, murder, and other diverse forms of moderate and severe juvenile delinquency are its major expressions. Its cost—in pain, money, lost opportunity, and diminished life-style—becomes manifest in the behavior of teachers kept too busy managing their classrooms to teach, in elderly persons self-sentenced to their apartments by fear of being mugged on the street, in monies spent on a juvenile justice system better spent elsewhere, in parents who are impotent and grieving for offspring now incarcerated though so recently children, and most especially in the wasted lives of the youngsters themselves. Unequivocally, youth violence is a major social problem in Western society.

It is a problem, however, to which many disciplines have responded creatively and energetically. Research and intervention efforts directed at the causes and remediation of youth violence are currently actively being pursued, as the present book will illustrate, in education, special education, psychology, sociology, legal studies, ecology, communications, neurophysiology, and other behavioral and social sciences. The problem is immense; the response is very substantial.

In the first seven chapters of the book, a variety of perspectives on programmatic interventions with violent youth are reviewed and evaluated. In chapter 1, Frank Wood provides a comprehensive assessment of special education programs with relevance for violent youth. Chapters 2 and 3 are both written by the same team of authors (William S. Davidson II, Leah K. Gensheimer, Rand Gottschalk, and Jeffrey P. Mayer) and focus respectively on social learning programs in the juvenile justice system and on diversion programs developed in the same service delivery framework. In chapter 4, Lawrence J. Lewandowski and Barbara Forsstrom-Cohen discuss the neurological bases of youth violence, while Vicki L. Agee describes institutional treatment programs for violent juveniles in chapter 5. Finally, to conclude the first part of the book, Arnold P. Goldstein describes recent work on psychological skill training with aggressive adolescents in chapter 6 and Berj Harootunian discusses the problem of school violence and vandalism in chapter 7.

The second part of the book contains six chapters and looks somewhat more broadly at youth violence. In chapter 8, Steven J. Apter and Cathy A. Propper describe an ecological perspective on youth violence, while chapter 9 is devoted to discussion of the relationship between social competence and youth crime by Richard J. Gable. In chapter 10, George Comstock provides an analysis of the relationship between television and films and youth violence. Barry Glick discusses an administrator's perspective on programming for violent youth in chapter 11, while Richard A. Ellison describes legal perspectives on youth violence in chapter 12. Finally, Lea Pulkkinen and Marketta Saastamoinen focus on cross-cultural perspectives on youth violence in chapter 13.

Acknowledgments

Joe and Ruth Begun brought to this book both financial support and their spirit of concern about youth violence and its remediation. Their aid has served us well, and well deserves our appreciation. To Diane Apter and Lenore Goldstein, interested professionals themselves, we owe thanks for feedback given, encouragement offered, and assistance provided. Connie Salvetti, our very talented secretary, helped put it all together, and did so with skill and grace. We gratefully acknowledge her effort.

1

Special Education for Disturbed Adolescents

Frank H. Wood

PROBLEM AND KNOWLEDGE BASE

Disturbed Behavior and the School

Does the school cause some students to become seriously enough disturbed to require special education, or, are some students intrinsically disturbed? With human behavior being complex in both causation and in interpretation, the most truthful simple answer to both questions is a qualified yes. Further discussion of the appropriate qualifications can be found elsewhere (Goldstein, Apter, & Harootunian, 1983, pp. 201–204). Disturbed behavior in schools is disturbance in a social system to which all of the actors in that social system, especially students, teachers, and administrators, contribute. There are differences in the effective social power of these actors (Wood, 1981), and the disturbance is often viewed as centering in those who are weakest, the students. When conflicts over needs and expectations arise, those of teachers and administrators take priority. Most special education programs are structured to achieve goals set by these dominant actors, teachers and administrators. But social roles assign them heavy responsibility for the well-being of students. Thus, they must structure the system so that the needs of all are being met—at least to some extent.

As already suggested, no complex social system will be free of "disturbance." Some disturbance in schools is to be expected, and the author professes an innate skepticism about any claims that it can be eliminated. The real issue is how to manage school disturbance while a process of conflict resolution and negotiation takes place between teachers and disturbed students.

In the case of an extremely dysfunctional system, one which is failing to meet needs of a sufficiently large group of those in possession of social power, resolution of disturbance may occur through collapse of the system, permitting reorganization into a new pattern. Despite widespread criticism of the schools in our society and the existence of theoretically sound alternatives, such as reliance on informal instruction or apprenticeship systems for the transmission of knowledge and skills, few seem ready to call for their dissolution. Instead, disturbance within the schools leads to efforts at modification or reform focusing on changes in expectations and attitudes of the actors supplemented by extrusion of individuals, usually students, regarded as foci of disturbance by those in possession of power. The extrusions temporarily release part of the tension that has accumulated within the system while the slow work of changing attitudes and expectations take place. While some of the changes that are negotiated within the system increase the school's capacity for accommodating "disturbers" of the system, others do not. Thus, to the extent that it has been effectively implemented, the "least restrictive environment" concept of Public Law 94–142 caused schools to increase their ability to meet the needs of students with defined disabilities in the regular classroom, but more recent changes such as requirements that candidates for regular diplomas pass minimum competency examinations have the effect of placing some of these students in a "handicapped" category, albeit for different reasons. Concern to adapt the system to provide a better fit for students who do not slip easily into the standard student role is temporarily forgotten when calls for raising the quality of education by raising standards become louder.

The belief of Americans that 10 to 12 years of "education" in a "school" is both a right and an obligation is inscribed in a series of laws and court decisions. The current issue is the extent to which disruptive student behavior can be countered by limiting exercise of that right. Recently, legislatures and courts are attempting to create rules to guide the decision makers who decide the conditions under which a student considered to be major disturber may be extruded from the regular system. The continuum of restrictions (special interventions) ranges from support assistance to the teacher while the target student remains in the regular classroom through resource or special class instruction to suspension, residential placement, or expulsion, the so-called "cascade" of options (Deno, 1970). While, on the one hand, some school systems have begun to codify lists of infractions for which the most extreme extrusion procedures, suspension and expulsion, are "required," the courts have tended to rule that placement in an alternative program of "special" education appropriate to the student's needs is the most severe action that may be taken if a student has been declared eligible because of special needs (Craft & Haussman, 1983).

The Nature of "Special" or "Alternative" Education

Special education is in some sense a "pocket" into which disturbers of the system may be slipped when they cannot be extruded completely from the system. Being placed in this pocket may not be in the best interests of the student, no matter how much those administering the regular system feel they have benefited by the student's departure. Although special programs were originally intended to be positive alternatives to the regular program, as the number of students assigned to alternative or adjunct special education programs increased in the 1950s and 1960s, criticism began to be heard (Dunn, 1968). This criticism culminated in the call to return mildly handicapped students to the mainstream (Madden & Slavin, 1983).

The critics do not question the good intentions of those who designed special education programs. "Special" and "alternative" are not intended by educators to be euphemisms, and the critics have not sought an end to special education programs. The criticism is intended to encourage a fairer balance between the desire of those responsible for managing the regular education system to be freed to primary responsibility for students seen as foci of disturbance in the regular system and the right of those students to the closest approximation to a nonsegregated school experience that is still appropriate. The problem of achieving an equitable compromise is particularly acute in the case of student to whom the most negative of labels, "emotionally disturbed" (Tringo, 1970) is applied. More likely than not, application of this label exposes the student to removal from the regular program to a more restrictive placement. In Minnesota, in 1982, a student labeled "emotionally disturbed" was five times more likely than a student labeled "learning disabled" to be in a segregated special class most of the day. Unnecessarily restrictive placements for disturbed youth are made more likely by the anger that becomes focused on them during the process of identification and labeling (Wood, 1981). This continues in spite of the legal guarantees of rights previously mentioned. The author shares the view expressed by Kauffman (1982):

> Can the right of all disturbed children to special education be assured by government decree? My belief is that that right can not be guaranteed and that attempts to guarantee it are and will invariably be sham . . . . current policy does not assure all disturbed children an appropriate education. (p. 1)

This is not the best of all possible worlds, and those in positions of power in schools sometimes use that power to deny the rights of disturbing, disturbed youth to a free, appropriate public education. However, few programs are deliberately planned to be abusive, and despite their flaws, the better programs which will be discussed later represent good faith compromises balancing student needs against those of teachers and administrators.

Research on the Characteristics and Efficacy of Special Programs

To help us in our efforts to improve the quality of educational programming, we periodically undertake a general review of the literature, gathering together the available written descriptions and evaluations of special and alternative programs and summarizing their findings. Usually, we also apply an announced standard of methodological soundness to the descriptions of the programs reviewed. Recent studies of this type include those of Nelson and Kauffman (1977), Topping (1983), and Grosenick and Huntze (1983). The latter was the most extensive and systematic of recent efforts to summarize this literature. Because their conclusions about the state of knowledge in this field were strongly negative, tending to cast in doubt any recommendations that might be based upon it, it seems important to describe both their process and conclusions in some detail.

Grosenick and Huntze's original search of the literature for reports on programs for emotionally disturbed, behaviorally disordered children and youth published from 1960 through 1983 yielded 703 possible references. Screening by the authors reduced the total number of studies to 457, of which 365 were located for further study. The 365 program descriptions and evaluations were reviewed to determine whether or not they met the eight criteria chosen by the reviewers to differentiate "programs" from the less complete descriptions of "strategies" or "techniques." Their eight criteria for a well-conceptualized program description, developed from those suggested by McCauley (1977), will be given as stated, because, in addition to being important in Grosenick and Huntze's selection process, they should be useful to others interested in preparing adequate descriptions and evaluations of the programs with which they are familiar. Grosenick and Huntze's (1983, pp. 3–4) criteria are as follows:

1. *Philosophy or Ideational Context.* A program for behaviorally disordered children and youth should have a well-articulated conceptual, philosophical and/or theoretical base which includes

a definition of disturbance, a description of population needs and a rationale for the program which is expressed in statements of belief, assumptions and/or principles.

2. *Program Goals*. Program goals should include general aims and purposes of the program with specific, measurable objectives of that program (objectives for the clients are not a substitute). The goals should be consistent with the realities, that is, with the philosophical perspective, the methods selected, the population served and the environmental setting.

3. *Population Definition*. This program element includes a delineation of student characteristics and needs, eligibility issues, and the program/child match considerations.

4. *Program Entry*. A program for behaviorally disordered children and youth should: (a) establish referral procedures (including referring persons or agencies, referral priorities, specification of referral steps, persons in the intake process and data to be included); (b) establish identification procedures (including methods, persons involved and steps in the sequence); and (c) adequately address due process issures (including parental involvement, child rights data access, independent evaluations, negotiation of objectives and plans and the right to counsel).

5. *Methods, Curriculum and Materials*. In addition to establishing parameters of the methods, curriculum, and materials, a program should describe those choices clearly, indicate their relationship to the program as a whole, delineate the role of the service provider within them, and organize them in such a manner that personnel can operate cohesively.

6. *Exit Procedures*. This element of a well-conceptualized program includes a delineation of (a) criteria for success, (b) the steps in the exit process, (c) the persons who make exit decisions, and (d) follow-up and tracking procedures.

7. *Evaluation*. Included here are evaluation of program components, evaluation of child progress, and delineation of the method for utilization of evaluation results for program change.

8. *Program Operation*. There are numerous related items that must be finalized in a complete program. These include: discussion of the physical facilities, including location and adequacy; delineation of program supervision and administrative responsibility; and consideration of financial issues, public relations efforts, replication possibilities, staffing issues, support personnel need and availability, and program size.

Among the 365 possible program descriptions reviewed, only 81 contained even minimal discussions of all eight criteria. Like Topping (1983), who cites Sindelar and Deno (1978) for further support, they apparently discovered "that the many descriptive studies often had no evaluation, but the few evaluative studies often were short on description, so the detailed nature of the program which had produced the effects specified remains something of a mystery" (p. 14).

Disappointed by the low quality of the studies thus selected for further analysis, Grosenick and Huntze decided against further synthesis and generalization from the reported findings. They concluded that while the literature provided some base for synthesizing information about possible intervention strategies, there was no base for generalizing about the conceptual frameworks on which programs were based or about program efficacy. They concluded their report by challenging the assumption that "the literature base is an ever growing repository of the wisdom of the field that is available to assist and guide us as we strive to provide services to children and youth who are handicapped by their behavior" (p. 22). Topping's (1983) reflective observation is that "special education policy has always been shaped more by politics than philosophy, and more by philosophy than evaluative evidence" (p. viii). The problem is not unique to special education. For example, Eisner (1984) offers his opinion that although "research might *influence* practice, whether it *informs* practice is quite another matter" (p. 448).

Perspective

These pessimistic conclusions serve as a *caveat emptor* to the readers of this paper. But, the author feels reasonably certain the limitations of present certain knowledge about program efficacy will not be a surprise to anyone working in the field. It is obvious that those most able to do the hard work of program description and evaluation are seldom provided either the time or the resources to do so. All of us owe a debt of gratitude to the few who take their personal time to describe briefly what they are doing and how it seems to be going for volumes like *Alternative Programs for Disruptive Youth* (Thomas, Sabatino, & Sarri, 1982). Yet, criticism of the quality of those descriptions after saying thank you is not being mean-spirited. Criticism, especially self-criticism, is necessary if we are to improve the quality of our special education response to the challenges presented by the educational needs of disruptive youth.

At the present time, what we have in the way of program description and evaluation does not justify what we are doing. Yet, we keep doing it. Why? Several plausible explanations can be adduced for the continuing creation and maintenance of programs for disruptive, disturbed youth in the absence of strong data supporting their efficacy. One of the more obvious, and cynical, draws from the concept of negative reinforcement: Behavior that results in the removal of an unpleasant person or event tends to persist or increase in frequency. This explanation may explain the support given by regular educators and administrators to the development of alternative programs. But, it is not an adequate explanation for the persistent efforts of those staffing such programs to assist their students to grow and learn. Some more positive reasons must be sought. A partial explanation in this case comes from the observation that most of the continuing programs are believed by those who staff them to be partly successful. Test-retest score comparisons, ratings, and observations often do support their beliefs that some of the students in their program are "improving," but because there is usually no basis for determining what gains might have occurred in the absence of special treatment, programs may continue even if their success rates are not larger than one might predict from the literature on spontaneous remission (see Topping, 1983, pp. 11–12), assuming, and it is a large assumption, that such rates are appropriate for the population served by these programs. The combination of relief to the regular system through removal of disruptive students and observed gains at some level by students in the alternative system serves to perpetuate special education for disturbed youth while we seek stronger support for conclusions about its effectiveness.

Having acknowledged a lack of good empirical foundation for the comments that follow, the author will be presenting selected material from program reports to fit a pattern of desirable practice based on his own experience. The program elements described are commonly found in the best of present programs. Their value as models is rooted to a large extent in the integrity of those who staff these good programs, professionals who are genuinely concerned about the youth with whom they work and are seeking to implement the best practice known to them. Until we have empirical proof that alternative procedures are superior, their recommendations are the best basis for our programs.

STUDENT NEEDS AND PROGRAM CHARACTERISTICS

Student Needs

"The general impression from this study is that teachers appear to have no trouble discriminating the problem behavior patterns of pupils identified as behaviorally disordered from those of unidentified peers" (Epstein, Cullinan, & Rosemier, 1983, p. 174). Epstein et al. based their conclusions on a comparision of teacher ratings of behaviorally disordered and normal adolescents. They echo the findings of many other researchers on problem behavior in schools. Like other recent studies (Achenbach & Edelbroch, 1978, 1979; Quay, 1977), Epstein et al. also noted that the problem behaviors described tended to cluster into two major factors, one associated with the externalizing of conflicts, perceived by others as characterized by aggressive, acting-out behavior, and the other by the internalizing of conflicts, leading to withdrawal or personality disturbances. Neither of these major clusters describes a discrete group of disturbed students, that is students showing high rates of acting-out behavior may also appear atypically withdrawn at other times.

A related body of research shows that teachers, as might be predicted from knowledge of the settings in which they work, are more disturbed by acting-out behavior than withdrawn behavior. Wickman's (1928) classic report of the differences between teacher and mental health clinician ratings of the seriousness of disturbed behavior, which shows that teachers, in contrast to mental health clinicians, rate acting-out behavior as more serious than with-drawn behavior, was used for years to arouse guilt feelings in teachers. Teachers, it was said, then and now, were insensitive to the long-range implications of inner emotional conflict. For example, Sprinthall and Sprinthall (1981) say:

> Even though educational psychologists have been trying to convince teachers to look beyond the obvious and recognize that withdrawn children may be a more serious problem than loud, active children, there is still a very strong tendency to equate activity and noise with a discipline problem and to ignore passivity. (pp. 230–231)

While this concern is well taken, later researchers have somewhat redressed the balance by pointing out that the fact teachers give a higher priority to the management of disruptive, acting-out behavior does not mean that they lack concern for the implications of social and emotional withdrawal (Algozzine, 1977; Beilin, 1959). Teachers are charged by the community with maintaining order in large groups of students so that instructional activity and learning may take place. When maintenance of order is a major challenge, as it is in many secondary classrooms, teachers may never get to their second order of priorities, which includes a concern for students who do not act out their disturbances so disruptively. Certainly, most of the programs described in the literature are designed to serve aggressive, acting-out students. Withdrawn behavior must be present in many of these students as an accompanying behavior pattern, but it is seldom in itself reason for referral or a focus for planning.

Not only are acting-out, conduct problems the predominate reason for referral of students to special education programs for the emotionally disturbed, they are also predicted by regular classroom teachers to be most characteristic of students returning from such programs. Schloss, Miller, Sedlack, and White (1983) found that teachers anticipated returning students would show, first, conduct problems, and second, personality problems. To help them manage students, they asked for ancillary support, including counseling, crisis teacher assistance, and administrative support, and assistance in developing behavioral monitoring and modification programs. Again, acting-out behavior was seen as the major challenge, and the anticipatory focus is on control of such behavior.

Probing more deeply, educators note more dynamic characteristics of the group of disturbed students referred for special education (Roth, 1977). For many, fundamental issues of trust of adults have never been resolved. They tend to be related to a strong attraction to peers and peer groups that strongly express anger and suspicion of the dominant values of the society controlled by adults. Paradoxically, progress toward establishment of a mature independent sense of self is frequently slow and uncertain (Erikson, 1968). The disturbed adolescents remain dependent while demanding independence.

Adults working with them find themselves trying to balance authoritative and nurturing behaviors. As we shall see, many educators try to structure a series of "levels" within their programs to accommodate the range of developmental needs they find in their students.

Sprinthall and Sprinthall (1981) postulated a series of four stages of cognitive, moral, and emotional growth which they related to the disciplinary procedures appropriate for each stage. In Stage I, students respond primarily to the use or threat of physical force. During Stage II, they respond to material consequences, both rewarding and punishing. Sprinthall and Sprinthall feel that these first two classes of interventions are only useful for a short time. Successful programs must move students on to Stage III, in which social group pressure is the effective means for control and promoting growth, and Stage IV, where individual decision making and responsibility for actions are characteristic.

The problem faced by educators of disturbed adolescents is that many of their students come to them with long histories of exposure to the disciplinary procedures described in Sprinthall and Sprinthall's Stages I and II, procedures whose maximum effectiveness may be long past. Yet, these students are not prepared to respond to the patterns of social control characteristic of Stages III and IV.

In addition to these conduct and personality problems, many seriously disturbed youths also have a history of failure at academic tasks. The target populations of the 16 alternative school programs described in Thomas, Sabatino, and Sarri (1982) show average to above average intelligence and widely varying achievement. McCauley and Erikson's (1982) description is typical:

> The students range from the lower 5 percentile ranks to the upper percentile ranks (90%) in reading, mathematics, language arts (spelling, writing, expression), language and speech, and general junior high school curriculum subjects. Approximately one-third of the students have been classified as learning disabled, language deficient, or educable mentally retarded in the past. (p. 42)

While behavioral needs may be the primary reason for referral for special services, academic performance differences are also prominent.

Range of Program Options

Like many other social welfare programs, special education programs were established to serve students whose needs were not being met in regular classrooms. The assumption of reform-minded educators was that students placed in special programs would show greater social and academic performance gains in their new settings than they could have achieved in their regular classroom. The movement was also accelerated by the belief that regular class teachers could instruct the remaining students more effectively after the "problem children" had been removed. As already mentioned, the assumption that special students were better served in special classes was brought into question in the 1960s and 1970s. One response has been to transform special education from a singletrack alternative program (the segregated special class) to a multitrack alternative system, conceptualized as a "cascade of services" (Deno, 1970), with options ranging from consultation provided to the regular classroom teacher through various degrees of part-time special programming to full-day or even residential special placement. The full cascade model was usually implemented first at the elementary level, partly in the belief that early intervention would lead to elimination of behavioral and emotional problems. Recently, there has been more rapid development at the secondary level.

Several factors provide impetus for the development of secondary programs. One is the "aging" of the population of the school-identified emotionally disturbed students. Some students placed in the elementary level class programs are eventually able to return full-time to regular classrooms. Others, however, continue to need at least part-time special programming. Students with a history of disturbed behavior, and those whose problems appear later, are tending to remain in school longer. Recent court decisions indicate that the right to education of a handicapped student extends to the age where a free public education is no longer guaranteed to any student or until a diploma is received, and severely circumscribe the authority of the school to suspend or expell for disturbed, disordered behavior (Craft & Haussman, 1983). Placement in private schools, especially those that are residential, has become more costly, making the local district day school program more attractive as an option to administrators.

Phoenix Union High School District's Desiderata Program, a special day-school program, opened its doors to a full enrollment of 36 students in 1978. Buck and Markson (1982) give this rationale:

> Prior to that time the Phoenix Union High School District was servicing SEH (Severely Emotionally Handicapped) students through private placement. This was proving to be quite expensive and each year tuition was being raised. It was felt by district administration and the board of education that a more cost-effective program could be created within the district as well as such a program could provide more intensive services to the student by drawing on the district resources.

> Another factor causing the district to consider creating this program was Operation Child Find. More and more students with severe emotional problems were being drawn to the district schools. Therefore, the district found itself placing increasingly more students in private programs. (p. 1)

A year later, the program was doubled in size.

Many of these programs require cooperation among several different social agencies. Students may be receiving services simultaneously from welfare, mental health, and correctional services. Coordination of such services is recognized as highly desirable, but is often difficult or nonexistent (Wood, 1982). Kennedy, Mitchell, Klerman, and Murray (1976) provide an interesting, brief account of the working through of disagreements over program eligibility, goals, and reintegration criteria in a secondary day-school program housed in a mental hospital, jointly staffed by hospital, public school, and mental health center personnel. Working agreements, once negotiated, must sometimes be altered when changes in funding and definitions of responsibility occur.

The curriculum of the traditional American high school places heavy emphasis on academic skill development. Remediation of academic skill deficiencies is, therefore, a major goal along with modification of social behavior in many programs described in the literature. However, it is a common experience for those responsible for these programs to come quickly to the conclusion that development of academic performance to a level permitting successful reintegration into regular high school classes is not a realistic goal for some of their students. In a typical account, Kennedy et al. (1976) state that "the primary goal shifted, therefore, to teaching 'survival' skills . . . . (and) the staff obtained funds for a vocational education program to provide skills and thus help students get jobs" (p. 717). Most of the programs surveyed included a strong prevocational or vocational emphasis in addition to the remediation component. The number of special education options for disturbed adolescents has grown rapidly during the past few years. Consultation and resource programs that aim to expand the accommodating power of the regular program have increased at the same time new day-school programs have been developed. It is hoped that fewer students than in the past are being pushed out of school at school-leaving age lacking both academic and social skills needed for employment (Sarri, 1982).

Desirable Staff Characteristics

Two aspects of staffing need consideration: those related to roles and those related to the desirable characteristics of those filling different roles. With regard to the matter of roles, it is clear that most of the apparently successful programs for disturbed adolescents are team efforts. Typical teams include an administrator, usually an educator in a school situation, but often a social worker or psychologist in a clinical situation. Besides teachers, the staff includes aides, social workers, and psychologists. Tasks assigned to these professional roles include counseling students and parents and liaison with the home, school, and community of the students. The focus of this discussion will be on desirable characteristics of those in the teacher role, which in many programs seems to include some counseling and liaison responsibilities. Lists of desirable teacher competencies have been developed by others (Polsgrove & Reith, 1979). Here the stress will be on less easily defined characteristics of personal style.

Bloom (1983) is one writer who has addressed this topic. Bloom notes that adolescence is a period of important, normal intergenerational conflict, which is manifested with particular intensity in relationships between disturbed adolescents and their teachers. Teachers must interact for long periods of time with students whose behavior is often frustrating or provocative. Those who carry loads of stress into the classroom may find that students can easily "hook" them into punishing, non productive behavior. Maintaining a flexible, constructive attitude requires the ability to avoid or defuse potentially troublesome situations. Bloom describes a number of challenges to mental health and suggests how they can be confronted.

Learning to use a cognitive-emotional strategy such as Rational-Emotive Therapy (Walen, DiGiuseppe, & Wessler, 1980) or Transactional Analysis (Harris, 1969) help some teachers deal constructively with emotionally arousing conflict. Schloss, Sedlack, Wiggins, and Ramsey (1983) report that teachers at a residential facility for behaviorally disturbed adolescents benefited from training in relaxation techniques and systematic desensitization procedures. The techniques chosen vary, but teachers who continued to work effectively with disturbed adolescents master and use procedures such as these which aid them to anticipate and avoid stress whenever possible and to shed its effects quickly when they appear.

What other interpersonal characteristics do experienced administrators look for in their teachers? Size and sex do not seem to be crucial factors for most tasks. More critical seems to be a high physical energy level and a determination to provide strong, constructive leadership to the group to which one is assigned. The emerging literature on social dominance in human beings and other social mammals provides a way of conceptualizing the importance of this kind of behavior in a teacher. Teachers who are effective, regardless of their expressed philosophy of education, move quickly to establish their position as the "alpha individual" in the classroom. This ability to establish dominance is more psychological than physical, for the true alpha individual uses his/her dominant position both to help the group have satisfying experiences and to minimize intergroup conflict. Informal conversation with program administrators suggests that while the ability to establish one's dominance in the group is a characteristic they seek in prospective teachers, they are not sure it is there until the teacher shows that ability by meeting the challenge of a particular group of students. There is a fine line between the positive social dominance of the alpha individual and the extremes on either side, abuse or ineffectiveness, and where a given teacher falls is only clearly revealed in on-the-job performance.

Teaching emotionally disturbed students is extremely hard work. Teachers are often young and have limited training (Schmid, Algozzine, Maher, & Wells, 1984). Lawrenson and McKinnon (1982) reported a high rate of turnover in their Iowa sample, which reported reasons stressing the difficulty of the job and lack of support from administrators. In a series of structured interviews with experienced, successful teachers of disturbed adolescents, the authors have found that teachers stress the importance of "liking the work" while at the same time acknowledging that there were times when they felt so exhausted by the physical and emotional effort required that they felt like quitting or transferring to something else for at least a period of resting. A sense of isolation and lack of respect from regular educators may also weaken morale (Knoblock & Goldstein, 1971). Clearly, dynamic characteristics such as those mentioned, however difficult to quantify, are as important as more trainable skills in determining classroom effectiveness with this group of students.

Program Goals and Individual Objectives

Special programs for emotionally disturbed adolescents are "alternative" programs in the sense that they are planned for students who have not been successful in the regular program. One might expect, therefore, that the stated goals for these programs would differ considerably from the goals for regular programs. However, despite the emphasis placed on the importance of showing differences by critics (Sabatino, 1982; Sarri, 1982), this is seldom the case.

The following project goals reported by Adams and Bielicki (1981, pp. 18–26)* are included as representative of goal statements from the better programs reviewed. These goals are measurable, and in the original report, the operationalizing procedures are specified.

It is expected that the mean of (observed behavioral) infractions will be significantly higher in the Fall than in the Spring . . . .

It was expected that the mean of the number of individual tokens awarded for the final quarter of the school year would be significantly higher than the mean number of individual tokens awarded during the first quarter (the number of days is equal) . . . .

It is expected that 60% of all second year students will maintain vocational mainstreaming status by adhering to provisions of behavior contracts . . . .

It was expected that a reduction in frequency of infractions from pre to post would be at least 50% for each of the . . . (observed) behaviors . . . as well as for all behaviors combined . . . .

It is expected that . . . the social behavior at the end of the student's first year in the program will be equal to that of other students enrolled in vocational programs . . . .

---

*Note. From *Alternative Design for Vocational and Necessary Cognitive Education for Secondary Emotionally Disturbed Students* (p. 18) by W. H. Adams and R. J. Bielicki, 1981, Salem, NJ: Salem County Vocational Technical Schools. Used by permission of the authors.

It is expected for the post-program means of Project students in verbal and quantitative achievement to be significantly higher than the pre-program means . . . .

It is expected that 75% of all Project students will achieve five of the six academic growth standards set for them . . . .

It is expected that 60% of Project students will achieve a minimum standard for quantitative and communication skills set for them by their teachers on a weekly basis . . . .

It is expected that 60% of Project students enrolled in prevocational shop will demonstrate hand tool skills, vocational safety, and complete shop projects at a minimum performance level . . . .

It was expected that 60% of Project students that are mainstreamed in vocational skills development will acquire the minimum skills of the occupational area of their enrollment . . . . (A final objective dealing with Project process has been omitted.)

Note that the standard referent for success in attaining most of these goals is the behavior of typical students and academic performance in the regular academic or vocational program. There is a strong tendency in many school systems to require that goals for programs labeled as alternatives be the same as those for the regular programs. References were made earlier to the comments by Kennedy et al. (1976) that when their program staff attempted to shift from a primary goal of preparation for reintegration into the regular school program to teaching "survival skills," the public school representatives on their interdisciplinary team were concerned about the deemphasis on academic skills. They believed that the long-run interests of the students necessitated better academic preparation. The vocational (survival skills) program was perceived as inadequate for students' needs because it trained "students for low-level jobs" (pp. 717–718). In this case, a compromise was eventually developed regarding school expectations for reentry behavior, which remained the overriding goal.

In most cases, program goals continue to reflect regular school priorities rather than being uniquely alternative. But, another opportunity for flexibility comes when goals or objectives are *established* for individual students. Student objectives are developed through two different procedures. They are either prespecified by the program staff or negotiated with individual students. Both of these procedures can be implemented simultaneously with the same student. Examples of prespecified individual goals are the Developmental Therapy Objectives Rating Form (M. Wood, 1979) and the STEPS Sequence (1977). Braaten (F. Wood, 1979) has developed a set of prespecified objectives based on an analysis on the needs and learning characteristics of seriously disturbed adolescents served in a Minneapolis Public School program. Although the domain of objectives is prespecified, selection of objectives for individual students can be individualized. The rationale and advantages of prespecified objectives assigned to students after teacher observation of individual student behavior has been discussed elsewhere by M. Wood (1979).

The major disadvantage of preset objectives are the limited allowances made for individual idiosyncrasy and the lack of student involvement in goal setting. Extreme individual differences can be accommodated by writing additional specific objectives for individuals, but a focus on teacher prespecification limits direct student involvement. As students develop cognitively and emotionally, their direct participation in objectives setting become desirable. Participation in objectives setting may even be identified as an appropriate higher level goal in a prespecified list. Several procedures for involving students in setting objectives have been developed.

One particularly useful approach is called Goal Attainment Scaling (GAS). This procedure has been described in some detail elsewhere (Carr, 1979; Maher, 1983). Goal Attainment

Scaling is a central feature of the SAIL Program for emotionally disturbed adolescents described by Balfour (1982).

> Goal Attainment Scaling is a goal-setting process that encourages individuals to set concrete, measurable goals that are realistically attainable. Staff assist students to select 6–15 individualized goals with at least one goal related to attendance and academic achievement in each class. Additional goals mutually negotiated by the student and staff relate to problem areas such as aggression, dependency, chemical abuse, hostility, passivity, suicide, responsibility, sexuality, peer relationships, authority conflicts, and delinquency. Students are also expected to select at least one goal focused on maintenance of a currently successful area of function or personal strength. (pp. 73–74)

In the GAS procedure, five different levels of success in meeting of objectives, rather than only one, are specified. The target level, one step higher than the current rate of accomplishment, is called the "expected" level. Below it are two levels, "somewhat" and "much less" than expected. The two higher levels are "somewhat" and "much more" than expected. While objectives are set individually and there is no common scale against which progress can be measured, "total goals achieved" can be counted as indicator of group progress. Whether or not they use this particular procedure, all of the better programs reviewed made use of some method for setting individual objectives.

Intervention: Social Behavior

There are no "silver bullet" remedies to disturbed social behavior of adolescence. Goldstein, Sprafkin, Gershaw, and Klein (1979) make the case well for prescriptive interventions matched to the characteristics of the individual or group. Goldstein (1978) has edited a book of papers in which this concept is applied to various areas of mental health and education. All good programs use a variety of different intervention procedures, some behavioral, others based on psychodynamic or psychoeducational concepts. Roth's statement is typical.

> The boys (in the residential treatment program) have in common a presenting problem of being unable to function in their home, school or community and a need for their residential treatment that is transitional rather than institutional. Since there is a broad spectrum of presenting problems, a wide array of treatment approaches is employed. A treatment approach deemed most effective in a given situation is used. The Transactional Analysis Group (which he is discussing), a recent addition to the program, augments rather than replaces already existing treatment methods. (p. 776)

Some frequently encountered elements in this array of interventions will be described here. For fuller discussion, readers may wish to consult one of a number of texts in the field including Brown, McDowell, and Smith (1981); Goldstein et al. (1983); Jones (1980); and McDowell, Adamson, and Wood (1982).

Levels Systems. Many programs use some form of levels, steps, or codes to group students in ways that relate their typical behavior to recurring rewards and privileges. In the Madison School Program described by Braaten (1979), students are grouped for instruction by level with substantial differences in curriculum between the third or entry level and the first or transition level. McCauley and Erikson (1982) describe a similar application of this concept. Julian and Weitzner (1982) note that at the Bellafaire School, students are also grouped in levels according to their assessed characteristics and needs. Teachers are matched to students according to their teaching styles. The lowest level is characterized by a highly structured classroom and a heavy reliance on behavioral interventions. At the second level, a directive but less structured approach is used. And, on the highest level, the intervention style is described as facilitative. The later approach is "employed with the students who are developmentally the most inner-directive and who possess the highest cognitive control" (p. 38).

Token/Points Systems. Many programs for adolescents provide rewards for appropriate behavior in the form of tokens or points, which can be used to purchase material objects, recreation opportunities, or free time (Thomas et al., 1982). The mechanics of setting up such programs have been described elsewhere in detail (Epstein, Cullinan, & Rose, 1980; Kazdin, 1977; Tomalesky & Jackson, 1984). Variations include a "response cost" feature, the taking away of points for inappropriate behavior rather than the reinforcement of appropriate behavior, or combinations of reinforcement and response cost (Kaufman & O'Leary, 1972; Phillips, Phillips, Fixsen, & Wolf, 1971). Backup reinforcers include both material objects and activities. In some cases, rewards are provided at home by parents (Stein, Ball, Conn, Haran, & Strizver, 1976).

In most systems, points are awarded to the individual whose behavior is judged appropriate. A variation of this is the *group* contingency program in which points earned by individuals are counted toward a group reward. When a sufficient number of points have been earned, the group receives the predetermined reward. In a group contingency program described by McCauley and Erikson (1982), the group points are awarded for such behaviors as being on time, finishing work on time, having materials ready, knowing and working on individual goals, being helpful to others, and participating in group lessons. Group contingency programs can be used in conjunction with individual contingency programs.

Time-Out and In-School Suspension. Time-out and in-school suspension are frequently mentioned as the most severe in-school sanctions for inappropriate behavior in programs for disturbed adolescents. Both procedures call for the removal of the student from the regular classroom environment to a special setting, usually drab and undecorated, where the usual rewards can not be earned or enjoyed. In the case of time-out, the special setting lacks work or recreational opportunities of any kind and is often somewhat stimulus deprived (no windows, closed door, muffled sound). The in-school suspension setting is usually a small, sparsely furnished classroom in which the student is expected to work on an assignment prepared by his/her teacher. While placement in a time-out room should be for a short period of time, not more than 1 hour, placement in an in-school suspension room may be for several days. Both procedures are intended to be unpleasant enough that the student will refrain in the future from the behavior that led to their application. As such, they are subject to easy abuse, and require thoughtful planning and administration (Garibaldi, 1978; Gast & Nelson, 1977; Polsgrove, 1983; Rutherford & Nelson, 1982; Wood & Braaten, 1983). Because the effectiveness of such interventions is so obviously related to the effectiveness of the entire program of which they are a part, efforts to determine their effectiveness alone have not been very successful. However, it could be said with confidence that high frequency use of either procedure for a particular student by a particular teacher means that one or both are failing to make progress and changes in the basic program are required.

It is this writer's opinion that time-out and suspension should be considered mainly as negative control procedures rather than as educational interventions. Among the most structured interventions, they are ineffective or counterproductive for teaching new appropriate behavior when compared with the other procedures discussed. Their use negatively reinforces a wide range of avoidance behavior in students. It would be preferable to discontinue the use of time-out and suspension in school situations entirely, but they are sometimes needed for controlling the behavior of highly aggressive or noncompliant students.

Suspension and Expulsion. The most extreme response of a system to a disruptive individual is to expell him/her entirely from a system. While adults in school may be negatively reinforced when a student is "out," they have thereby lost any opportunity for facilitating that student's learning and growth. Recent court decisions on cases challenging suspension or expulsion of students with special needs seem to present the following argument: The school has the obligation to provide an appropriate program for students who have been identified as eligible for special education. A temporary suspension is to be considered in part of that special education program, that is, it is a different special education placement. If challenged, the school must be able to demonstrate that the suspension was either a necessary, short-term measure (up to 5 days), taken while a more suitable placement was being developed, or that educational benefit was to be expected of this suspension. More permanent expulsion of a student for behavior associated with his/her handicapping condition, which may be severe behavioral disorder or emotional disturbance, is not permitted. Expulsion is not an appropriate educational placement because it deprives the student of the right to an education. This is an area where the law is still in the process of change. Craft and Haussmann (1983) present a review of its current state.

Social Skills Training. Despite the lack of strong data to support the efficacy of their practice, most highly regarded programs for disturbed adolescents follow a pattern similar to that noted earlier in the discussion of developmental stages and program levels. The more intrusive, behavioral interventions mentioned receive greater emphasis for students perceived to be at "lower" levels of development, and as students mature, great stress is placed on developing self-management skills through cognitively mediated interventions. These interventions aim at changing the student's inner behaviors, thoughts, and feelings. These techniques may be demonstrated to produce changes in subjects' behavior in experimental situations. What is lacking is clear evidence that they are *the* component producing the changes in students enrolled in special education programs where a variety of different approaches are being used. Because the different models of social skills training tend to have many common factors, this review will stress generic characteristics with illustrative references to specific programs.

One procedure used is the teaching of self-management of behavior. While many students develop self-management skills without instruction, these skills must often be taught to disturbed youth (Polsgrove, 1979). To become skilled in self-management, students must first learn to monitor their own behavior. This is usually taught in connection with instruction in a simple method for behavior recording. For example, students might tally the number of times they make an inappropriate comment during a discussion or remember to raise their hand to receive recognition from the teacher before speaking out. Accuracy can be encouraged by offering bonus points for close agreement with the tally kept by the teacher. The final stage of self-management is self-reward. Teachers sometimes find it difficult to implement self-reward systems, because it means that they must alter their directive style. For example, if students are permitted to reward themselves with free time for completing their assignments, they must be able to take that free time at the beginning of the work period if they choose to do so rather than waiting until the end. Teachers need to hold their tongues as students experiment with what works for them. Of course, students who have reached this level of self-management are probably long since back in the regular classroom!

Another group of teacher interventions are concerned with teaching social skills. These procedures use a sequence of modeling, role play or rehearsal, and assigned practice to teach skills that disturbed individuals or groups have been observed to lack. Goldstein et al. (1979) provide excellent instruction and examples for teaching skills to adolescents. The general research regarding the effectiveness of skill training has been reviewed by Gresham (1981) and will be discussed more fully in the section on program evaluation.

Counseling Interventions. Many special education programs for the adolescent mention the use of counseling as an intervention. The details of the procedures used are seldom given in published reports. Buck and Markson's (1982) description of the counseling program in the Desiderata Program is typical.

> Every student is required to be involved in a homeroom group. The social worker, teacher, and instructional aide hold a weekly group used to discuss student interaction, student-staff inter- action, and numerous other topics that may come out in the course of the school year. The student strongly identifies with this group as he/she assembles with it every morning at nine o'clock for homeroom and class, once a week for a structured group session, as well as meeting with them at the end of every school day to regroup, relax, and exchange information with the homeroom staff as to how the day went. (p. 5)

Goldstein (1978) has pointed out the value of the prescriptive approach to therapy. While the programs reviewed do not seem to apply different approaches systematically enough to be considered prescriptive, many can be characterized as eclectic, using and combining techniques drawn from counseling approaches such as Rational-Emotive Therapy (Zionts, 1983), Positive Peer Culture (Vorrath & Brendtro, 1974), Reality Therapy (Glasser, 1965), and the Life Space Interview (Fagen & Long, 1981) among others. Counseling programs developed in specific situations have been described by Balfour and Harris (1979), Balfour (1982), Larsen (1978), and Rutherford (1976). These models share a cognitive-emotional approach to the treatment of behavior disorders, emphasizing the working out of alternative solutions to group or individual problems in a context strongly reflecting the reality of social expectations without necessarily approving or disapproving them. "You do this; this (bad thing for you) is what happens. If you change your behavior, the chances are good that this (better thing for you) will happen." The amount of confrontation used varies from program to program.

It was noted earlier that more structured interventions are recommended for use with adolescents who are in earlier stages of cognitive, emotional, and moral development. Several programs demonstrate application of this concept. For example, Braaten (1979) describes these differences in the counseling program for students at different levels of the Madison School Program.

> Individual and group counseling are an important part of the program . . . . Initially, nearly all of the counseling is one-to-one. As the student progresses, supportive individual counseling continues, but the emphasis shifts to group sessions . . . . The type of counseling provided is problem solving, personally supportive, and reality oriented. (p. 160)

Academic and Vocational Training

Reference has already been made of the conflict in goals that develops in some programs (Kennedy et al., 1976). Whether or not they meet the criteria for classification as learning disabled, many disruptive students have histories of academic failure and achieve poorly on standardized tests (Bullock & Reilly, 1979; Schwartz & Wall, 1979). For these students, curriculum planned to assist in career development (Gable, 1984; Fink & Kokaska, 1983), or even directed toward instruction in what Kennedy et al. (1976) call "survival skills" is more appropriate than the typical secondary academic program.

Whether or not they have the skills to achieve academically, disturbed adolescents are often not motivated by either a vocationally oriented, career-development curriculum or an academic curriculum. This is particularly true of the disruptive youth who are placed in special education programs. Most chronically disruptive students do not accept their teachers' definition of a "meaningful, satisfying work life." Thus, they reject much of the curriculum that will facilitate attainment of such a life. Chronically disruptive youth "ain't buying," either because they already have knowledge and skills that provide them with a meaningful satisfying work life of their own choosing, or because they feel that conformity to the behavior norms of the school that is the price for participation in the typical workplace is too painful and the payoffs too uncertain to be attractive. Successful education for disturbed youths requires overcoming well-established tendencies for resistance to learning adult-approved behavior as well as providing opportunities to learn new skills.

Trying to meet the conflicting expectations and goals for special programs held by regular school administrators, parents, students, and their own staffs, administrators of special education programs must make compromises. Some programs are strongly vocationally oriented in the traditional sense. Adams and Bielicki (1981) report that their program included academic instruction for students provided by teachers trained to teach learning disabled students together with prevocational shop activities and vocational training in the student's choice of seven occupational programs. Buck and Markson (1982) describe a program in which decisions on placement in an academic or prevocational emphasis track are based on assessment of achievement and estimates of student potential.

Special effort is given to providing programs that are motivating to students. To try to break down student resistance, which often takes the form of declaring that the traditional curriculum is "irrelevant," educators have tried different approaches. One approach is to expand program content to cover skill areas with which their analysis suggests youth need to cope successfully in our present society. Examples would be courses on drugs, sexuality, ethnic history, crafts, music, cooking, and child care, presented in ways that provide for active student participation and offer direct reinforcement of learning. Another approach is to place students in a situation where they need skills only the staff can teach if they are to accomplish goals set by the situation itself, the so-called "wilderness camping" or "survival" curriculum. This approach has roots that go back many years (Loughmiller, 1965). Brown and Simpson (1976) applied similar ideas in a program which culminated with a student-planned week-long wilderness expedition. Griffin reported his evaluation of a long-term residential therapeutic camp (1981). Berry and Learch (1979) have described their program, which is based on teaching students the skills needed to operate the oceangoing vessel on which they are at sea. Revising curriculum to achieve greater relevance is successful unless the students' rejection is based on a deeply held, generally negative attitude toward what the school has to offer.

Parent Involvement

All programs recognize the importance of working cooperatively with parents. Two patterns for involving parents seem to exist. In one pattern, program staff seek to obtain parental support for efforts to achieve program goals. Few such efforts are successful, even when the desirability of the goals is fully shared by parents, and staff members may be left feeling frustrated and angry. In the other pattern, program staff attempt to provide family support on the assumption that families will be better able to help the program achieve its goals when their own problems are less pressing. The later strategy seems preferable.

Most parents of disturbed adolescents have largely depleted their own reserves of energy. One program administrator, when asked what word he would use to describe the parents of his students, replied *exhausted*. Kroth (1978, 1981) offers a number of suggestions about constructive approaches about family involvement. Sharing responsibility for young people whose behavior is punishing and anxiety-producing is not the best basis for a good relationship between parents and teachers. Kroth says:

> The creative minds of parents and professionals will be put to the test . . . to develop innovative ways of fostering and maintaining cooperative relationships. Some old attitudes will die hard. The idea of blaming parents for children's problems and the concept that parents do not care need to be put to rest. There are many benefits to be gained for the students by concentrating on the strengths that parents and professionals possess. (1981, p. 138)

Here is a suggested sequence of priorities for working with parents. First, commit yourself to understanding each student's parents with their unique needs, problems, and strengths before making any demands on them. Second, learn to communicate with parents to build greater understanding. Remember to share positive as well as negative events from their student's school experience. Finally, only after a good level of understanding has been achieved, offer to teach parents more active ways for working cooperatively with the school to promote their student's growth. Even at this stage, be prepared to deal patiently with their reluctance to be involved. At all stages, monitor parent/student interaction at home to the extent that is possible without being too intrusive. Some "helpful" parents become abusive under pressure; others move even further toward abandonment of responsibility for their child's behavior. Professionally trained staff find it difficult to work constructively with disturbed adolescents; no parent is a professional where his/her child is concerned.

Program Evaluation

Each of the programs from which information has been drawn in preparing this overview of recommended educational practices collects data that show their students, as a group, make progress while in the program. The designs used in evaluation are those usually described as preexperimental. To meet the requirement of an experimental or quasi-experimental design, program staff would need to provide data collected from appropriate comparison groups. Only this way is it possible to dismiss alternative explanations for observed gains or decrements in performance. Gains could have occurred in the absence of any special intervention or as the result of an intervention not under the control of the program staff. Collecting data on a second population for comparison purposes greatly increases the cost of program evaluation. Thus, use of appropriate quasi-experimental design for the evaluation of special education programs for disturbed adolescents is not common.

Even with these problems, it should still be possible to use more adequate evaluation designs than those used by many programs. A positive example is provided by Adams and Bielicki (1981), who report the use of a form of discrepancy evaluation (Brinkerhoff, Brethower, Hluchyji, & Nowakowski, 1983) by the staff of Project ADVANCE. Prior to the initiation of the project, measurable program goals were specified. These goals were quoted earlier in this chapter. Program success was measured in terms of progress relative to these preestablished goals. While such a design does not permit the elimination of the alternative hypotheses of no treatment or effective alternative treatments, it does provide a quantitative perspective on program accomplishment. Wider use of such designs is encouraged.

Very few programs provide data collected during follow-up of program graduates. Again, the major factors are probably expense and lack of staff time. This lack of information on maintenance of gains is particularly unfortunate because the literature regarding maintenance of gains achieved during experimental sessions is discouraging.

Gresham (1981) reviewed the literature on social skills training and concluded that evidence was lacking regarding generalization and maintenance of trained social skills. The social skills literature is cited because much of the work being done in social skills training uses a cognitive-behavioral approach (Kendall & Hollon, 1979; Meichenbaum, 1977) in an effort to increase generalization and maintenance beyond the limited effects observed following strictly behavioral interventions. Rimm and Masters (1979) suggest that generalization is made more likely "by the incorporation of the specific training to promote generalization, and careful assessment of discriminations, particularly inappropriate ones, that the individual under treatment . . . may make" (p. 269). Gresham (1981) suggests, "Training for generalization should receive as much attention and emphasis as training for the acquisition of social skills if mainstreaming efforts are to be successful in facilitating teacher and peer acceptance of handicapped children" (p.168). Goldstein et al. (1979) suggest that transfer is enhanced by overlearning of new skills, increasing the variety of stimulus (teaching) situations used in training, seeking to maximize the similarity between training situations and the situations to which generalization is wished, development of the reinforcement potential of transfer situations, and teaching the student to self-reinforce. All of these remain suggestions. Like the methods described, they are for the most part "best guesses" whose potential remains to be solidly demonstrated.

Ideally, every program director should plan to describe and evaluate his/her program so as to meet the criteria offered by McCauley (1977) which were quoted earlier. Given limited resources, priorities should be set. The author would place the highest priority on adequate description of program, students, staff, interventions used, and institutional context. The second priority should be given to assessment of student change in the program as measured against preestablished goals. Third priority should go to follow-up studies on generalization and maintenance of observed changes. Careful attention to these three priorities will do much to establish the internal validity of the program, answering the basic question, "Are we getting a positive outcome for our expenditures of funds and staff effort?"

The step from this point up to a strong quasi-experimental design is a large and expensive one. This is a fourth priority, one which would be wasteful to attempt before a sound program foundation has been laid. For the sake of being able to make more confident statements about what does and does not work in special education programs for disturbed adolescents, the author would like as many program staffs as possible to take this fourth step. But, as an educator concerned about the erosion of services, which at least appear to be beneficial to some of the present student population with special needs, and aware of the inherent difficulty of effective field evaluation, he will be satisfied if the field does a better job of addressing the first three priorities mentioned.

FUTURE PROSPECTS

The right of disturbed adolescents to a free, appropriate, public education until graduation or until the age of 21 (older in some states) is well-established in legislation and case law. Efforts by schools to limit the exercise of this right by explusion for disability-related problem behavior have been limited by lower court decisions, although a definitive body of case law has not yet developed. However, efforts to limit indirectly exercise of that right persist through the establishment of competency examinations, limitation of the credit toward graduation allowed for special class participation, and provision of programs that are such a poor match for student needs that they encourage students to give up their right to an education voluntarily by dropping out of school.

Recent statements by President Ronald Reagan (McGrath, 1984), and Theodore Sizer, the former Dean of Harvard School of Education (1984), should serve as a warning to those of us who believe that present special education programs, with all their limitations, are still worth defending. While neither of these influential leaders are attacking special education programs directly, their suggestions that greater priority be given to the educational needs of conforming, high achieving students and punitive steps be taken against students who find school an uncomfortable fit are alarming to those sensitive to the needs of special students. Disturbed students continue to need all the intelligent, hard-working, and self-critical friends they can find. To the extent that we learn to describe better our special education programs and can demonstrate their efficacy more adequately, we will be better friends to them than we are at present.

REFERENCES

Achenbach, T.M., & Edelbrock, C.S. (1978). The classification of child psychopathology: A review and analysis of empirical efforts. *Psychological Bulletin, 85*, 1275–1301.

Achenbach, T.M., & Edelbrock, C.S. (1979). The child behavior profile: II. Boys aged 12–16 and girls aged 6–11 and 12–16. *Journal of Consulting and Clinical Psychology, 47*, 223–233.

Adams, W.H., & Bielicki, R.J. (1981). *Alternative design for vocational and necessary cognitive education for secondary emotionally disturbed students*. Salem, NJ: Salem County Vocational Technical Schools. (ERIC Document Reproduction Service No. ED 204 947)

Algozzine, B. (1977). The emotionally disturbed child: Disturbed or disturbing. *Journal of Abnormal Child Psychology, 5*, 205–211.

Balfour, M.J. (1982). SAIL Project (Student Advocates Inspire Learning): Special education support service for dropout-prone adolescents. In M.A. Thomas, D.A. Sabatino, & R.C. Sarri (Eds.), *Alternative programs for disruptive youth* (pp. 71–75). Reston, VA: Council for Exceptional Children.

Balfour, M.J., & Harris, L.H. (1979). Middle class dropouts: Myths and observations. *Education Unlimited, 1*, 12–16.

Beilin, H. (1959). Teachers' and clinicians' attitudes toward the behavior problems of children: Reappraisal. *Child Development, 30*, 9–25.

Berry, R.S., & Learch, A.N. (1979). Victory at sea: A marine approach to rehabilitation. *Federal Probation, 43*, 44–47.

Bloom, R.B. (1983). The effects of disturbed adolescents on their teachers. *Behavioral Disorders, 8*, 209–218.

Braaten, S. (1979). The Madison School Program: Programming for secondary level severely emotionally disturbed youth. *Behavioral Disorders, 4*, 153–162

Brinkerhoff, R.O., Brethower, D.M., Hluchyji, T., & Nowakowski, J.R. (1983). *Program evaluation*. Hingham, MA: Kluwer Boston.

Brown, G.B., McDowell, R.L., & Smith, J. (Eds.). (1981). *Educating adolescents with behavior disorders*. Columbus, OH: Charles Merrill.

Brown, W.K., & Simpson, B.F. (1976). Confrontation of self through outdoor challenge: Pennsylvania's outdoor experience for juvenile offenders. *Behavioral Disorders, 2*, 41–48.

Buck, M.T., & Markson, H.J. (1982). *Desiderata programs: A unit of Phoenix Union High, District*

#210. Phoenix, AZ: Phoenix Union High School District. (ERIC Document Reproduction Service No. ED 217 667)

Bullock, L.M., & Reilly, T.F. (1979). A descriptive profile of the adjudicated adolescent. In R.B. Rutherford, Jr., & A.G. Prieto (Eds.), *Monograph in Behavioral Disorders* (pp. 153–161). Reston, VA: Council for Exceptional Children.

Carr, R.A. (1979). Goal attainment scaling as a useful tool for evaluating progress in special education. *Exceptional Children, 46,* 88–95.

Craft, N., & Haussmann, S. (1983). Suspension and expulsion of handicapped individuals. *Exceptional Children, 49,* 524–527.

Deno, E. (1970). Special education as developmental capital. *Exceptional Children, 37,* 229–237.

Dunn, L.M. (1968). Special education for the mentally retarded: Is much of it justified? *Exceptional Children, 35,* 5–22.

Eisner, E.W. (1984). Can educational research inform educational practice? *Phi Delta Kappan, 65,* 447–452.

Epstein, M.H., Cullinan, D., & Rose, T.L. (1980). Applied behavior analysis and behaviorally disordered pupils: Selected issues. In L. Mann, & D. Sabatino (Eds.), *The fourth review of special education.* New York: Grune and Stratton.

Epstein, M.C., Cullinan, D., & Rosemier, R.A. (1983). Behavior problems of behaviorally disordered and normal adolescents. *Behavioral Disorders, 8,* 171–175.

Erikson, E. (1968). *Identity: Youth and crisis.* New York: Norton.

Fagen, S.A., & Long, N.J. (Eds.). (1981). Life space interviewing [Special issue]. *Pointer, 25* (2).

Fink, A.H., & Kokaska, C.J. (Eds.). (1983). *Career education for behaviorally disordered students.* Reston, VA: Council for Exceptional Children.

Gable, R.A. (1984). A program for prevocational instruction for adolescents with severe behavioral disorders. In S. Braaten, R.B. Rutherford, Jr., & C.A. Kardash (Eds.), *Programming for adolescents with behavioral disorders* (pp. 59–68). Reston, VA: Council for Exceptional Children, Council for Children with Behavioral Disorders.

Garibaldi, A.M. (Ed.). (1978). *In-school alternatives to suspension.* Washington, DC: Department of Health, Education, and Welfare, National Institute of Education.

Gast, D.L., & Nelson, C.M. (1977). Legal and ethical considerations for the use of time-out in special education settings. *Journal of Special Education, 11,* 457–467.

Glasser, W. (1965). *Reality therapy: A new approach to psychiatry.* New York: Harper and Row.

Goldstein, A.P. (Ed.). (1978). *Prescriptions for child mental health and education.* New York: Pergamon Press.

Goldstein, A.P., Apter, S.J., & Harootunian, B. (1983). *School violence.* Engelwood Cliffs, NJ: Prentice-Hall.

Goldstein, A.P., Sprafkin, R.P., Gershaw, N.J., & Klein, P. (1979). *Skillstreaming the adolescent.* Champaign, IL: Research Press.

Gresham, F.M. (1981). Social skills training with handicapped children: A review. *Review of Educational Research, 51,* 139–176.

Griffin, W.H. (1981). *Evaluation of a residential therapeutic camping program for disturbed children.* Pensacola, FL: University of West Florida, Educational Research and Development Center. (ERIC Document Reproduction Service No. 204 041)

Grosenick, J.K., & Huntze, S.L. (1983). *More questions than answers: Review and analysis of programs for behaviorally disordered children and youth.* Columbia, MO: University of Missouri-Columbia, Department of Special Education, National Needs Analysis/Leadership Training Project.

Harris, T. (1969). *I'm OK, You're OK.* New York: Harper and Row.

Jones, V. (1980). *Adolescents with behavior problems: Strategies for teaching, counseling, and parent involvement.* Boston: Allyn and Bacon.

Julian, V., & Wietzner, R.P. (1982). Bellafaire School. In M.A. Thomas, D.A. Sabatino, & R.C. Sarri (Eds.), *Alternative programs for disruptive youth* (pp. 31–39). Reston, VA: Council for Exceptional Children.

Kauffman, J.M. (1982). Social policy issues in special education and related services for emotionally disturbed children and youth. In M.M. Noel & N.G. Haring (Eds.), *Progress or change: Issues in educating the emotionally disturbed: Vol. 1. Identification and program planning* (pp. 1–10). Seattle, WA: University of Washington, Program Development Assistance System.

Kaufman, K.F., & O'Leary, K.D. (1972). Reward, cost, and self-evaluation procedures for disruptive adolescents in a psychiatric hospital school. *Journal of Applied Behavior Analysis, 5,* 293–309.

Kazdin, A.E. (1977). *The token economy.* New York: Plenum Press.

Kendall, P.C., & Hollon, S.D. (Eds.). (1979). *Cognitive behavioral interventions: Theory, research, and procedures.* New York: Academic Press.

Kennedy, J., Mitchell, J.B., Klerman, L.V., & Murray, A. (1976). A day school approach to aggressive adolescents. *Child Welfare, 55,* 712–724.

Knoblock, P., & Goldstein, A.P. (1971). *The lonely teacher.* Boston: Allyn and Bacon.

Kroth, R.L. (1978). The role of the family. In J.B. Jordan (Ed.), *Exceptional students in secondary schools* (pp. 45–54). Reston, VA: Council for Exceptional Children.

Kroth, R.L. (1981). Involvement with parents of behaviorally disordered adolescents. In G.B. Brown, R.L. McDowell, & J. Smith (Eds.), *Educating adolescents with behavior disorders* (pp. 123–139). Columbus, OH: Charles E. Merrill.

Larsen, E.D. (1978). FOCUS: A successful secondary school program for dealing with disaffected. In J.B. Jordan (Ed.), *Exceptional students in secondary schools* (pp. 111–120). Reston, VA: Council for Exceptional Children.

Lawrenson, G.M., & McKinnon, A.J. (1982). A survey of classroom teachers of the emotionally disturbed: Attrition and burnout factors. *Behavioral Disorders, 8,* 41–49.

Loughmiller, C. (1965). *Wilderness road.* Austin, TX: Hogg Foundation for Mental Health.

Madden, N.A., & Slavin, R.E. (1983). Mainstreaming students with mild handicaps: Academic and social outcomes. *Review of Educational Research, 53,* 519–569.

Maher, C.A. (1983). Goal Attainment Scaling: A method for evaluating special education services. *Exceptional Children, 49,* 529–536.

McCauley, R.W. (1977, May). Elements of educational programming. *Iowa Perspectives,* pp. 1–4.

McCauley, R.W., & Erikson, J.A. (1982). Longfellow Education Center. In M.A. Thomas, D.A. Sabatino, & R.C. Sarri (Eds.), *Alternative programs for disruptive youth* (pp. 41–54). Reston, VA: Council for Exceptional Children.

McDowell, R.L., Adamson, G.W., & Wood, F.H. (Eds.). (1982). *Teaching emotionally disturbed children.* Boston: Little, Brown, and Company.

McGrath, E. (1984, January). Preparing to wield the rod. *Time,* p. 57.

Meichenbaum, D.M. (1977). *Cognitive Behavior Modification: An integrative approach.* New York: Plenum Press.

Nelson, C.M., & Kauffman, J.M. (1977). Educational programming for secondary school age delinquent and maladjusted pupils. *Behavioral Disorders, 2,* 102–113.

Phillips, E.L., Phillips, E.A., Fixsen, D.L., & Wolf, M.M. (1971). Achievement place: Modification of behaviors of predelinquent boys within a token economy. *Journal of Applied Behavior Analysis, 4,* 45–59.

Polsgrove, L. (1979). Self control: Methods for child training. *Behavioral Disorders, 4,* 116–130.

Polsgrove, L. (Ed.). (1983). Aversive control in the classroom [Special issue]. *Exceptional Education Quarterly, 3*(4).

Polsgrove, L., & Reith, H.S. (1979). A new look at competencies required by teachers of emotionally disturbed and behaviorally disordered children and youth. In F.H. Wood (Ed.), *Teachers for secondary school students with serious emotional disturbance* (pp. 25–46). Minneapolis: University of Minnesota, Special Education Programs.

Quay, H.C. (1977). Measuring dimensions of deviant behavior: The Behavior Problem Checklist. *Journal of Abnormal Child Psychology, 5,* 277–287.

Rimm, D.C., & Masters, J.C. (1979). *Behavior therapy: Techniques and empirical findings* (2nd ed.). New York: Academic Press.

Roth, R. (1977). A Transactional Analysis group in residential treatment of adolescents. *Child Welfare, 56*, 776–786.

Rutherford, R.B., Jr. (1976). Behavioral decision model for delinquent and predelinquent adolescents. *Adolescence, 11*, 97–106.

Rutherford, R.B., Jr., & Nelson, C.M. (1982). Analysis of the response contingent time-out literature with behaviorally disordered students in classroom settings. In R.B. Rutherford, Jr. (Ed.), *Severe behavior disorders of children and youth* (pp. 79–105). Reston, VA: Council for Children with Behavioral Disorders.

Sabatino, D.A. (1982). Issues and concerns: Problems with alternative schools. In M.A. Thomas, D.A. Sabatino, & R.C. Sarri (Eds.), *Alternative programs for disruptive youth* (pp. 7–20). Reston, VA: Council for Exceptional Children.

Sarri, R.C. (1982). Introduction. In M.A. Thomas, D.A. Sabatino, & R.C. Sarri (Eds.), *Alternative programs for disruptive youth* (pp. 1–6). Reston, VA: Council for Exceptional Children.

Schloss, P.J., Miller, S.R., Sedlak, R.A., & White, M. (1983). Social-performance expectations of professionals for behaviorally disordered youth. *Exceptional Children, 50*, 70–72.

Schloss, P.J., Sedlak, R.A., Wiggins, S.E., & Ramsey, D. (1983). Stress reduction for professionals working with aggressive adolescents. *Exceptional Children, 49*, 349–354.

Schmid, R., Algozzine, B., Maher, M., & Wells, D. (1984). Teaching emotionally disturbed adolescents: A study of selected teacher and teaching characteristics. *Behavioral Disorders, 9*, 105–112.

Schwartz, S.L., & Wall, S.A. (1979). The relationship between learning disabilities and juvenile delinquency. In R.B. Rutherford, Jr. & A.G. Prieto (Eds.), *Monograph in Behavioral Disorders* (pp. 162–173). Reston, VA: Council for Exceptional Children.

Sindelar, P.T., & Deno, S.L. (1978). The effectiveness of resource programming. *Journal of Special Education, 12*, 17–28.

Sizer, T.R. (1984). *Horace's compromise: The dilemma of the American high school.* New York: Houghton Mifflin.

Sprinthall, N.A., & Sprinthall, R.C. (1981). *Educational psychology: A developmental approach* (3rd ed.). Reading, MA: Addison-Wesley.

Stein, E.M., Ball, H.E., Jr., Conn, G.T., Haran, J., & Strizver, C.L. (1976). A contingency management day program for adolescents excluded from public schools. *Psychology in the Schools, 13*, 185–191.

STEPS: Sequential Tasks for Educational Planning. (1977). Palo Alto, CA: VORT Corporation.

Thomas, M.A., Sabatino, D.A., & Sarri, R.C. (Eds.). (1982). *Alternative programs for disruptive youth.* Reston, VA: Council for Exceptional Children.

Tomalesky, M., & Jackson, R. (1984). The safety harbor exceptional student centers: Multiphasic academic/therapeutic program model. In S. Braaten, R.B. Rutherford, Jr., & C.A. Kardash (Eds.), *Programming for adolescents with behavioral disorders* (pp. 52–58). Reston, VA: Council for Exceptional Children, Council for Children with Behavioral Disorders.

Topping, K.J. (1983). *Educational systems for disruptive adolescents.* New York (London): Croon Helm, St. Martin's Press.

Tringo, J.L. (1970). The hierarchy of preference toward disability groups. *Journal of Special Education, 4*, 295–306.

Vorrath, H.H., & Brendtro, L.K. (1974). *Positive peer culture.* Chicago: Aldine.

Walen, S.R., DiGiuseppe, R., & Wessler, R.L. (1980). *A practitioner's guide to rational-emotive therapy.* New York: Oxford.

Wickman, E.K. (1928). *Children's behavior and teacher's attitudes.* New York: Commonwealth Fund.

Wood, F.H. (1981). Influence of personal, social, and political factors on the labeling of students. In F.H. Wood (Ed.), *Perspectives for a new decade: Education's responsibility for seriously disturbed and behaviorally disordered children and youth* (pp. 45–62). Reston: VA: Council for Exceptional Children.

Wood, F.H. (1982). Cooperative full service delivery to emotionally disturbed students. In M.M. Noel & N.G. Haring (Eds.), *Progress or change: Issues in educating the emotionally disturbed: Vol. 1:*

Identification and program planning (pp. 115–134). Seattle, WA: University of Washington, Program Development Assistance System.

Wood, F.H., & Braaten, S. (1983). Developing guidelines for the use of punishing interventions in the schools. *Exceptional Education Quarterly, 3*, 68–75.

Wood, F.H., & Kayser, T.F. (1982). Perspectives on chronically disruptive students. In A.H. Fink & C.J. Kokaska (Eds.), *Career education for behaviorally disordered students* (pp. 26–41). Reston, VA: Council for Exceptional Children.

Wood, M.M. (Ed.). (1979). *The developmental therapy objectives: A self-instructional workbook* (3rd ed.). Baltimore: University Park Press.

Zoints, P. (1983). The rational-emotive approach. *Pointer, 27*, 13–17.

2

Social Learning Treatment within Juvenile Justice: A Meta-Analysis of Impact in the Natural Environment

Jeffrey P. Mayer
Leah K. Gensheimer
William S. Davidson II
Rand Gottschalk

INTRODUCTION

Approaches to the problem of juvenile delinquency have been characterized by a struggle between a desire to assist youth in eliminating criminal behavior and the need to protect society from wrongdoing (Krisberg & Austin, 1978). After a long history of idiosyncratic processing in the adult system, a separate legal apparatus was established for the handling of juvenile cases with the broad goals of keeping the offending youth away from the potentially harmful influences of the adult correctional system, and providing humane conditions and rehabilitative treatment for the youth. Thus, the juvenile court system was to provide a parent-like and corrective function. This demanded a situation associated with procedural informality and intensive, rehabilitative intervention (Mennel, 1972; Schultz, 1973). More recently, these historical developments in society's response to juvenile delinquency have come under attack on several grounds.

First, the juvenile justice system was criticized for failing in the execution of the *parens patriae* doctrine. The Supreme Court in 1967 reinstituted procedural formality in the juvenile courts, claiming that the exchange of legal rights for parent-like treatment was not working. Second, both the underlying assumptions of and the effectiveness of intervention approaches were called into question. Several reviews of the research literature suggested that traditional treatment approaches were not particularly effective in solving the problem of juvenile crime (Grey & Dermody, 1972; Kahn, 1965; Lipton, Martinson, & Wilkes, 1975; Romig, 1978). Typically, recidivism rates for juvenile institutions remained high (Scarpitti & Stephenson, 1971). Others concluded that treatment approaches relied too heavily on individual difference assumptions, and that, in fact, most of the research underpinning intervention efforts had measured characteristics of the legal system rather than juvenile behavior itself (Blakely & Davidson, 1982). Some suggested that treatment integrity was consistently compromised, and thus desired outcomes were not achieved (Sechrest & Redner, 1978).

It was in the content of this chaotic situation that the application of social learning principles to juvenile corrections began. For several reasons, it was hoped that the new approach offered by behavior modification would assist in establishing the legitimacy and positive character of juvenile treatment. This chapter, utilizing the recently developed methods of meta-analysis (Glass, McGraw, & Smith, 1981; Hunter, Schmidt, & Jackson, 1982), will attempt to summarize the effectiveness of behavioral intervention in the juvenile justice system. First, the emergence of behavioral interventions within the juvenile justice system will be briefly described, including a discussion of previous literature reviews, the theoretical context, and criticisms of the behavioral approach. Next, the specific methods of the meta-analysis will be detailed. Finally, the results of the meta-analysis and their implications will be presented and discussed.

THE EMERGENCE OF BEHAVIORAL APPROACHES

Behavioral approaches represent only one of many treatment regimens that have been employed in the treatment of juvenile delinquency. Some modes of treatment (i.e., individual and group therapy, vocational training, etc.), are driven by theories that emphasize individual differences. Within this approach, it was argued that youth with certain psychological and physiological characteristics would tend to exhibit delinquent behavior. The goal of these treatments was to remove the individual deficits that were presumed to be the cause of delinquent acts. The classic study in this area compared delinquent with nondelinquent youth on a large number of personality, physiological, and social variables (Glueck & Glueck, 1951). Other theorists, each influencing the practice of treatment to some extent, have made comparisons between delinquent and nondelinquent youth based on patterns of socialization (Smith & Ausnew, 1974); moral development (Prentice, 1972); communication within the family (Alexander & Parsons, 1973); learning disabilities (Broder, Dunivant, Smith, & Sutton, 1981); social skills (Gaffney & McFall, 1981); interpersonal contingencies (Stuart, 1971); intelligence (Mednick & Christianson, 1977); and problem-solving skills (Spivack & Schure, 1982). Thus, individual differences approaches have been very influential in the design of rehabilitative treatment for juvenile offenders.

Other modes of treatment have stressed that the source of delinquent behavior can be found in the environment. In this case, intervention efforts have been guided by theories that focus on environmental, rather than individual, differences. Culture, social structure, and institutions influence the formation of delinquency according to this approach. Important theoretical and empirical work in this area has included blocked opportunity to legitimate goals (Cloward & Ohlin, 1960); poor functioning in the educational system (Elliot & Voss, 1974; Polk & Schaefer, 1972); and labeling theory (Glaser, 1975; Matza, 1969; Richette, 1969). Many intervention strategies were influenced by the environmental differences approach, including diversion from the court system, community-based treatment, altering contingencies among family and peer groups, and other system-level and second-order change approaches.

Behavioral approaches focus on changing aspects of the social and physical environment such that appropriate prosocial behaviors increase, and inappropriate antisocial behaviors decrease. Even at its earliest stages of application, many advantages of behavioral technology within the juvenile justice system were apparent. The first examples of the application of behavioral principles to juvenile justice occurred in the early 1960s. Stumphauser (1976) reviewed some of this early work in institutions (Cohen, 1968; Jesness & Derisi, 1973); in clinics (Alvord, 1971; Patterson, 1971; Stuart, 1971); and in community settings (Buehler,

1973; Fo & O'Donnell, 1974; Tharp & Wetzel, 1969). In any case, great optimism existed that behavioral approaches offered promise because of the disillusionment associated with the apparent ineffectiveness of existing approaches, and the seemingly inherent compatibility between the juvenile legal system and social learning approaches.

Behavioral approaches required the clear specification of behaviors targeted for change. This concern for specifiable behavioral acts, overt as opposed to unobservable events, and the importance of behavioral consequences involved terms and concepts familiar to the juvenile justice system (Steketee, 1973). Also, behavioral procedures emphasized the importance of parents, program staff, caseworkers, teachers, and other "nonprofessionals" as change agents. The field of treatment for juvenile offenders had always been faced with the unavailability of expensive professionals. Utilizing nonprofessionals in the natural environment, therefore, was an important asset of the behavioral approach. Behaviorist suggestions that nonprofessionals could do the job allowed them access to the juvenile system (Tharp & Wetzel, 1969). An additional asset of the behavioral approach was that the primary goal of intervention was to increase desired or socially appropriate behaviors. More traditional interventions had focused on removing undesirable performances, and other deficits attributable to individual differences. In fact, the lack of emphasis on etiology by behaviorists was viewed as another advantage of the approach.

Finally, it can be argued that behaviorists gained access to juvenile delinquents by default. Positions in juvenile justice were not popular with human service professionals (Saul & Davidson, 1982). Psychologists, in particular, had not been very active in interventions with juvenile delinquents. Thus, the field was to some extent interested in new approaches. Additionally, available empirical evidence suggested that juvenile delinquents did not appear to be positively affected by psychotherapy (e.g., Grey & Dermody, 1972; Levitt, 1971). Hence, when the general behavioral movement was gaining momentum in the mid-1960s, behaviorists were willing and able to provide alternatives to traditional intervention in the juvenile justice system.

The rapid emergence of behavioral approaches, therefore, was fostered for several important reasons, including a focus on well-defined and observable behaviors and events, ease of applicability by nonprofessional service providers, disregard for elaborate and unuseful etiological paradigms, and a focus on increasing the behavioral repertoire of juveniles, rather than eliminating existing personality defects.

In general, existing reviews of social learning approaches with delinquent youth have reported positive results (Blakely & Davidson, 1982; Braukman, Fixsen, Phillips, & Wolf, 1975; Davidson & Seidman, 1974; Nietzel, Winett, MacDonald, & Davidson, 1977; Redner, Snellman, & Davidson, 1982; Stumphauser, 1971). However, these reviews have also pointed to several methodological and substantive shortcomings. First, the internal validity of the reported studies has been characterized as poor. For example, Davidson and Seidman (1974) expressed concern that only 82% of the studies reviewed included a no-treatment control group, and only 36% reported the use of a reversal design. Therefore, the generally positive results needed to be viewed in light of the lack of experimental rigor. The use of control groups was considered extremely important given the high potential for biasing maturational effects with a youthful target group.

Second, the existing reviews indicated that intermediate behaviors were the targets of intervention almost to the exclusion of delinquent acts themselves. This focus on within-program, rule-following behavior pointed to the lack of external validity in the findings, and the lack of follow-up data (Emery & Marholin, 1977), and laid on the table issues brought up in other settings that concerned the role of behavioral procedures in producing conformity (Winett & Winkler, 1972). The question still remained whether the transfer from change agent implemented contingencies to natural contingencies was being affected (Burchard & Hartig, 1976). More evidence was needed concerning both response and stimulus generalization (e.g., positive recidivism results would imply that both were occurring); sufficient evidence already existed to confirm the legitimacy of reinforcement theories with juvenile samples (Blakely & Davidson, 1982; Emery & Marholin, 1977; Stumphauser, 1976).

Each of these existing reviews employed a narrative approach. Most provided a synopsis of a large number of studies, and took "votes" on each study. Tallies were kept of the positive, negative, or insignificant impact of each of the interventions included in the review. The voting method of accumulation represents a way of assessing the direction and frequency of results across studies. However, it does not allow an assessment of the magnitude of effects. In the present study, methods of research accumulation developed by Glass, McGraw, and Smith (1981) and Hunter, Schmidt, and Jackson (1982) were applied to the juvenile delinquent social learning treatment literature. These review procedures included an estimation of the magnitude of treatment impact (i.e., the effect size), and estimate error introduced by sampling or measurement artifacts. Additionally, several methodological and intervention-related characteristics of the studies were coded. Thus, another advantage of meta-analysis is the ability to examine the relationships between study characteristics and a quantitative estimate of intervention impact. Problems that have been cited with this methodology of research accumulation include the replicability of the study selection process, collapsing across diverse dependent variables, collapsing across studies with different degrees of experimental rigor, and lack of adequate information in the literature to allow a complete and accurate assessment of effect size.

THE PRESENT REVIEW

Sample of Studies

This review was based on studies obtained from a computer search of *Psychological Abstracts* from 1967 to 1983, as well as a mail campaign to prominent authors requesting unpublished manuscripts. The computer-based search used the following key words: juvenile delinquents, treatment, intervention, and outcome. The unpublished studies were included to counter arguments that the published literature primarily includes studies with positive results, and ignores less successful research; the so-called "file drawer" problem (Rosenthal, 1979).

To be included in the present review, a study had to have the following characteristics:

1. Dependent variables were assessed that would demonstrate generalization across time, behavior, or setting. Studies examining behaviors within the treatment setting were excluded.
2. Only studies involving adjudicated youth were included. Those involving pre-delinquents, troubled youth, underachievers, and so on, with no court or police contact, were excluded.
3. The study had to specifically report on an application of a behavioral procedure, such as a token economy, modeling, behavioral contracting, positive reinforcement, or contingency management.

This process resulted in a total sample of 34 studies. Several studies examined multiple treatment interventions within one research design. The meta-analysis procedures allow the comparison of only two groups in a given experimental/control design, regardless of whether a no-treatment or treatment-as-usual comparision group was employed. Differences between treatments within a given study are handled by coding the same study separately for each treatment. Because of this, the results of 39 distinct research designs were included in the meta-analysis database.

Coding methods

The 39 studies were divided among the authors and coded according to the procedures described here.

A number of investigator, subject, intervention, and methodological characteristics were coded: Table 2.1 presents a summary of these study characteristics. This step provides for a broad description of the studies that were included in the review. Further, it is possible to examine relationships between some study characteristics and effect size.

For each dependent outcome variable in each study, several pieces of information were recorded. These included method of data collection, size and type of reliability, length of follow-up period, and number of subjects and effect size for both pre/post and experimental/control comparisons. Additionally, a "vote count" tally of positive, negative, or insignificant effects was also coded.

Effect sizes were calculated for three types of dependent variables: recidivism, behavior, and attitudes. Recidivism included arrests, court contacts, and other archival indicants of official involvement in the juvenile justice system. Behavior included rule compliance, adherence to predetermined behavioral regimens, measures of prosocial behavior, and school and work attendance. The attitude dependent variable was an accumulation across a number of more highly specified outcomes, including academic performance (e.g., achievement tests, grades), self-esteem, locus of control, ratings of adjustment, and other cognitive and attitudinal outcomes. Finally, an overall effect size was calculated which collapsed

Table 2.1. Study Characteristics

Subject Characteristics
1. Adjudicated—coded yes/no.
2. Percent male.
3. Average age.

Intervention Characteristics
1. Setting—whether the intervention took place in an institution, community residential program, or community/nonresidential setting.
2. Duration—the average length of the intervention in weeks.
3. Intensity—the average number of hours of intervention.

Investigator Characteristics
1. Discipline of authors.
2. Investigator had influence over treatment process—coded none, to some extent, to a great extent.

Methodological Characteristics
1. Implementation measurement—was there assessment of intervention integrity?
2. Evidence of unplanned variability in intervention—was there evidence of lack of compliance or other problems in treatment integrity?
3. Multiple baseline used—coded yes/no.
4. Reversal conditions used—coded yes/no.
5. Description of control group—coded as no treatment, treatment as usual, subjects as own control (pre/post designs), or no control group.
6. Assignment of subjects to treatment—coded as random, matching, or nonrandom.
7. Assignment of interveners to participants—coded as random, matching, or nonrandom.

across all dependent variables present in each design, and then collapsed across all designs to produce a single pre/post and a single experimental/control effect size. This index reflected a global estimate for the entire meta-analysis data set. An overall "voting method" summary of the studies was calculated in a similar fashion.

Calculation of Effect Sizes

Both pre/post and experimental/control effect sizes were coded for each dependent variable within each design. Basically, three different approaches were used in obtaining effect sizes. The first, a standardized mean difference, was calculated by subtracting the experimental group post-mean from the control group post-mean (or the pre-mean) and dividing by the control group standard deviation (or the pre-standard deviation). Many single-subject design studies did not report sufficient statistical information to use this formula. In cases where specific behavioral outcomes were plotted across time, pre/post effect sizes were calculated by treating baseline and reversal intervals (i.e., when contingencies were *not* enforced) as pre-data, and treatment intervals (i.e., when contingencies were enforced) as post-data.

In other studies with less than ideal information reported, one of two other methods was used. If significance level and sample size, but no means or standard deviation, were reported, then the following formula from Glass et al. (1981) was used:

$$\text{Effect size} = t\sqrt{1/n + 1/n} \quad ,$$

converting F into t if necessary. If success on a particular dependent variable could be dichotomized within each two-group design, then an effect size was obtained by comparing the proportion of success in the experimental group (or post-interval) with the proportion of success in the control group (or the pre-interval) using the probit transformation table provided by Glass, McGraw, and Smith (1981). As mentioned previously, a voting method count of effectiveness was coded for each dependent variable within each design as well.

For eight cases, two of the authors coded the same study to produce an estimate of interrater reliability. Across all variables included in the meta-analysis coding, the exact agreement reliability was 86%.

RESULTS

Descriptive Findings

The publication dates of the reviewed studies ranged from 1971 to 1982 with a mode of 1976. Ninety-five percent of the studies were published in journals. The remainder were found in book chapters or were unpublished technical reports.

Table 2.2 describes the investigator, subject, intervention, and methodological characteristics of the reviewed studies. Sixty-four percent of the studies were authored by psychologists. Sociology, social work, and criminal justice departments were also represented. There also appeared to be a substantial amount of experimenter influences in the studies. Sixty-two percent of the studies were coded as having a great extent of experimenter influence on the design and implementation of the treatment.

The youth included in the studies tended to be male, 14 ½ years of age on the average, and had had some prior contact with the juvenile justice system. A total sample size of 607 subjects for pre/post designs, and 1,207 subjects for experimental/control designs was obtained across all studies.

Table 2.2. Descriptive Findings

Investigator Characteristics	
1. Percent of authors who are psychologists	64%
2. Extent of experimenter influence on the treatment	
Great influence	62%
Some influence	29%
No influence	9%
Subject Characteristics	
1. Average percent of subjects who are males	81%
2. Average age	14 years, 7 months
3. Percent of studies involving adjudicated youth	88%
Intervention Characteristics	
1. Setting	
Institutional	36%
Community residential	33%
Community non-residential	24%
2. Length of treatment	
Duration	
Mean weeks	17.8
Median weeks	8.8
Intensity	
Mean hours	55.5
Median hours	72.5
3. Use of token economy	54%
4. Use of behavioral contracting	46%
5. Use of positive reinforcement	85%
6. Use of modeling	56%
Methodological Characteristics	
1. Studies including some measurement of treatment implementation	31%
2. Studies reporting unplanned variation in treatment	13%
3. Studies including reversal design	8%
4. Studies including multiple baseline design	31%
5. Type of control group	
No treatment	28%
Treatment as usual	36%
Other	36%
6. Studies including random assignment of subjects to treatment	36%
7. Studies including random assignment of change agents	3%

The setting of the intervention was somewhat evenly distributed across total institutions, community-based residential programs, and community nonresidential programs. The duration and intensity of treatment was not long-term in character. The average intervention lasted approximately 9 weeks, and provided 55.5 hours of direct contact. The use of token economies, behavioral contracting, modeling, and positive reinforcement dominated the types of intervention techniques employed. It should be noted that two or more of these intervention types could have been included in a single study.

Methodological Characteristics

Thirty-one percent of the studies reported some measurement of the implementation of the treatment. Thirteen percent reported that unplanned variation in the treatment model had occurred. Because implementation was infrequently monitored, it is possible that additional unwanted treatment variation occurred, but went undetected. The strength and integrity of interventions is clearly an issue that deserves more attention (Sechrest & Redner, 1978).

Multiple baseline designs were reported in 31% of the studies, and reversal designs in 8%. When a control group design was reported, 28% used a no-treatment control, 36% compared the treatment to other existing services, and the remainder used subjects as their own control. Only 36% included random assignment of subjects to treatment. Hence, the degree of internal validity within the reviewed studies was not outstandingly high. Less than half the studies included solid evidence that the effects observed were actually attributable to treatment. The proportion of studies including these important methodological safeguards was nearly identical to those reported by Davidson and Seidman (1974) a decade ago.

The role of change agent characteristics was practically never monitored. There was no examination of the relationship between change agent characteristics and treatment effectiveness, and only one study attempted to control for potential change agent characteristic confounds through random assignment.

Effectiveness Results

Recall that the "voting method" of review involved coding each result for each reported dependent variable as a positive effect, no effect, or a negative effect. Table 2.3 presents the "vote count" findings, including the number of distinct designs upon which the frequencies were based (the N column). These findings indicate a high degree of effectiveness for behavioral interventions, for the recidivism, behavior, and attitudinal outcomes, as well as the collapsed overall results. No substantial differences existed whether a pre/post or an experimental/control design was employed. An overwhelming majority of the studies reported positive effects of treatment, while only a small proportion reported nonsignificant or negative effects.

A somewhat different story emerged when the meta-analytic effect size results were considered. Table 2.4 presents the quantitative effect sizes for the aggregated results and for each of the three outcomes. Column A reports the number of distinct designs, and column B the number of subjects for that category. Column C includes the unweighted mean effect size across studies, calculated by using the methods explained previously. Because an effect size based on a larger number of subjects should be a better estimate of the true effect size, each effect size was weighted by the appropriate sample size, and

Table 2.3. "Voting Method" Results

Dependent Variable	N	Positive Effect	No Effect	Negative Effect
Overall				
Pre/Post	23	19(83%)	3(13%)	1(4%)
EC	26	23(88%)	1(4%)	2(8%)
Recidivism				
Pre/Post	4	3(75%)		1(25%)
EC	19	12(63.2%)	5(26.3%)	2(10.5%)
Behavior				
Pre/Post	17	13(76.5%)	2(11.8%)	2(11.8%)
EC	17	14(82.4%)	1(5.9%)	1(11.8%)
Attitudes				
Pre/Post	9	7(77.8%)	1(11.1%)	1(11.1%)
EC	13	7(53.8%)	5(38.5%)	1(7.7%)

Table 2.4. Effect Size Results

Dependent Variable	A	B	C	D	E	F	G
Overall							
Pre/Post	21	607	1.23	1.04	.61	21%	−.49 to 2.57
EC	23	1207	.64	.52	.04	66%	.12 to .93
Recidivism							
Pre/Post	3	183	.60	1.08	.72	10%	−.58 to 2.74
EC	17	1080	.50	.33	.11	37%	−.31 to .97
Behavior							
Pre/Post	15	259	1.43	1.26	1.29	22%	−.99 to 3.49
EC	14	480	.57	.63	.58	17%	−.87 to 2.11
Attitudes							
Pre/Post	6	355	.54	.62	.10	40%	.01 to 1.23
EC	8	274	.61	.32	.20	38%	−.55 to 1.18

A = number of designs reporting this dependent variable
B = number of subjects reflected in the effect size
C = the mean effect size
D = the weighted mean effect size
E = corrected variance of the effect size
F = % of observed variance due to sampling error
G = 95% confidence interval around the effect size

a mean (column D) and a variance (column E) were computed. Using formulas developed by Hunter, Schmidt, and Jackson (1982), a ratio between variance due to sampling error and the observed variance was computed. Column F indicates the proportion of the observed variance that was attributable to sampling error. Finally, the 95% confidence interval around the weighted mean effect size was computed (column G). The confidence interval was computed by subtracting the variance attributable to sampling error from the total variance. This corrected variance was used in computing the confidence intervals. Hunter et al (1982)) claim that if 75% or more of the observed variance is due to sampling or other biases, then all variance should be considered artifactual. Unfortunately, measurement reliability was reported so infrequently that an estimation of bias due to measurement unreliability was impossible.

Table 2.4 indicates that both the unweighted and weighted mean effect sizes were uniformly positive, and in some cases greater than 1. Five of the weighted mean effect sizes were larger than the unweighted ones; for the remaining three effect sizes, the opposite was true. Whether the weighted effect sizes were larger or smaller than the unweighted effect sizes depended on the proportion of positive effect sizes that had large versus small sample sizes within each subset of studies. An effect size of 1 implies that the experimental (or post-group) mean was 1 standard deviation above the control (or pre-group) mean. The weighted mean effect sizes ranged from 0.32 to 1.26. The weighted experimental/control effect sizes (those with the most internal validity) ranged from 0.32 to 0.63. The behavior outcome weighted experimental/control effect size was largest. The effect size variances ranged from 0.04 to 1.29. Although in some cases the proportion of variance due to sampling error was substantial, in no instance did the proportion exceed 75%. In all but two cases, the confidence intervals included 0, and ranged into negative values. The confidence intervals for the overall experimental/control effect size and the pre/post attitude effect size included only positive values. In all cases, the confidence intervals were skewed more strongly into the positive range.

Table 2.5. Correlations of Effect Size with Selected Study Characteristics

Study Characteristic	Pre/Post Effect Size	EC Effect Size
% male	.04, $n=20$, ns	.26, $n=23$, ns
Age	-.09, $n=18$, ns	-.06, $n=23$, ns
Duration	-.20, $n=17$, ns	.02, $n=18$, ns
Hours contact	-.20, $n=18$, ns	.07, $n=18$, ns
Token economy	.35, $n=21$, .05	.21, $n=23$, ns
Behavioral contracting	.12, $n=21$, ns	.23, $n=23$, ns
Positive reinforcement	-.10, $n=21$, ns	-.25, $n=23$, ns
Modeling	.11, $n=21$, ns	.17, $n=23$, ns
Unplanned treatment variation	.14, $n=21$, ns	.06, $n=23$, ns
Measure of implementation	.17, $n=21$, ns	.00, $n=23$, ns
Experimenter influence	.17, $n=16$, ns	.29, $n=20$, ns
Random assignment of subjects	.23, $n=21$, ns	-.12, $n=23$, ns

Table 2.5 presents the intercorrelations between several study characteristics and effect size. The only statistically significant correlation suggested that the use of token economies was positively associated with pre/post effect size.

Finally, the correlations between the "vote count" results and the meta-analytic effect size results were uniformly positive and significant. Nevertheless, the "vote count" results seemed to provide a more positive conclusion concerning the effectiveness of social learning intervention with juvenile delinquents, when compared to the effect size results.

SUMMARY AND DISCUSSION

The present work collected information from 39 studies reporting behavioral interventions within the juvenile justice system in an effort to summarize their effectiveness. Both "vote count" and effect size methods of research accumulation were employed in assessing recidivism, behavioral, and attitudinal outcomes. The typical study included in the review involved an adjudicated male sample in a residential setting; treatment involved token economies. modeling, contracting, or some other application of social learning theory.

Given observations that behavioral treatments have not demonstrated sufficient generalization across behaviors and settings (Emory & Marholin, 1977; Stumphauzser, 1978), it is very significant that the study selection process for this review eliminated studies that used behavior in the treatment setting as the dependent variable. This step removed from the review most of the studies where the strength of behavioral treatment seems to lie, at least according to some past reviewers of the literature. On the other hand, it is critical to examine long-term outcomes when judging the effectiveness and importance of different intervention techniques. In essence, this review presents a tough test for the behavioral literature involving juvenile delinquents because historically, many studies were overly concerned with demonstrating the law of effect, rather than examining impact on legal and natural environment behavior outcomes.

The "vote count" accumulation results agreed with past reviews suggesting that behavioral approaches were for the most part highly effective. The results of the effect size method presented a more mixed picture. Although all mean effect sizes were positive, and in some cases over 1 in magnitude, all but two of the reported confidence intervals included 0. The weighted experimental/control effect sizes were perhaps most telling because they concerned designs that, in general, possessed more internal validity. Every pre/post effect size was substantially larger than its experimental/control counterpart, suggesting that it was more difficult for the interventions to "work" when additional threats to validity were ruled out. Although it is encouraging to note that the lower bound of the overall experimental/ control confidence interval was as high as 0.12, 66% of the effect size variance was attributable to sampling error.

The highest experimental/control effect size was for the behavior outcome category, with only 17% of the corrected effect size variance due to sampling error. The pre/post behavior outcome had the lowest number of subjects per study, suggesting that many single-subject designs were included in this category. This may explain why the variance and confidence interval for this outcome-design combination were so large. Overall, it appears that the treatments were moderately effective, although this conclusion must be moderated by the fact that the effect size variances were large, and the confidence intervals broad. More studies with more subjects are necessary to get a closer estimate of the true effect size. Eliminating studies that measured behaviors within the treatment setting limited the scope of this review, and consequently study and subject sizes. However, it also meant that the review concerned an extremely important issue: efficacy with long-term, policy-relevant outcomes.

Methodologically, this literature continues to display serious shortcomings. Implementation of the treatment was infrequently measured. Less than half the studies employed designs with good internal validity, whether single-subject or group designs. Unfortunately, the influences of such methodological shortcomings are entangled in the reported overall effect, and will continue to be until more high quality research becomes available.

One shortcoming the meta-analysis has highlighted is the poor reporting of results in the literature. It was frequently difficult to discern the major methodological characteristics of many studies. For example, such basic dimensions as intervention length and intensity were uncodable 20% and 57% of the time, respectively. In addition to indicating troublesome reporting practices, this situation produced missing data rates which made examination of the interrelationships between methodological characteristics and effect size difficult. Only the use of token economies correlated significantly with effect size. More critical were the difficulties experienced in extracting sufficient information to make effect size calculations. The practice of reporting only significance levels without reporting means and variances is problematic. This is particularly at issue when examining nonsignificant findings, which are frequently reported without any statistical documentation. These problems, as well as difficulties associated with collapsing across diverse dependent variables, prevented further exploration of study characteristic–effect size relationships, and rendered the meta-analysis database much less complete than ideal.

Overall, the results of the present study suggest that future social learning treatment research efforts with juvenile delinquents should examine long-term outcomes more frequently and more rigorously, and that reporting practices should become more thorough.

REFERENCES

Alexander, J.F., & Parsons, B.V. (1973). Short-term behavioral intervention with delinquent families: Impact on family process and recidivism. *Journal of Abnormal Psychology, 81*, 219–225.

Alvord, J.R. (1971). The home token economy: A motivational system for the home. *Corrective Psychiatry and Journal of Social Therapy, 17*, 6–13.

Blakely, C., & Davidson, W.S. (1982). Behavioral approaches to delinquency: A review. In P. Karoly (Ed.), *Adolescent behavior disorders* (pp. 241–272). New York: Pergamon Press.

Broder, P.K., Dunivant, N., Smith, E.C., & Sutton, L.P (1981). Further observations on the link between learning disabilities and juvenile delinquency. *Journal of Education Psychology, 73*, 838–850.

Braukman, C.J., Fixsen, D.L., Phillips, E.L., & Wolf, M.M. (1975). Behavioral approaches to treatment in crime and delinquency. *Criminology, 13*, 299–331.

Buehler, R.E. (1973). Social reinforcement experimentation in open social systems. In J.S. Stumphauser (Ed.), *Behavior therapy with delinquents*, (pp. 250–262). Springfield, IL: Charles C Thomas.

Burchard, J.D., & Hartig, P.T. (1976). Behavior modification and juvenile delinquency. In H. Leiterberg (Ed.), *Handbook of behavior modification and behavior therapy*. Englewood Cliffs, NJ: Prentice-Hall.

Cloward, R., & Ohlin, L. (1960). *Delinquency and opportunity*. Glencoe, IL: The Free Press.

Cohen, H.L. (1968). Educational therapy: The design of learning environments. *Research in Psychotherapy, 3*, 21–58.

Davidson, W.S., & Seidman, E. (1974). Studies of behavior modification and juvenile delinquency. *Psychological Bulletin. 81*, 998–1011.

Elliot, D.S., & Voss, H.L. (1974). *Delinquency and dropout*. Lexington, MA: Lexington Press.

Emery, R.E., & Marholin, D. (1977). An applied analysis of delinquency. *American Psychologist, 32*, 860–871.

Fo, W.S., & O'Donnell, C.R. (1974). The buddy system: Relationship and contingency conditions in a community intervention program for youth with nonprofessionals as behavior change agents. *Journal of Consulting and Clinical Psychology, 42*, 163–169.

Gaffney, L.R., & McFall, R.M. (1981). A comparison of the social skills in delinquent and nondelinquent adolescent girls using behavioral role-playing inventory. *Journal of Consulting and Clinical Psychology, 49*, 959–967.

Glaser, D. (1975). *Strategic criminal justice planning*. Washington, DC: U.S. Government Printing Office.

Glass, G.V., McGraw, G., & Smith, M.L. (1981). *Meta-analysis in social research.*. Beverly Hills, CA: Sage.

Glueck, S., & Glueck, E. (1951). *Unraveling juvenile delinquency*. Cambridge, MA: Harvard University Press.

Grey, A.L., & Dermody, H.E. (1972). *Reports of casework failure. Social Casework, 16*, 207–212.

Hunter, J., Schmidt, F., & Jackson, G. (1982). *Cumulating research findings across studies*. Beverly Hills, CA: Sage.

Jesness, C.F., & DeRisi, W.J. (1973). Some variations in techniques of contingency management in a school for delinquents. In J.S. Stumphauser (Ed.), *Behavior therapy with delinquents* (pp. 196–235). Springfield, IL: Charles C Thomas.

Kahn, A.J. (1965). A case of premature claims. *Crime and Delinquency, 20*, 233–240.

Krisberg, B., & Austin, J. (1978). *The children of Ishmael*. Palo Alto, CA: Mayfield Press.

Levitt, E.L. (1971). Research on psychotherapy with children. In A. Bergin & S.L. Garfield (Eds.), *Handbook of psychotherapy and behavior change* (pp. 474–494). New York: Wiley.

Lipton, D., Martinson, R., & Wilks, J. (1975). *The effectiveness of correctional treatment: A survey of treatment evaluation studies.*. New York: Praeger.

Matza, D. (1969). *Becoming deviant*. Englewood Cliffs, NJ: Prentice-Hall.

Mednick, S., & Christiansen, S.O. (1977). *Biosocial basis of criminal behavior*. New York: Gardner Press.

Mennel, R.M. (1972). Origins of the juvenile court. *Crime and Delinquency, 18*, 58–78.

Nietzel, M.T., Winett, R.A., MacDonald, M.L., & Davidson, W.S. (1977). *Behavioral approaches to community psychology*. New York: Pergamon Press.

Patterson, G.R. (1971). *Families: Application of social learning to family life*. Champaign, IL: Research Press.

Polk, K., & Schaefer, W.K. (Eds.). (1972). *Schools and delinquency*. Englewood Cliffs, NJ: Prentice-Hall.

Prentice, N.M. (1972). The influence of live and symbolic modeling on promoting moral judgements of adolescent delinquents. *Journal of Abnormal Psychology*, 80, 157–161.

Redner, R., Snellman, L., & Davidson, W.S. (1982). A review of behavioral methods in the treatment of delinquency. In R.J. Morris & T. Kratochwill (Eds.), *Practice of therapy with children: A textbook of methods* (pp. 193–220). New York: Pergamon Press.

Richette, L.A. (1969). *The throwaway children*. Philadelphia: Lippincott.

Romig, V.A. (1978). *Justice for our children*. Lexington, MA: D.C. Heath.

Rosenthal, R. (1979). The "file drawer problem" and tolerance for null results. *Psychological Bulletin*, 86, 638–641.

Saul, J., & Davidson, W. (1982). Child advocacy in the juvenile court: A clash of paradigms. In G. Melton (Ed.), *Child advocacy*. Beverly Hills, CA: Sage.

Scarpitti, F., & Stephenson, R.M. (1971). Juvenile court dispositions. *Crime and Delinquency, 17*, 142–151.

Schultz, J.L. (1973). The cycle of juvenile court history. *Crime and Delinquency, 19*, 457–476.

Sechrest, L., & Redner, R. (1979). Strength and integrity of treatments. In *Review of criminal evaluation results* (pp. 19–62). Washington, DC: National Criminal Justice Reference Service, U.S. Department of Justice.

Smith, P.M., & Ausnew, H.R. (1974). Socialization as related to delinquency classification. *Psychological Reports, 34*, 677–678.

Spivack, G., & Schure, M.B. (1982). The cognition of social adjustment. In B.B. Lahey & A.E. Kazdin (Eds.), *Advances in child clinical psychology* (pp. 139–164). New York: Plenum Press.

Steketee, J.P. (1973). *Community and behavioral approaches to delinquency: The court's perspective*. Paper presented at the American Psychological Association Convention, Montreal, Canada.

Stuart, R.B. (1971). Behavioral contracting within the families of delinquents. *Journal of Behavior Therapy and Experimental Psychiatry, 2*, 1–11.

Stumphauser, J. (1971). *Behavior therapy with delinquents*. Springfield, IL: Charles C Thomas.

Stumphauser, J.S. (1976). Modifying delinquent behavior: Beginnings and current practices. *Adolescence, 11* (41), 14–28.

Stumphauser, J. (1978). *Progress in behavior therapy with delinquents*. Springfield, IL: Charles C Thomas.

Tharp, R., & Wetzel, R. (1969). *Behavior modification in the natural environment*. New York: Academic Press.

Winett, R.A., & Winkler, R.C. (1972). Current behavior modification in the classroom: Be still, be quiet, be docile. *Journal of Applied Behavior Analysis, 5*, 499–509.

STUDIES USED IN THE META-ANALYSIS

Alexander, R.N., Corbett, T.F., & Smigel, J. (1976). The effects of individual and group consequences on school attendance and curfew violations with predelinquent adolescents. *Journal of Applied Behavioral Analysis, 9*, 221–226.

Alexander, J.F., & Parsons, B.V. (1973). Short-term behavioral intervention with delinquent families. *Journal of Abnormal Psychology, 81*, 219–225.

Braukmann, C.J., Fixsen, D.L., Phillips, C.L., & Wolf, M.M. (1974). An analysis of a selection interview training package for predelinquents at Achievement Place. *Criminal Justice & Behavior, 1*(1), 30–42.

Davidson, W.S., & Robinson, M.R. (1975). Community psychology and behavior modification. *Corrective and Social Psychiatry, 21*, 1–12.

Davidson, W.S., Seidman, E., Rappaport, J., Berck, P.L., Papp, N.A., Rhodes, W., & Herring, J. (1977). Diversion programs for juvenile offenders. *Social Work Research and Abstracts, 13*(2), 40–49.

Davidson, W.S., & Wolfred, T.R. (1977). Evaluation of a community-based behavior modification program for prevention of delinquency: The failure of success. *Community Mental Health Journal, 13,* 296–306.

Eitzen, D.S. (1974). Impact of behavior modification techniques on locus of control of delinquent boys. *Psychological Reports, 35,* 1317–1318.

Eitzen, D.S. (1975). The effects of behavior modification on the attitudes of delinquents. *Behavior Research and Therapy, 13,* 295–299.

Eitzen, D.S. (1976). The self-concept of delinquents in a behavior modification treatment program. *Journal of Social Psychology, 90,* 203–206.

Eller, B.F., & Stone, J. (1979). Corrective procedures for academic failure and school truancy with a delinquent adolescent male. *Corrective and Social Psychiatry and Journal of Behavior Technology, 25,* 21–24.

Emshoff, J.G., Redd, W.H., & Davidson, W.S. (1976). Generalization training and the transfer of prosocial behavior in delinquent adolescents. *Behavior Therapy and Experimental Psychiatry, 7,* 141–144.

Hendrix, C.E., & Heckel, R.V. (1982). The effects of a behavioral approach on modifying social behavior in incarcerated male delinquents. *Journal of Clinical Psychology, 36,* 77–79.

Hobbs, T.R., & Holt, M.M. (1976). The effects of token reinforcement on the behavior of delinquents in cottage settings. *Journal of Applied Behavior Analysis, 9,* 189–198.

Holt, M.M., & Hobbs, T.R. (1979). Comparative effectiveness of behavior modification and transactional analysis programs for delinquents. *Journal of Consulting and Clinical Psychology, 43,* 758–779.

Kifer, R.E., Lewis, M.A., Green, D.R., & Phillips, E.L. (1974). Traianing predelinquent youths and their parents to negotiate conflict situations. *Journal of Applied Behavior Analysis, 7,* 357–364.

Kirigin, K.A., Braukmann, C.J., Atwater, J.D., & Wolf, M.M. (1982). An evaluation of teaching-family group homes for juvenile offenders. *Journal of Applied Behavior Analysis, 15,* 1–16.

Kirigin, K.A., Wolf, M.M., Braukmann, C.J., Fixsen, D.L., & Phillips, E.L. (1979). Achievement Place: A preliminary outcome evaluation. In J.S. Stumphauser (Ed.), *Progress in behavior therapy with delinquents* (pp. 118–145). Springfield, IL: Charles C Thomas.

Klein, N., Alexander, J., & Parsons, B. (1977). Impact of family systems intervention on recidivism and sibling delinquency: A model of primary prevention and program evaluation. *Journal of Consulting and Clinical Psychology, 45,* 469–474.

O'Donnell, C.R., & DeLeon, J.L. (1973). A contingency program for academic achievement in a correctional setting: Gains and time in school. *Journal of Community Psychology, 1,* 285–287.

Ollendick T.H., & Hersen, M. (1979). Social skills training for juvenile delinquents. *Behavior Research and Therapy, 17,* 547–554.

Parsons, B.V., & Alexander, J.F. (1973). Short-term family intervention. *Journal of Consulting and Clinical Psychology, 41,* 195–201.

Reid, J.B., & Patterson, G.R. (1976). A study of institutional treatment programs. *International Journal of Offender Therapy and Comparative Criminology, 20,* 165–173.

Sarason, I.G. (1976). A modeling and informational approach to delinquency. In E. Ribes-Inesta & A. Bandura (Eds.), *Analysis of delinquency and aggression* (pp. 71–93). Hillsdale, NJ: Erlbaum.

Sarason, I.G., & Ganzer, V. (1973). Modeling and group discussion in the rehabilitation of juvenile delinquents. *Journal of Counseling Psychology, 20,* 442–449.

Sloane, H.N., & Ralph, J.L. (1973). A behavior modification program in Nevada. *International Journal of Offender Therapy and Comparative Criminology, 17,* 290–296.

Spence, S.H., & Marzillier, J.S. (1979). Social skills training with adolescent male offenders I: Short-term effects. *Behavior Research and Therapy, 17,* 7–16.

Spence, S.H., & Marzillier, J.S. (1981). Social skills training with adolescent male offenders II: Short-term, long-term and generalized effects. *Behavior Research and Therapy, 19,* 348–368.

Stuart, R.B. (1971). Behavioral contracting within the families of delinquents. *Journal of Behavior Therapy and Experimental Psychiatry, 2,* 1–11.

Weathers, L., & Liberman, R.P. (1975). Contingency contracting with families of delinquent adolescents. *Behavior Therapy, 6*, 356–366.

Weinrott, M.R., Jones, R.R., & Howard, J.R. (1982). Cost effectiveness of teaching family programs for delinquents. *Evaluation Review, 6*, 173–201.

Wener, J.S., Minkin, N., Minkin, B.L., Fixsen, D.L., Phillips, E.L., & Wolf, M.M. (1975). Intervention package: Analysis to prepare juvenile delinquents for encounters with police officers. *Criminal Justice and Behavior, 2*, 55–85.

Willner, A.G., Braukmann, C.J., Kirigin, K.A., & Wolf, M.M. (1977). Achievement Place: A community treatment model for youths in trouble. In Marholin D. (Ed.), *Child behavior therapy* (pp. 239–273). New York: Gardner Press.

3

Diverting Youth from the Juvenile Justice System: A Meta-Analysis of Intervention Efficacy

Leah K. Gensheimer
Jeffrey P. Mayer
Rand Gottschalk
William S. Davidson II

INTRODUCTION

Violence and aggression have plagued civilization since its conception. Manifestations of these behaviors have taken many forms, from a child's deliberate refusal to obey a parent's request to a brutal beating inflicted upon another human being. Theorists have offered various causal explanations for such actions (Bandura, 1973; Dollard, Doob, Miller, Mower, & Sears, 1939; Rule & Nesdale, 1976) and others have attempted to operationalize them (Bandura, 1976; Berkowitz, 1974; Feshbach, 1970; Novaco, 1979). Although there is great disparity among writers regarding the forms, theories, and definitions of these antisocial responses, a general consensus does exist regarding the prevalence of violence/aggression in American society and the public's fear of being victims of these acts.

Violence and aggression have been the focus of much research over the past two decades. The result has been a plethora of publications which attempt to explain the phenomenon and/or present methods of prediction, control, and treatment (Goldstein & Krasner, 1983; Goldstein, Carr, Davidson, & Wehr, 1981; Hays, Roberts, & Solway, 1981; Stuart, 1981). At the forefront of this interest is concern over the prevalence of acts socially defined as criminal and/or delinquent among contemporary youth.

> The criminal deviance of juveniles is one of the major problems confronting contemporary society. Slightly less than half the persons arrested for serious offenses are under eighteen years of age. Arrests of young people have doubled over the last decade, as compared to relatively minor increases for those eighteen and over. And recent self-report studies suggest that the social demographic correlates of delinquency are expanding to include female, middle-class, majority, and rural juveniles as well as male, lower-class, minority, and urban youths. Thus, the contemporary crime problem is largely attributable to the actions of juveniles. (Lundman & Scarpitti, 1978, p. 207)

The paragraph quoted above is a typical introduction to the vast number of articles and chapters on delinquency. Statements regarding the widespread prevalence of violent crime among youth and increasing trends are used to substantiate the serious crime problem in America and the need for intervention in any number of forms, ultimately dictated by the bias of the particular author/investigator. Although evidence exists that demonstrates a tapering off of the rate of juvenile crime in recent years (Laub, 1983; Zimring, 1979), delinquency has persisted as a major contemporary issue. Whether this is in part due to public fear of being victimized or due to pure humanitarian concern over our country's youth, the result has been continued expenditures of finances and energies toward seeking effective approaches to the prevention and control of juvenile deviance.

While the juvenile justice system represents one approach to the prevention of violence in American society (Blakely & Davidson, 1981), it has also largely been criticized as a contributory factor to further involvement in crime (Gold & Williams, 1969). As a result, much attention has been directed toward alternative approaches and strategies in the handling of juvenile offenders apart from the traditional system. Diversion is such an alternative approach, one which has gained much momentum since its conception almost two decades ago.

This chapter will assess the efficacy of diversion practices with juvenile delinquents through a meta-analysis of the research literature. Prior to proceeding with the actual analysis, a brief discussion of the history of the juvenile justice system will be presented, focusing on events leading up to the diversion reform movement. Next, the concept of diversion will be clarified and the current status of diversion practices will be discussed. A rationale for the present literature review will be provided followed by a description of the meta-analysis methods used, based upon the works of Hunter, Schmidt, and Jackson (1982) and Glass, McGraw, and Smith (1981). Finally, results of the meta-analysis will be presented and implications for diversion interventions with juvenile offenders will be drawn.

EVENTS PRECEDING THE DIVERSION MOVEMENT

The evolution of the juvenile justice system can be viewed as a series of reform movements dating back to the early 1800s, marked by the establishment of the first House of Refuge in 1825 (Krisberg & Austin, 1978). This reformation was prompted by society's concern over the inhumane treatment of youths in adult correctional facilities and their failure to reduce delinquency and provide the public with the protection it demanded. These concerns have persisted over the past century and a half and are credited for many of the changes in our country's handling of juvenile offenders. The reform schools initiated by the Child Savers of the Industrial era, the creation of the first juvenile court in 1899, and the establishment of procedural safeguards to protect the constitutional rights of juveniles during the 1960s were all prompted by concerns over the welfare of children and society's protection against lawlessness.

Many of the structures and practices associated with the contemporary juvenile justice system are largely an outgrowth of the 1960s. The civil rights movement prompted concern over the rights of various minority groups and revitalized interest in what had become an overlooked segment of the population—children. This was a decade where established social institutions were critically examined for their merit in providing adequate and effective services. The juvenile justice system was one of many institutions to fall prey to public scrutiny. Concerns that prompted changes nearly a century before resurfaced. In general, the system came under attack for having failed to fulfill its primary objectives of preventing and treating delinquency. More specifically, criticisms focused on the system's failure to ameliorate crime and tendency to exacerbate the problem instead; the inhumane and ineffective treatment of juveniles; the bureaucratic and overburdened court system; the denial to youth's constitutional rights; and the sentiment that the system was focusing on the wrong population through its almost unlimited jurisdiction upheld by the *parens patriae* philosophy (Carter & Klein, 1976; Davidson, Snellman, & Koch, 1981; Lemert, 1976).

In addition to criticisms of the traditional practices of processing and handling juveniles, the 1960s brought about a general rethinking of the delinquency problem (Clarke, 1974). The popularized opportunity theory and findings from studies based on self-report data, which revealed the widespread nature of delinquency across social statuses, spurred an antidelinquency campaign. Proponents of this crusade did not view delinquency as a problem warranting governmental action; rather, it was seen as nonproblematic behavior to be solved by restraining public policy in the form of narrowing what constitutes juvenile offenses and diverting youths from the system (Clarke, 1974). A hands off policy emerged with recommendations to leave youths alone and for "judicious/planned nonintervention" (Lemert, 1971; Schur, 1973).

Overall disillusionment with the practices of the system and the redefinition of deviant behavior prompted the search for alternative approaches to existing methods of prevention and control. Diversion was one such approach. During the late 1960s and throughout the 1970s diversion came to take the lead among alternative strategies.

THE DIVERSION MOVEMENT

The concept of diversion is not new. It has long been a part of the American criminal justice system (Carter & Klein, 1976) with roots going back to early reform movements. Historically, the juvenile justice system was established for the purpose of diverting children away from the formal system imposed on the hardened adult population, and toward a more humane system intended to take the best interest of the child into consideration. Further, diversion has been viewed as an inherent and necessary process of the system (Klein, 1976a; Nejelski, 1976; Binder, 1977). The almost unlimited discretionary powers held by agents of each component of the juvenile justice system (i.e., police, court officials, correctional personnel) allow for much filtering out/turning away of youths from further system penetration. As a consequence of such applications, a great deal of definitional variation exists in the literature and much discussion surrounds the ambiguity of "diversion" (for example, see Binder, 1977; Cressey & McDermott, 1976; Klein, 1979). In an attempt not to get "caught in the web of definitional variations" (Carter & Klein, 1976), diversion in the context of this article will mean the formal channeling of youths away from further penetration into the juvenile justice system to an alternative nonjudicial means of handling the juvenile. Therefore, our definition is broad and includes common "warn and release" practices as well as a wide variety of activities/services offered to juveniles instead of the formal court process.

The impetus of current diversion practice is attributed to the President's Commission on Law Enforcement and Administration of Justice (1967). The task force was formed to prepare a broad-based report on crime and delinquency and make recommendations for national policies. In the area of delinquency, the commission recommended a narrowing of the juvenile courts' jurisdiction over cases and supported the use of dispositional alternatives for juvenile offenders that would avoid the stigma associated with formal processing, urging the establishment of Youth Service Bureaus and community-based treatment programs. In addition, the commission advocated increased efforts on the part of the federal, state, and local governments to finance the establishment of such programs. Incited by the commission's report, diversion quickly "caught on" and was endorsed by public officials, the American Bar Association, and various national commissions (Dunford, Osgood, & Weichselbaum, 1981). In 1973 the National Advisory Commission on Criminal Justice Standards and Goals advocated the use of diversionary programs and in the following year diversion was embodied in congressional policy and was implemented by federal and state funds (Lemert, 1981).

The years following the commission's report were characterized by a proliferation of diversion programs. Diversion brought society promise for correcting the various short-comings of the juvenile justice system. It was assumed that diversionary practices would protect youths from the abuses of the system; reduce the excessive number of children processed through the overburdened courts; avoid the negative effects of labeling and stigmatization; foster a reduction in recidivism rates among juveniles; promote a sense of community responsibility for its youth; and provide financial relief for the system by reducing the costs of processing delinquency cases (Carter & Klein, 1976; Lemert, 1981). This enthusiasm over the merits of diversion, however, was short-lived.

CURRENT STATUS OF DIVERSION PROGRAMS: A NEED FOR META-ANALYSIS

Seventeen years have elapsed since the diversion reform movement began. During this time, diversion interventions have become a nationally accepted alternative to traditional processing of juvenile offenders. However, as with various other so-called reform practices instituted throughout the history of the justice system, diversion also has undergone critical examination and subsequently has been attacked for failing to fulfill its primary objectives. Following the surge in diversion programming, articles sharply criticizing its practices and policies widely appeared in the professional literature. Numerous criticisms have been waged against this form of intervention. In general, these attacks have centered on diversion failing to fulfill its intended purposes of reducing the negative effects of labeling or stigmatization, widening rather than narrowing social control over youths, and impeding youth's rights and due process safeguards (Blomberg, 1980; Lemert, 1981; Rausch & Logan, 1983). Other issues raised have included the definitional ambiguity of "diversion," overrepresentation of minority and poor groups among diversion clients, poorly established rational/conceptual framework, costs, and implementation issues (Bullington, Sprowls, Katkin, & Phillips, 1978; Cressey & McDermott, 1973; Davidson et al., 1981; Klein, 1979).

Similarly, during this time period reviews of the efficacy of diversion programs with juvenile offenders began to appear. Conclusions drawn by reviewers of the literature have generally painted a pessimistic view for the promise of diversionary efforts. Diversion interventions have been described as being noneffective, as showing little evidence of positive impact, and as producing mixed results (Dunford et al., 1981; Gibbons & Blake, 1976; Romig, 1978). These reviews have consistently pointed out numerous methodological flaws that plague diversion research and various implementation issues that impede the ability to draw definite conclusions regarding the effectiveness of diversion (Binder, 1977; Dunford et al., 1981).

This chapter will seek to assess the efficacy of diversion approaches in the treatment of juvenile offenders using the methods of meta-analysis proposed by Hunter et al. (1982) and Glass et al. (1981). Meta-analysis was developed in response to the perceived need to bring specificity, standardization, and replicability to the process of literature reviews. Typically, reviewers summarized a body of research literature by either overall impression or vote counting. Reviews were often concluded by statements on the percentage of studies that demonstrated the hypothesized relationship. Debates following such reviews often centered on disagreements over the method of review. Essentially, arguments have arisen over the replicability of the study review process (Smith, Glass, & Miller, 1980). An advantage of meta-analysis is the specification of procedures for the conversion of results from different studies into a common metric. A common issue with previous review procedures was the replicability of conclusions due to differences in outcome variables, research designs, and statistical standards. Once outcome variables have been converted to a standard metric, an examination of the relationship, if any, between outcomes and other study characteristics becomes possible. This allows the reviewer to address a series of interesting questions. The most germane questions are what impact does diversion interventions have on juvenile delinquents and what is the size of the observed effect? In other words, across studies, how strong is the relationship between diversion interventions and desired outcomes? Further, one could examine whether particular intervention or methodological characteristics contribute to more positive or negative outcomes. In addition, this review will provide an opportunity to resolve some of the ambiguity surrounding the concept of diversion. A systematic look at subject and intervention characteristics across studies will allow for general statements regarding "who" diversion clients are and what types of services they are actually being provided.

Two basic assumptions underlie the methods of quantitative meta-analysis used here. First, the most important question to be addressed is the efficacy of diversion approaches to juvenile delinquents compared to no-treatment or treatment as usual controls. To the extent that other specific interventions are included in treatment as usual groups, this review will address the efficacy of diversion approaches relative to these other treatments. A second assumption is that the aggregation of results across studies allows for drawing stronger conclusions than any individual study by compensating for methodological flaws inherent in a particular study. If a number of studies, all with different methodological flaws, come to the same conclusion, then one could have confidence in that conclusion. Because this review will examine some of the methodological characteristics of the research, it will be possible to see to what extent the literature taken as a whole addresses particular methodological problems.

METHOD

Domains Covered

This review and meta-analysis is a culmination of published and unpublished literature on diversion interventions with delinquent youth from 1967 through 1983. Studies were selected for inclusion in this review based on several criteria. First, only outcome studies were included. This meant the study had to assess dependent variables that showed evidence of generalization whether it be across time, behavior, or setting. Investigations that merely reported results on behaviors within the treatment setting were excluded on the grounds of being process studies. Second, only studies that included officially delinquent youth were included. This criteria demanded that the subject be youth who were referred by juvenile/family officials or by the police for official delinquency. Specifically excluded were studies involving "troubled youth, maladjusted youth, antisocial youth, underachieving children, and adjustment reactions of adolescents." It was felt that such work would broaden the review in unreliable ways. Third, only those studies that involved diversion from the formal juvenile justice system were included.

The meta-analysis was based on studies collected from two sources, a computer based search of *Psychological Abstracts* and through personal correspondence with known experts in the field of delinquency research. The computerized search was based on the following key words: juvenile delinquents, treatment, intervention, and outcome studies. This search produced abstracts for 643 studies. In an attempt to broaden the covered domain to include unpublished works, letters requesting copies of technical reports, reprints, and other manuscript forms of outcome studies with delinquent youths were mailed to 60 investigators. From this procedure, 117 studies were added to our collection. Abstracts were read by the authors and studies that were not outcome studies of interventions with juvenile delinquents were excluded. Of the 760 studies, 175 appeared to be outcome studies with juvenile delinquents. The 175 studies were then read for potential coding and inclusion in the review. From the 175 studies, 103 were actually codable for a meta-analysis on all types of interventions, the findings of which are the topic of another article (Davidson, Gottschalk, Gensheimer, & Mayer, 1984). The diversion studies for the present review were selected on an a priori basis. These studies are a subset of those coded from the more comprehensive review and were selected based on the criteria that the intervention included diversion from the formal juvenile justice system. Procedures used for calculating effect size for this meta-analysis required comparisons between two groups. Therefore, complex designs had to be reduced and were coded multiple times. As a result, 44 research designs were coded and treated as distinct studies.

Coding Procedures for the Meta-Analysis

The 44 studies were divided among the four authors and coded according to the procedures described below. The methods specified by Glass et al. (1981) and Hunter et al. (1982) were followed. Overall, the goal of coding was to capture important characteristics of the study and to specify a standard metric for outcome results.

Study Characteristics. Table 3.1 presents a summary of the study characteristics that were coded. These variables represented a coding of the characteristics of the subjects, the location of the intervention in the juvenile justice system, the components of the intervention, the relationship of the investigator and change agent to the intervention, and the characteristics of the methodology. Coding of such variables allowed for a description of the literature on which the assessment of outcome effect size was based. It also allowed for an examination of the relationship of some study characteristics and effect size.

Effect Size Calculations. This meta-analysis involved five potential effect size indices for each of the several different types of outcome variables. First, an overall effectiveness rating was assigned to each study based on the overall conclusions drawn by the authors of this meta-analysis. Second, a general rating was assigned to each study based on the overall conclusion presented by the author of the specific study. Third, a specific rating of effectiveness was assigned to each dependent variable within each study. This third rating was based on the conclusion drawn in the study concerning effects on the specific dependent variable in question. These three indices of effectiveness were done on a 3-point scale of positive effect, no effect, and negative effect. These methods represent three distinct versions of what others have called the ballot box or voting methods of literature review. Fourth, standardized effect scores were calculated for reported pre/post changes for each dependent

Table 3.1. Study Characteristics

Subject Dimensions
  1. Adjudicated—coded yes/no.
  2. Percent male.
  3. Average age.

Relationship to Juvenile Justice System
  1. Intervention inside system—coded yes/no.
  2. Intervention included diversion–coded yes/no.

Intervention Components
  1. Setting—whether the intervention took place in an institution, community residential program, or community/nonresidential setting.
  2. Duration—the average length of the intervention in weeks.
  3. Intensity—the average number of hours of intervention.
  4. Primary type of intervention—coded once per study for behavioral, educational/vocational, individual psychotherapy, casework/probation, and other nonspecific.
  5. Types of intervention present—coded multiple timers per study for group therapy, modeling/role playing, token economies, academic, positive reinforcement, behavioral contracting, service brokerage, probation, vocational, intensive casework, advocacy, psychodynamic therapy, client centered therapy, transactional analysis, cognitive therapy, and reality therapy.

Characteristics of Investigator
  1. Discipline of authors.
  2. Intervener had influence over treatment process—coded none, to some extent, to a great extent.
  3. Investigator had influence over treatment process—coded none, to some extent, to a great extent.

Methodological Characteristics
  1. Implementation measurement—was there assessment of intervention integrity?
  2. Evidence of unplanned variability in intervention—was there evidence of lack of compliance or other problems in treatment integrity?
  3. Data collectors blind to experimental conditions/hypotheses—coded yes/no.
  4. Description of control group—coded as no treatment, treatment as usual, subjects as own control (pre/post designs), or no control group.
  5. Assignment of subjects to treatment—coded as random, matching, or nonrandom.
  6. Assignment of interveners to participants—coded as random, matching, or nonrandom.

variable within the study; and fifth, calculated effect sizes for experimental/control group differences for each dependent variable were also derived. In general, these quantitative effect sizes were calculated by subtracting the experimental group post-mean from the control group post-mean (or experimental group pre-mean) and dividing by the control group standard deviation (or the pre–standard deviation). This yielded an effect size index in standard deviation units. Table 3.2 summarizes the variables that were coded for each dependent variable within each study. Types of dependent variables coded included recidivism (up to three per study), self-report delinquency,program behaviors (up to two per study), vocational behavior, academic performance (up to two per study) social behavior (up to two per study), school or work attendance (up to two per study), attitudinal variables (up to two per study), self-esteem, ratings of global adjustment, and other cognitive variables. Two other coding rules must be mentioned. Studies that reported no data (e.g., case studies) were included in the "ballot box" ratings. Studies that reported "no significant findings" on a particular dependent variable were coded as having reported a 0.00 effect size. This was selected as the best estimate (the population mean) of nonsignificant effect sizes. Assuming a zero effect size when the effect statistic is uncomputable is a very conservative way to deal with missing data.

Table 3.2. Calculation of Effect Size

For each of the following types of dependent variables, ratings were made for each study when sufficient data was present.

1. Recidivism—these outcomes included arrests, court charges, or other indicants of official involvement in the juvenile justice system for illegal behavior. Up to three recidivism outcomes were coded per study.
2. Self report delinquency—this outcome included self-reports of illegal acts.
3. Program behavior—this outcome included assessments of within-program behavior such as subsequent diagnoses, rates of release, violations of probation, rates of rule compliance, etc. Up to two program behavior outcomes were coded per study.
4. Vocational behavior—this outcome included assessment of job or employment related performance.
5. Academic behavior—this outcome included assessments of academic performance such as achievement tests, grades, etc. Up to two academic behavior outcomes were coded per study.
6. Other social behavior—this outcome included assessments of other interpersonal performances. Up to two social behavior outcomes were coded per study.
7. School/work attendance—this outcome included assessments of attendance in school or a job. Up to two attendance outcomes were coded per study.
8. Self-concept—this outcome included assessments of self-esteem and self-concept.
9. Other attitudinal—this outcome included assessments of other attitudes.
10. Other cognitive—this outcome included assessments of other cognitive variables.
11. Ratings of global adjustment—this outcome included ratings or reports of nonspecific adjustment not covered under above variables categories.

Variables coded for each dependent variable.

1. Method of data collection—coded as behavioral observation, archival, self-report, paper and pencil, interview, rating of someone else.
2. Reliability assessment—type of reliability reported, if any.
3. Size of reliability of assessment.
4. Research design for specific dependent variable.
5. Length of follow-up period in weeks.
6. Number of subjects for pre/post comparison.
7. Significance level of pre/post comparison.
8. Effect size for pre/post comparison.
9. Effectiveness rating of pre-post change for specific dependent variable.
10. Number of experimental subjects for experimental/control comparisons.
11. Number of control subjects for experimental/control comparison.
12. Significance level for experimental control comparison.
13. Effect size for pre/post comparison.
14. Effectiveness rating of pre-post change for specific dependent variable.

One tenth of the studies were coded independently by two authors. The interrater agreement rate was 86%.

RESULTS

Description of the Studies

The characteristics of the studies and programs included in the meta-analysis are summarized in Table 3.3. This table has been divided into several sections describing investigators, subjects, interventions, relationship to the juvenile justice system, and methodological

Table 3.3. Description of Studies

Characteristics	Number (n)	Percentage
Study		
Publication date:		
1971	1	
1972	2	
1973	2	
1975	2	
1976	3	
1977	6	
1978	2	
1979	1	
1980	9	
1981	14	
1982	2	
Publication form:		
Journal	20	45
Book	4	9
Other (e.g., technical reports, unpublished manuscripts)	20	45
Investigator		
1. Discipline of principal investigator:		
Psychology	18	41
Criminal Justice	13	30
Other	13	30
2. Service deliverer influence:		
Great amount of influence	11	37
Some influence	16	53
No influence	3	10
3. Experimenter/evaluator influence:		
Great amount of influence	12	28
Some influence	4	9
No influence	27	63
Subject		
1. Average percent male	—	73
2. Average age	14.6 years	
3. Studies with adjudicated youth	31	70
Relationship to the Juvenile Justice System		
Intervention outside system	33	77
Intervention		
1. Setting		
Institutional	1	2
Community residential	4	9
Community nonresidential	39	89
2. Average Duration		
Mean number of weeks	18.31	
Median number of weeks	15.00	
Range	4–52	
3. Average Intensity		
Mean number of hours	37.16	
Median number of hours	15.13	
4. Primary Type of Intervention		
Non-specific	17	39

(continued)

Table 3.3. Description of Studies (*continued*)

Characteristics	Number (n)	Percentage
Group psychotherapy	11	25
Case work/probation	6	14
Behavioral	6	14
Educational/vocational	2	5
Individual psychotherapy	2	5
5. Type of Intervention Used		
Service brokerage	20	45
Group therapy	18	41
Academic	16	36
Vocational	16	36
Advocacy	15	34
Intensive casework	8	18
Modeling role play	6	14
Behavioral contracting	5	11
Positive reinforcement	5	11
Token economy	3	7
Probation	3	7
Psychodynamic	2	5
Cognitive	2	5
Client centered	1	2
Methodological		
1. Studies measuring implementation	19	43
2. Evidence of unplanned treatment variation	11	25
3. Studies including blind data collectors	1	2
4. Control group type		
No treatment	21	48
Treatment as usual	19	43
Other	4	9
5. Studies including random assignment to treatment	19	43
6. Studies including random assignment of intervener		0

characteristics. Where appropriate, the number of studies that included the specific feature and overall percentages are presented.

The first section of Table 3.3 lists publication dates and forms of the studies included in the review. As implied from the span of dates, investigations on the efficacy of diversion programs is a relatively recent activity with studies appearing only over the last decade. This is to be expected, because the origin of the contemporary diversion movement is routinely attributed to the 1967 President's Commission on Law Enforcement and Administration of Justice. The first outcome study appeared 4 years after the commission's report, a time when legislative and executive branches of the government had begun to actively endorse the recommendations of the commission. Although the 1980s appear marked by heightened interest in diversion research, the figures may be somewhat misleading. The majority of studies associated with 1980 and 1981 were part of two large-scale evaluation projects. These comprehensive reports evaluated a sample of different diversion programs to assess the impact of this type of general intervention strategy. Therefore, based on the coding criteria previously described, these reports contained several distinct codable studies. With respect to the publication form, only slightly more than half (55%) of the studies were published works located in journals or books. The remaining 45% were comprised of technical reports and unpublished manuscripts.

Researchers were predominately psychologists (41%) or were associated with the criminal justice field (30%). Social work was the only other discipline represented to any noticeable extent, authoring 7% of the studies. In all but three studies, the service deliverers had some to a great amount of influence within the system in which the intervention took place. This implies that the diversion literature is characterized by interventions using change agents who are central to the setting rather than bringing in "outsiders" to carry out the intervention. This finding was consistent with that found in a more broad-based review of all the treatment outcome literature with juvenile delinquents, among which diversion programs comprised one of the many types of interventions reviewed (Davidson et al., 1984). A look at the extent of influence the investigator had in the design and implementation of diversion programs revealed quite a different finding. In almost two thirds of the studies, the investigator had no influence whatsoever over treatment. This indicated that research on the efficacy of diversion programs was conducted by evaluators external to the intervention setting.

An examination of subject characteristics indicated that diversion clients were predominately adjudicated, male youths whose average age was 14½ years old. It was surprising that 70% of the studies involved subjects labeled as adjudicated youth. This implied some formal processing despite the diversion classification of the study. Further, nearly one fourth of the studies involved interventions that took place inside the system, a finding that tends to conflict with more conservative definitions of diversion programs.

Interventions typically took place in community nonresidential settings. It is worth mentioning, however, that 11% of the diversion programs reviewed involved a residential treatment setting. The length of interventions ranged from 4 to 52 weeks. On an average, the intervention consisted of 18.31 weeks. Due to the positively skewed nature of this data set, however, a better estimate would be the median value of 15 weeks. Likewise, the mean number of contact hours of each youth with the service deliverer was 37.16 hours, whereas the median was 15.13 hours of service.

For the majority of studies, almost 40%, the primary mode of intervention fell within the "nonspecific" category. Twenty-five percent of the studies were coded as having offered group psychotherapy as its primary service. Both casework/probation and behavioral intervention were reported as the primary type of intervention in 14% of the studies. Finally, educational/vocational and individual psychotherapy were each cited in 5% of the studies.

To provide a clearer picture of the activities and services offered under the rubric of diversion, specific intervention types observed in the literature were also coded. Unlike the primary mode of intervention, a study could be coded in multiple intervention categories. The data substantiate the ambiguity and diversity of diversion programs. The practice of referring subjects to other community resources/programs (service brokerage) was the most common intervention used. Group therapy was also highly employed. Other interventions used in over a third of the studies were academic, vocational, and advocacy training. The use of behavioral techniques were used in slightly over 10% of the programs.

Several major methodological shortcomings were revealed among this sample of studies. Over 40% provided some measurement of program implementation, but only one fourth provided evidence of unplanned treatment variation. Procedures that would allow for drawing unambiguous conclusions on the efficacy of diversion programs were, for the most, absent. Less than half of the studies included random assignment of subjects to experimental conditions and none addressed the possible influence of the service deliverer or treatment effects. Further, in only one study were data collectors blind to the nature of the investigation.

Effectiveness Results

Rated Effectiveness. A summary of rated effectiveness ("ballot box" ratings) for each dependent variable is presented in Table 3.4. In general, the data suggest that diversion intervention had no effect on outcome measures. In terms of the overall rating of effectiveness, over half of the studies were judged to have had no effect by both our ratings and by those authoring the investigation. The relationship between these two ratings was significant at the .001 level ($r = .67$). This finding is consistent across all outcome variables except for the pre/post comparison among attitudinal measures and experimental/control comparison for school/work attendance.

Quantitative Effectiveness. The preceding conclusions were substantiated by the quantitative effect sizes calculated for this sample of studies. Table 3.5 displays the quantitative effect sizes for the overall set of studies and for each of several types of dependent variables. Prior to discussing the results, an explanation of Table 3.5 is required. The overall effect size is the calculated effect size averaged across all dependent variables. In order to produce a respectable number of studies for effect size calculations among the specific outcome

Table 3.4. Rated Effectiveness

Variable	No. of Studies	Negative Effect (Percentage)	No Effect (Percentage)	Positive Effect (Percentage)
Overall Ratings of Effectiveness				
Our rating	44	7	52	41
Author's rating	44		52	48
Calculated Overall Effectiveness Vote				
Pre/post vote	25	20	36	44
E/C Vote	41	5	41	54
Recidivism				
Pre/post vote	13	31	39	31
E/C Vote	38	5	47	47
Self-Report Delinquency				
Pre/post vote	16	6	94	0
E/C Vote	18	6	89	6
Program Behavior				
Pre/post vote	11	36	46	18
E/C Vote	13	15	39	46
Social Behavior				
Pre/post vote	4	50		50
E/C Vote	2	50		50
Attitude Measure				
Pre/post vote	17		47	53
E/C Vote	21		91	10
Attendance				
Pre/post vote	3	100		
E/C Vote	7	29		71
Self-Esteem				
Pre/post vote	17		76	24
E/C Vote	18		89	11

Table 3.5. Calculated Effect Size

Variable	A	B	C	D	E	F	G
Calculated Overall Effectiveness							
Pre/post	16	4,438	.40	.12	.30	5%	−0.43 to 0.67
E/C	35	13,233	.40	.21	.23	17%	−0.24 to 0.66
Recidivism							
Pre/post	7	2,188	.26	−.23	.32	11%	−0.86 to 0.39
E/C	31	10,210	.44	.26	.28	14%	−0.28 to 0.81
Behavioral Outcomes							
Pre/post	6	1,189	.11	.73	.42	5%	−0.53 to 1.99
E/C	5	320	.16	−.08	.04	60%	−0.48 to 0.33
Attitudinal Outcomes							
Pre/post	8	390	.53	.50	0	100%	—
E/C	2	26	.65	—	—	—	—

Note: Column A = Number of studies reporting the dependent variable
Column B = Number of subjects across studies
Column C = The mean effect size (This represents effect sizes calculated for each study added together and divided by number of studies having a calculable effect size for that particular variable. Therefore, this value does not correct for sample sizes).
Column D = The weighted mean effect size
Column E = The corrected variance of the effect size
Column F = % of observed variance due to sampling error
Column G = 95% confidence interval for effect size

variables, several dependent measures were combined. Recidivism was left as a single-outcome variable. The behavioral outcomes, however, are a combination of program behaviors, social behaviors, and school/work attendance. The attitudinal outcomes reflect a combination of both attitudinal and self-esteem measures.

As shown in Table 3.5, neither the overall effect size nor those calculated for each dependent variable approach an appreciable value. For only two variables (behavioral and attitudinal outcomes) did the weighted effect size reach a half a standard deviation above the control or pre-group mean. It is also important to note that these involved pre/post comparisons and thus are plagued with numerous threats to interval validity. Further evidence of the finding of no effect rests in column G. For all variables, confidence intervals surrounding the corrected effect sizes include 0 and range into negative values.

Overall, the results drawn from both the qualitative ratings of effectiveness and those obtained from quantitative methods lead to the conclusion that diversion interventions produce no effects with youths diverted from the juvenile justice system.

Moderator Variables

Correlational analyses were performed to examine the relationship of study characteristics with the calculated mean effect size and rated effectiveness. From this line of investigation, three interesting relationships emerged. First, the subjects' age was inversely related to the calculated mean effect size ($r = -.35; p = .038$). The older the subject, the less likely the intervention would have a positive effect. A similar relationship was found between age and the global effectiveness rating, however, this relationship did not reach statistical significance ($r = -.21; p = .115$). Second, the hours of contact with a service deliverer (amount of intervention) was found to be significantly related to the calculated mean effect size. This implied the greater number of contact hours between the youth and the service deliverer, the greater positive effect on outcome measures ($r = .69$; $p = .001$). A similar but nonsignificant relationship was observed between the number of contact hours and the global effectiveness rating ($r = .19$; $p = .175$). Finally, there was a significant correlation between the investigator's influence in the design and implementation of treatment and the calculated mean effect size ($r = .76$; $p = .001$). A significant relationship between investigator's influence and the global effectiveness rating was also found ($r = .56$; $p = .001$).

DISCUSSION

The primary purpose of this review was to assess the efficacy of diversion interventions with juvenile delinquents. Meta-analysis was used to determine what effect this alternative to traditional procedures has on various desired outcomes (e.g., recidivism, attitudinal, behavioral). This method of review provided a standardized approach to examine the outcome literature on diversion programs across studies. Overall, findings from this analysis do not provide substantial evidence for the efficacy of diversion programs. Results from both rated effectiveness and those obtained from quantitative methods lead to the conclusion that diversion interventions produce no strong positive nor strong negative effects with youth diverted from the juvenile justice system.

Isolated from other information secured from this review process, these results could be discouraging to advocates of the diversion movement. Based on these conclusions, researchers can pursue one of two avenues. One route is to abandon diversion efforts entirely on grounds that it has shown to be ineffective. The alternative is to seek means of improving diversion efforts. The first route is ill-founded. It is important to note that while no strong positive relationship existed between diversion interventions and the desired outcomes, no strong negative effects were observed either. Viewed in conjunction with the well-established literature on the detrimental effects of traditional approaches to treating juvenile offenders, findings of this review should prompt researchers to pursue the alternative route. A closer examination of the study characteristics and some of their relationships with the observed outcomes provide directions for future diversion programming and evaluation. This discussion will focus on three specific areas: diversion clients, the need for increased program specificity, and improved evaluation methods.

Based on the sample of studies reviewed, the typical diversion clients were adjudicated, 14½-year-old male youths. The fact that the majority were adjudicated implied some form of formal processing by the system had occurred. This presents severe limitations in our examination of diversion interventions. It is impossible to determine how far into the system those youths went before they were "referred out" to a diversion program, and further, what impact this contact had on the overall results. Despite the care taken in selecting studies based on rigid criteria, this review could be seriously criticized for having failed to adequately target "diversion" clients. Although purely speculative, it is possible that positive effects of diversion were cancelled by negative influences on traditional processing. Future evaluations need to control for this variable so the pure effects of diverting youths from traditional procedures can be ascertained.

In the search for "who" might benefit most from diversion approaches, correlational analyses were performed to isolate subject dimensions related to more positive or negative outcomes. From this line of investigation, age was found to be inversely related to the calculated mean effect size. The older the subject, the less likely intervention would have a positive effect. This finding can be viewed from two perspectives. One interpretation is that the younger the individual, the more amenable s/he is to treatment. This interpretation would support the prevention model of targeting individuals for intervention at an early age and suggests greater attention be focused on diverting adolescents at a younger age from the system. The second interpretation centers around the theory that adolescents outgrow deviant behavior. This implies the older the youth, the less likely s/he will engage in juvenile deviance, in other words, there is a maturational effect. Until research more systematically examines the moderator effect of age on outcomes of diversion programs, it is too premature to make any recommendations regarding at what age juveniles would benefit most from diversion interventions.

A common criticism waged against diversion is its ambiguous nature. A wide range of services and activities are offered under the diversion rubric, as well as great variation in the intensity of the interventions. Data from this review showed diversion clients received an average of 15 hours of intervention over the course of approximately 4 months. It is interesting to note that the hours of contact with a service deliverer (amount of intervention) was significantly related to the calculated mean effect size. The greater number of contact hours between the youth and the service deliverer, the greater positive effect on outcome measures. Proper interpretation of this finding is difficult to make. On the one hand, it would appear to support the treatment model approach to juvenile delinquency and suggests further development of service oriented programs versus the more radical movement toward diversion without services. On the other hand, there is little evidence to support the value of services per se. The number of hours of contact was demonstrated to be related to positive outcome. There may be no connection whatsoever between this variable and the particular services provided by the change agents. Attention effects may have played a role in the finding, or the mere fact that the diverted youths were off the street that many hours more than their counterparts, and therefore had less opportunity to get into trouble, are alternative explanations for this relationship. Investigations that adequately control such variables as hours of contact, attention, and services provided are needed to guide future diversion programming.

This raises another important issue regarding program specificity. An auxiliary purpose of this review was to clarify some of the ambiguity surrounding the diversion literature by systematically recording the various services and activities offered by diversion agents. This procedure has failed to provide much more information than other reviews. The primary mode of intervention for the majority of programs were classified as "nonspecific." Whether this was a function of services actually being ambiguous, or the failure of investigators to adequately document pertinent information cannot be determined. Regardless of the reason, this severely constrains making recommendations in favor of one approach over another. This is further complicated by the large percentage of programs referring clients to other community agencies to receive services (service brokerage). These clients could have received any of a wide variety of interventions. If the overall results of this review were different, that is, a positive or a negative effect was demonstrated, because of the large number of studies falling within these categories, it would be difficult to determine what characteristics of the program moderated the effect. Little information is currently available to properly guide program development on what type of services/activities diversion programs should offer clients, if any. Investigators need to be sensitive to this issue and make a diligent effort toward providing sufficient documentation of what they are evaluating. Without knowledge on the specific interventions provided, or not provided, the dissemination of effective programs would be impossible.

The final area in need of improvement is in evaluation methods. The lack of sound research designs, the use of non-blind data collectors, comparison with nonequivalent control groups, and nonrandomly assigned subjects and/or service deliverers characterizes most of the literature. Such methodological shortcomings compromise results and prevent drawing definitive conclusions on the efficacy of diversion interventions. The prevalence of such poor methodology may be because of the general absence of investigators' influence in program design and implementations. In two thirds of the studies reviewed, the investigators had no influence over treatment. Perhaps this is a function of the post hoc nature of much diversion research, wherein the investigator is called in from the outside to evaluate an already existing program, and thus is often confronted with various external constraints impeding the use of adequate research methods. Further examination of predictive value of the investigator's influence on outcome revealed a significant correlation between this variable and the calculated mean effect size and the global effectiveness rating. This implies that the greater the amount of influence the investigator has in designing and implementing the intervention, the greater the chance of producing a positive effect. Although experimenter bias might contribute to this relationship, the value of investigators taking a more active role in planning and implementing interventions cannot be overlooked. Researchers must become involved with program evaluations a priori. Their involvement from the start of program development will help circumvent some of the methodological flaws that currently exist in the literature.

It has been 17 years since the explosion of the contemporary diversion movement. Although some have argued that diversion is nothing more than a "fad" (Cressey & McDermott, 1973; Gibbons & Blake, 1976), an existence of almost two decades of experience negates this as just a passing craze. There are some serious issues surrounding the current status of diversion practices; however, it is premature to abandon this alternative approach to traditional juvenile justice practices. Diversion is a necessary and inseparable part of the system (Binder, 1977; Nejelski, 1976), which still holds promise as a valuable alternative to the prevention and control of juvenile deviance.

REFERENCES

Bandura, A. (1973). Social learning theory of aggression. In J. Knutson (Ed.), *In control of aggression* (pp. 201–250). Chicago: Aldine Publishing Co.

Bandura, A. (1976). Social learning analysis of aggression. In E. Ribes-Inesta & A. Bandura (Eds.), *Analysis of delinquency and aggression* (pp. 203–232). Hillsdale, NJ: Lawrence Erlbaum Associates.

Berkowitz, L. (1974). Some determinants of impulsive aggression: Role of mediated associations with reinforcement for aggression. *Psychological Review, 81*, 165–176.

Binder, A. (1977). Diversion and the justice system: Evaluating the results. In A. W. Cohn (Ed.), *Criminal justice planning and development* (pp. 117–129). Beverly Hills, CA: Sage Publications.

Blakely, C., & Davidson, W.S. (1981). Prevention of aggression. In A. P. Goldstein, E. G. Carr, W. S. Davidson, & P. Wehr (Eds.), *In response to aggression. Methods of control and prosocial alternatives* (pp. 319–345). New York: Pergamon Press.

Blomberg, T.G. (1980). Widening the net: An anomaly in the evaluation of diversion programs. In M. W. Klein & K. S. Teilmann (Eds), *Handbook of criminal justice evaluation* (pp. 572–592). Beverly Hills, CA: Sage Publications.

Bullington, B., Sprowls, J., Katkin, D., & Phillips, M. (1978). A critique of diversionary juvenile justice. *Crime and Delinquency, 24*(1), 59–71.

Carter, R.M., & Klein, M.W. (Eds.). (1976). *Back on the street: The diversion of juvenile offenders*. Englewood Cliffs, NJ: Prentice-Hall.

Clarke, S.H. (1974, September). Juvenile offenders and delinquency prevention. *Crime and Delinquency Literature*, 377–399.

Cressey, D.R., & McDermott, R.A. (1976). Diversion: Background and definition. In R. M. Carter & M. W. Klein (Eds.), *Back on the street: The diversion of juvenile offenders* (pp. 67–73). Englewood Cliffs, NJ: Prentice-Hall.

Davidson, W.S., Gottschalk, R., Gensheimer, L., & Mayer, J. (1984). *Interventions with juvenile delinquents: A meta-analysis of treatment efficacy*. Washington, DC: National Institute of Justice.

Davidson, W.S., Snellman, K., & Koch, J.R. (1981). Current status of diversion research. Implications for policy and programming. In R. Roesch & R. R. Corrado (Eds.), *Evaluation and criminal justice policy* (pp. 103–121). Beverly Hills, CA: Sage Publications.

Dollard, J., Doob, L., Miller, N., Mower, O., & Sears, R. (1939). *Frustration and aggression*. New Haven: Yale University Press.

Dunford, F.W., Osgood, D.W., & Weichselbaum, H.F. (1981). *National evaluation of diversion projects: Final report*. (Grant Number 78-JN-AX-0037). Washington, DC: National Institute of Juvenile Justice and Delinquency Prevention.

Feshbach, S. (1970). Aggression. In P. H. Mussen (Ed.), *Carmichaels manual of child psychology* (Vol. 2, pp. 159–259). New York: Wiley.

Glass, G.V., McGraw, G., & Smith, M.L. (1981). *Meta-analysis in social research*. Beverly Hills, CA: Sage Publications.

Gibbons, D.C., & Blake, G.F. (1976). Evaluating the impact of juvenile diversion programs. *Crime and Delinquency, 22*, 411–420.

Gold, M., & William, J. (1969). The effect of "getting caught": Apprehension of the juvenile offender as a cause of subsequent delinquencies. *Prospectus: A Journal of Law Reform 3*, 1–12.

Goldstein, A., Carr, E.G., Davidson, W.S., & Wehr, P. (1981). *In response to aggression. Methods of control and prosocial alternatives*. New York: Pergamon Press.

Goldstein, A.P., & Krasner, L. (1983). *Prevention and control of aggression*. New York: Pergamon Press.

Hays, J.R., Roberts, T.K., & Solway, K.S. (1981). *Violence and the violent individual*. New York: Spectrum Publications.

Hunter, J., Schmidt, F., & Jackson, G. (1982). *Cumulating research findings across studies*. Beverly Hills, CA: Sage Publications.

Klein, M.W. (1976a). Issues in police diversion of juvenile offenders. In R. M. Carter & M. W. Klein (Eds.), *Back on the street: The diversion of juvenile offenders* (pp. 73–104). Englewood Cliffs, NJ: Prentice-Hall.

Klein, M.W. (1976b). On the front end of the juvenile justice system. In R. M. Carter & M. W. Klein (Eds.), *Back on the street: The diversion of juvenile offenders* (pp. 307–313). Englewood Cliffs, NJ: Prentice-Hall.

Klein, M.W. (1979). Deinstitutionalization and diversion of juvenile offenders: A litany of impediments. In N. Morris & M. Tonry (Eds.), *Crime and justice. An annual review of research* (Vol. 1, pp. 145–201). Chicago: The University of Chicago Press.

Krisberg, B., & Austin, J. (Eds.) (1978). *The children of Ishmael*. Palo Alto, CA: Mayfield Publishing Co.

Laub, J.H. (1983). Trends in serious juvenile crime. *Criminal justice and behavior, 10*, 485–506.

Lemert, E.M. (1981). Diversion in juvenile justice: What hath been wrought? *Journal of Research in Crime and Delinquency, 18*(1), 34–46.

Lemert, E.M. (1976). Instead of court: Diversion in juvenile justice. In R. M. Carter & M. W. Klein (Eds.), *Back on the streets: The diversion of juvenile offenders* (pp. 123–155). Englewood Cliffs, NJ: Prentice-Hall.

Lemert, E.M. (1971). *Instead of court: Diversion in juvenile justice*. Rockville, MD: National Institute of Mental Health.

Lundman, R.J., & Scarpitti, F.R. (1978). Delinquency prevention: Recommendations for future projects. *Crime and Delinquency, 24*, 207–220.

Nejelski, P. (1976). Diversion: The promise and the danger. *Crime and Delinquency, 22*, 393–410.

Novaco, R.W. (1979). The cognitive regulation of anger and stress. In T. C. Kendall & S. D. Hollon (Eds.), *Cognitive behavioral interventions: Theory, research and procedure*. New York: Academic Press.

President's Commission on Law Enforcement and Crime (1967, February). *The Challenge of Crime in a Free Society*. Washington, DC: U.S. Government Printing Office.

Rausch, S. P., & Logan, C.H. (1983). Diversion from juvenile court. Panacea or Pandora's box? In J. R. Kluegel (Ed.), *Evaluating juvenile justice* (pp. 19–30). Beverly Hills, CA: Sage Publications.

Romig, D.A. (1978). Diversion from the juvenile justice system. In D. A. Romig (Ed.), *Justice for our children* (pp. 117–123). Lexington, MA: Lexington Books, D.C. Health & Company.

Rule, B.G., & Nesdal, A.R. (1976). Emotional arousal and aggressive behavior. *Psychological Bulletin, 83*, 851–863.

Schur, E. (1973). *Radical nonintervention: Rethinking the delinquency problem*. Englewood Cliffs, NJ: Prentice-Hall.

Smith, M.L., Glass, G., & Miller, T.I. (1980). *The benefits of psychotherapy*. Baltimore: Johns Hopkins University Press.

Stuart, R.B. (1981). *Violent behavior: Social learning approaches to prediction, management and treatment*. New York: Brunner/Mazel.

Zimring, F. (1979). American youth violence: Issues and trends. In N. Morris & M. Tonry (Eds.), *Crime and justice. An annual review of research* (Vol. 1, pp. 67–107). Chicago: University of Chicago Press.

STUDIES USED IN THE META-ANALYSIS

Baron, R., & Feeney, F. (1973). *Preventing delinquency through diversion: The Sacramento County Probation Department 601 Diversion Project. A second year report*. Davis, CA: University of California at Davis, Center on Administration of Criminal Justice.

Baron, R., & Feeney, F. (1973). *The Sacramento County Probation Department 602 Diversion Project. A first year report*. Davis, CA: University of California at Davis, Center on Administration of Criminal Justice.

Collingwood, T.R., & Genthner, R.W. (1980). Skills training as a treatment for juvenile delinquents. *Professional Psychology, 11*, 591–598.

Collingwood, T.R., Williams, H., & Douds, A. (1976). An HRD approach to police diversion for juvenile offenders. *Personnel & Guidance Journal, 54*(8), 435–437.

Cotton, M., Fein, D., & Cotton, S. (1976). Effectiveness of a community based treatment program in modifying aggressiveness of delinquent behavior. *Corrective and Social Psychiatry and Journal of Behavior Technology, Methods & Therapy, 22*(2), 35–38.

Davidson, W.S. II, Koch, J.R., Lewis, R.G., & Wresinski, M.D. (1981). *Evaluation strategies in criminal justice*. New York: Pergamon Press.

Davidson, W.S., Seidman, E., Rappaport, J., Berck, P.L., Rapp, N.A., Rhodes, W., & Merring, J. (1977). Diversion programs for juvenile offenders. *Social Work Research and Abstracts, 13*(2), 40–49.

Douds, A.F., & Collingwood, T.R. (1978). Management by objectives: A successful application. *Child Welfare, LV11*(3), 181–185.

Dunford, F.W., Osgood, D.W., & Weichselbaum, H.F. (1981). *National Evaluation of Diversion Projects: Final Report*. (Grant Number 78-JN-AX-0037). Washington, DC: National Institute of Juvenile Justice and Delinquency Prevention.

Elliot, D.S., & Blanchard, S. (1975). *An impact study of two diversion projects*. Paper presented at American Psychological Association, Chicago.

Fryrear, J.L., Nuell, L.R., & Ridley, S.D. (1974). Photographic self-concept enhancement of male juvenile delinquents. *Journal of Consulting and Clinical Psychology, 42*, 915.

Garber, J., Tapp, J.T., Dundar, M., Tulkin, S., & Jens, K. (1976). A psycho-educational therapy program for delinquent boys: An evaluation report. *Journal of Drug Education, 6*, 331–342.

Gilbert, G.R. (1977). Alternative routes: A diversion project in the juvenile justice system. *Evaluation Quarterly, 1*(1), 301–318.

Haapanen, R., & Rudisill, D. (1980). *The evaluation of youth service bureaus: Final report*. Sacramento, CA: Department of the Youth Authority.

Eitzen, D.S. (1975). The effects of behavior modification on the attitudes of delinquents. In J.S. Stumphauser (Ed.), *Progress in behavior therapy with delinquents* (pp. 146–155). Springfield, IL: Charles C Thomas.

Kirigin, K.A., Wolf, M.M., Braukmann, C.J., Fixsen, D.L., & Phillips, E.L. (1979). Achievement Place: A preliminary outcome evaluation. In J.S. Stumphauser (Ed.), *Progress in behavior therapy with delinquents*. Springfield, IL: Charles C Thomas.

Lipsey, M.W., Cordray, D.S., & Berger, D.E. (1981). Evaluation of a juvenile diversion program: Using multiple lines of evidence. *Evaluation Review, 5*, 283–306.

Palmer, T., Bohnstedt, M., & Lewis, R. (1978). *The evaluation of juvenile diversion projects: Final report*. Sacramento, CA: Department of the Youth Authority.

Quay, H.C., & Love, C. (1977). The effect of juvenile diversion program on rearrests. *Criminal Justice and Behavior, 4*, 377–396.

Severy, L.J., & Whitaker, J.M. (1982). Juvenile diversion: An experimental analysis of effectiveness. *Evaluation review, 6*, 753–774.

Stuart, R.B. (1971). Behavioral contracting with the families of delinquents. *Journal of Behavior Therapy and Experimental Psychiatry, 2*, 1–11.

Venezia, P.S. (1972). Unofficial probation: An evaluation of its effectiveness. *The Journal of Research in Crime and Delinquency, 9*, 149–170.

Willner, A.G., Braukmann, C.J., & Kirigin, K.A. (1977). Achievement Place: A community treatment model for youth in trouble. In D. Marholin II (Ed.), *Child behavior therapy* (pp. 239–273). New York: Gardner Press.

4
Neurological Bases of Youth Violence

Lawrence J. Lewandowski
Barbara Forsstrom-Cohen

This chapter will highlight research that has attempted to link aggressive or violent behavior in animals and humans, particularly youth, with neurophysiological mechanisms. Although the background for this chapter is drawn largely from neuroscience research, the content is summarized and simplified for students in social and behavioral sciences who are unfamiliar with neuroscience methods. Thus, many controversial issues in neuroscience will not receive adequate discussion, and conclusions drawn from such research may not reflect the opinions of all scientists in the area. It is hoped that the overview presented here will for the most part capture current findings and viewpoints, while allowing the reader to determine the relative validity, importance, and utility of the various research contributions.

Violence is undoubtedly a heterogeneous phenomenon which seems to have no single etiology and which is manifested in many different forms. Violence is a form of human aggression that involves inflicting damage on people or property. Most students of violent behavior adopt an interactive viewpoint which admits potential contributions from both nature and nurture or physiology and environment. Mezzich (1969) has developed a multiaxial diagnostic model to address the complex factors involved in youth violence. Despite the acknowledgment of both physiological and environmental influences, investigators tend to lean toward one or the other of these dimensions, and try to understand a part of the youth violence phenomenon. The result is usually a better understanding of the part, but not necessarily how it relates to the whole phenomenon. Such is the case with the neurophysiological aspects of violence. While, for example, we might better understand the pharmacologic action that inhibits or facilitates aggressive propensities, we cannot assert that specific neurochemical processes underlie all forms of violence. Consequently, we are faced with a wealth of correlative information indicating relationships between violent behavior and brain chemistry, activity, and damage. It seems a safe assertion to make that not all violence is induced by some form of brain dysfunction, nor are all forms of brain dysfunction likely to lead to violent behavior. Although violence and brain dysfunction are not perfectly correlated, the relationship between the two is interesting and heavily researched. The remainder of this chapter will address the interaction of violence with neuroanatomical, neurochemical, neuroendocrine, neuropsychiatric, and neuropsychological factors.

The brain is the command center for human behavior and as such is ultimately responsible for our actions. It is assumed, therefore, that we all have the equipment for aggressive and violent behavior (Moyer, 1980). When behavior is aberrant in this fashion, scientists and practitioners are compelled to beg the question as to whether or not brain activity has been altered, either temporarily or permanently. This is most readily witnessed in cases of brain damage and alcohol or substance abuse. In these instances, the inhibitory and facilitory nature of the nervous system is thrown out of balance, and usually behavior changes will accompany. In order to better understand the neurological mechanisms involved in such brain-behavior alterations, let us briefly review some brain structures and their general functions.

A common and simplistic anatomic breakdown of brain structures involves three major brain divisions. First, there is the brain stem which, among other things, includes structures necessary for life maintenance and various automatic, arousing, and orienting functions. Superior to the brain stem is the "old" or "limbic" brain, which consists of various subcortical brain structures involved in many functions. These functions include primitive, emotionally based behaviors such as sex, smell, fight or flight reactions, and food seeking. In lower phylogenetic species, this degree of brain development represents the highest level of neural control, and thus the limbic brain is sometimes referred to as the reptilian brain (Sagan, 1980). Some reptiles are noted for their aggressive instincts, which can be predictably triggered with little apparent neural capacity to inhibit the aggression.

Surrounding the limbic brain is the "new" brain or "neocortex." In higher animals, such as humans, cortical development has increased the organism's capacity to behave adaptively. Increased cortical development corresponds with greater regulation and modulation of limbic and other lower brain structures. Thus, most humans do not act on mere sexual or aggressive instinct, but rather have the capacity to think, plan, delay, and inhibit.

In fact, the entire network of brain structures operates on a principle of inhibition and facilitation. The principle is best exemplified by the neurochemical processes of neural transmission. With neurotransmitter chemicals as the messengers, the brain can send inhibitory or facilitory messages to any part of the central nervous system. The interaction of these inhibitory and facilitory chemical messages, which differentially affect various parts of the brain, essentially constitutes the underlying dynamics of behavior. When we interfere with the natural electrochemical activity of the brain, we usually alter behavior. This has been demonstrated in countless ways. For example, malnutrition, sensory deprivation, electrical stimulation, chemical intervention, and brain lesions can all affect brain activity and behavior. A small portion of these induced behavior changes include aggressive or violent behavior. In addition, we know that when these brain alterants are applied to specific brain areas, one may induce selective impairment in behavior. Thus, chemical, electrical, and neuroanatomical trauma in various brain areas will give rise to different forms of aggressive or violent behavior.

Obviously, the relationship between neurophysiology and violent behavior is complex and multifaceted. To begin to understand the broad electrical, chemical, and neuroanatomical basis of this relationship, let us first briefly review the extensive research on animal aggression.

ANIMAL STUDIES OF AGGRESSION

Space does not permit an exhaustive review of the many types of aggression of specific animals and the different methods used to study them. It should suffice to say that research findings depend upon the type of aggressive behavior being studied, the species and age of the animal, the method employed, and the part of the nervous system explored. Most of the animal studies on aggression have been conducted in laboratories rather than natural settings, under the influence of chemical, electrical, or surgical stimulation. In general, the findings indicate that there are different types of aggression (i.e., predatory, fear-induced, dominance, irritable) subserved by different, yet perhaps overlapping, neurophysiological mechanisms (Moyer, 1968).

For the past 50 years, investigators have used surgical and electrical stimulation techniques to evoke or inhibit aggressive actions in animals. The most common sites for such stimulation have been the limbic brain and temporal lobes, particularly the amygdala, hypothalamus, and hippocampus. In a well-known study, Kluver and Bucy (1937) removed both temporal lobes (including the amygdala and hippocampus) in rhesus monkeys and found that they became nonaggressive, hypersexual, and hyperoral. Since then, many studies of aggression have focused on the amygdala and its involvement in determining whether a stimulus should be avoided or attacked. It has been suggested that systems for escape behavior and irritable aggression are controlled by overlapping areas of the amygdala. In contrast to the taming result of removing the amygdala, other studies have indicated that lesions in certain portions of the hypothalamus or amygdala may actually increase attack behavior (Egger & Flynn, 1963). It appears that the site and extent of just amygdaloid lesions can affect aggressive behavior in various ways.

In addition to amygdaloid involvement, septal lesions may cause an animal to display wild and vicious aggressive behavior (Brady & Nauta, 1953), referred to as "septal rage." Electrical stimulation of the tegmentum or hypothalamus can cause another condition of strong emotionality called "sham rage." At high levels of stimulation, an animal shows an increased tendency toward vicious, nondirected attack behavior. In addition to these heavily researched limbic brain sites, aggressive propensities have been increased after frontal lobe lesions (Bandler & Chi, 1972).

Somewhat apart from surgical and electrical brain alterations are the effects on aggression by hormones and neurotransmitters. In both cases, a reciprocal relationship exists between physiology and behavior. Administration of certain hormones (i.e., testosterone) or drugs (i.e., apomorphine) may both increase the incidence of aggressive behavior, and in untreated animals, these chemicals may be found in greater concentrations after aggression has been induced in a noninvasive manner (Essman, 1980). In this way, experience can shape the biochemical balance of the organism, which in turn affects the organism's sensitivity to stimuli, and consequently may establish a low biochemical threshold for violent behavior. The effect of experience on biochemistry is less well-known than the effects of drugs on behavior. It appears that environmental stimuli can change the sensitivity of the nervous system, or that physiological changes can affect sensitivities toward certain stimuli. There is no question that many types of aggressive behaviors can be inhibited or facilitated by particular drugs or hormones that affect neural transmission (Mandel, Kempf, Mack, Haug, & Puglisi-Allegra, 1980). This has been demonstrated in animals and humans with a variety of chemical agents (i.e., alcohol, amphetamines, and benzodiazymes).

The number of biobehavioral studies of animal aggression is impressive. Although not directly generalizeable to the human species, research on nonhuman animals has afforded opportunities for carefully controlled invasive studies that could not be performed on humans. The extent of research in this area has also provided for the convergence of surgical, electrical, and biochemical data that link certain brain systems to various forms of aggression. In some cases, these relationships are consistent across species, including humans. Based upon the manipulation of aggression in animals, investigators have shaped theories and research about the human brain and its role in violent behavior.

NEUROPHYSIOLOGICAL CORRELATES
OF AGGRESSION IN HUMANS

The study of brain lesion effects on human aggression has been limited to naturally occurring lesions, temporal lobectomy for intractable seizures, and frontal lobectomy in criminals and the mentally ill. Structural changes in human brain tissue resulting from disease, tumor, and surgery have been linked in some cases to violent behavior. Tumors in the hypothalamus (Reeves & Blum, 1969) and other parts of the limbic system (Blumer, Williams, & Mark, 1974) have been associated with increased excitability, irritability, and aggression. Abnormal aggressiveness and violence have been related to temporal lobe tumors, such as in the case of Charles Whitman, the mass murderer from the University of Texas. Sweet, Ervin, and Mark (1969) reported on two violent patients with temporal lobe tumors. Scoville, Dunsmore, Liberson, Henry, and Pepe (1953) demonstrated that bilateral temporal lobectomy decreased social interaction and aggressiveness. Temporal lobe lesions may also result in paroxysmal symptoms such as affective disturbance or epileptoid features in conjunction with violence.

Frontal lobe tumors seem to have a less direct involvement in aggression. Frontal lesion symptomatology includes indifference, lack of planning ability, mood/personality changes, inflexibility, and cognitive-memory disturbances (Kolb & Wishaw, 1984). Such changes in mental ability could underlie violent behavior. Over the years, a number of unmanageable mental patients and violent criminal offenders have been subjected to frontal lobectomy and lobotomy. These cases are quite variable, but in general, such surgery tends to cause affective lability, inattention, lack of initiative, and relatively passive behavior. It appears that when brain damage occurs in associative and integrative cortical areas, certain perceptual and cognitive processes are restricted from exerting their normal contributing influence on behavior. By reducing cortical control of human behavior, whether by damage or alcohol intoxication, we begin to approach the unmodulated reptilian brain. In other words, we remove our ability to reason, plan, inhibit, or modify behavior, thus allowing primitive impulses free expression.

One way to more directly influence or curtail violent behavior is to remove the amygdala. Studies of amygdala ablation have repeatedly demonstrated a reduction in uncontrolled violence in a variety of patients (Heimburger, Whitlock, & Kalsbeck, 1966; Narabayashi, 1972; Vaernet & Madsen, 1970). It does appear that the amygdala plays a major role in the neural system for animal and human aggression.

Although not related strictly to the amygdala, patients with temporal lobe lesions, particularly bilaterally, often have psychomotor epilepsy. While it seems rare that violent behavior accompanies a seizure, uncontrolled assaultive behavior has been known to occur between seizures of some epileptics (Gastaut, 1954; Serafetinides, 1970). In addition, a greater incidence of epilepsy and electroencephalogram (EEG) abnormalities have been found in delinquent and criminal populations (Knott, 1965; Lewis & Balla, 1976), especially among the more violent individuals (Williams, 1969). Other investigators have not found a relationship between EEG abnormalities and violent behavior (Arthurs & Cahoon, 1964; Rodin, 1973), casting doubt on the EEG as a useful discriminator of violent patients. The interpretation of this relationship remains open. It appears that electrical abnormalities can coincide with pathology in the brain, which in turn disrupts the neural systems underlying aggressive behavior. In this way, both epilepsy and/or violence may be results of a neurophysiological abnormality, frequently in the temporal lobes. Monroe (1978) has extended this line of thinking by his description of an episodic dyscontrol syndrome. He suggests that many or most violent persons have some type of brain dysfunction that is detectable through neurological and psychological testing. This position has yet to be sufficiently investigated.

When we stop to consider the widespread effects that alcohol can have on brain function and behavior, we are immediately reminded of the chemical nature of our nervous systems. It is now well recognized that neural activity is governed by more than 20 neurotransmitters which can be selectively influenced by certain drugs (Kolb & Wishaw, 1984). This process is the basis of psychopharmacology, in which certain conditions of mental illness, epilepsy, and brain disorders are effectively treated. Although most of our knowledge about the neurochemical substrates of aggressive behavior is based on animal research, there have been various clinical treatment studies with humans that indicate positive drug effects on aggressive patients. Leventhal and Brodie (1981) have provided a summary of these pharmacologic interventions which are listed below:

1. Lithium carbonate appears to be a drug of major promise for some populations of violent patients. This observation is based on the neuropharmacology of lithium as it affects behavior. Clinical trials have confirmed the potential efficacy of this compound.
2. The anticonvulsants (diphenylhydantoin or phenytoin and carbamazepine) have a demonstrated ability to control some forms of violent and aggressive behavior. The agents appear to be particularly useful in the treatment of such behaviors when they are episodic and/or associated with EEG abnormalities, although these do not appear to be necessary indications for these agents.
3. Antipsychotic medications including phenothiazines, butyrophenones, thioxanthines, and oxyindoles appear to have potential benefit in the treatment of nonpsychotic violent patients.
4. Antidepressants may be effective in the control of violence seen in some depressed patients.
5. The psychostimulants appear to have a very circumscribed role in the treatment of violence in the minimal brain dysfunction (MBD) patient. There is an inherent, albeit small, risk of precipitating a paranoid psychosis with these agents.
6. The minor tranquilizers, specifically the benzodiazepines, probably have a limited role, if any, in the management of violent or aggressive behavior given their potential to produce aggression.
7. Antiandrogen agents may be effective in the treatment of male sex offenders whose violence is related to perpetration of a sex act.

It should be obvious that neurochemical factors play a major part in human behavior. Changes in neurochemistry follow, accompany, and cause alterations in behavior. It is not always clear which comes first. Nevertheless, to fully understand the underpinnings of human violence, we will need to more clearly delineate the neurochemical causes and treatment of such behavior.

An area of research that is tangential to the neurological bases of violence, yet related physiologically, is the study of genetic factors. This research is clouded by the fact that most of it has been conducted on populations of criminals. In general, investigators have noted a higher rate of criminal behavior among individuals born to a criminal parent and given up for adoption at an early age than among other adopted persons born to noncriminal parents (Eichelman, Elliot, & Barchas, 1981). As in most of these studies, there is no distinction made between violent and dyssocial behavior. Studies of criminal behavior of twins show a monozygotic concordance rate of about 33% to 60% (Christiansen, 1968;

Rosenthal, 1971) which is higher than that of dizygotic pairs. Such studies must be interpreted cautiously, however, because both genetic and environmental factors are involved.

Another type of genetic research has explored the relationship between chromosomal abnormality and antisocial and violent behavior. There have been reports of murderers and violent criminals who have an XYY karyotype (Shah, 1970). When populations of prisoners and mentally disordered offenders are surveyed, a disproportionate number of individuals with 47 XXY and 47 XYY karyotypes is found (Casey et al., 1966). However, a more recent study of such subjects reported an increase in crime rate, decrease in intelligence, but no increase in violent behavior compared to control subjects (Witkin et al., 1976).

There is sparse evidence relating human violence to chromosomal anomalies. Conditions such as Down or Turner syndrome, for example, demonstrate no increased incidence of violent behavior. The data on XYY males are confounded and suspect. It is possible that such a chromosomal abnormality is associated with other neurophysiological mechanisms (i.e., neuroendocrine function) which in some cases may play a part in what is observed to be increased aggression.

The role of endocrine physiology in behavior, particularly violent behavior, is not well-known. Hormone concentrations rise and fall during certain periods of early childhood, with a considerable increase in gonadatropins and gonadal steroids during puberty. The rise in hormone levels during puberty appears to not only affect physical changes, but also behavior. Medical cases in which hormone levels are manipulated have reported marked behavioral changes. Among the changes accompanying hormone level fluctuation are irritability, anxiety, hostility, and depression (i.e., seen in premenstrual syndrome). Efforts to relate endocrine function/dysfunction to increased human aggression have been inconclusive. Most of the controversy surrounds the relationship of male testosterone and aggression. Some studies have yielded evidence correlating higher testosterone levels in aggressive versus nonaggressive prisoners (Ehrenkratz, Bliss, & Sheard, 1974), and a group of rapists who were rated as most violent (Rada, Laws, & Kellner, 1976). Monti, Brown, and Corriveau (1977), however, found no significant relationship between testosterone levels and questionnaire ratings of aggression. Studies like these have obvious limitations and generally focus on adult populations who have had more time than youths to learn how to adjust and control their drive states.

A large literature exists that associates aggression and certain types of mental illness. Most of the youth and adults who are violent and receive a psychiatric classification are considered psychopathic or sociopathic. A small proportion of such criminals are ever diagnosed as psychotic (Wolfgang & Ferracuti, 1967). Guze (1976) found sociopathy, alcoholism, and drug dependence, but not schizophrenia, manic-depression, or neurosis to be prevalent in the criminal population. Gillies (1976) reported on studies in England that showed a high proportion of mental illness in murderers.

For the most part, violent offenders tend to have antisocial personality disorders. Whether such disorders are part genetic, hormonal, neurochemical, or environmental is not clearly understood. It is possible, as with other types of mental illness (i.e., schizophrenia, depression, drug psychosis) that organic brain alterations chemically or structurally underlie an increased disposition toward mental disturbance and violence.

NEUROLOGICAL CORRELATES OF YOUTH VIOLENCE

The neurophysiological research pertaining to animal and human aggression is abundant, and although not conclusive, certainly persuasive. There is little doubt that violence is to some degree a neurobehavioral phenomenon. Bearing the summary of brain-violence relationships in mind, one must consider to what extent all this information generalizes to the youth population. Because the young nervous system is more similar to than different from that of the adult, we may assume that, to some extent, the same brain-behavior relationships exist in young adults and children. By this, we mean that brain damage, drug intoxication, neuroendocrine or chemical imbalance, and even genetic factors may play a significant role in the violent behavior of youth.

In reviewing the surveys of violent youngsters/delinquents, two things stand out: first, that the patterns of youth violence differ somewhat from adult violence patterns; and second, that youths engage in a variety of forms of violent crime. Patterns of youth violence appear to have changed little over the past two decades. While the number of youth violent crimes has been steadily increasing, the overrepresentation of blacks among violent adolescents remains constant. Tinklenberg and Ochberg (1981) studied 95 violent adolescents in California between 1973 and 1977 and found that most of the violence occurred on the weekends, particularly between 8 p.m. and 2 a.m., either in a residence or on the street. These data are similar to those collected by Wolfgang (1958) in Philadelphia. However, the percentage of felony-related violence reported by Wolfgang was 10%, and that by Tinklenberg and Ochberg 37%. This high proportion also differs from adult crime statistics, which indicate that about 10% of aggravated assaults are felony related (Mulvihill & Tumin, 1969). Another difference between youth and adult patterns of violence is that most victims of youth violence are unknown or casually acquainted with the assailant, while adult violence tends to involve a much higher proportion of family members and friends. These data may be due in part to a substantial amount of gang violence perpetrated by adolescents, in which victims are not family or friends. This may also account in part for the fact that most victims of youth violence are about the same age as the assailant. Perhaps the most revealing statistic in the Tinklenberg and Ochberg (1981) study is the relationship of drugs (61% of offenders had taken alcohol and/or drugs shortly before the assault), and weapons (over half used a gun) to a violent act. Based on their extensive study, Tinklenberg and Ochberg (1981, pp. 136–137) outline five major types of youth violence:

1. Instrumental. This form of violent crime involves acts that are planned, dispassionate, purposeful, and motivated by a calculated decision to eliminate or harm the victim.
2. Emotional. Violent acts in this category are "hot blooded," angry, or performed in extreme fear. They are impulsive and usually occur among intimates.
3. Felonious. The felonious category includes those assaultive acts that are committed in the course of another crime. Injuring the victim is not premeditated.
4. Bizarre. This term refers to insane and severely psychopathic crimes. These crimes may be associated with brain damage, mental retardation, psychosis, or serious personality disorder, and characterized by irrational, excessive, and sometimes sadistic dimensions.
5. Dyssocial. In certain violent subcultures, criminal aggression is the norm. These acts are often associated with membership in an ethnic youth gang and are part of ongoing vendettas against other gangs. However, the violence may also be directed against innocent bystanders who happen to be on the wrong turf.

Although only one of the five categories of violence suggests a neurological or neuro-psychiatric etiology for violent crime, one can speculate that there are possible neurological factors that underlie the other types of violence. It is plausible that many premeditated, impulsive, felonious, and dyssocial violent acts are related to subtle neurological problems (i.e., electrical irregularity, minimal brain dysfunction, learning disability, etc.), and transient changes in brain state (i.e., drugs, altered consciousness). The research that connects neurological factors to youth violence is not as convincing as the research on animals or adult humans. In fact, there have been few studies of youth offenders applying a neuroscience perspective. Thus, the studies reviewed later in this chapter will also include neuropsychological findings among violent youths.

Before beginning the review, it is important to delineate some of the difficulties with presenting the research on violent youth. First, there is a paucity of research concerning the neurological functioning of violent youth; in particular, there is little research on the biological bases of the violence. This includes the obvious reason that invasive research cannot readily be performed on humans. Second, the population that has been studied most often is that of youthful offenders or "delinquents." A problem with studying such a population is its heterogeneous makeup; some of the delinquents have been arrested, others not, and some have been severely violent while others have been arrested for status crimes. When investigators do not sort out or estimate the number of delinquents who commit violent crimes, it becomes difficult to interpret the relationship between violence and those neurobiological or neuropsychological factors under investigation. Third, the research methods vary, and therefore, data are hard to compare across studies. For instance, much of the neurobiological data are gathered from single case studies where invasive techniques have been applied. Often the studies on delinquency have used samples ranging from small to large groups of offenders where inferential research techniques were used.

With limitations duly noted, by far the most often cited measure of neurobiological dysfunction related to youth violence is an abnormal EEG. This research literature encompasses the controversy about the relationship of epilepsy, and in particular, temporal lobe epilepsy, to violence. There are several eloquently described cases of adolescents with abnormal electrical activity in the brain who are prone to rage attacks. Mark and Ervin (1970) describe two such cases. One is the story of Julia, who had a history of "brain disease" beginning with encephalitis at 2 years of age. Subsequently, she developed seizures, often followed by periods of panic and disorientation. During several of these, she also became violent. Surgery to remove a destructive lesion to the amygdala, where irregular activity was recorded, resulted in only two outbreaks of violence in the first year following the operation, and none the second. The second case is a 13-year-old double murderess. No unusual brain activity was documented initially, but invasive techniques uncovered abnormal activity in the hippocampal area. The girl was known to be unduly upset by children's cries, and it was under these conditions that she murdered her stepsister. An experiment revealed that recorded children's cries sparked seizure activity in her temporal lobe which was accompanied with anxious and angry behavior. The authors cite these cases of seizure activity as evidence for brain disease as a possible underlying cause for violent outbursts.

Ounsted (1969) also cites temporal lobe epilepsy as being related to rage outbursts and violence. He followed 100 children with temporal lobe epilepsy for a decade. Of these, 36 children were found to have rage outbursts. The etiology of the epilepsy for those who experienced violent outbursts was generally from trauma or severe febrile convulsions. No relationship could be found between frequency of seizures and likelihood of rage attacks. As there was some relationship to disordered homes and violent episodes, Ounsted concluded that rage behavior in those with temporal lobe epilepsy is ". . . probably. . . of multifactored origin" (p. 241).

Serafetinides (1965) studied 100 patients who had surgery to alleviate symptoms of temporal lobe epilepsy. Twenty-seven patients fell within the youth age range, with 19 of them acting aggressively. Although the study does not sufficiently delineate the effectiveness of surgical intervention for the youth population, correlative data exist to suggest that temporal lobe epilepsy in youth can be related to aggression.

During the last decade, Lewis and colleagues have studied the relationship between epilepsy and juvenile delinquency. Some of the research has pertained to violent delinquents; it is this research that will be emphasized. Lewis (1976) reviewed the charts of all children with psychomotor epileptic symptoms referred to a juvenile court clinic over a 2-year period. Eighteen adolescents or 6% of the total sample screened exhibited epileptic symptoms. Fourteen of the subjects had histories of violent behavior. Electroencephalograms were obtained for 14 of the subjects. Eleven of these were abnormal, with three indicating temporal lobe abnormalities. Of these three, two children had violent histories.

Lewis, Shanok, Pincus, and Glaser (1979) reported results of EEGs as part of a more inclusive study of psychiatric, neurological, psychological, and abuse factors of violent juvenile delinquents. They found that the violent offenders differed significantly from the nonviolent youths in psychomotor epileptic symptomotology. They also compared the youths on amount of violence, dividing the violent group into two sections: more violent and less violent. When this was done, 30% of the more violent group displayed grossly abnormal EEGs, while the second group showed no such abnormality.

Lewis, Pincus, Shanok, and Glaser (1982) reported results of a study on 97 incarcerated youths and the relationship of psychomotor epilepsy to violence. The youths were rated on a scale of violence based on their participation in aggressive acts and given physical examinations and interviews to determine epileptic symptoms. Seventy-eight percent of the boys had one or more symptoms of epilepsy. Electroencephalogram data were those reported in the 1979 study: There were more youths in the more violent group with gross EEG abnormalities. There was also a significant correlation between number of psychomotor symptoms and increased degree of violence. They extended their study further by identifying those youths who had psychomotor seizures, finding 18 in the study. The relationship of their aggressive acts to seizure activity was as follows: Five clearly committed violence during seizures; in six cases it was unclear whether violence had occurred during seizure activity; and seven subjects had committed all violence while in control of themselves. All five who had committed aggressive acts during seizures had also been violent when seizures were not occurring.

Lewis and her colleagues have also explored the relationship of medical histories to delinquency. Lewis and Shanok (1977, 1979) found that delinquent children suffered more adverse medical histories than nondelinquent children, and that psychiatrically referred delinquents had more serious medical histories than nonreferred delinquents. Their medical problems included a greater number of perinatal difficulties, seizures, physical abuse incidents, and face and head injuries. Lewis et al. (1979) found the group of violent adolescents to have more neurological impairments than the nonviolent delinquents. The more violent youths in that group had also sustained greater degrees of physical abuse from parents or parent substitutes than the less violent group. Of the 18 epileptic subjects in the 1982 study, 16 had histories of severe central nervous system trauma and/or perinatal difficulties. These ranged from severe falls to ingestion of a toxic substance causing convulsions. Penner (1982), in his review of health problems in the causation of juvenile delinquency, supports the information set forth by Lewis et al. (1979, 1982) that delinquents often have aberrant health histories.

Another factor that has been related to delinquency and violent behavior is hyperactivity. Mark and Ervin (1970) state, "The typical severe hyperkinetic brain-injured child is indiscriminately aggressive and impulsively violent" (p. 57). In Japan, Narabayashi (1972) per-formed bilateral amygdalotomy on such children and reported a reduction in hyperkinesis and assaultive behavior as well as an increase in behavior that is more conducive to training and management in school and home. Ounsted (1969) reported a relationship between hyperactivity and rage outbursts in children with temporal lobe epilepsy, although he cau-tioned:

> It is perhaps more significant to view the coin from the opposite side and to say that of the thirty six children who had rage outbursts less than a half had the hyperkinetic syndrome. Thus both hyperkinesis and catastrophic rage can exist independently of one another. (p. 239)

Other researchers also have found a relationship between hyperactivity and delinquency. Lewis and Balla (1976) reported a high incidence of hyperactivity among delinquent youth, as did Cantwell (1975). Mendelson, Johnson, and Stewart (1971) also found that delin-quency often followed early hyperactivity. This suggests that hyperactivity may be a common central nervous system precursor to delinquency. Regarding the relationship of hyperactivity to violent youth, however, the results must be viewed with caution because of the heter-ogeneity of the groups.

Another area that has been examined in the search for biological reasons for youth violence is that involving research of hormonal levels and imbalances. The primary thrust in this area has been investigating the relationship of sex hormones (i.e., testosterone and estrogen) to violent behavior. Olweus, Mattsson, Schalling, and Low (1980) examined the testosterone levels of a group of normal adolescents in relation to aggression, physical characteristics, and personality variables. A correlation was found between testosterone and the verbal and physical aggression scales utilized. They reported that ". . . dimensions reflecting intensity or frequency of aggressive responses to provocation and threat were most clearly related to testosterone" (p. 263). Mattsson, Schalling, Olweus, Low, and Svens-son (1980) conducted an experiment on plasma testosterone, aggressive behavior, and personality dimensions in male delinquents. Forty serious recidivist offenders participated. Twenty-one of the juveniles were detained for violent offenses. The delinquents had a slightly higher mean testosterone level, approaching the .1 level of significance. The seven subjects that were rated as the most violent had significantly higher testosterone levels than the remaining delinquents.

Mann (1984) presented a review of the literature surrounding hormonal involvement in female delinquency. Her work centered mainly on the research of Dalton (1960a, b; 1961) conducted with British school girls and female prisoners. Although Dalton reports positive results in terms of a relationship between menstrual cycle (low levels of hormones) and "naughty" and delinquent behavior, Mann is very convincing in suggesting caution when reviewing the results. She presented more rigorously gathered data (Ellis & Austin, 1971) that suggested that female prisoners were more irritable during the paramenstruum (pre-menstrual plus menstrual days). They did not, however, find differences in overt aggres-siveness as reported by the prison officers. As the previous studies suggest, the question of the relationship of hormone level and aggression in youth is still in need of elucidation.

There has been similar disagreement as to whether or not psychiatric disorders are more prevalent in the delinquent population (Guze, 1976). Lewis (1976), in a retrospective chart-review study, found 16 of 18 delinquents with epileptic symptoms to also suffer from delusions. Nine of the children had experienced hallucinations. Also, "Violence was more common in the psychomotor epileptic children evaluated than in other children referred to the court" (p. 1398). In the study of violent offenders, Lewis et al. (1979) found that significantly more violent delinquents suffered from paranoid symptoms, and were loose, rambling, and illogical in their thinking than were nonviolent delinquents.

Studies like these hold open the possibility that various neural systems, perhaps working improperly, may underlie much of disordered behavior, particularly violence. Investigators have looked for other evidence of dysfunctional neural systems and in the process have turned to neuropsychology. Neuropsychological investigations of select groups of children over the past two decades have resulted in a technology for accurately assessing children with brain damage, brain dysfunction, and brain normality (Selz & Reitan, 1979). A number of investigators have applied this technology to delinquent and violent youths. It is becoming widely accepted that a substantial number of these youngsters manifest neuropsychological deficits.

In one of the earlier studies, Wolff and Hurwitz (1966) found that children with learning disorders and juvenile delinquents demonstrated more signs of minor neurological insta- bilities as compared to normal children. Hurwitz, Bibace, Wolff, and Rowbatham (1972) followed this line of research and demonstrated that both delinquent and learning disabled boys were significantly delayed in motor development relative to normal peers. Berman and Siegal (1976) administered the Halstead-Reitan Neuropsychological Battery to delin- quents and controls and found significant differences favoring the controls on almost every measure. They also noted that the deficits found in the delinquent children were similar to those found in neurologically impaired children, particularly regarding higher level verbal and nonverbal conceptual abilities.

Spellacy (1977) administered the neuropsychological battery from the University of Vic- toria to 40 violent and 40 nonviolent delinquent adolescent males. He found the nonviolent group to out-perform the violent group on 25 of 31 variables, and that the battery of neuropsychological tests could reliably discriminate the violent subjects. No particular pat- tern or set of diagnostic rules was extracted for extended validation, however.

Krynicki (1978) also administered a series of neuropsychological tests to male adolescents who had either a history of multiple assaults, less than two assaults, or organic brain syndrome. He found that several variables distinguished between the highly assaultive and other two groups: EEG abnormality, degree of hand dominance, perseveration errors on a visuomotor task, and verbal short-term memory. Krynicki also suggested that his results support a hypothesis of frontal and left hemisphere brain dysfunction related to repetitive violent behavior.

Voorhees (1981) supports the hypothesis of frontal area involvement in delinquents. He administered Luria's Neuropsychological Investigation to a group of male and female adolescent delinquents and controls. The delinquent group was statistically inferior on 9 of the 11 measures, particularly when tasks required sustained attention, symbolic manip- ulations, and complex abstract abilities. The delinquent groups performed well on simple tactile and motor tasks.

A recent study by Yeudall, Fromm-Auch, and Davies (1982) differed slightly in findings from previous studies. Yeudall et al. examined 99 delinquents and 47 controls of both sexes using the Halstead-Reitan Battery and 12 additional neuropsychological tests. They found a greater number of abnormal profiles within the delinquent groups (84% v. 11%); however, these results indicated frontal lobe dysfunction primarily of the right hemisphere. They explain their right instead of left frontal finding as a function of their sample, which had a low percentage of violent adolescents and a high percentage of delinquents exhibiting characteristics of depression. Although they did not completely replicate the findings of previous studies, they too found significant neuropsychological deficits in the delinquent population. And once again, the deficits were associated with frontal lobe functioning.

The hypothesis of frontal lobe dysfunction in juvenile delinquents was initially advanced by Pontius (1972). Based largely on the notions of frontal lobe function proposed by Luria and Homskaya (1964), Pontius notes that the "frontal lobe system" mediates the formation of plans of action and the ability to continuously evaluate, alter, or reprogram actions as situations and demands change. The loss of this high level ability is notable in frontal lesion patients (Luria, 1973), some types of minimal brain dysfunction (Pontius, 1973), and juvenile delinquency (Pontius, 1972). Pontius, as well as Luria (1973) and Golden (1981) have described maturational periods that are important for the development of the frontal lobe system. The first period is 0 to 3 years, during which the frontal areas become increasingly linked to the reticular activating system governing arousal, attention, and activity. Trauma to the nervous system during this early period is thought to result in attention deficit disorders, hyperactivity, and other behavior disorders. The second developmental period is between 12 and 20 years of age. Injury or dysfunction during this period may result in the inability to achieve adult maturity in terms of reasoning, planning, judgment, acting responsibly, developing relationships, conceptual thinking, and modulating impulses.

The frontal lobe dysfunction hypothesis for delinquency is far from being accepted as true. Even those who propose the idea (Pontius & Ruttiger, 1976) found only about half of their delinquent youths to be deficient in planning and flexibility, while 30% of the normal youths were similarly deficient. This may suggest that frontal lobe functioning is not well-developed in much of the youth population. The fact that Krynicki (1978), Pontius and Ruttiger (1976), Voorhees (1981), and Yeudall et al. (1982) all find evidence of subtle frontal lobe deficiency in delinquents indicates the need for more research on the issue. Appeloff (1985) recently completed a study in which nonviolent delinquents were compared to nondelinquents on a variety of frontal lobe sensitive neuropsychological tests. She found no differences between the groups and no evidence of frontal lobe dysfunction in delinquents. Perhaps in time we will be able to discriminate violent youth who have evidence of frontal lobe dysfunction and determine characteristics of the brain deficiency that may respond to individualized treatment.

In a chapter on youth violence it would be remiss to neglect a topic that is currently considered of research importance in the area of delinquency: the relationship between delinquency and learning problems. Many of the factors mentioned thus far as correlates of youth violence are the same as those used to describe children and adolescents with learning disabilities. In fact, there may be a considerable overlap between these two populations. In 1977, the office of the Comptroller General of the U.S. reported on the extent of learning problems among institutionalized delinquent youth. Of the sample of 129 delinquents, the report concluded that 3% were slow learners, 19% had limited potential, and 77% were underachievers. Of these underachievers, 26% had endogenous learning problems, while 51% had primarily exogenous learning problems— those based on emotional factors. A similar project conducted by the Association of Children with Learning Disabilities (1978) reported a larger percentage of learning disabled children (32%) in a sample of delinquents than in a public school sample (16%). In an overview of this issue, Lane (1980) concluded that the relationship between juvenile delinquency and learning disabilities is still unclear. Murray (1976) also concluded that the link between delinquency and learning disabilities is clouded, particularly because of difficulties with definitions of the phenomena. The connection between violence, delinquency, and learning disabilities is yet to be explained and certainly warrants extensive research.

In summary, the following is a partial listing of the correlates that have been found in relation to youth violence: abnormal EEGs, temporal lobe epilepsy, other types of seizure activity, head trauma, perinatal difficulties, hyperactivity, a history of child abuse, variability in hormone levels, psychiatric difficulties, and neuropsychological deficits. It must be remembered that many of these relationships were found on varying, often ill-defined populations, assessed using less than optimal research methods. Much of the information is inferential and none of it has been replicated sufficiently to render it as scientific "truth."

Although much of the evidence linking youth violence with neurological dysfunction is tentative, one is struck by the weight of findings. It should be apparent that many violent youths are not fully intact individuals. As a group, these youngsters are at greater risk for medical problems, neurological impairment, learning problems, psychiatric disorders, and social disorganization than their peers. It is not difficult to surmise that these factors lower the threshold for aggressive or violent behavior. We might assume that this is a result of underdeveloped or dysfunctional higher order brain controls. Whether these neurologically based controls are developmentally deficient (e.g., genetic or congenital problems) and or acutely deactivated (e.g., alcohol intoxication), the result is a youngster who is less likely to inhibit impulses or turn away from stimuli (i.e., gang fight) that engender violence. Youngsters with this constitutional bias toward violence are easy prey for corrupting societal influences. Once a pattern of maladaptive (violent) behavior is begun, it becomes part of one's neural and psychological repertoires. Thus, the neurological foundation for violence is built, the low threshold is set, and without intervention the neural system will continue to operate at that low threshold for violence.

The research on youth violence does not lead to a natural conclusion. As mentioned, the investigation of the neural bases of youth violence has only just begun. The research to date has linked violence in youth to a variety of neurophysiological factors, most of which seem weakly related to violent youth or apply to a small portion of that population. The more convincing scientific research on brain and violence is borrowed from studies of animals and human adults. Consequently, one is left to infer from a diverse set of studies that the neural underpinnings of youth violence range from primary (i.e., irritating temporal lobe lesion) to secondary (i.e., perceptual and cognitive dysfunction) to temporary (i.e., alcohol intoxication factors). In each case, one must consider a complex of biological, developmental, and environmental factors. Controlling these factors in research in order to assess the neural underpinnings of youth violence is a monumental task not yet achieved. It is hoped that intensified neuroscience research efforts with this population will further delineate contributing factors, develop a technology for early identification and subtyping, and find better methods of prevention and treatment.

REFERENCES

Appellof, E. (1985). *Prefrontal functions in juvenile delinquents.* Unpublished doctoral dissertation. Syracuse University, Syracuse, N.Y.

Arthurs, R.G., & Cahoon, E.B. (1964). A clinical and electroencephalographic survey of psychopathic personality. *American Journal of Psychiatry, 120,* 875–877.

Bandler, R.J., & Chi, C.C. (1972). Effects of olfactory bulb removal on aggression: A reevaluation. *Physiology and Behavior, 8,* 207–211.

Berman, A., & Siegal, A.W. (1976). Adaptive and learning skills in juvenile delinquents: A neuropsychological analysis. *Journal of Learning Disabilities, 9,* 51–58.

Blumer, D.P., Williams, H.W., & Mark, V.H. (1974). The study and treatment, on a neurological ward of abnormally aggressive patients with focal brain disease. *Confinia Neurologica, 36,* 125–176.

Brady, J.V., & Nauta, W.J.H. (1953). Subcortical mechanisms in emotional behavior: Affective changes following septal forebrain lesions in the albino rat. *Journal of Comparative and Physiological Psychology, 46,* 339–346.

Cantwell, D.P. (1975). *The hyperactive child: Diagnosis, management and current research.* New York: Spectrum.

Casey, M.D., Blank, C.E., Street, D.R.R., Segall, L.J., McDougall, J.H., McCraft, P.J., & Skinner, J.C. (1966). XYY chromosomes and antisocial behavior. *Lancet, 2,* 859–860.

Christiansen, K. (1968). Thresholds of tolerance in various population groups illustrated by results from a Danish criminological twin study. In A. de Reuck (Ed.), *The mentally abnormal offender* (pp. 107–116). Boston: Little Brown.

Comptroller General of the United States. (1977). *Learning disabilities: The link to delinquency should be determined, but schools should do more now.* Washington, DC: General Accounting Office.

Dalton, K. (1960a). Effect of menstruation on school girls' weekly work. *British Medical Journal, 1,* 326–328.

Dalton, K. (1960b). School girls' behavior and menstruation. *British Medical Journal, 2,* 1647–1649.

Dalton, K. (1961). Menstruation & crime. *British Medical Journal, 2,* 1752–1753.

Egger, M.D., & Flynn, J.P. (1963). Effect of electrical stimulation of the amygdala on hypothalmically elicited attack behavior in cats. *Journal of Neurophysiology, 26,* 705–720.

Ehrenkrantz, J., Bliss E., & Sheard, M.H. (1974). Plasma testosterone: Correlation with aggressive behavior and social dominance in man. *Psychosomatic Medicine, 36,* 469–475.

Eichelman, B., Elliot, G.R., & Barchas, J.D. (1981). Biochemical, pharmacological, and genetic aspects of aggression. In D. Hamburg & M. Trudeau (Eds.), *Biobehavioral aspects of aggression* (pp. 51–84). New York: Liss.

Ellis, D.P., & Austin, P. (1971). Menstruation and aggressive behavior in a correctional center for women. *Journal of Criminal Law, Criminology and Police Science, 62,* 388–395.

Essman, W.B. (1980). Drug effects upon aggressive behavior. In L. Valzelli & L. Morgese (Eds.), *Aggression and violence: A psychobiological and clinical approach. Proceedings of the St. Vincent Conference* (pp. 150–165). Milan, Italy: Saint Vincent.

Gastaut, H. (1954). Interpretation of the symptoms of psychomotor epilepsy in relation to physiologic data on rhinencephalic function. *Epilepsia, 3* (3), 84–88.

Gillies, H. (1976). Homicide in the west of Scotland. *British Journal of Psychiatry, 128,* 105–127.

Glaser, G.H., & Dixon, M.S. (1956). Psychomotor seizures in childhood: A clinical study. *Neurology, 6,* 646–655.

Golden, C. (1981). The Luria-Nebraska children's battery: Theory and formulation. In G. Hynd & J. Obrzut (Eds.), *Neuropsychological assessment of the school-age child* (pp. 277–302). New York: Grune & Stratton.

Guze, S.B. (1976). *Criminality and Psychiatric Disorders.* New York: Oxford University Press.

Guze, S.B., Goodwin, D.W., & Crane, J.B. (1969). Criminality and psychiatric disorders. *Archives of General Psychiatry, 20,* 583–591.

Healy, W., & Bronner, A.F. (1926). *Delinquents and criminals, their making and unmaking: Studies in two American cities.* New York: Macmillan.

Heimberger, R.F., Whitlock, C.C., & Kalsbeck, J.E. (1966). Stereotaxic amygdalotomy for epilepsy with aggressive behavior. *Journal of the American Medical Association, 198,* 165–169.

Hurwitz, I., Bibace, R.M., Wolff, P.H., & Rowbotham, B.M. (1972). Neuropsychological function of normal boys, delinquent boys, and boys with learning problems. *Perceptual and Motor Skills, 35,* 387–394.

Kluver, H., & Bucy, P.C. (1937). "Psychic blindness" and other symptoms following bilateral temporal lobectomy in rhesus monkeys. *American Journal of Physiology, 119,* 352–353.

Knott, J.R. (1965). Electroencephalograms in psychopathic personality and murders. In W. Wilson (Ed.), *Applications of electroencephalography in psychiatry* (pp. 19–29). Durham, NC: Duke University Press.

Kolb, B., & Wishaw, I.Q. (1984). *Fundamentals of human neuropsychology. San Francisco: Freeman Press.*

Krynicki, V.E. (1978). Cerebral dysfunction in repetitively assaultive adolescents. *Journal of Nervous and Mental Disease, 166*, 59–67.

Lane, B.A. (1980). The relationship of learning disabilities to juvenile delinquency: Current status. *Journal of Learning Disabilities, 13,* 425–434.

Leventhal, B.L., & Brodie, H.K. (1981). The psychopharmacology of violence. In D. Hamburg & M. Trudeau (Eds.), *Biobehavioral aspects of aggression* (pp. 85–106). New York: Liss.

Lewis, D.O. (1976). Delinquency, psychomotor epileptic symptoms, and paranoid ideation: A triad. *American Journal of Psychiatry, 133,* 1395–1398.

Lewis, D.O., & Balla, D.A. (1976). *Delinquency and psychopathology.* New York: Grune & Stratton.

Lewis, D.O., Pincus, J.H., Shanok, H.P.H., & Glaser, G.H. (1982). Psychomotor epilepsy and violence in a group of incarcerated adolescent boys. *American Journal of Psychiatry, 139,* 882–887.

Lewis, D.O., & Shanok, S.S. (1977). Medical histories of delinquent and nondelinquent children: An epidemiological study. *American Journal of Psychiatry, 134,* 1020–1025.

Lewis, D.O., & Shanok, S.S. (1979). Medical histories of psychiatrically referred delinquent children: An epidemiological study. *American Journal of Psychiatry, 136,* 231–233.

Lewis, D.O., Shanok, S.S., Pincus, J.H., & Glaser, G.H. (1979). Violent juvenile delinquents: Psychiatric, neurological, psychological and abuse factors. *Journal of the American Academy of Child Psychiatry, 18,* 307–319.

Luria, A.R. (1973). *The working brain: An introduction to neuropsychology.* New York: Basic Books.

Luria, A.R., & Homskaya, E.D. (1964). Disturbance in the regulative role of speech with frontal lobe lesions. In J. Warren & K. Akert (Eds.), *The frontal granular cortex and behavior* (pp. 353–371). New York: McGraw-Hill.

Mandel, P., Kempf, E., Mack, G., Haug, M., & Puglisi-Allegra, S. (1980). Neurochemistry of experimental aggression. In L. Valzelli & L. Morgese (Eds.), *Aggression and violence: A psychobiological and clinical approach. Proceedings of the St. Vincent Conference* (pp. 61–69). Milan, Italy: St. Vincent.

Mann, C.R. (1984). *Female crime & delinquency.* University, AL: University of Alabama Press.

Mark, V.H., & Ervin, F.R. (1970). *Violence and the brain.* New York: Harper & Row.

Mattsson, A., Schalling, D., Olweus, D., Low, H., & Svensson, J. (1980). Plasma testosterone, aggressive behavior, and personality dimensions in young male delinquents. *Journal of American Academy of Child Psychiatry, 19,* 476–490.

Mendelson, W., Johnson, N., & Stewart, M.A. (1971). Hyperactive children as teenagers: A follow-up study. *Journal of Nervous and Mental Disease, 153,* 273–279.

Mezzich, A. (1969). Exploring diagnostic formulations for violent delinquent adolescents: Conceptual considerations. *Bulletin of the American Academy of Psychiatry and Law, 10,* 61–67.

Monroe, R.R. (1978). *Brain dysfunction in aggressive criminals.* Toronto: Heath.

Monti, P.M., Brown, W.A., & Corriveau, D.P. (1977). Testosterone and components of aggressive and sexual behavior in man. *American Journal of Psychiatry, 134,* 692–694.

Moyer, K.E. (1968). Kinds of aggression and their physiological basis. *Communications in Behavioral Biology, 2,* 65–87.

Moyer, K.E. (1980). A physiological model of aggression with implications for control. In L. Valzelli & L. Morgese (Eds.), *Aggression and violence: A psychobiological and clinical approach* (pp. 72–78). *Proceedings of the Saint Vincent Conference.* Milan, Italy: St. Vincent.

Mulvihill, D.J., & Tumin, M.M. (1969). *Crimes of violence* (a staff report submitted to the National Commission on the Causes and Prevention of Violence). Washington, DC: U.S. Government Printing Office.

Murray, C.A. (1976). *The link between learning disabilities and juvenile delinquency.* Washington, DC: Law Enforcement Assistance Administration.

Narabayashi, H. (1972). Stereotaxic amygdalectomy. In D. Eleftheriou (Ed.), *The neurobiology of the amygdala* (pp. 459–483). New York: Plenum.

Olweus, D., Mattsson, D., Schalling, D., & Low, H. (1980). Testosterone, aggression, physical, personality dimensions in normal adolescent males. *Psychosomatic Medicine, 42*, 253–269.

Ounsted, C. (1969). Aggression and epilepsy: Rage in a child with temporal lobe epilepsy. *Journal Psychosomatic Research, 13*, 237–242.

Penner, M.J. (1982). The role of selected health problems in the causation of juvenile delinquency. *Adolescence, 27*, 347–368.

Pontius, A.A. (1972). Neurological aspects in some types of delinquency especially among juveniles. *Adolescence, 7*, 289–308.

Pontius, A.A. (1973). Conceptual model of minimal brain dysfunction. *Annals of the New York Academy of Sciences, 205*, 61–63.

Pontius, A.A., & Ruttiger, K.F. (1976). Frontal lobe system maturational lag in juvenile delinquents shown in narratives tests. *Adolescence, 11*, 509–518.

Rada, R.T., Laws, D.R., & Kellner, R. (1976). Plasma testosterone levels in the rapist. *Psychosomatic Medicine, 38*, 257–268.

Reeves, A.G., & Blum, F. (1969). Hyperphagia, rage and dementia accompanying a ventromedial hypothalmic neoplasm. *Archives of Neurology, 20*, 616–624.

Rodin, E.A. (1973). Psychomotor epilepsy and aggressive behavior. *Archives of General Psychiatry, 28*, 210–213.

Rosenthal, D. (1971). A program of research on heredity in schizophrenia. *Behavior Science, 16*, 191–201.

Sagan, C. (1981). *Cosmos*. New York: Random House.

Scoville, W.B., Dunsmore, R.H., Liberson, W.T., Henry, C.E., & Pepe, A. (1953). Observations on medical temporal lobotomy uncotomy in the treatment of psychotic states. *Proceedings of the Association of Research on Nervous and Mental Diease, 31*, 347.

Selz, M., & Reitan, R.M. (1979). Rules for neurological diagnosis: Classification of brain function in older children. *Journal of Consulting and Clinical Psychology, 47*, 258–264.

Serafetinides, E.A. (1965). Aggressiveness in temporal lobe epileptics and its relation to cerebral dysfunction and environmental factors. *Epilepsia, 6*, 33–42.

Serafetinides, E.A. (1970). Psychiatric aspects of temporal lobe epilepsy. In E. Neidmeyer (Ed.), *Epilepsy, modern problems in pharmopsychiatry* (pp. 155–169). New York: Karger.

Shah, S.A. (1970). *Report on the XYY chromosomal abnormality* (U.S. Public Health Service Publication No. 2103). Washington, DC: U.S. Government Printing Office.

Spellacy, F. (1977). Neuropsychological differences between violent and nonviolent adolescents. *Journal of Clinical Psychology, 33*, 966–969.

Sweet, W.H., Ervin, F., & Mark, V.H. (1969). The relationship of violent behavior to focal cerebral disease. In S. Garattini & E.B. Sigg (Eds.), *Aggressive behavior* (pp. 336–352). New York: Wiley.

Tinklenberg, J.R., & Ochberg, F.M. (1981). Patterns of adolescent violence: A California sample. In D. Hamburg & M. Trudeau (Eds.), *Biobehavioral aspects of aggression* (pp. 121–140). New York: Liss.

Vaernet, K., & Madsen, A. (1970). Stereotoxic amygdalotomy and basofrontal tractotomy in psychotics with aggressive behavior. *Journal of Neurology, Neurosurgery and Psychiatry, 33*, 858–863.

Voorhees, J. (1981). Neuropsychological differences between juvenile delinquents and functional adolescents: A preliminary study. *Adolescence, 16*, 57–66.

Williams, D. (1969). Neural factors related to habitual aggression. Consideration of differences between those habitual aggressives and others who have committed crimes of violence. *Brain, 92*, 503–520.

Witkin, H.A., Mednick S.A., Schulsinger, F., Bakkestrom, E., Christiansen, K., Goodenough, D., Hirschhorn, K., Lundstein, D., Owen, D., Phillip, J., Rubin, D., & Stoking, M. (1976). Criminality in XYY and XXY men. *Science, 193*, 547–555.

Wolff, P.H., & Hurwitz, I. (1966). The choreiform syndrome. *Developmental Medicine and Child Neurology, 8*, 160–165.

Wolfgang, M.E. (1958). *Patterns in criminal homicide*. Philadelphia: University of Pennsylvania.

Wolfgang, M.E., & Ferracuti, F. (1967). *The subculture of violence*. London: Tavistock Publications.
Yeudall, L.T., Fromm-Auch, D., & Davies, P.D. (1982). Neuropsychological impairment of persistent delinquency. *Journal of Nervous and Mental Disease, 170,* 259–265.

5
Institutional Treatment Programs for the Violent Juvenile
Vicki L. Agee

INTRODUCTION

Institutional treatment for the violent juvenile is known for its rarity. The majority of violent juveniles are passed from one program to another until they end up in an adult correctional setting, where they usually receive no treatment at all. Both the mental health systems and the youth correctional systems find the violent juvenile aversive, although there have been a few programs that have attempted to deal with this very difficult population.

The rationalization presented by the majority of mental health professionals is that most violent juveniles have "character disorders" and thus are not amenable to treatment. Yochelson and Samenow (1977) state that institutions have failed in their attempts to treat characterological problems because they have applied the same methods to treat them that they have used with noncharacterological patients. They cite Miller and Kenney (1966), who stated, "No one has ever demonstrated that problems of delinquency can be successfully treated on a large scale in a psychiatric facility. We cannot treat misbehavior" (p.47).

Yochelson and Samenow (1977) also cite Silber (1974), who agrees that the traditional psychiatric approaches do not fit for the characterological patient: "Mental hospitals have the wrong 'set' for treating felons: they perceive the patient as helpless and disturbed. Most criminals are not out of contact with reality, but rather are deviant in social values and behavior" (p. 241).

Unfortunately, the diagnosis of "character disorder" in adolescence often has been broadened to include any behavior disorder, and behavior disorders are by far the most predominant symptomatology of adolescence. Schizophrenia is a disease that appears most often in late adolescence and early adulthood, but is not a common diagnosis in the adolescent years. Most treatment programs in mental hospitals are designed, therefore, for the rare schizophrenic adolescent, plus those equally rare adolescents who have no outstanding behavior disorders.

Why is it that mental hospitals seem to have such difficulty in dealing with behavior disorders? One would assume that with their staffing patterns (which are rich compared to correctional settings) and their access to psychotropic medications, they would have little difficulty in handling behavior disorders. What seems to occur confirms what the authors cited earlier conclude: The mental health system does not understand much about dealing with the violent juvenile, and to date most have been unable to redesign their treatment approaches to deal with this population.

The youth correctional system generally finds itself heir to youths who are rejected from the mental health systems because they are "non-amenable to treatment." Sometimes, of course, they receive youths who have not had mental health evaluations directly from the courts, and sometimes they receive them after they are rejected, but the majority of violent adolescents end up in our nation's youth correctional systems. The majority of the youth correctional systems, unfortunately, are even more poorly prepared to deal with them than the mental health systems. Their staffing patterns are traditionally at custodial level only, and staff pay, staff training, and administrative support are totally inadequate for the job they are required to do, that is, to treat the youth whom the mental health system has been unable to treat.

Almost anyone who has worked in an institution that deals with youths with severe behavior disorders knows that there are two ways to leave a treatment program. One is by improving behavior, and the other is to misbehave so badly that the program rejects the youth. This contributes to the "hot potato" syndrome in dealing with violent youths. Each move usually becomes a regressive one in that youths are likely to find themselves in programs that limit their freedom to increasing degrees.

Unfortunately, the majority of violent youths do not see each institutional change as a regressive move, but as a victory for refusing to allow others to control them. As explained in Agee (1979), it doesn't take long for them to feel invulnerable to any attempts at changing their behavior through treatment. And this compounds the already difficult treatment problem.

Tennenbaum (1978) stated that staff perception of "dangerousness" within a juvenile institution was inversely related to a desire to work with a youth. Bewildered and frightened staff are often presented with the dilemma of having to both manage and treat behavior in youths who have a long history of perceiving reinforcement for: (a) acting out violently against others; (b) having a deviant value system; and (c) sabotaging attempts at treatment. There is little wonder that few programs have been designed to work with this type of youth.

REPRESENTATIVE INSTITUTIONAL TREATMENT PROGRAMS

With the exception of the author's program, the Closed Adolescent Treatment Center, most treatment programs for the violent adolescent are fairly new, particularly those that specialize in treatment of the violent juvenile sex offender. The following are some examples of programs in mental health facilities, youth correctional facilities, and joint mental health–youth correctional facilities. The first example is of a mental health facility for violent juveniles.

Thistletown Regional Centre, Syl Apps Campus (475 Iroquois Shore Road, Oakville, Ontario L6J5E8), Clark Deller, Director

The Syl Apps program was in the planning stage for several years before opening in 1981. Planners visited several programs in the United States and Canada and did considerable research and staff training before opening their doors. The program is contained in two cottages, each with a capacity of 8 to 10 youths. It is unusual in that it is a mental health program specifically designed for violent youth. Usually, more than half the youths in the program at any time are sex offenders (either rapists or child molestors) and the rest are assorted other violent offenders. As is typical of mental health programs, the staffing ratio is quite high. There are 14 direct care staff in each unit of eight youths. The treatment approach is an eclectic one, and still in the developing stage.

In recent years, some youth correctional institutions decided to concentrate their most difficult youths in one cottage in order to protect them from influencing the "average" delinquents. They soon found it necessary to staff this type of cottage more highly than the usual single (or occasionally double) coverage of line staff. This was necessary if for no other reason than to prevent this collection of dangerous youths from assaulting staff and each other and escaping. It was found to be particularly necessary if any semblance of treatment was to take place. Even with increased staffing ratios, the staff-client ratio generally remained well below that of a mental health program, and the facility and all ancillary resources are generally of the austere nature reserved for correctional settings.

In spite of the drawbacks, several programs of this nature have survived and even flourished in correctional settings. As an example, the Lookout Mountain Center in Golden, Colorado (which originally was the boys' training school), has two such units, Oak and Blue Spruce. The former is described here as a program example.

The Oak Unit, Lookout Mountain Treatment Center (Golden, Colorado 80401), Darlene Miller, PhD, Director and John Davis, Treatment Team Coordinator

The Oak Unit has been in existence for 8 years. The staffing ratio of 14 staff to 18 youths is higher than the usual ratio at the institution of 11 staff to 24 youths in a cottage. The Oak Unit receives some of its violent incorrigible clients directly from the courts and some are transferred from other cottages after revealing strong resistance to treatment attempts. The treatment approach is mainly group-therapy oriented. All of the youths meet together in a community group three times a week, although group meetings may be called several times a day if there is a disturbance in the peer culture. In addition to the community group, the youths are involved in skill building groups which meet four times a week. These groups vary in content, but are educational as well as therapeutic. Samples of areas of concentration in skill building groups are: human sexuality; assertiveness training; values clarification; drugs and alcohol; social survival skills; and relationship awareness training.

Because there is a large number of sex offenders in the program, the sex offenders also have a separate group that meets four times a week. The emphasis in sex offender group is to raise awareness of victims and to teach the offenders to recognize thinking patterns in their rape cycles and change them.

In many respects, a combination approach to working with the violent juvenile is ideal. State mental health systems often have the resources in the way of staff, and in some respects in theoretical background, and the correctional systems often have the youths themselves. In addition, although lacking resources, the correctional staff often have the right "set" for working with the violent juvenile. For example, because they have long experience at being on the receiving end of youths that no one else wants to treat, they have experience with a wide variety and degree of disturbance that is often denied to mental health staff in settings with selective admission policies. For another, because they are particularly familiar with character disorders in juveniles, understanding of their cognitive processes is unlikely to be as naive and easily influenced as that of staff who don't work constantly with skilled manipulators. Finally, because they work in a correctional area, they are more likely to be capable of dealing with violent acting-out behavior because it is a fairly constant companion to their jobs.

The Closed Adolescent Treatment Center (CATC) described in the following paragraphs is an example of a program that began as a combined effort between mental health and youth correctional institutions to provide treatment for the violent juvenile.

The Closed Adolescent Treatment Center (3900 South Carr, Denver, Colorado 80235), Vicki Agee, PhD, Director

The CATC was opened in 1972 on the grounds of a youth correctional institution. It was funded by a Law Enforcement Assistance Act (LEAA) grant and was designed to be a cooperative program between Colorado's Division of Mental Health and Division of Youth Services to treat the youths (both male and female) who were considered the most violent and incorrigible in the state. The staff was hired by the Fort Logan Mental Health Center and they provided supervision. The facility and all ancillary services were provided by the Division of Youth Services. The original facility had a capacity of 18 youths, but after the first year of the program, it was moved to a facility that housed 26 youths. The total number of staff was 26. Staffing around the clock and on weekends, there are an average of three to five staff members on any shift.

The clients at the CATC are all violent offenders committed by the courts. As is similar in most programs for the violent offender, about half the population are sex offenders. Another fourth of the population are murderers, and the remainder are assorted other violent offenders.

The treatment program at the CATC is extremely complex, but centers around the therapeutic community concept. The major therapeutic modality is group therapy, and group meetings are held daily. The peer group is guided by staff in treating each other, and treatment is considered to go on at all times. The groups are homogeneous groupings based on Marguerite Warren's Differential Diagnostic Typology, Interpersonal Maturity Level Theory (1966). Staff are also matched with students for treatment purposes using this typology. Therefore, group, individual, family therapy, and all treatment planning are done by matched staff.

In addition to the daily groups, there is a separate sex offenders group (very similar to that at Oak Unit) and a separate group for murderers. Both of these groups meet once a week, and are in addition to the daily therapy groups. Other programming involves a remedial school program; a life skills program; recreational and occupational therapy; and an intensive community reintegration program.

During the first 3 years of the program, the Law Enforcement Assistance Administration also funded a separate independent research study which essentially did a cost-benefit analysis of the program. The study was quite complex, although the number of subjects was small. The results indicated that the unit was quite cost effective. Since the study was completed, the only research has been on recidivism to adult corrections, with the average recidivism being 33%.

After the LEAA funding ended, the CATC was funded by the State of Colorado. For purposes of efficiency, it was placed totally within the Division of Youth Services, rather than remaining a joint program. The philosophy of the program remains one of a joint mental health–youth correctional approach.

In many treatment programs, sex offenders are separated from the rest of the violent juvenile offenders and treatment programs are designed specifically for sexual disorders. Knopp (1982), of the Prison Research Education/Action Project, described examples of these homogeneous programs, as well as the programs that combine violent juvenile offender populations in her review of treatment programs for adolescent sex offenders.

Reasoning for separating the population of sex offenders from other violent offenders usually revolves around the need for protection. Sex offenders (particularly child molesters) are usually at the bottom of the peer hierarchy in an institution. This culture mirrors that which is found in adult correctional institutions. Probably this is one of the reasons sex offenders characteristically deny vehemently that they are guilty (even if they were apprehended in the act). Separating the populations then presumably makes the juvenile sex offender feel physically safe from harm from other offenders, and also contributes to lessened emotional stress stemming from peer rejection.

It should be noted that some programs, such as the Closed Adolescent Treatment Center and Oak Cottage at Lookout Mountain School, have a combined approach. That is, although the violent juvenile offender population is a mixed offense group, the sex offenders in each program have separate therapy groups to work on their sexual problems. Both programs, however, have a rich enough staffing ratio to provide the physical protection the sex offender seems to need.

The following program, the Intensive Change Sex Offenders' Program, is located in a unit for violent juvenile offenders, but is even more of a separate program than the CATC and Oak programs.

The Intensive Change Sex Offenders' Program, Maine Youth Center (675 Westbrook Street, South Portland, Maine 04106), David Berenson, Unit Director

The Maine Youth Center is the state's only juvenile institution, and the Intensive Change Sex Offenders' Program (ICSOP) is a part of the Cottage 1 program on grounds, which is primarily for violent offenders. There are 30 adolescents in the Cottage 1 program, and about 20% to 30% are sex offenders. Most of the latter are in the ICSOP program.

The ICSOP uses an eclectic treatment approach based mainly on the work of Yochelson and Samenow (1976, 1977) and William Glasser (1981). In addition, they have a therapeutic community approach called the Intensive Peer Culture. Youths are held responsible for each other's treatment, and this process is taught by and carefully supervised by staff. The Yochelson and Samenow approach is used in the treatment program to analyze inappropriate thinking patterns and to learn deterrents to these patterns. A daily journal of the youths' thought processes is kept and carefully analyzed for criminal personality thinking errors. To assist in their analysis of thought patterns, the Glasser BCP Model (1981) is used as a tool to help in learning.

The ICSOP is a fairly new program in the process of developing, but already is using some unique and promising approaches to working with the sex offender.

CHARACTERISTICS OF TREATMENT PROGRAMS FOR THE VIOLENT JUVENILE OFFENDERS

With only a few exceptions, the programs designed to treat the violent juvenile offender have many aspects in common. Most, for example, have as a major treatment emphasis a therapeutic community, or positive peer culture approach. Second, most have structured treatment programs that provide youths with ongoing behavioral feedback. Third, most use a team management approach with staff and have a high quality (and quantity) of staff. Fourth, most have developed a discipline system that is prompt, and have some sort of specialized approach in working with the sex offender portion of the violent juvenile offender population. Finally, most of the programs feel that a secure setting and adequate time for treatment are critical in their success. Each of these areas will be discussed in more detail in order to describe the philosophical sets that seem to be important in working with this very difficult population.

The Therapeutic Community Concept

Dr. Maxwell Jones (1953) was an early pioneer in the treatment of the sociopathic patient. His therapeutic community approach was one that would be replicated, expanded upon, and eventually become a popular approach with many different patient populations in addition to character disorders. At about the same time, the Highfields Program in New Jersey (Weeks, 1958) was developing the concept of Guided Group Interaction, and this concept also spread rapidly and was expanded upon. The numerous self-help groups in institutional settings and in the community were generally versions of these positive peer culture or therapeutic community approaches.

Examples of such programs are: Synanon, Delancy Street, Elan, and Vision Quest. These programs are quite different and designed for different populations (the first two generally for drug abusers, and the last two for adolescents with behavior problems), but all revolve around the concept that peers are responsible for treating each other. Harry Vorrath and Larry Brentro were leaders in utilizing these concepts in youth correctional settings and describe the concepts in their book, *Positive Peer Culture* (1974).

There is much similarity between the "therapeutic community" concept and that of the "positive peer culture" as described earlier (Agee & McWilliams, 1984, pp. 283–284*). They both espouse the following treatment approaches or philosophies:

1. The concept that the patient is responsible for his behavior. This may not seem to be a particularly radical concept, now, but in the heyday of the medical model, the patient was considered "sick" and therefore needed "treatment" applied by doctors. The therapeutic community rests on the understanding that the patient is capable of taking an active role in his own treatment.

2. The concept that the positive peer group is the most effective mode of treatment. A positive peer group is a group whose values and interactions reinforce thinking and behavior which is consistent with that of the core culture (e.g., integrity, hard work, mutual support, division of labor, etc.). A negative peer group, of course, reinforces values which are not only counter to

---

*Note. From "The Role of Group Therapy and the Therapeutic Community in Treating the Violent Juvenile Offender" (pp. 283–284) by V. Agee and B. McWilliams, 1984. In R. Mathais (Ed.), *Violent Juvenile Offenders.* San Francisco, CA: National Council on Crime and Delinquency. Copyright 1984 by National Council on Crime and Delinquency. Used with permission.

society in general, but which are usually harmful both to members of the group itself, and to others. Typical examples are the "con code" which exists in some psychiatric settings. The therapeutic community is designed to create a positive peer culture which in turn confronts negative behavior in its members and teaches positive behaviors.

3. The individual patient and the positive peer culture are held responsible for the treatment and management of the unit. The degree to which this takes place varies considerably in different treatment settings, but all therapeutic communities reject the medical model concept of a passive patient who is cared for by the nursing staff. The patient is held responsible for managing his own affairs and that of the group. In self-help settings such as the drug treatment program, Synanon, this responsibility was more or less considered to be a lifetime one. After successful treatment, patients would become treaters and continue living in the program permanently. In many mental health programs, the responsibility ended when the short term of hospitalization was over.

4. The responsibility of the staff in a therapeutic community is to help create and maintain the positive peer culture by careful guiding of its functioning. The staff in all therapeutic communities functions as a team and is itself expected to be a role model of a positive peer culture. The team model replaces the traditional hierarchy of the medical model—with the physician or psychiatrist making all of the decisions, the nurse supervising the implementation, and the psychiatric technician carrying out the direct care. Although the management system varies considerably from setting to setting, all therapeutic communities promote considerable input into treatment and programming at all levels of staff.

During the past 20 years, many felt that the therapeutic community–positive peer culture approach was the final answer for treating disturbed youth. The most obvious benefit was the use of peer pressure to control and, it was hoped, provide treatment to the youths in the program. The typical power struggle between adolescents and adults is increased greatly in a population of disturbed adolescents. In a therapeutic community, however, the control battle is avoided. The group values revolve around the philosophy of "we" rather than staff versus peers, or peers versus each other. Like an ideal extended family, problems are handled within the group, as they affect everybody. The youth who has had longstanding problems with interpersonal relationships learns how to meet the expectations of others and how to establish meaningful friendships. The youth who has successfully resisted becoming a contributing member of society cannot avoid the social framework in the therapeutic community. It pervades his or her existence, and it does this during a life phase when peer influence is paramount in importance. In addition, the therapeutic community confronts and attempts to reverse negative delinquent subculture values in youths before they become as habitual as they are in much of the adult criminal population.

If the therapeutic community approach is so ideal for working with juvenile offenders, why isn't it in general use in institutions? And, in fact, why was it considered a failure in many programs that attempted to use it? There is no simple answer, but there are some general problems that typically arise when attempting to use the approach.

One of the major problems revolved around the conflict between the treatment philosophies of the medical model versus those of the therapeutic community. Those who espouse the medical model see their patients as having primarily intrapersonal disorders, and thus they emphasize the one-to-one relationship between the patient and therapist. The therapeutic community model was originally designed for sociopaths with a major focus on treatment of interpersonal problems. Group therapy was thus the treatment of choice. In addition, the medical model stressed the use of psychotropic medications to control behavior, while the therapeutic community model resists the use of medications because they mask the behaviors that the group must observe in order to change. Also, the medical model stresses the shortest possible treatment time, so that patients are released as soon as minimal behavioral control is achieved. Therapeutic communities, on the other hand, take time to develop and cannot thrive where there is a rapid turnover in population. Finally, the power or authority in a medical model treatment program always rests in the physician, whatever the actual formal role of that person. Therapeutic communities cannot function effectively unless the power source in the program rests in the group leader, and thus with the group itself. This is to ensure that the group can realistically meet the expectation that it is responsible for the unit; it cannot be responsible for something it cannot control.

These are just a few of the major conflicts between the medical model and the therapeutic community model, but it can be seen that the two do not combine well at all. Unfortunately, what occurred in many psychiatric settings was an attempt to combine the philosophies with negative results. Sacks and Carpenter (1974), in their article on "The Pseudotherapeutic Community," describe what occurred in many settings.

In addition, there were conflicts with the traditional correctional organization when the therapeutic community approach was used in youth correctional facilities. The fairly rigid hierarchy of authority and pervasive distrust of mental health staff made it almost impossible to provide the individual units with the autonomy and support necessary to establish therapeutic communities. One example is the typical division in correctional settings between "group life" and treatment staff. The former handle security, discipline, and daily living experiences. The latter see the inmates on a periodic basis for therapy and then return them to their various living units. This usually results in the therapist being the "good guy" who is seen as a sympathetic listener, and the group life staff being the "bad guys" who enforce rules. Obviously there is no way to model a team or positive culture approach to the peer group with this type of staff structure.

For a time during the 1960s and 1970s, the therapeutic community approach was used with many other populations besides the "sociopaths" for which it was originally designed. The problem with this, of course, was some types of patients do not have the internal resources to be therapeutic with each other. Chronic schizophrenics, for example, may marginally exist in a therapeutic community, but they are certainly not capable of running one. Because of their thinking disorders, they are totally self-involved. Their problems are intrapersonal. Although they may learn rudimentary responses in a therapeutic community, they do not change their thinking patterns, and might even experience undue stress from the unrealistic expectations on their interpersonal skills.

At first glance, the violent juvenile offender, with his or her usual long history of sabotaging attempts at intervention and poor interpersonal relationships, would seem to be about as likely to benefit from a therapeutic community as a schizophrenic. The vital difference is that while the interpersonal skills of the violent juvenile offender are characteristically poor, the majority of them can be taught the behaviors necessary to be therapeutic with each other.

Unfortunately, this requires very special circumstances. Therapeutic communities are extraordinarily difficult to create and maintain, particularly with a population skilled in creating a negative peer culture. Nevertheless, the approach has not only been seen to be feasible, but the treatment of choice in most settings working with the violent juvenile offender.

Structured Treatment Programs

Many of the original therapeutic communities had very little, if any, structure, and in fact, some practitioners felt structure was counter to the philosophy. Harry Vorrath and Larry Brentro (1974), for example, were strongly adverse to using any ancillary treatment techniques with their positive peer culture, particularly the structure of "behavior modification" or point and level systems. What structure did exist in many programs was unidimensional. That is, the structure was limited to daily or weekly time schedules (e.g., Community Group was held at a certain time on a certain day). If there was any written program at all, it usually gave the schedule, the philosophy of the unit, and some rules (there was usually little said about consequences of breaking the rules).

The developers of treatment programs for the population of violent delinquents generally design an intricate, extremely structured written treatment program as a critical adjunct to the therapeutic community. There are several complex reasons for this, but the major one is the need to address the problem that the majority of the youths have character disorders and typically have manipulated or intimidated to avoid numerous previous attempts at treatment. Usually they are particularly expert at avoiding unidimensional type programs. For example, if they were in a program where it was necessary to earn points to progress through a program, they quickly became adept at "point scoring" while continuing their usual negative behaviors when there was no one around to score them down. In programs where there was strictly group therapy approach, they often became adept at appearing very sincere and therapeutic in group, and then becoming their usual intimidating selves outside of group, or around staff that was not involved in group.

To clinicians skilled in working with this population, every facet of the program must have a system that backs it up in such a fashion that it is very difficult for a youth to avoid the pressure of critically examining his or her behavior. For example, a youth may earn enough points from a scoring system to qualify him or her to move up a level in the program. However, the peer group may not approve the promotion because they feel the behavioral changes were not genuine. In this example, the youth quickly realizes that "point scoring with staff" is not enough, and must also impress his or her peer group with behavioral changes. To further expand the concept, the program may require that a youth make a commitment to the group to use some positive behavior alternatives and be confronted at any time outside of group by peers for not following up on these commitments. The ideal therapeutic community is a pervasive concept. The quality of interpersonal relationships is the major focus during all waking hours, not just during formal therapy times. For example, it is considered as important for the youths to learn how to relate while washing dishes as it is while telling their innermost secrets in group therapy. Therefore, the unidimensional schedule of daily activities is of minor importance. The total emphasis in all activities is on relationships—who is relating to whom, about what, and what is the quality of the interaction. This added dimension provides a depth that was missing in some previous attempts at establishing therapeutic communities with this population.

Another problem that often occurred in unsuccessful attempts to treat the population of violent juvenile offenders with a therapeutic community model was the lack of emphasis on victim awareness. The traditional mental health system considers its first responsibility to be to the patient, rather than to the community. Workers within this system usually take a very protective nurturing stance with their clients which is definitely not appropriate with the character disorder type of patient, who is looking for any excuse to deny responsibility for misbehavior. Rather than changing harmful behaviors, the result was more often that the behaviors were reinforced, as they often received much kindly attention and support after acting out. It was Glasser (1965) who first began emphasizing the importance of making the patient feel responsible for his or her own behavior, and apparently many of his insights were achieved from working with a population of delinquent girls. This concept has been expanded upon in most current treatment programs that work with violent juvenile offenders, so that the whole process of becoming acutely aware of the negative effects of their behaviors on their victims is a major part of the treatment process.

Adding further intensity to the treatment programs are such significant additions to the program as family therapy; one-to-one relationships with assigned staff; recreational and occupational therapy programs; life skills and community reentry programs; and the educational program. Unfortunately, it is not possible to discuss all of these program components in a short article. The important point to be made is that most treatment programs for the violent juvenile offenders are all-inclusive in order to provide the support and guidance to nourish a positive peer culture.

Team Management Approaches with Staff

Quality of staff (and to some extent quantity) is also seen to be a critical factor in developing and maintaining a treatment program for violent juvenile offenders. A positive peer culture cannot exist in the absence of a positive staff culture. Even if hiring is of necessity via a typical civil service, the staff culture must be such that high quality people are attracted to the system, and once hired usually make a long-term commitment to the unit.

In addition to selecting people who are personally exceptional, staff selection must also be keyed toward people who function well in a team system. There are some individuals who may be excellent therapists in their own right, but who just cannot relinquish enough autonomy to function as a member of a team and therefore cannot contribute to a therapeutic community with violent juvenile offenders. The concept requires that staff work so closely together as to almost appear to be a gestalt organism. This is because for one thing, they must appear as role models of cooperative interpersonal relationships to the peer group; and for another, the violent juveniles are obviously dangerous, and maximum safety is achieved through cohesion.

In an ideal family, the parents present a united front to their offspring. In the therapeutic community, the same thing must occur. Violent juvenile offenders usually have much experience at being able to split staff (and their own parents) and set them up against each other in an effort to divert attention from their negative behaviors. Ideally, in a team setting, there are very strong values against allowing this to happen, and attempts to do so are promptly confronted.

The team approach is very similar to the highly touted Japanese system of management. For one thing, staff in these programs usually make a long-term commitment to the job. Second, they are generalists. That is, no matter what one's training or experience, everyone has many of the same tasks. For example, the team's special education teachers may conduct the education program for part of the day but also have other tasks, such as supervising daily living experiences; disciplining youth; having one-to-one caseloads; and participating in all treatment planning. Similarly, the team psychiatric nurses may spend a small percentage of their time on medical responsibilities, but the majority of their time is spent in treatment and supervision of the peer culture. Third, all staff have input into the treatment planning and carrying it out. Although in most therapeutic communities there is a hierarchy (with the group leader being at the apex), staff at all levels participate in decision making and planning. As with the Japanese system, the administrative staff of these programs generally see that their function is to provide the resources for the staff to do their job in the highest quality manner possible. This provides the critical support necessary for staff to devote their energies to treatment rather than to resisting authority as they do in many settings.

A final staffing consideration that is considered a strong asset in some programs that treat the violent juvenile offender (such as the CATC) is the matching of staff and students along certain personality dimensions. At the Closed Adolescent Treatment Center, this matching is done on the basis of Marguerite Warren's (1961, 1983) Interpersonal Maturity Level Theory and is a complex concept. At least on an intuitive level, the matching seems to greatly facilitate staff–student relationships, and thereby aid in the treatment process.

Effective Discipline Systems

Partly due to their violent and intimidating behavior, and partly due to an acquired skill at sabotaging attempts at controlling them, teaching the violent juvenile offender self-discipline is an overwhelming task. However, as William Glasser (1965) has stated in his Reality Therapy theory, the need for self-discipline is one of four basic needs to be met in order to learn responsible behavior. Often the violent juvenile offender has to have almost a complete resocialization in order to achieve this goal.

The concept of giving "natural and logical consequences" as developed by Dreikurs and Grey (1970) has been helpful in designing discipline systems in treatment settings with the violent offender. Of course, it is difficult to provide "natural" consequences for misbehavior in an institutional setting, but it is possible to design a system that provides consequences that are as logical as possible, and certainly prompt and effective. Gadow and McKibbon (1984, p. 315) summarize the design of such a system as follows:

> First, it is necessary in working with the violent juvenile to have a treatment program which clearly spells out the structure of the program, including the rules which are designed to promote socialization and the offenses which are considered serious and not to be tolerated. The consequences for these major and minor offenses are spelled out in detail in the program, in order to provide the consistency that did not occur in the childhood of the offenders. It is vitally important that this structure be very detailed and that the youths know that certain behaviors will inevitably result in certain consequences, and there is no way that they can manipulate or intimidate their way out of the consequences.

> In a therapeutic community, such as the CATC, the positive peer culture sets the standards as to what is acceptable and non-acceptable in their peer culture, although this process is guided by staff, and is done within the structure of the overall treatment program. All staff and peers are expected to confront misbehavior, whether it is behavioral or attitudinal, as soon as it occurs. This is such a strong value in the peer culture that the person who does not confront negative behavior is considered equally guilty as the person who is misbehaving. The rationale of course is to teach the value that stopping people from hurting themselves or others is a caring thing to do in our society.

The concept of applying logical consequences requires two philosophical steps. The first is to help the youths reach the level of "ownership," or accepting that the problem is theirs. The second step is to have them learn good decision making by looking at the consequences of their decisions, both for themselves and for others. Neither step is easy. The first step, for example, is confounded by the habitual stance of the violent juvenile offender of projecting blame for his behavior. As Yochelson and Samenow (1976) describe the thinking pattern, they display the "victim stance" whenever they are caught at some misbehavior. That is, they claim that they themselves are the victim of the behavior. They usually have long histories of having been rewarded for not "owning" their behavior by having consequences removed or lightened.

Regarding the second step, character disorders are renowned for their so-called "inability to learn from experience." Whatever the source of this behavior, it is seen in an enormous resistance to even attempting behavioral alternatives to their usual aggressive, harmful behavior. For this reason, the discipline has to be structured enough to be resistant to strong attempts to manipulate, intimidate, or escape from the consequences in the program.

At the same time, the system has to do this without inhumane consequences, and in fact with less acceptable consequences than the typical family is allowed.

The programs that are successfully treating violent juvenile offenders have mastered the ability to control negative behavior and also, in the majority of cases, to have youths learn to discipline themselves.

Specialized Treatment for the Juvenile Sex Offender

As stated in the section on program descriptions, most treatment programs for the violent juvenile offender, whether or not they mix offense groups, have portions of the program specifically directed toward the sexual problems of the juvenile sex offender. Knopp (1982) summarizes the components of most of the programs for sex offenders as follows:

> Presently, program components include *family therapy*; various types of *education in human sexuality*, sometimes for the entire family; *victim awareness* exercises, including empathy training, accountability and responsibility acceptance, and familiarity with cycles of victimization; *interpersonal social skills development*, which teaches communication, socialization, and group work; *anger management*, which deals with conflict resolution and negotiating skills; *grief work*, which helps work through personal victimization and trauma; *journal keeping*, which teaches how to record thought processes and fantasies and encourages writing autobiographical materials; *survival skills*, which include stop-thought processes and day-to-day living skills; *sex-role expectations*, which educate about "macho" sex-role stereotyping; and *general education*, which includes a high school diploma and vocational and occupational therapies. Some programs also have *alcohol dependency groups* or refer adolescents to community self-help groups for chemical dependents. Programs increase in structure and intensity in line with the seriousness of the offense and violence exhibited by the offender. (p. 37)

Lane and Zamora (1984) describe five fairly distinct phases of their treatment of juvenile sex offenders. They are: (a) penetrating the denial and dealing with the sexual assaults the youths committed; (b) identifying the individual's rape cycle and working with the daily manifestations of the cycle; (c) working with unresolved emotional issues (particularly their own victimization if they were sexually abused in early childhood); (d) retraining in the areas of skill deficits; and (e) reentry into the community.

Because treatment of the juvenile sex offender is in a developing phase, as is the treatment of the violent offender in general, most programs only have tentative data about their effectiveness. However, the results to date show a great deal of promise in the ability to successfully intervene in the sex offender's behavior in adolescence.

A Secure Setting and Adequate Time for Treatment

Although the degree of security varies in different programs, it is generally accepted that violent juvenile offenders must be treated in secure settings. The basic reason for this is for the protection of the community. Most violent delinquents have developed a pattern under pressure to escape if at all possible, and they, of course, experience considerable pressure in most successful treatment programs. Again, unlike the nurturing, protective environment of traditional mental health programs, the programs for the violent juvenile offenders are confrontive, structured, and emphasize consequences for irresponsible behavior. The pressure of critically examining their behavior and changing is likely to make life fairly uncomfortable for the violent juvenile offender, and increase attempts to return to their previous lives full of criminal excitement. Many programs that did not actively attempt to prevent escapes were eventually terminated due to backlash from the general public and their lawmakers. In treating the violent delinquent, staff must realize that their top priority is to ensure the safety of the community.

In addition, successful treatment of the violent juvenile offender is not possible in short-term settings. Unfortunately, many earlier attempts at treatment failed because the violent offender was not kept in the program long enough to see if surface behavior changes would last over time. This was contributed to both because of the pressure of space problems and also because of the philosophy that short-term treatment is the best choice for any client population. Unfortunately, most violent juvenile offenders become quite "psychologically sophisticated" over their careers in various treatment settings, so they often are successful at pretending to "go along with program" and experience great insight until staff feels they are ready for release. Another common tactic is to intimidate or act out enough that staff will release, transfer, or allow them to escape. The result, of course, is that the violent offender is left with the feeling that once again he or she has "beaten the system."

It is impossible to define what enough time is, of course, as it varies with each individual. In ideal programs, the treatment program is designed with a level system wherein the youth earns increased freedom along with increased responsibility, and is unable to leave the program until his or her behavior has improved and maintained over enough time that the changes appear to be permanent. Testing the youth with a slow transition period into the community is also a part of the ideal program. Again, violent offenders with long offense histories are highly unlikely to really benefit from short-term intervention.

PROGRAM DEVELOPMENT EFFORTS

Although the statistics indicate a "leveling off" in the incidence of violent juvenile crime, the leveling off is at a level much too high for community safety. As Heide (1979) indicated in her study of adolescent arrests for murder and non-negligent homicide in the United States, between 1960 and 1975, such crimes increased more than 200%. As summarized by Empey (1979) and Isralowitz (1979), there is a growing disenchantment with the juvenile justice systems, and rapidly increasing tendencies to send dangerous juveniles to adult correctional settings. Fortunately, the experts in juvenile corrections are strongly resisting this move and generally are using what meager resources most have to develop long-term, intensive, secure treatment programs for violent juvenile offenders within the juvenile system. Numerous states and provinces in Canada are in the process of developing treatment programs specifically for this population. Notable at this current time are the states of Utah, New Mexico, Michigan, and Mississippi, whose programs for the violent offender are in the initial stages after long and intensive planning. Many other states are in the planning process, or already have some capacity to treat the violent juvenile offender. It is clear to experts in the field that intensive treatment efforts are far preferable in most cases to sending a youth to an adult custodial setting.

REFERENCES

Agee, V. (1979). *Treatment of the violent incorrigible adolescent*. Lexington, MA: Lexington Books.

Agee, V., & McWilliams, B. (1984). The role of group therapy and the therapeutic community in treating the violent juvenile offender. In R. Mathias (Ed.), *Violent juvenile offenders: An anthology*. Newark, NJ: National Council on Crime and Delinquency.

Dreikurs, R., & Grey, L. (1970). *A parent's guide to child discipline*. New York: Hawthorne Books, Inc.

Empey, L.T. (Ed.). (1979). *The future of childhood and juvenile justice*. Charlottesville, VA: University Press of Virginia.

Gadow, D., & McKibbon, J. (1984). Discipline and the institutionalized violent delinquent. In R. Mathias (Ed.), *Violent juvenile offenders: An anthology*. Newark, NJ: National Council on Crime and Delinquency.

Glasser, W. (1965). *Reality therapy*. New York: Harper & Rowe.

Glasser, W. (1981). *Stations of the mind*. New York: Harper & Rowe.

Heide, F. (1979). Juvenile justice: The second revolution. *Crime and Delinquency, 25*, 299–318.

Isralowitz, R.E. (1979). Deinstitutionalization and the serious juvenile offender. *Juvenile and Family Court Journal, 30*, 21–35.

Jones, M. (1953). *The therapeutic community*. New York: Basic Books.

Knopp, F.H. (1982). *Remedial intervention in adolescent sex offenses: Nine program descriptions*. Syracuse, NY: Safer Society Press.

Lane, S., & Zamora, P. (1984). A method for treating the adolescent sex offender. In R. Mathias (Ed.), *Violent juvenile offenders: An anthology*. Newark, NJ: National Council on Crime and Delinquency.

Miller, R.B., & Kenney, E. (1966). Adolescent delinquency and the myth of hospital treatment. *Crime and Delinquency, 12*, 38–48.

Sacks, M., & Carpenter, W. (1974, May). The pseudotherapeutic community: An examination of antitherapeutic forces on psychiatric units. *Hospital and Community Psychiatry, 25*, 315–318.

Silber, D.E. (1974). Controversy concerning the criminal justice system and its implications for the role of mental health workers. *American Psychologist, 29*, 239–244.

Tennenbaum, D.J. (1978). Dangerousness within a juvenile institution. *Journal of Criminal Justice, 6*, 329–345.

Vorrath, H., & Brentro, L.K. (1974). *Positive peer culture*. Chicago: Aldine Publishing Company.

Warren, M. (1983). Applications of interpersonal maturity theory to offender populations. In W. Laufer & J. Day (Eds.), *Personality theory, moral development and criminal behavior* (pp. 23–164). Lexington, MA: Lexington Books.

Weeks, H.A. (1958). *Youthful offenders at Highfields*. Ann Arbor: The University of Michigan Press.

Yochelson, S., & Samenow, S. (1976). *The criminal personality, Vol. 1, A profile for change*. New York: Jason Aronson.

Yochelson, S., & Samenow, S. (1977). *The criminal personality, Vol. 2, The change process*. New York: Jason Aronson.

6
Psychological Skill Training and the Aggressive Adolescent
Arnold P. Goldstein

Until the early 1970s, there existed three major psychological approaches designed to alter the behavior of aggressive, unhappy, ineffective, or disturbed individuals: psychodynamic/psychoanalytic, humanistic/nondirective, and behavior modification. Each of these diverse psychotherapeutic orientations found concrete expression in interventions targeted to aggressive youth—the psychodynamic in psychoanalytically oriented individual psychotherapy (Guttman, 1970), activity group therapy (Slavson, 1964), and the varied array of treatment procedures originally put forth by Redl and Wineman (1957); the humanistic/nondirective in the individual psychotherapy of Carl Rogers (1957), the alternative educational programs offered by Gold (1978), and the approach to school discipline put forth by Dreikurs, Grunwald, and Pepper (1971); and the behavior modification in a wide variety of interventions reflecting the systematic use of contingency management, contracting, the training of teachers and parents as behavior change managers, and related techniques (O'Leary, O'Leary, & Becker, 1967; Patterson, Cobb, & Ray, 1973; Walker, 1979). Although each of these therapeutic philosophies differs from the others in several major respects, one of their significant commonalities is the shared assumption that patients have somewhere within themselves, as yet unexpressed, the effective, satisfying, nonaggressive, or healthy behaviors whose expression was among the goals of the therapy. Such latent potentials, in all three approaches, would be realized by the patient if the therapist was sufficiently skilled in reducing or removing obstacles to such realization. The psychoanalyst sought to do so by calling forth and interpreting unconscious material blocking progress-relevant awareness. The nondirectivist, who believes that the potential for change resides within the patient, sought to free this potential by providing a warm, empathic, maximally accepting therapeutic environment. And the behavior modifier, by means of one or more contingency management procedures, attempted to see to it that when the latent desirable behaviors or approximations thereto did occur, the patient received contingent reinforcement, thus increasing the probability that these behaviors would recur. Therefore, whether sought by means of interpretation, therapeutic climate, or by dint of offering contingent reward, all three approaches assumed that somewhere within the individual's repertoire resided the desired, effective, sought-after goal behaviors.

In the early 1970s, an important new intervention approach began to emerge—psychological skill training, an approach resting upon rather different assumptions. Viewing the helpee more in educational pedagogic terms rather than as a patient in need of therapy, the psychological skills trainer assumed he or she was dealing with an individual lacking, deficient, or at best weak in the skills necessary for effective and satisfying interpersonal functioning. The task of the skills trainer became, therefore, not interpretation, reflection, or reinforcement, but the active and deliberate teaching of desirable behaviors. Rather than an intervention called psychotherapy, between a patient and psychotherapist, what emerged was training, between a trainee and a psychological skills trainer.

The roots of the psychological skills training movement lay within both education and psychology. The notion of literally seeking to teach desirable behaviors has often, if sporadically, been a significant goal of the American educational establishment. The Character Education Movement of the 1920s and more contemporary Moral Education and Values Clarification programs are but a few of several possible examples. Add to this institutionalized educational interest in skills training, the hundreds of interpersonal and planning skills courses taught in America's over 2,000 community colleges, and the hundreds of self-help books oriented toward similar skill-enhancement goals which are available to the American public, and it becomes clear that the formal and informal educational establishment in America provided fertile soil and explicit stimulation within which the psychological skills training movement could grow.

Much the same can be said for American psychology, as it too laid the groundwork in its prevailing philosophy and concrete interests for the development of this new movement. The learning process has above all else been the central theoretical and investigative concern of American psychology since the late 19th century. This focal interest also assumed major therapeutic form in the 1950s, as psychotherapy practitioners and researchers alike came to view psychotherapeutic treatment more and more in learning terms. The very healthy and still expanding field of behavior modification grew from this joint learning-clinical focus, and may be appropriately viewed as the immediately preceding context in which psychological skills training came to be developed. In companion with the growth of behavior modification, psychological thinking increasingly shifted from a strict emphasis on remediation to one that was equally concerned with prevention, and the bases for this shift included movement away from a medical model concept toward what may most aptly be called a psychoeducational theoretical stance. Both of these thrusts—heightened concern with prevention and a psychoeducational perspective—gave strong added impetus to the viability of the psychological skill training movement.

Perhaps psychology's most direct contribution to psychological skills training came from social learning theory, and in particular from the work conducted by and stimulated by Albert Bandura. Based upon the same broad array of modeling, behavioral rehearsal, and social reinforcement investigations that helped stimulate and direct the development of our own approach to skill training, Bandura (1973) comments:

The method that has yielded the most impressive results with diverse problems contains three major components. First, alternative modes of response are repeatedly modeled, preferably by several people who demonstrate how the new style of behavior can be used in dealing with a variety of . . . situations. Second, learners are provided with necessary guidance and ample opportunities to practice the modeled behavior under favorable conditions until they perform it skillfully and spontaneously. The later procedures are ideally suited for developing new social skills, but they are unlikely to be adopted unless they produce rewarding consequences. Arrangement of success experiences particularly for initial efforts at behaving differently, constitute the third component in this powerful composite method . . . . Given adequate demonstration, guided practice, and success experiences, this method is almost certain to produce favorable results. (p. 253)

Other events of the 1970s provided still further fertile ground for the growth of the skills training movement. The inadequacy of prompting, shaping, and related operant procedures for adding new behaviors to individuals' behavioral repertoires was increasingly apparent. The widespread reliance upon deinstitutionalization which lay at the heart of the community mental health movement resulted in the discharge from America's public mental hospitals of approximately 400,000 persons, the majority of whom were substantially deficient in important daily functioning skills. Furthermore, it had grown clear that what the American mental health movement had available to offer lower social class clients—adult, adolescent, or child—was grossly inadequate in meeting their psychotherapeutic needs. These factors, that is relevant supportive research, the incompleteness of operant approaches, large populations of grossly skill deficient individuals, and the paucity of useful interventions for a large segment of American society—all in the context of historically supportive roots in both education and psychology—came together in the thinking of the present writers and others as demanding a new intervention, something prescriptively responsive to these several needs. Psychological skill training was the answer, and a movement was launched.

Our involvement in this movement, a psychological skill training approach we have termed Structured Learning, began in the early 1970s. At the time, and for several years thereafter, our studies were conducted in public mental hospitals with long-term, highly skill-deficient, chronic patients. As our research program progressed, and demonstrated with regularity successful skill enhancement effects (Goldstein, 1981), we shifted in our focus from teaching a broad array of interpersonal and daily living skills to adult, psychiatric inpatients to a more explicit concern with skill training for aggressive individuals, especially aggressive adolescents. A not insubstantial body of literature has in fact directly demonstrated that delinquent and other aggressive youngsters display widespread interpersonal, planning, aggression management, and other psychological skill deficiencies. Freedman, Rosenthal, Donahoe, Schbundy, and McFall (1978) examined the comparative skill competence levels of a group of juvenile delinquents and a matched group (age, IQ, social background) of nonoffenders in response to a series of standardized role-play situations. The offender sample responded in a consistently less skillful manner. Spence (1981) constituted comparable offender and nonoffender samples, and videotaped their individual interviews with a previously unknown adult. The offender group evidenced significantly less (a) eye contact, (b) appropriate head movements, and (c) speech, as well as significantly more fiddling and gross body movement. Conger, Miller, and Walsmith (1965) add further to this picture of skill deficiency. They conclude from their evidence that juvenile delinquents, as compared to nondelinquent cohorts

. . . had more difficulty in getting along with peers, both in individual one-to-one contacts and in group situations, and were less willing or able to treat others courteously and tactfully, and less able to be fair in dealing with them. In return, they were less well liked and accepted by their peers. (p. 442)

Not only are adjudicated delinquents discriminable from their nondelinquent peers on a continuum of skill competence, but much the same is true for youngsters who are "merely" chronically aggressive. Patterson, Reid, Jones, and Conger (1975) observe:

. . . the socialization process appears to be severely impeded for many aggressive youngsters. Their behavioral adjustments are often immature and they do not seem to have learned the key social skills necessary for initiating and maintaining positive social relationships with others. Peer groups often reject, avoid, and/or punish aggressive children, thereby excluding them from positive learning experiences with others. (p. 4)

YV-D*

As Patterson et al. (1975) appear to be proposing, the social competence discrepancy between delinquent or aggressive youngsters and their nondelinquent, nonaggressive peers has early childhood roots according to evidence provided by Mussen, Conger, Kagan, and Gerwitz (1979). Boys who became delinquent in their longitudinal study were appraised by their teachers as less well-adjusted socially than their classmates as early as third grade. They appeared less friendly, responsible, or fair in dealing with others, and more impulsive and antagonistic to authority. Poor peer relations—less friendly toward classmates, less well-liked by peers—were further developmental predictors of later delinquency. Thus, it may be safely concluded that psychological skill deficiencies of diverse—especially inter-personal—types markedly characterize both the early development and adolescent nature of delinquent and aggressive youngsters to a degree that significantly differentiates them from their nondelinquent, nonaggressive peers.

STRUCTURED LEARNING

As is true of almost all current forms of psychological skills training, the Structured Learning approach consists of the didactic procedures recommended by Bandura (1973) based upon empirical, social learning research. These procedures, which we now wish to describe briefly, are (a) modeling, (b) role playing, (c) performance feedback, and (d) transfer training.[1]

Procedures

Modeling. Structured Learning requires first that trainees be exposed to expert examples of the behaviors we wish them to learn. The five or six trainees constituting the Structured Learning group are selected based upon their shared skill deficiencies. Each potentially problematic behavior is referred to as a skill. Each skill is broken down into four to six different behavioral steps. The steps constitute the operational definition of the given skill. Using either live acting by the group's trainers or audiovisual modeling displays, actors portray the steps of that skill being used expertly in a variety of settings relevant to the trainee's daily life. Trainees are told to watch and listen closely to the way the actors in each vignette sequentially portray the skill's behavioral steps.

Role Playing. A brief spontaneous discussion almost invariably follows the presentation of a modeling display. Trainees comment on the steps, the actors, and, very often, on how the situation or skill problem portrayed occurs in their own lives. Because our primary goal in role playing is to encourage realistic behavior rehearsal, a trainee's statements about his or her individual difficulties using the skill being taught can often develop into material for the first role play. To enhance the realism of the portrayal, the main actor is asked to choose a second trainee (co-actor) to play the role of the significant other person in his or her life who is relevant to the skill problem.

The main actor is asked to briefly describe the real skill problem situation and the real person(s) involved in it, with whom he or she could try these behavioral steps in real life. The co-actor is called by the name of the main actor's significant other during the role

---

[1] An extended description of the procedures that constitute Structured Learning, in format tailored to adolescent trainees, is presented in *Skillstreaming the Adolescent* (Goldstein, Sprafkin, Gershaw, & Klein, 1980).

play. The trainer then instructs the role players to begin. It is the trainers' main responsibility, at this point, to be sure that the main actor keeps role playing and that he or she attempts to follow the behavioral steps while doing so.

The role playing is continued until all trainees in the group have had an opportunity to participate—even if the same skill must be carried over to a second or third session. It should be noted that while the framework (behavioral steps) of each role play in the series remains the same, the actual content can and should change from role play to role play. It is the skill-deficiency problem as it actually occurs, or could occur, in each trainee's real-life environment that should be the content of the given role play. When completed, each trainee should be better armed to act appropriately in the given reality situation.

Performance Feedback. Upon completion of each role play, a brief feedback period ensues. The goals of this activity are to let the main actor know how well he or she followed the skill's steps or in what ways he or she departed from them, to explore the psychological impact of this enactment on the co-actor, and to provide the main actor with encouragement to try out his or her role play behaviors in real life. In these critiques, the behavioral focus of Structured Learning is maintained. Comments must point to the presence or absence of specific, concrete behaviors, and not take the form of general evaluative comments or broad generalities.

Transfer and Maintenance of Training. Several aspects of the Structured Learning sessions described here have, as their primary purpose, augmentation of the likelihood that learning in the training setting will transfer to the trainee's actual real-life environment, and endure there over time. These procedures will be described in detail later in this chapter.

Skills

By means of the four procedures just described, we have systematically taught aggression-relevant skills to delinquent adolescents, and other highly aggressive individuals. Our investigations of the effectiveness of these combined procedures are presented in *Psychological Skill Training* (Goldstein, 1981). These 50 antisocial-inhibiting or prosocial-enhancing Structured Learning skills, and their component behavioral steps include:

Asking for Help
1. Decide what the problem is.
2. Decide if you want help with the problem.
3. Identify the people who might help you.
4. Make a choice of helper.
5. Tell the helper about your problem.

Giving Instructions
1. Define what needs to be done and who should do it.
2. Tell the other person what you want him or her to do, and why.
3. Tell the other person exactly how to do what you want done.
4. Ask for his or her reaction.
5. Consider his or her reactions and change your direction if appropriate.

Expressing Affection
1. Decide if you have warm, caring feelings about the other person.
2. Decide whether the other person would like to know about your feelings.
3. Decide how you might best express your feelings.

4. Choose the right time and place to express your feelings.
5. Express affection in a warm and caring manner.

Expressing a Complaint
1. Define what the problem is, and who's responsible.
2. Decide how the problem might be solved.
3. Tell that person what the problem is and how it might be solved.
4. Ask for a response.
5. Show that you understand his or her feelings.
6. Come to agreement on the steps to be taken by each of you.

Persuading Others
1. Decide on your position and what the other person's is likely to be.
2. State your position clearly, completely, and in a way that is acceptable to the other person.
3. State what you think the other person's position is.
4. Restate your position, emphasizing why it is the better of the two.
5. Suggest that the other person consider your position for a while before making a decision.

Responding to the Feelings of Others (Empathy)
1. Observe the other person's words and actions.
2. Decide what the other person might be feeling, and how strong the feelings are.
3. Decide whether it would be helpful to let the other person know you understand his or her feelings.
4. Tell the other person, in a warm and sincere manner, how you think he or she is feeling.

Following Instructions
1. Listen carefully while the instructions are being given.
2. Give your reactions to the instructions.
3. Repeat the instructions to yourself.
4. Imagine yourself following the instructions and then do it.

Responding to Persuasion
1. Listen openly to the other person's position.
2. Consider the other person's possible reasons for that position.
3. Ask the other person to explain anything you don't understand about what was said.
4. Compare the other person's position with your own, identifying the pros and cons of each.
5. Decide what to do, based on what will benefit you most in the long run.

Responding to Failure
1. Decide if you have failed.
2. Think about both the personal reasons and the circumstances that have caused you to fail.
3. Decide how you might do things differently if you tried again.
4. Decide if you want to try again.
5. If it is appropriate, try again, using your revised approach.

Responding to Contradictory Messages
1. Pay attention to those body signals that help you know you are feeling trapped or confused.
2. Observe the other person's words and actions that may have caused you to have these feelings.
3. Decide whether that person's words and actions are contradictory.
4. Decide whether it would be useful to point out the contradiction.
5. Ask the other person to explain the contradiction.

Responding to a Complaint
1. Listen openly to the complaint.
2. Ask the person to explain anything you don't understand.
3. Show that you understand the other person's thoughts and feelings.

4. Tell the other person your thoughts and feelings, accepting responsibility if appropriate.
5. Summarize the steps to be taken by each of you.

Preparing for a Stressful Conversation
1. Imagine yourself in the stressful situation.
2. Think about how you will feel and why you will feel that way.
3. Imagine the other person in the stressful situation. Think about how that person will feel and why he or she will feel that way.
4. Imagine yourself telling the other person what you want to say.
5. Imagine the response that that will elicit.
6. Repeat the above steps using as many approaches as you can think of.
7. Choose the best approach.

Determining Responsibility
1. Decide what the problem is.
2. Consider possible causes of the problem.
3. Decide which are the most likely causes of the problem.
4. Take actions to test out which are the actual causes of the problem.

Responding to Anger
1. Listen openly to the other person's angry statement.
2. Show that you understand what the other person is feeling.
3. Ask the other person to explain anything you don't understand about what was said.
4. Show that you understand why the other person feels angry.
5. If it is appropriate, express your thoughts and feelings about the situation.

Setting Problem Priorities
1. List all the problems that are currently pressuring you.
2. Arrange this list in order, from most to least urgent problems.
3. Take steps (delegate, postpone, avoid) to temporarily decrease the urgency of all but the most pressing problem.
4. Concentrate on the most pressing problem.

Dealing with Being Left Out
1. Decide if you're being left out (ignored, rejected).
2. Think about why the other people might be leaving you out of something.
3. Decide how you could deal with the problem (wait, leave, tell the other people how their behavior affects you, talk with a friend about problem).
4. Choose the best way and do it.

Dealing with an Accusation
1. Think about what the other person has accused you of (if it is accurate, inaccurate, if it was said in a mean way or in a constructive way).
2. Think about why the person might have accused you (have you infringed on his or her rights or property?).
3. Think about ways to answer the person's accusations (deny, explain your behavior, correct other person's perceptions, assert, apologize, offer to make up for what happened).
4. Choose the best way and do it.

Dealing with Group Pressure
1. Think about what the other people want you to do and why (listen to other people, decide what the real meaning is, try to understand what is being said).
2. Decide what you want to do (yield, resist, delay, negotiate).
3. Decide how to tell the other people what you want to do (give reasons, talk to one person only, delay, assert).
4. Tell the group what you have decided.

RESEARCH RESULTS

Concurrent with or following our development of the Structured Learning approach to psychological skills training, a number of similar programmatic attempts to enhance social competency emerged. Those that focused at least in large part on aggressive youngsters and their prosocial training include Life Skills Education (Adkins, 1970, 1974); Social Skill Training (Argyle, Trower, & Bryant, 1974); AWARE: Activities for Social Development (Elardo & Cooper, 1977); Relationship Enhancement (Guerney, 1977); Teaching Conflict Resolution (Hare, 1976); Developing Human Potential (Hawley & Hawley, 1975); Interpersonal Communication (Heiman, 1973); and Directive Teaching (Stephens, 1978). The instructional techniques that constitute each of these skills training efforts derive from social learning theory and typically consist of instructions, modeling, role playing, and performance feedback—with ancillary use in some instances of contingent reinforcement, prompting, shaping, or related behavioral techniques. Developing in part out of the empirical tradition of behavior modification, it is not surprising that psychological skill training efforts came under early and continuing research scrutiny. Table 6.1 summarizes the existing body of psychological skills training investigations involving aggressive adolescent and preadolescent subjects.

The 30 investigations that constitute Table 6.1 are essentially all of the psychological skills training studies conducted to date with aggressive youngsters. Two-thirds are of multiple-group design; the remainder are single-subject studies. Psychological skills training is operationally defined in almost an identical manner across all of these investigations— almost always a combination of instructions, modeling, role playing, and performance feedback. Study subjects are either adjudicated juvenile delinquents, status offenders, or chronically aggressive youngsters studied in secondary school settings. While target skills have varied across investigations, for the most part they have concerned interpersonal behaviors, prosocial alternatives to aggression, and aggression-management or aggression-inhibition behaviors. As Spence (1979) correctly notes, the single-case studies have tended toward microskill training targets—eye contact, head nods, and the like—and the multiple group studies have sought to teach more macroskill competencies, for example, coping with criticism, negotiation, and problem solving. Results, for skill acquisition, have been quite consistently positive. Aggressive adolescents are able to learn a broad array of previously unavailable interpersonal, aggression-management, affect-relevant and related psychological competencies via the training methods examined here. Evaluation for maintenance and transfer of acquired skills yields a rather different outcome. Many studies test for neither. Those that do combine to report a mixed result. Our own investigative efforts in this regard (Goldstein, 1981) point to the not surprising conclusion that generalization of skill competency across settings (transfer) and time (maintenance) are very much a direct function of the degree to which the investigator/trainer implemented as a part of the training effort procedures explicitly designed to enhance transfer and/or maintenance. We will examine an array of such procedures in a later section. To summarize our view of empirical efforts to date—psychological skills training with aggressive adolescents rests on a firm investigative foundation—a variety of investigators, designs, subjects, settings, and target skills is providing a healthy examination of the effectiveness of such training. Skill acquisition is a reliable outcome, but the social validity of this consistent result is tempered substantially by the frequent failure—or at least, indeterminacy—of transfer and maintenance. In the sections that follow, we wish to address several issues relevant to the future course of psychological skills training research, directing our attention as we do so to means for further clarifying the optimal nature of such training, further refining the quality of its investigation, and further improving the efficacy of its outcomes.

Table 6.1. Psychological Skills Training Research with Adolescent and Preadolescent Trainees

Investigator	Design	Treatment	Trainees	N	Setting	Target	Outcome
Bornstein, et al. (1980)	Single case: Multiple base-line	Instructions Modeling Role play Feedback	Aggressive adolescent inpatients	4	Psychiatric hospital	Assertiveness	Increase in skill performance contingent on training; decrease in aggression, maintained at 6 months.
Braukmann, et al. (1973)	Single case: Multiple base-line	Instructions Modeling Role play Feedback	Juvenile delinquents	2	Family group home	Heterosexual interaction skills (head nods, attending, etc.)	Increase in skill performance; contingent on training; increase in female contact at parties.
Braukmann, et al. (1974)	Single case: Multiple base-line	Instructions Modeling Role play Feedback	Juvenile delinquents	6	Family group home	Interview skills (posture, eye contact, etc.)	Increase in skill performance contingent on training.
De Lange (1981)	Multiple group: Training, no training	Modeling Role play Feedback	Juvenile delinquents	50	Residential institution	Assertiveness	No significant between-condition differences.
Elder, et al. (1979)	Single group: Multiple base-line	Instructions Modeling Role play Feedback	Aggressive adolescent	4	Psychiatric hospital	Assertiveness, Anger control	Increase in skill performance con-tingent on training, decrease in aggression, maintained at 6 months.
Greenleaf (1977)	Multiple group: Training (present vs. absent), transfer pro-gramming (pre-sent vs absent), attention con-trol, brief instructions control	Modeling Role play Feedback	Aggressive adolescents	43	Secondary school	Helping others	Both training conditions> Controls on study skill acquisition and maintenance.

(Continued)

Table 6.1. Psychological Skills Training Research with Adolescent and Preadolescent Trainees (*Continued*)

Investigator	Design	Treatment	Trainees	N	Setting	Target	Outcome
Gross, et al. (1980)	Single group: Multiple baseline	Instructions Modeling Role play Shaping	Juvenile delinquent	10	Group home	Prosocial responsiveness (responding to criticism, responding to teasing)	Increase in skill performance contingent on training, reduced truancy at post, 2 months & 1 year.
Hazel (1981)	Multiple group: Training, no training	Instructions Discussion Modeling Role play Feedback	Juvenile delinquents	24	Probation office	Giving feedback, negotiation, resisting peer pressure, etc.	Training > Controls on study skills, maintained at 2 months.
Hollin & Courtney (1983)	Multiple group: Training - 8 weeks, training - 4 days no training control, non-referred control	Instructions Modeling Role play Feedback	Juvenile delinquents	15	Residential institution	Conversation skills (eye contact, listening, initiating). Conflict avoidance skills.	No significant between-condition differences.
Hollin & Henderson (1981)	Multiple group: Training, no training	Instructions Modeling Role play Feedback	Juvenile delinquents	14	Residential institution	Conversation skills, non-verbal communication skills	No significant between-condition differences.
Hummel (1980)	Multiple group: Training (single or combined skills), varied or constant stimulus conditions	Modeling Role play Feedback	Aggressive adolescents	47	Secondary school	Negotiation, Self-control	All training under varied stimulus conditions >. All training under constant stimulus conditions.
Kifer, et al. (1974)	Single case: Multiple baseline	Instructions Role play Feedback	Juvenile delinquents and their parents	3	Family group home	Negotiation skills (expressing opinion, reaching agreement)	Increase in skill performance contingent on training.

Study	Design	Training components	Population	N / Setting	Skills	Outcomes
Lee (1979)	Multiple group: Training, attention control, no training control	Instructions Modeling Role play	Aggressive adolescents	30 Secondary school	Aggression-control skills, assertiveness	Training > Controls on assertiveness, no significant between-condition differences on aggression-control skills.
Litwack (1976)	Multiple group: Training & anticipation of serving as a trainer, training, brief instructions control	Modeling Role playing Feedback	Aggressive adolescents	40 Secondary school	Following instructions, Expressing a compliment	Both training conditions> Controls on both study skills Training & helper role structuring training.
Long & Sherer	Multiple group: Training, discussion control, no training control	Modeling Role playing Feedback	Juvenile delinquents	30 Probation counseling	Communication, affective and aggression-relevant	Training and discussion groups increasing significantly in internality.
Maloney, et al. (1976)	Single case: Multiple baseline	Role play Contingent reinforcement	Juvenile delinquents	4 Family group home	Conversation skills, (posture, volunteering answers)	Increase in skill performance contingent on training - by peers or by teaching parents.
Matson, et al. (1980)	Single group: Multiple baseline	Instructions Modeling Role Play Feedback Contingent reinforcement	Aggressive adolescent inpatients	4 Residential institution	Conversation skills, (eye contact, choosing content, etc.)	Increase in skill performance contingent on training maintained at 3 months.
Minkin, et al. (1976)	Single Case: Multiple baseline	Instructions Modeling Role play	Juvenile delinquents	4 Family group home	Conversation skills, (asking questions, giving feedback)	Increase in skill performance contingent on training.

(Continued)

Table 6.1. Psychological Skills Training Research with Adolescent and Preadolescent Trainees (*Continued*)

Investigator	Design	Treatment	Trainees	N	Setting	Target	Outcome
Ollendick & Hersen (1979)	Multiple group: Training, discussion control, no training	Instructions Modeling Role play Feedback	Juvenile delinquents	27	Residential institution	Interpersonal accomodation skills, verbal and nonverbal	Training > Controls on study skills, reduction in state anxiety, increase in internal locus of control.
Pentz (1980)	Multiple group: brief instruction control, no training control; Training by teacher, parent or peer; Aggressive vs. passive trainees	Modeling Role play Feedback	Aggressive & unassertive adolescents	90	Secondary school	Assertiveness	All training conditions > Controls on study skill acquisition and transfer, teacher trainers, parent or peer trainers on skill acquisition.
Robin (1981)	Multiple group: Training, family therapy, wait-list control	Instructions Modeling Role play Feedback	Adolescents from conflicted families	33	Clinic	Problem solving communication skills	Training > Control on all study skills, Training Therapy on behavioral skills, maintained at 10 weeks.
Robin, et al. (1977)	Multiple group: Training, wait list control	Instructions Discussion Modeling Role play Feedback	Adolescents from conflicted families & their parent	24	Clinic	Problem solving communications skills	Training > Control on study skills, no transfer to home.
Sarason & Ganzer (1973)	Multiple group: Training, discussion control, no training control	Modeling Role play Feedback	Juvenile delinquents	192	Residential institution	Prosocial problem solving	Training > Control on study skills.
Sarason & Sarason (1981)	Multiple Group: Training-live modeling, training video modeling, no training control	Instructions Modeling Role play Feedback	Adolescents in school with high dropout and delinquency levels	127	Secondary school	Job interview, resisting peer pressure, asking for help, dealing with frustration	Training-live modeling > Controls on job interview skills, training (both types) controls on problem

Study	Design	Training components	N / Setting	Target skills	Outcomes
					solving skills, no significant between condition differences on other study skills.
Shoemaker (1979)	Multiple group: Training discussion control, no training control	Instructions Discussion Role play Feedback Contingent reinforcement	30 Residential institution	Assertiveness	Training > Controls on study skill, no generalization to interview situation.
Spence & Marzillier (1979)	Single case: Multiple baseline	Instructions Modeling Role play Feedback	5 Residential institution	Conversation skills (eye contact, head movement, listening)	Increase in nonverbal skills performance contingent on training, maintained at 2 weeks.
Spence & Marzillier (1981)	Multiple group: Training, attention placebo control, no training control	Instructions Modeling Role play Feedback	76 Residential institution	Coping with criticism & teasing, Inviting friendships	Training > Controls on study skills
Spence & Spence (1980)	Multiple group: Training, attention control, no training control	Modeling Role play Feedback	44 Residential institution	Nonverbal skills (e.g., eye contact), Interaction skills e.g., dealing with teasing)	Training > Controls on study skills. No maintenance at 6 months.
Thelen, et al. (1976)	Multiple group: Training, didactic control, baseline control	Modeling Role play Feedback	6 Group home	Conflict resolutions skills (coping with accusations, expressing positive feelings)	Increase in skill performance contingent on training not maintained at 2 weeks.

All rows under N/Setting marked "Juvenile delinquents" population.

(Continued)

Table 6.1. Psychological Skills Training Research with Adolescent and Preadolescent Trainees (*Continued*)

Investigator	Design	Treatment	Trainees	N	Setting	Target	Outcome
Trief (1976)	Multiple group: Training (cognitive, affective or combined aspects of skill), attention control, brief instructions control	Modeling Role play Feedback	Juvenile delinquents	58	Residential institution	Perspective taking	All training conditions > Controls on study skill acquisition and transfer
Werner, et al. (1975)	Multiple group: Training, no training control	Instructions Modeling Role play Feedback	Juvenile delinquents	6	Family group home	Prosocial communication with police officers (eye contact, cooperation, and expression of reform)	Pre-post training increase on study skills for Training and Control groups.

RESEARCH ISSUES AND CONCLUSIONS

Experimental Design

As noted earlier, existing psychological skills training research has relied upon either multiple-group or single-subject designs. The respective advantages and limitations of these
two strategies have been amply considered elsewhere (Hersen & Barlow, 1976; Kazdin,
1978, 1980) and will not be examined further here—save to assert that utilization of both
in combination seems far preferable to us than what is now typically the case, that is, sole
reliance on one approach or the other.

There are a number of additional experimental design issues relevant to skills training
research worth examining. Although it is true, as Table 6.1 reveals, that most skills training
to date is operationally defined by the procedures of instructions, modeling, role playing,
and performance feedback, we most strongly do not recommend this treatment package
as somehow "final." On the contrary, our view of skills training—or any psychological
intervention—is that its components optimally will perpetually evolve and never reach a
sense of completion or closure. The modest success of skills training with regards to transfer
and maintenance effects is, by itself, sufficient basis for being sharply dissatisfied with its
customary operational definition. What needs to be added to the "basic foursome," and
what optimally ought be deleted is best tested, respectively, by what Kazdin (1980) has
described as constructive and dismantling treatment designs. He comments:

> With the constructive approach the investigator usually begins with a basic treatment component
> that is relatively narrow or circumscribed in focus. Research is conducted that adds various
> ingredients to the basic treatment to determine what enhances treatment effects. As research
> continues, effective components are retained and a large treatment package is constructed.
> (p. 87)

> The dismantling treatment strategy refers to analyzing the components of a given treatment . .
> . . Once a treatment package has been shown to "work," research may begin to analyze the
> precise influence of specific components . . . . To dismantle a given technique, individual treatment
> components are eliminated or isolated from treatment. Comparisons usually are made across
> groups that receive the treatment package or the package minus the specific components.
> (p. 84)

Skillful utilization of combinations of constructive and dismantling designs reflect what
we feel to be the optimal experimental design strategy at this stage of the development of
the psychological skills training research literature. Given the paucity of successful reports
of transfer and maintenance, treatment components explicitly designed toward such ends
are prime candidates for additions in a constructive treatment design. We will examine
several such components later in this paper. Prompting, shaping, and discussion opportunities are treatment components that have been added in some of the studies summarized
earlier, and a few have dropped the instructions or the modeling components, but in no
instance were these additions or deletions evaluated comparatively in either a constructive
or dismantling design. In implementing such designs, we believe there exist two planes
along which potentially viable treatment components may be experimentally added and
deleted. Horizontal additions and deletions refer to new treatment components utilized with
the trainee himself or herself. In our current Structured Learning research (Spatz-Norton,
1984; Zimmerman, 1984) we are seeking by a constructive design strategy to discern whether
the potency of our basic psychological skills training package (modeling, role playing,
performance feedback, transfer training) will be significantly increased if, in addition to our
attention to the direct teaching of prosocial behavior (by the four components), we also

seek to simultaneously teach prosocial values (by means of Kohlberg's [1973] moral education techniques) and aggression-inhibitors (relaxation and self-statement disputation), that is, not only what to do instead of aggression (prosocial values and behaviors), but also how to manage or reduce the aggression itself. These few horizontal components are but mere examples of the potential array of other existing or to-be-developed techniques that can be meaningfully tested as possible additions to existing operational definitions of psychological skills training.

But skills training does not occur in an environmental vacuum. There are always several other players on the stage of interpersonal competency—parents, peers, employers, siblings, friends, teachers, strangers, and antagonists. Rather than simply seek to train the main actor—the psychological skills training trainee—we may also intervene vertically and seek to have a direct impact on any and all of those figures in the trainee's real world whose own behavior may significantly influence trainee skill competency. With reference to aggressive adolescents, our recent *School Violence* (Goldstein, Apter, & Harootunian, 1984) is an example of such a systems or vertical intervention research strategy. School violence, we held, would yield most fully when, in addition to the several suggested interventions targeted directly to the aggressive youngster, equally energetic attention was directed to the teachers involved; the school's administration; the youngster's parents, the school board, and other relevant persons in the school's community; and even at the broader state and federal levels. We have not yet tested this particular highly comprehensive implementation of a constructive treatment design, but share it here as an extended example of a research strategy we feel may be particularly fruitful when used in a psychological skills training context.

Prescriptive Utilization

The efficacy of psychological skills training may also be enhanced by adherence, in both its investigation and implementation, to a prescriptive, tailored, or differential ingredients strategy. Here the effort is made to be responsive to trainee learning styles, group-relevant behaviors, and personality characteristics when defining the specific training procedures to be used and deciding how they will be implemented; the spacing, duration, and pacing of the group's sessions; the trainers to be employed; the skills to be taught—their difficulty, sequencing, and relevance to trainee motivation; and other training parameters. In short, prescriptive utilization of psychological skills training seeks to discern and employ optimal characteristics of the training enterprise *for particular trainees*. This research and practice strategy parallels directly analogous viewpoints productively advanced earlier with regard to education (Cronbach, 1967; Harootunian, 1978; Hunt, 1972; Stern, 1970) and psychotherapy (Goldstein, 1978; Goldstein & Stein, 1976; Magaro, 1969). There are in particular a number of aspects of psychological skills training we wish to highlight as especially heuristic targets of this prescriptive viewpoint, that is, dimensions of the skill training enterprise whose individualization may be particularly enhancing of trainee skill competency. All of these suggestions, however, are speculative products of skills training experiences, and are in need of direct empirical scrutiny.

There is, first, the nature of trainees' skill deficiencies. It is not enough, as Bellak (1979), Michaelson and Wood (1980), and others have argued, to employ multimodal deficit assessment techniques—behavioral observation, role-play tests, skill inventories, structured interviews—in order to seek to reliably identify in *which* skills the youngster is deficient. It is also necessary, we would propose, to be prescriptively responsive in our remedial efforts to the fact that there are three different ways in which an individual may be deficient in any given skill. Ladd and Mize (1983) comment:

First, children may lack knowledge or concepts of appropriate social behavior . . . . or they may possess concepts atypical of their peer group . . . . At least three forms of social knowledge may be represented in a skill concept, each of which is viewed as necessary for effective social functioning: (a) knowledge of appropriate goals for social interaction, (b) knowledge of appropriate strategies for reaching a social goal, and (c) knowledge of the context(s) in which specific strategies may be appropriately applied . . . . Second, children may lack, perhaps as a result of insufficient practice of the skills, actual behavioral abilities . . . . Finally, some children may be deficient in giving themselves feedback about their interpersonal encounters. Specifically, these children may lack the ability (a) to monitor and evaluate their own behavior and its effects on others . . . and (b) to make inferences or attributions about their interpersonal successes and failures that are conducive to continued effort, adaptation, and self-confidence in social interactions. (pp. 129–130)

Selection of target skills, it thus follows, might optimally reflect not only such typical parameters as the skill(s) in which the trainee is deficient, the degree of deficiency, and the interpersonal and environmental contexts in which the deficiency manifests itself, but also the particular nature (knowledge, behavior, feedback) of the deficit. To do so has clear and direct implications for the prescriptive specification of just what is to be taught the trainee.

Our decade-long experience with Structured Learning, across a variety of trainee populations, has provided a lengthy series of additional leads for studying the prescriptive individualization of the skills training process. We have employed, and formally investigated, Structured Learning with aggressive adolescents, typical and special needs children, adult psychiatric patients, developmentally disabled adults, career felons, geriatric clients, teachers, nurses, police, and industrial managers. In all instances, our basic procedures were modeling, role playing, performance feedback, and transfer training. Yet, also in all instances, we have energetically sought to adapt these four skills training components to the particular receptivity channels and optimal learning styles of the particular trainees involved. Depending in large measure on such trainee qualities, our modeling displays have been either audio, video, or live; role playing has varied in length, simplicity, and repetitiveness; performance feedback has been directive, especially gentle, or lengthy; and transfer training has been operationalized as a function of the trainee's available community resources, homework opportunities, and abstraction capacity. A more concrete sense of what we mean by such prescriptive implementation is captured in the following excerpt from our *Trainer's Manual* (Goldstein, Sprafkin, Gershaw, 1976) for Structured Learning with adult psychiatric inpatients:

> . . . with long-term hospitalized patients—whose attention span is short and whose motivation for skill enhancement is low—we have adapted the procedures set forth earlier in this manual by (1) having the trainers be more active and participate more directly in role playing, (2) having the trainers offer social (and token or material) reinforcement more frequently and for lesser skill increments, (3) having the trainers begin thinning of reinforcements later, (4) having shorter and more repetitive group sessions, (5) having fewer trainees per group, (6) paying more relative attention to simpler levels of a given skill, (7) allowing more total time per skill, and (8) requiring less demanding homework assignments. (p. 16)

Analogously, with aggressive adolescents, we have in our practice prescriptively evolved toward (a) groups no larger than five or six, (b) briefer initial structuring of group procedures, (c) live modeling by the trainers, (d) use of two or three different vignettes when modeling, (e) heightened levels of trainer activity, directiveness and control, (f) increased use of token or material reinforcers, (g) employment of visual depictions of target skill steps, (h) added reliance on pre-announced rules for group management, (i) certain of the same modifications noted above as apparently optimal for adult psychiatric patients and, of course, (j) adolescent-relevant target skills and (k) adolescent-experienced skill trainers.

Trainee Motivation

We believe that psychological skills training research and practice have not given sufficient attention to the relevance of trainee motivation for skill competency and its development. It is as if, in Hullian terms of several years ago, our focus has been almost exclusively on habit strength at the expense of drive, in a context in which, as Hull (1943) amply demonstrated, behavior was a multiplicative function of both. We feel it important that future investigative efforts in this domain seek to redress this imbalance, and thus examine means for the substantial enhancement of skill competency motivation—a matter very often of special relevance for aggressive adolescents. In addition to appropriate contingent reinforcement, whose functioning in a skills training context is well established, trainee motivation may be enhanced in conjunction with three different events which unfold sequentially during the skills training process: (a) the establishment of the trainer–trainee relationship, (b) selection of appropriate target skills, and (c) establishment of certain motivation-relevant group parameters.

Trainer–trainee relationship. It is a truism in such interpersonal influence contexts as psychotherapy, counseling, and education that client or student motivation to do "the work" of the process is in part driven by the steam of a positive relationship with the change agent involved. Ladd and Mize (1983) comment in this regard:

> ...as in any pedagogical undertaking, it is likely that the success of a social skill training program also depends on the quality of the relationship established between the child and the instructor. Even the most well-designed and all-inclusive training program may be rendered ineffective if it is conducted in an overly didactic, mechanical, and uninviting manner. Rarely, however, have previous social skill training investigators alluded to instructor characteristics or the instructor–child relationship as important aspects of the skill training process. (p. 153)

Thus, it might seem, we ought to appropriately conclude—consistent with the prevailing truism for other change endeavors—that a warm, close, personal, empathic, trainer–trainee relationship may well substantially potentiate skill acquisition in aggressive adolescent trainees. But all truisms are not necessarily true and, in fact, by their very comprehensiveness may deny or minimize the opportunity for a differentiated, prescriptive perspective on such matters. A host of clinicians have speculated that therapeutic progress of diverse sorts with aggressive adolescents would, in fact, be advanced by a very different kind of (especially initial) helper–helpee relationship—one of *low* empathy, high impersonality, and careful avoidance of emotional exploration (Dean, 1958; Goldstein, Heller, & Sechrest, 1966; Redl & Wineman, 1957; Schwitzgebel, 1967; Slack, 1960). Edelman and Goldstein (1984) examined this proposition empirically, and indeed found quite substantial support for the prescriptive utility in such pairings of low empathy (plus high genuineness) helper behavior. Thus, we indeed support the generalization that trainee motivation and consequent skill acquisition are likely influenced substantially by the quality of the trainer–trainee relationship. But precisely what kind(s) of relationships are optimal in this context remains very much an open question—with considerable speculation and some beginning evidence combining to point to a type of relationship quite different from that characteristically aspired to in most other change endeavors.

Skill selection. Which skills shall be taught, and who will select them? This is as much a motivational as a tactical question, for to the degree that youngsters are enabled to anticipate learning skill competencies they feel they need, they discern as presently deficient but of likely utility in their real-world relationships, their motivation is correspondingly enhanced. We have operationalized this perspective in our Structured Learning skills training by means of a process we call "negotiating the curriculum." First, we avoid the option of serving as unilateral skill selector for the trainee. In doing so, we concur with Schinke (1981) who observes, "Seldom recognized in interpersonal skills training with adolescents is how values influence client referral and problem definition. Decisions about desirable skills are weighted by personal preferences, moral judgments, and ethical constraints" (p. 81).

We similarly avoid the cafeteria-like option of denying the potential value of our skill-relevant expertise and knowledge and laying out the entire skill curriculum, and simply asking the trainer to select those he or she wishes. Either unilateral approach, we feel, is inadequate—the first delimits trainee motivation, the second denies trainer expertise. Instead, we use a means that allows both parties to actively participate. We begin by having the trainer (if he/she knows the trainee well) and the trainee each *independently* complete their respective versions of the Structured Learning Skills Inventory (Goldstein, Sprafkin, Gershaw, & Klein, 1980). Then, much the same as in a meeting between an academic advisor and a student to juxtapose and reconcile their respective views of the student's tentative course program for the next semester, skills trainer and trainee compare, contrast, examine, and select from their Skills Inventories in such a manner that trainer beliefs about what the trainee needs, and trainee beliefs about his/her own deficiencies and desired competencies are mutually reflected. Such is our applied procedure. We feel it to be motivation-enhancing. Whether it in fact serves this important function is indeed an investigative question worth careful examination.

Group procedures. Our concern stated earlier in optimizing trainee participation in the skill selection process is an example of seeking to enhance the trainee's task-associated *intrinsic* motivation. But extrinsic task characteristics may also profitably be mobilized toward the goal of maximizing inducements for active, on-task trainee participation. While we as yet have little empirical evidence in support of the group procedure recommendations we are about to make, they indeed appear to us to be reliable extrinsic means for enhancing trainee motivation. Where are the group sessions held? In most schools and institutions we try to seek a special place, associated in the trainee's thinking with particular privileges or opportunities, for example, teacher's lounge, student center, recreation area—and yet not a place so removed in its characteristics from the typical skill application settings in which trainees function as to reduce the likelihood of skill transfer. When will the group meet? If it is not judged to be too great an academic sacrifice, we attempt to schedule skills training sessions when what the youngsters will have missed in order to attend the sessions is an activity he/she does not especially enjoy (including certain academic subjects), rather than free play, lunch, gym, or the like. Who will lead the group? For our initial, program-initiating groups in particular, we seek as trainers those teachers, cottage parents, members of the institutional staff, or others who we deem to be most stimulating, most tuned to the needs and behaviors of aggressive adolescents (but not the most overtly empathic, for reasons described earlier), and in general most able to capture and hold the attention of participating youngsters. Because the impact of the initial meeting(s) of the initial group bears upon not only the motivation and performance of trainees in *that* group, but also, rapidly through the school's or institution's grapevine, upon the interest, motivation and, eventually, performance of youngsters who constitute subsequently formed groups, the group leadership skills of the first trainers employed can have far-reaching motivational consequences. Which skill shall be taught first? This is a crucial decision, one of special relevance to trainee motivation. In addition to reflecting the give and take of the negotiated skill curriculum, the first skill taught is optimally one very likely to yield immediate, real-world reward for the trainee. It must "work"; it must pay off. While some trainers prefer to begin with the simpler conversational skills, as a sort of warm-up or break-in, our preference is to try to respond to both simplicity and reward potential. The "felt need" of the trainee for the near-future value of a given skill, therefore, weighs especially heavily in our initial, skill selection decisions.

Transfer and Maintenance Enhancement

Trainee change in prosocial directions, even when prescriptively wrought, means rather little if such change is essentially limited in its occurrence to the training setting. Failure to transfer therapeutic gains from training to application settings constitutes one of, if not the most, significant yet unsolved problems in the field of psychotherapy and behavior change in general, and in the skills training domain as well. Research clearly points to the conclusion that a very substantial proportion of therapeutic change is limited to the therapy or training setting, with minimal "real-life" value accruing to the participating patients (Ford & Urban, 1963; Goldstein, 1973; Goldstein et al., 1966; Gruber, 1971; Kazdin, 1975). While efforts at "programming generalization" by teaching systematic problem-solving skills and coping strategies (Mahoney, 1974; Walker & Buckley, 1972) or circumventing the need for "transfer" by providing in vivo treatment (Drum & Figler, 1973; Goldstein et al., 1966; Hsu, 1965; Weiner, Becker, & Friedman, 1967) have moderated this pessimistic conclusion somewhat with reference to certain behavior modification therapies, it largely applies even there. Thus, failure of transfer remains a most serious and pervasive psychotherapeutic and psychoeducational problem. In the sections that follow, we wish to describe a number of procedures which, because of their transfer-enhancement potential, we are currently actively implementing and evaluating in our research program.

Provision of general principles. Transfer of training has been demonstrated to be facilitated by providing trainees with general mediating principles governing successful or competent performance on the training and criterion tasks. This procedure has typically been operationalized in laboratory contexts by providing subjects with the organizing concepts, principles, strategies, or rationales that explain or account for the stimulus–response relationships operative in *both* the training and application settings (Duncan, 1959; Goldbeck, Bernstein, Hellix, & Marx, 1957). The same transfer-enhancement effect, under other rubrics, has been reported in studies of learning sets (Harlow, 1949), deutero-learning (Ruesch, 1957), advance organizers (Ausubel, 1963), and pre-task instructions (Masters & Branch, 1969; Whalen, 1969). There are, furthermore, a variety of at least partially successful attempts to capitalize upon this procedure in psychotherapeutic contexts. Examples of such efforts include clarification of therapy-relevant role expectations by means of pretherapy structuring (Goldstein, 1971), successive structuring (Rotter, 1954), or role induction/anticipatory socialization interviews (Hoehn-Saric et al., 1964; Orne & Wender, 1968); the use of ambiguity-reducing communications (Kanfer & Marston, 1963); teaching of coping and problem-solving strategies (Mahoney, 1973); and by supplying the patient with written materials describing the typical course and content of the contemplated treatment (Heck, Gomez, & Adams, 1973; Kovel, 1976; Wolberg, 1954). The provision of general principles to adolescent, Structured Learning trainees is being operationalized in our investigations by the presentation in verbal, pictorial, and written forms of appropriate information governing skill instigation, selection, and implementation principles.

Response availability. Transfer of training has been shown to be enhanced by procedures that maximize criterion response availability. It has been well-established by now that, other things being equal, the response that has been emitted most frequently in the past will be emitted on subsequent occasions. This finding derives from studies of the frequency of the evocation hypothesis (Underwood & Schulz, 1960), the spew hypothesis, and research on preliminary response training (Atwater, 1953; Cantor, 1955; Gagne, Baker & Foster, 1950; Mandler & Heinemann, 1956). This general result, which Mandler (1954) summarizes as " . . . learning to make an old response to a new stimulus showed increasing positive transfer as degree of original training was increased" (p. 411), is also consistent with research on overlearning. Overlearning is a procedure whereby learning is extended over more trials than are necessary merely to produce *initial* changes in the subject's behavior. The over-learning or repetition of successful skill enactment in the typical Structured Learning session is quite substantial, with the given skill taught and its behavioral steps or learning points (a) modeled several times on audiotape and pictorially, (b) role-played one or more times by the trainee, (c) observed live by the trainee as each other group member role-plays it, (d) read by the trainee from a blackboard and on his or her skill card, (e) written by the trainee in his or her trainee's notebook, (f) practiced in vivo one or more times by the trainee in response to adult and/or peer leader coaching, and (h) practiced in vivo one or more times by the trainee in response to skill-oriented, intrinsically interesting stimuli introduced into his or her real-life environment (e.g., we are presently constructing Structured Learning skill development games and comic books). We have demonstrated the efficacy of overlearning for transfer-enhancement purposes in the context of Structured Learning in studies conducted by Lopez, Hoyer, & Goldstein (1980).

Identical elements. In perhaps the earliest experimental concern with transfer enhancement, Thorndike and Woodworth (1901) concluded that when there was a facilitative effect of one habit on another, it was to the extent that, and because, they shared identical elements. Ellis (1965) and Osgood (1953) have more recently emphasized the importance for transfer of similarity between the stimulus and response aspects of the training and application tasks. The greater the similarity of physical and interpersonal stimuli in the therapy setting and the cottage, school, home, or other setting in which the skill is to be applied, the greater the likely transfer. Awareness of this principle of transfer enhancement has already been acted upon in the context of psychotherapy by investigators and clinicians who have (a) literally moved the therapy out of an office setting and into the patient's real-life, problem-relevant environment (Jones, Kahn, & Wolcott, 1964; Lazarus, 1966; Stevenson, 1962); (b) enhanced the physical "real-lifeness" of the office setting (Hsu, 1965; Jones, 1960; Walker, Allenson, & Johnson, 1971); or (c) conducted treatment in such a manner that the significant others for the designated "patient" were also present and participants in the therapy, as in marital or family therapy.

The "real-lifeness" of Structured Learning is operationalized in a number of ways. These operational expressions of identical elements include:

1. The representative, relevant, and realistic content and portrayal of the models, protag-onists, and situations on the modeling tapes, all designed to be highly similar to what aggressive, low-income adolescents face in their daily lives;
2. The physical props used in and the arrangement of the role-playing setting as similar to real-life settings;
3. The choice, coaching, and enactment of the co-actors or protagonists as similar to real-life figures;

4. The manner in which the role-plays themselves are conducted (a) to be as responsive as possible to the real-life interpersonal stimuli in response to which the trainee will actually need the given skill, and (b) as behavioral rehearsal of that skill as he or she actually plans to employ it;

5. The in vivo homework, coached, practiced and intrinsically interesting skill-relevant stimuli described earlier;

6. The use of peer leaders who are drawn from "natural" peer leaders residing in the same cottage as the trainee; and

7. The training of living units (all the members of a given cottage) as a unit.

The transfer-enhancing potency of identical elements has been established in conjunction with Structured Learning by Guzzetta (1974) and Wood (1977).

Stimulus variability. Callentine and Warren (1955), Duncan (1958), and Shore and Sechrest (1961) have each demonstrated that positive transfer is greater when a variety of relevant training stimuli are employed. Kazdin (1975) has commented in this regard:

> One reason that behaviors are not maintained and do not transfer to new settings is that the clients readily form a discrimination between conditions in which reinforcement (or punishment) is and is not delivered. Behavior becomes associated with a narrow range of cues. As soon as the program is withdrawn or the setting changes, clients discriminate that the desirable behavior is no longer associated with certain consequences. Thus, responses are not maintained and do not transfer to new situations. One way to program response maintenance and transfer of training is to develop the target behavior in a variety of situations and in the presence of several individuals. If the response is associated with a range of settings, individuals, and other cues, it is less likely to be lost when the situations change. (p. 211)

We, too, have commented earlier on this approach to transfer enhancement, as it might be implemented in individual psychotherapy, by suggesting that each patient interact with more than one psychotherapist.

> The employment of several different therapists may . . . greatly increase the breadth of stimuli or the complexity of the total stimulus pattern to which the patient is exposed. The different personalities, styles, and even appearances of the separate therapists should become stimuli or cues for the desired responses. Since, presumably, all the therapists would be reinforcing responses in the same general class, the response class would become conditioned to a variety of interpersonal stimuli, and since the exact form of the response is assumed to vary more when emitted in the presence of the varying stimuli, greater response generalization should occur . . . (Goldstein et al., 1966, p. 232)

The transfer enhancing consequences of operationalizations of stimulus variability in psychotherapeutic contexts have been at least partially confirmed in investigations of round robin therapy (Holmes, 1971), rotational therapy (Slavin, 1967), rotational group therapy (Frank, 1973), multiple impact therapy (MacGregor, 1964), and use of multiple therapists (Dreikurs, Schulman, & Mosak, 1952; Hayward, Peters, & Taylor, 1952; Whitaker, Malone, & Warkentin, 1956). Stimulus variability is implemented in our Structured Learning groups by use of (a) rotation of group leaders across groups, (b) rotation of trainees across groups, (c) having trainees re-role-play a given skill with several co-actors, (d) having trainees re-role-play a given skill across several relevant settings, and (e) use of multiple homework assignments for each given skill. Hummel's (1980) investigation examining stimulus variability effects associated with Structured Learning for aggressive preadolescents was, we feel, an important first step in establishing the value in a skills training context of this potent transfer enhancer.

Programmed reinforcement. Given successful implementation of both appropriate skill training procedures and the transfer enhancement technique examined earlier, positive transfer may still fail to occur. As Agras (1967), Gruber (1971), Patterson (1963), Tharp and Wetzel (1969), and literally dozens of other investigators have shown, stable and enduring performance in application settings of newly learned skills is very much at the mercy of real-life reinforcement contingencies. Kazdin (1975) observes in this regard:

> The everyday social environment does not usually provide consequences as systematically as does the programmed environment in which a behavior modification program is conducted. Typically, desirable behaviors go unreinforced in the natural environment. Rather, punishment is delivered for not performing desirable behaviors . . . . An individual who leaves a programmed setting in which reinforcement was delivered might not respond in a similar fashion in the community where reinforcement is intermittent and unsystematic . . . . Socially appropriate behaviors may not be automatically maintained by the social environment after programmed contingencies are withdrawn for another reason. Behaviors which are deviant or disruptive are likely to receive attention or notice in everyday settings such as at home and at school. Bizarre behaviors may be reinforced rather than extinguished in the natural environment because of the attention they receive. Thus, it is no surprise that appropriate behaviors usually are not maintained once a behavior modification program is abruptly withdrawn and do not transfer to everyday situations. (p. 217)

Kazdin responds to the foregoing state of affairs by reviewing a series of procedures used by others to build in or program response maintenance and transfer of training:

1. Training relatives or other individuals in the client's environment.
2. Substituting "naturally occurring" reinforcers.
3. Intermittent reinforcement.
4. Delay of reinforcement.
5. Gradually removing or fading the contingencies.

Each of these means for seeking to program transfer enhancement is being implemented and evaluated in our research program.

1. Training significant others in the trainee's real-life environment. We have begun to examine transfer enhancement by this method in our examination of the effectiveness of peer versus adult leaders. Our purpose in the utilization of peer leaders was twofold. First, we predict such leaders will serve as effective teachers, developing high levels of skill acquisition during the training setting phase of Structured Learning. Second, and relevant to programmed transfer enhancement, the presence of the "natural" peer group leader in the cottage, or other residential or institutional application setting adds a powerful in vivo ally in the skill acquisition, maintenance, and transfer endeavor. But we do not wish to stop at this for, however influential, peer leaders usually consist of only one or two persons per setting, may be transitory, and even when in residence may be unavailable when in vivo reinforcement of competent skill performance is appropriate. Thus, in settings in which it has been possible, for each and every skill taught, *all* group trainees are also being taught how and when to observe, coach, prompt, and reward competent performance of the skill by others. Analogous training is provided cottage parents, group leaders, or other significant adults in the skill application setting. We thus seek, by training peer leaders, other peers, and significant adults present, to provide trainees with an interpersonal environment that reliably rewards prosocial behavior and responds to antisocial behavior with refresher, in vivo teaching of the prosocial skill alternatives. Our systematic and extensive use of homework assignments, it should be noted, is relevant here in that the regular enactment of newly learned skills can provide the occasions for dispensing by such real-life figures of appropriate, contingent reinforcement, occasions that otherwise may not occur with sufficient frequency.

Finally, we are very much aware of the research literature that demonstrates convincingly the effective role that can be played by parents as contingency managers (e.g., Johnson & Katz, 1973; O'Dell, 1974; O'Leary et al., 1967; Patterson & Gullian, 1972; Reid & Patterson, 1976; Tramontana, 1980; Wahler, 1969). They are an especially important real-life resource for transfer enhancement; their further study and utilization seems particularly warranted.

2. Substituting "naturally occurring" reinforcers. The phrase *naturally occurring reinforcers* usually refers to generally or at least not infrequently available social reinforcers, that is, praise, attention, a smile, and other common, everyday nonmaterial expressions of approval or interest. While we most certainly applaud the use of such reinforcement, use it heavily for skill acquisition purposes in the Structured Learning sessions themselves, and approve of its substitution for tangible reinforcers as a means toward transfer enhancement, our definition and use of the phrase *naturally occurring* reinforcers is rather different. We have asked ourselves and others the Premackian question of what aggressive youngsters do volitionally in their real-life settings when they are given a range of free choices and opportunities. We have also spent a great deal of time talking with and observing such youngsters toward this end in their various cottage and institutional settings. Our goal has been to determine what is intrinsically interesting, motivating, or attractive to them that can also be "captured" or constructed by us in order to provide additional, in vivo skill training which by its content or context, aggressive youngsters will find interesting and by involvement with which, skill use will be rewarded. Thus, our definition of *naturally occurring reinforcers,* rather than relying directly upon social reinforcement, is operationalized by means of the Structured Learning games and comic books which we have under development. Each consists of materials providing further instruction in and opportunities for real or imagined practice of the full array of prosocial skills described earlier.

3. Altered conditions of reinforcement. The conditions governing the scheduling and delivery of reinforcement have clearly been shown to influence response maintenance and transfer. Once a response is well-established in the original training context, resistance to extinction is increased if reinforcing consequences can then be delivered intermittently (Kale, Kaye, Whalen, & Hopkins, 1968; Kazdin & Polster, 1973). It seems probable that behavior may also be maintained by gradually increasing the delay between reinforcement and the performance of the skill behaviors (Cotler, Applegate, King, & Kristal, 1972). Kazdin (1975) comments:

> . . . most reinforcers available in the social environment are delayed. Thus, it is important to wean a client from immediate reinforcement. Behavior should be well established before invoking long delays . . . . Eventually, reinforcement may be withdrawn entirely or delivered only after a long delay. (p. 225)

Thus, Kazdin (1975) proposes, in addition to intermittent and delayed reinforcement, response maintenance and transfer may also occur even if the systematically applied consequences are gradually removed or faded altogether. Intermittency, delay and fading of reinforcement as transfer enhancing procedures should be systematically incorporated and evaluated in psychological skills training programs. Finally, it should be noted that still other potential means exist for the enhancement of skill transfer and maintenance, some of which we have already examined successfully in a skills training context. These include

(a) structuring trainees into the role of trainer (Litwack, 1976; Solomon, 1978), use of coping rather than mastery models (Fleming, 1976), teaching selected skills in tandem (Hummel, 1980), skill mastery pretraining induction (Solomon, 1978), and—as yet untested in our research program—various self-management techniques (Karoly & Kanfer, 1982), stimulus control techniques (Marholin & Touchette, 1979), and the building of transfer-enhancing social support networks (Heller, 1979) and ecological climates (Price, 1979).

Future Directions

We believe psychological skills training is an important movement with a substantial future as an effective intervention strategy. Its investigators are asking many questions; many of the questions are the heuristic ones to ask. And some are even yielding useful answers. In our view, the future of psychological skills training will be especially bright if investigators more frequently choose to operate—theorize, hypothesize, investigate— *within* the main-streams of contemporary psychology. Stated otherwise, there is much to benefit psycho-logical skills training if it interfaces closely with ideas and findings not only in clinical psychology, which has been its history, but also in developmental, experimental, social, and community psychology. Developmental psychology may be an especially worthwile context from which to seek questions relevant to skills training, for it is here that there now is such substantial empirical concern with social competence and its naturalistic development. Reflecting both this same viewpoint, as well as the prescriptive stance we articulated earlier, Ladd and Mize (1983) comment:

> There is a need for future investigators to tailor intervention efforts to the developmental level and individual needs of the learner . . . . Learner characteristics such as the child's developmental level, social class, and specific skill deficits will necessarily dictate the selection of target skills, training components, and the methodology used to foster the acquisition of social skills. (p. 152)

Socialization practices, modeling effects, sex-associated barriers and accomplishments, peer group influences, and parenting practices are but a few of the age and stage related contemporary concerns of the developmental psychologist that may bear importantly upon the effectiveness of psychological skill training.

The course and outcome of psychological skills training may be influenced not only by developmental characteristics of its recipients, but—as our social psychology colleagues have long demonstrated—also by qualities of the group format in which it is typically implemented. As such, we urge upon the investigator of this intervention approach a heightened familiarity with and utilization of research findings on the consequences of varying levels of group cohesiveness, diverse group leadership styles, group size, group phases and equilibrium processes, open versus closed membership patterns, emergent communication patterns within the group, persuasion and resistance thereto in what is, in part, an interpersonal influence arena, and related social-psychological concerns.

We heard earlier in this chapter from the experimental psychologist, in our earlier ex-amination of transfer and maintenance enhancement. Essentially all of the techniques elucidated there derive originally from research in the verbal learning laboratory or similar experimental psychological contexts. Because psychological skills training is at its root a teaching–learning activity, we strongly suspect there is much more of special value to be drawn from the concepts and findings of contemporary experimental psychology.

Finally, we turn to community psychology and its prevailing concern with prevention. Almost all applications of psychological skills training, including those targeted to children and adolescents, have been remedial and not preventive. Our collective efforts, investigative and applied, have been directed toward accurately identifying and effectively training youngsters with demonstrable skills deficits. Exceedingly little attention has been directed toward children and adolescents at risk, but not manifestly deficient in psychological skills. Exceedingly little attention has been directed toward psychological skills training with very young children and we have generally also failed to attend to youngsters *in anticipation* of their skill needs requisite to mastering the formidable array of developmental hurdles over which we all must pass—in school; at play; at home; in the community; with peers, family, and authority figures. As we observed elsewhere:

> Love, sex, and peer relationships are likely to require social skills (e.g., having a conversation, listening, joining in), skills for dealing with feelings (e.g., dealing with fear, expressing affection, understanding the feelings of others), and skills useful for dealing with stress (e.g., dealing with embarrassment, preparing for a stressful conversation, responding to failure). School-related tasks demand proficiency at yet other skills, in particular, planning skills (e.g., goal setting, gathering information, decision making). School settings also require daily success at tasks involving both peers (e.g., dealing with group pressure) and authority figures (e.g., following instructions). Similarly, work settings are also multifaceted in their task demands and, hence, in their requisite skills, especially those requiring planning and stress management. For many youngsters, whether at school, at work, or elsewhere, the skill demands placed upon them will frequently involve the ability to deal satisfactorily with aggression, either their own or someone else's. In these instances, skills to be mastered may include self-control, negotiation, and dealing with group pressure. (Goldstein et al., 1980, pp. 5–6)

Thus it can be seen that "normal" developmental hurdles are both high and numerous. Deficit prevention research and application, following both the spirit and much of the substance of community psychology, seems to us to be an especially valuable future path.

REFERENCES

Adkins, W.R. (1970). Life skills: Structured counseling for the disadvantaged. *Personnel and Guidance Journal, 49*, 108–116.

Adkins, W.R. (1974). Life coping skills: A fifth curriculum. *Teachers College Record, 75*, 507–526.

Agras, W.S. (1967). Behavior therapy in the management of chronic schizophrenia. *American Journal of Psychiatry, 124*, 240–243.

Argyle, M., Trower, P., & Bryant, B. (1974). Explorations in the treatment of personality disorders and neuroses by social skill training. *British Journal of Medical Psychology, 47*, 63–72.

Atwater, S.K. (1953). Proactive inhibition and associative facilitation as affected by degree of prior learning. *Journal of Experimental Psychology, 46*, 400–404.

Ausubel, D.P. (1963). *The psychology of meaningful verbal behavior*. New York: Grune & Stratton.

Bandura, A. (1973). *Aggression: A social learning analysis*. Englewood Cliffs, NJ: Prentice-Hall.

Bellack, A.S. (1979). Behavioral assessment of social skills. In A.S. Bellack & M. Hersen (Eds.), *Research and practice in social skill training*. New York: Plenum.

Bornstein, M., Bellack, A.S., & Hersen, M. (1980). Social skills training for highly aggressive children. *Behavior Modification, 4*, 173–186.

Braukmann, C.J., & Fixsen, D.L. (1975). Behavior modification with delinquents. In M. Hersen, R.M. Eisler, & P.M. Miller (Eds.), *Progress in behavior modification* (Vol. 1, pp. 191–231). New York: Academic Press.

Braukmann, C.J., Maloney, D.M., Fixsen, D.L., Phillips, E.L., & Wolf, M.M. (1974). Analysis of a selection interview training package for predelinquents at Achievement Place. *Criminal Justice & Behavior, 1*, 30–42.

Braukmann, C.J., Maloney, D.M., Phillips, E.L., & Wolf, M.M. (1973). *The measurement and modification heterosexual interaction skills of predelinquents at Achievement Place*. Unpublished manuscript, University of Kansas.

Callantine, M.F., & Warren, J.M. (1955). Learning sets in human concept formation. *Psychological Reports, 1,* 363–367.

Cantor, J.H. (1955). Amount of pretraining as a factor in stimulus pre-differentiation and performance set. *Journal of Experimental Psychology, 50,* 180–184.

Conger, J.J., Miller, W.C., & Walsmith, C.R. (1965). Antecedents of delinquency, personality, social class, and intelligence. In P.H. Mussen, J.J. Conger, & J. Kagen (Eds.), *Readings In Child Development and Personality.* New York: Harper and Row.

Cotler, S.B., Applegate, G., King, L.W., & Kristal, S. (1972). Establishing a token economy program in a state hospital classroom: A lesson in training student and teacher. *Behavior Therapy, 3,* 209–222.

Cronbach, L.J. (1967). How can instruction be adapted to individual differences? In R.M. Gagne (Ed.), *Learning and individual differences* (pp. 17–38). Columbus, OH: Charles C. Merrill.

Dean, S.I. (1958). Treatment of the reluctant client. *American Psychologist, 13,* 627–630.

De Lange, J.M., Lanham, S.L., & Barton, J.A. (1981). Social skills training for juvenile delinquents: Behavioral skill training and cognitive techniques. In D. Upper and S. Ross (Eds.), *Behavior group therapy, 1981: An annual review.* Champaign, IL: Research Press.

Dreikurs, R., Grunwald, B.B., & Pepper, F.C. (1971). *Maintaining sanity in the classroom.* New York: Harper & Row.

Dreikurs, R., Schulman, B.H., & Mosak, H. (1952). Patient-therapist in multiple psychotherapy: Its advantages to the therapist. *Psychiatric Quarterly, 26,* 219–227.

Drum, D.J., & Figler, H.E. (1973). *Outreach in counseling.* New York: Intext Educational Publication.

Duncan, C.P. (1958). Transfer after training with single versus multiple tasks. *Journal of Experimental Psychology, 55,* 63–72.

Duncan, C.P. (1959). Recent research on human problem solving. *Psychological Bulletin, 56,* 397–429.

Edelman, E., & Goldstein, A.P. (1984). Prescriptive relationship levels for juvenile delinquents in a psychotherapy analog. *Aggressive Behavior, 10,* 269–278.

Elardo, P., & Cooper, M. (1977). *AWARE: Activities for social development.* Reading, MA: Addison-Wesley.

Elder, J.P., Edelstein, B.A., & Narick, N.N. (1979). Adolescent psychiatric patients: Modifying aggressive behavior with social skills training. *Behavior Modification, 3,* 161–178.

Ellis, H. (1965). *The transfer of learning.* New York: Macmillan.

Fleming, D. (1976). *Teaching negotiation skills to pre-adolescents.* Unpublished doctoral dissertation, Syracuse University, Syracuse, NY.

Ford, D.H., & Urban, H.B. (1963). *Systems of psychotherapy.* New York: Wiley.

Frank, R. (1973). Rotating leadership in a group therapy setting. *Psychotherapy: Theory, Research and Practice, 10,* 337–338.

Freedman, B.J., Rosenthal, R., Donahoe, C.P., Schbundy, D.G., & McFall, R.M. (1978). A social behavioral analysis of skill deficits in delinquent and nondelinquent adolescent boys. *Journal of Consulting and Clinical Psychology, 46,* 1448–1462.

Gagne, R.M., Baker, K.E., & Foster, H. (1950). Transfer to a motor skill from practice on a pictured representation. *Journal of Experimental Psychology, 39,* 342–354.

Gold, M. (1978). Scholastic experiences, self-esteem, and delinquent behavior: A theory for alternative schools. *Crime and Delinquency, 7,* 290–309.

Goldbeck, R.A., Bernstein, B.B., Hellix, W.A., & Marx, M.H. (1957). Application of the half-split technique to problem solving tasks. *Journal of Experimental Psychology, 53,* 330–338.

Goldstein, A.P. (1971). *Psychotherapeutic attraction.* New York: Pergamon Press.

Goldstein, A.P. (1973). *Structured learning therapy: Toward a psychotherapy for the poor.* New York: Academic Press.

Goldstein, A.P. (Ed.). (1978). *Prescriptions for child mental health and education.* New York: Pergamon.

Goldstein, A.P. (1981). *Psychological skill training.* New York: Pergamon Press.

Goldstein, A.P., Apter, S., & Harootunian, B. (1984). *School violence.* Englewood Cliffs, NJ: Prentice-Hall.

Goldstein, A.P., Heller, K., & Sechrest, L.B. (1966). *Psychotherapy and the psychology of behavior change.* New York: Wiley.

Goldstein, A.P., Sprafkin, R.P., & Gershaw, N.J. (1976). *Skill training for community living: Applying structured learning therapy.* New York: Pergamon Press.

Goldstein, A.P., Sprafkin, R.P., Gershaw, N.J., & Klein, P. (1980). *Skillstreaming the adolescent.* Urbana, IL: Research Press.

Goldstein, A.P., & Stein, N. (1976). *Prescriptive psychotherapies.* New York: Pergamon Press.

Greenleaf, D. (1977). *Peer reinforcement as transfer enhancement in structured learning therapy.* Unpublished masters thesis, Syracuse University, Syracuse, NY.

Gross, A.M., Brigham, T.A., Hopper, C., & Bologna, N.C. (1980). Self-management and social skills training. *Criminal Justice and Behavior, 7,* 161–184.

Gruber, R.P. (1971). Behavior therapy: Problems in generalization. *Behavior Therapy, 2,* 361–368.

Guerney, B.G., Jr. (1977). *Relationship enhancement.* San Francisco: Jossey-Bass.

Guttman, E.S. (1970). Effects of short-term psychiatric treatment for boys in two California Youth Authority institutions. In D.C. Gibbons (Ed.), *Delinquent behavior.* Englewood Cliffs, NJ: Prentice-Hall.

Guzzetta, R.A. (1974). *Acquisition and transfer of empathy by the parents of early adolescents through structured learning training.* Unpublished doctoral dissertation, Syracuse University, Syracuse, NY.

Hare, M.A. (1976). *Teaching conflict resolution situation.* Paper presented at the meeting of the Eastern Community Association, Philadelphia.

Harlow, H.F. (1949). The formation of learning sets. *Psychological Review, 56,* 51–65.

Harootunian, B. (1978). Teacher training. In A.P. Goldstein (Ed.), *Prescriptions for child mental health and education.* New York: Pergamon Press.

Hawley, R.C., & Hawley, I.L. (1975). *Developing human potential: A handbook of activities for personal and social growth.* Amherst, MA: Education Research Associates.

Hayward, M.L., Peters, J.J., & Taylor, J.E. (1952). Some values of the use of multiple therapists in the treatment of psychoses. *Psychiatric Quarterly, 26,* 244–249.

Hazel, J.S., Schumaker, J.B., Sherman, J.A., & Sheldon-Wildgen, J. (1981). *ASSET: A social skills program for adolescents.* Champaign, IL: Research Press.

Heck, E.T., Gomez, A.G., & Adams, G.L. (1973). *A guide to mental health services.* Pittsburgh: University of Pittsburgh Press.

Heiman, H. (1973). Teaching interpersonal communications. *North Dakota Speech and Theatre Association Bulletin, 2,* 7–29.

Heller, K. (1979). The effects of social support. In A.P. Goldstein & F.H. Kanfer (Eds.), *Maximizing treatment gains.* New York: Academic Press.

Hersen, M., & Barlow, D.H. (1976). *Single case experimental designs: Strategies for studying behavior change.* New York: Pergamon Press.

Hoehn-Saric, R., Frank, J.D., Imber, S.D., Nash, E.H., Stone, A.R., & Battle, C.C. (1964). Systematic preparation of patients for psychotherapy effects on therapy behavior and outcome. *Journal of Psychiatric Research, 2,* 267–281.

Hollin, C.R., & Courtney, S.A. (1983). A skill training approach to the reduction of institutional offending. *Personality and Individual Differences, 4,* 257–264.

Hollin, C.R., & Henderson, M. (1981). The effects of social skills training of incarcerated delinquent adolescents. *International Journal of Behavioral Social Work and Abstracts, 1,* 145–155.

Holmes, D.S. (1971). Round robin therapy: A technique for implementing the effects of psychotherapy. *Journal of Consulting and Clinical Psychology, 37,* 324–331.

Hsu, J.J. (1965). Electro-conditioning treatment for alcoholics. *Quarterly Journal for the Study of Alcoholism, 26,* 449–459.

Hull, C. (1943). *Principles of behavior.* New York: Appleton-Century-Crofts.

Hummel, J.W. (1980). *Teaching preadolescents alternatives to aggression using structured learning training under different stimulus conditions.* Unpublished doctoral dissertation, Syracuse University, Syracuse, N.Y.

Hunt, D.E. (1972). Matching models for teacher training. In B.R. Joyce & M. Weil (Eds.), *Perspectives for reform in teacher education* (pp. 111–140). Englewood Cliffs, NJ: Prentice-Hall.

Johnson, C.A., & Katz, R.C. (1973). Using parents as change agents for their children: A review. *Journal of Child Psychology and Psychiatry, 14,* 181–200.

Jones, M.C. (1960). A laboratory study of fear: The case of Peter. In H.J. Eysenck (Ed.), *Behavior therapy and neurosis* (pp. 45–51). New York: Pergamon Press.

Jones, N.F., Kahn, M.W., & Wolcott, O. (1964). Wearing street clothing by mental hospital personnel. *International Journal of Social Psychiatry, 10,* 216–222.

Kale, R.J., Kaye, J.H., Whalan, P.A., & Hopkins, B.L. (1968). The effects of reinforcement on the modification, maintenance, and generalization of social responses of mental patients. *Journal of Applied Behavior Analysis, 1,* 307–314.

Kanfer, F.H., & Marston, A.R. (1963). Determinants of self-reenforcement in human learning. *Journal of Experimental Psychology, 66,* 245–254.

Karoly, P., & Kanfer, F.H. (1982). *Self-management and behavior change.* New York: Pergamon.

Kazdin, A.E. (1975). *Behavior modification in applied settings.* Homewood, IL: Dorsey Press.

Kazdin, A. (1978). Methodological and interpretive problems of single-case experimental designs. *Journal of Consulting and Clinical Psychology, 46,* 629–642.

Kazdin, A. (1980). *Research design in clinical psychology.* New York: Harper & Row.

Kazdin, A.E., & Polster, R. (1973). Intermittent token reinforcement and response maintenance in extinction. *Behavior Therapy, 4,* 386–391.

Kifer, R.E., Lewis, M.A., Green, D.R., & Phillips, E.L. (1974). Training predelinquent youths and their parents to negotiate conflict situations. *Journal of Applied Behavior Analysis, 7,* 357–364.

Kohlberg, L. (1973). *Collected papers on moral development and moral education.* Cambridge, MA: Center for Moral Education, Harvard University.

Kovel, J. (1976). *A complete guide to therapy.* New York: Pantheon.

Ladd, G.W., & Mize, J. (1983). A cognitive-social learning model of social-skill training. *Psychological Review, 90,* 127–157.

Lazarus, A.A. (1966). Behavior rehearsal vs. non-directive therapy vs. advice in effecting behavior change. *Behavioral Research and Therapy, 4,* 209–212.

Lee, D.Y., Hollbery, E.T., & Hussard, H. (1979). Effects of assertion training on aggressive behavior on adolescents. *Journal of Counseling Psychology, 26*(5), 459–461.

Litwack, S.W. (1976). *The helper therapy principle as a therapeutic tool: Structured learning therapy with adolescents.* Unpublished doctoral dissertation, Syracuse University.

Lopez, M.A., Hoyer, W.J., Goldstein, A.P., Gershaw, N.J., & Sprafkin, R.J. (1980). Effects of over-learning and incentive on the acquisition and transfer of interpersonal skills with institutionalized elderly. *Journal of Gerontology, 35,* 403–408.

Magaro, P.A. (1969). A prescriptive treatment model based upon social class and premorbid adjustment. *Psychotherapy: Theory, research and practice, 6,* 57–70.

Mahoney, M.J. (1973). *Cognition and behavior modification.* Cambridge: Ballinger.

Maloney, D.M., Harper, T.N., Braukmann, C.J., Fixsen, D.L., Phillips, E.L., & Wolf, M. (1976). Teaching conversation-related skills to pre-delinquent girls. *Journal of Applied Behavior Analysis, 9,* 371.

Mandler, G. (1954). Transfer of training as a function of degree of response overlearning. *Journal of Experimental Psychology, 47,* 411–417.

Mandler, G., & Heinemann, S.H. (1956). Effect of overlearning of a verbal response on transfer of training. *Journal of Experimental Psychology, 52,* 39–46.

Marholin, D., & Touchette, P.E. (1979). The role of stimulus control and response consequences. In A.P. Goldstein & F.H. Kanfer (Eds.), *Maximizing treatment gains.* New York: Academic Press.

Masters, J.C., & Branch, M.N. (1969). A comparison of the relative effectiveness of instructions, modeling and reinforcement procedures for inducing behavior change. *Journal of Experimental Psychology, 80,* 364–368.

Matson, J.L., Esveldt-Dawson, K., Andrasik, F., Ollendick, T.H., Petti, T., & Hersen M. (1980). Direct, observational, and generalization effects of social skills training with emotionally disturbed children. *Behavior Therapy, 11,* 522–531.

Michelson, L., & Wood, R. (1980). Behavioral assessment and training of children's social skills. *Progress in Behavior Modification, 9,* 241–291.

Minkin, N.M., Braukmann, C.J., & Minkin, B.L. (1976). The social validation and training on conversation skills. *Journal of Applied Behavior Analysis, 9,* 127–139.

Mussen, P.H., Conger, J.J., Kagan, J., & Gerwitz, J. (1979). *Psychological development: A life-span approach.* New York: Harper & Row.

O'Dell, S. (1974). Training parents in behavior modification. *Psychological Bulletin, 81,* 418–433.

O'Leary, O.D., O'Leary, S., & Becker, W.C. (1967). Modification of a deviant sibling interaction pattern in the home. *Behavioral Research and Therapy, 5,* 113–120.

Ollendick, T.H., & Hersen, M. (1979). Social skills training for juvenile delinquents. *Behavioral Research and Therapy, 17,* 547–555.

Orne, M.I., & Wender, P.H. (1968). Anticipatory socialization for psychotherapy: Method and rationale. *American Journal of Psychiatry, 124,* 1202–1212.

Osgood, C.E. (1953). *Method and theory in experimental psychology.* New York: Oxford University Press.

Patterson, G.R. (1963). *The peer group as delinquency reinforcement agent.* Unpublished manuscript, University of Oregon, Child Research Laboratory, Eugene, OR.

Patterson, G.R., Cobb, J.A., & Ray, R.S. (1973). A social engineering technology for retraining the families of aggressive boys. In H.E. Adams & I.P. Unikel (Eds.), *Issues and trends in behavior therapy* (pp. 221–243). Springfield, IL: Charles C Thomas.

Patterson, G.R., & Gullion, M.E. (1972). *Living with children.* Champaign, IL: Research Press.

Patterson, G.R., Reid, J.G., Jones, R.R., & Conger, R.E. (1975). *A social learning approach to family intervention* (Vol. 1). Eugene, OR: Catalise.

Pentz, M.A. (1980). Assertion training and trainer effects on unassertive and aggressive adolescents. *Journal of Counseling Psychology, 27,* 76–83.

Price, R.H. (1979). The social ecology of treatment gains. In A.P. Goldstein & F.H. Kanfer (Eds.), *Maximizing treatment gains* (pp. 348–379). New York: Academic Press.

Redl, F., & Wineman, D. (1957). *The aggressive child.* New York: Free Press.

Reid, J.B., & Patterson, G.R. (1976). The modification of aggression and stealing behavior of boys in the home setting. In E. Ribes-Inesta & A. Bandura (Eds.), *Analysis of delinquency and aggression* (pp. 123–145). Hillsdale, NJ: L. Erlbaum Associates.

Robin, A.L. (1981). A controlled evaluation of problem solving communication training with parent-adolescent conflict. *Behavior Therapy, 12,* 593–609.

Robin, A.L., Kent, R., O'Leary, D., Foster, S., & Prinz, R. (1977). An approach to teaching parents and adolescents problem solving communication skills: A preliminary report. *Behavior Therapy, 8,* 639–643.

Rogers, C.R. (1957). The necessary and sufficient conditions of therapeutic personality change. *Journal of Consulting Psychology, 21,* 95–103.

Rotter, J.R. (1954). *Social learning and clinical psychology.* Englewood Cliffs, NJ: Prentice-Hall.

Ruesch, J. (1957). *Disturbed communication.* New York: Norton.

Sarason, I.G., & Ganzer, V.J. (1973). Modeling and group discussion in the rehabilitation of juvenile delinquents. *Journal of Counseling Psychology, 20,* 442–449.

Sarason, I.G., & Sarason, B.R. (1981). Teaching cognitive and social skills to high school students. *Journal of Consulting and Clinical Psychology, 49,* 908–918.

Schinke, S.P. (1981). Interpersonal-skills training with adolescents. In M. Hersen, & A. Bellack (Eds.), *Progress in Behavior Modification,* pp. 65–111 (Vol. 11). New York: Academic Press.

Schwitzgebel, R.L. (1967). Short-term operant conditioning of adolescent offenders on socially relevant variable. *Journal of Abnormal Psychology, 72,* 134–142.

Shoemaker, M.E. (1979). Group assertion training for institutionalized male delinquents. In J.S. Stumphauser (Ed.), *Progress in behavior therapy with delinquents* (pp. 91–117). Springfield, IL: Charles C Thomas.

Shore, E., & Sechrest, L. (1961). Concept attainment as a function of number of positive instances presented. *Journal of Educational Psychology, 52,* 303–307.

Slack, C.W. (1960). Experimenter-subject psychotherapy: A new method of introducing intensive office treatment for unreachable cases. *Mental Hygiene, 44,* 238–256.

Slavin, D.R. (1967). *Response transfer of conditioned affective responses as a function of an experimental analogue of rational psychotherapy.* Unpublished doctoral dissertation, Northwestern University, Evanston, IL.

Slavson, S.R. (1964). *A textbook in analytic group psychotherapy.* New York: International Universities Press.

Solomon, E. (1977). *Structured learning therapy with abusive parents: Training in self-control.* Unpublished doctoral dissertation, Syracuse University, Syracuse, NY.

Spatz-Norton, C. (1984). *The effect of self-statements and structured learning training of empathy upon aggressive behavior and pro-social conflict resolution in aggressive elementary school aged males.* Unpublished master's thesis, Syracuse University, Syracuse, NY.

Spence, A.J., & Spence, S.H. (1980). Cognitive changes associated with social skills training. *Behavioral Research and Therapy, 18*, 265-272.

Spence, S.H. (1979). Social skills training with adolescent offenders: A review. *Behavioral Psychology, 7*, 49–57.

Spence, S.H. (1981). Differences in social skills performance between institutionalized juvenile male offenders and a comparable group of boys without offence records. *British Journal of Clinical Psychology, 20*, 163–171.

Spence, S.H., & Marziller, J.S. (1979). Social skills training with adolescent male offenders: Short-term effects. *Behavioral Research and Therapy, 17*, 7–16.

Spence, S.H., & Marziller, J.S. (1981). Social skills training with adolescent male offenders— II: Short-term, long-term and generalized effects. *Behavioral Research and Therapy, 19*, 349–368.

Stern, G.G. (1970). *People in context.* New York: Wiley.

Stephens, T.M. (1978). *Social skills in the classroom.* Columbus, OH: Cedars Press.

Stevenson, I. (1962). The use of rewards and punishments in psychotherapy. *Comprehensive Psychiatry, 3*, 20–28.

Tharp, R.G., & Wetzel, R. (1969). *Behavior modification in the natural environment.* New York: Academic Press.

Thelen, M.A., Fry, R.A., Dollinger, S.L., & Paul, S.C. (1976). Use of videotaped models to improve the interpersonal adjustment of delinquents. *Journal of Consulting and Clinical Psychology, 44*, 492.

Thorndike, E.L., & Woodworth, R.S. (1901). The influence of improvement in one mental function upon the efficiency of other functions, *Psychological Review, 8*, 247–261.

Tramontana, M.G. (1980). Critical review of research on psychotherapy outcome with adolescents: (1967–1977). *Psychological Bulletin, 88*, 429–450.

Trief, P. (1976). *The reduction of egocentrism in acting-out adolescents by structured learning therapy.* Unpublished doctoral dissertation, Syracuse University, Syracuse, NY.

Underwood, B.J. (1951). Associative transfer in verbal learning as a function of response similarity and degree of first-list learning. *Journal of Experimental Psychology, 42*, 44–53.

Wahler, R.G. (1969). Setting generality: Some specific and general effects of child behavior therapy. *Journal of Applied Behavior Analysis, 2*, 239–246.

Walker, H.M. (1979). *The acting-out child: Coping with classroom disruption.* Boston: Allyn & Bacon.

Walker, R., Allenson, E.A., & Johnson, M.E. (1971). OT CHIRP: A method of early assignment of hospital psychiatric patients to paid work. *Rehabilitation Literature, 32*, 360–364.

Walker, H.M., & Buckley, N.K. (1972). Programming generalization and maintenance of treatment effects across time and across settings. *Journal of Applied Behavior Analysis, 5*, 209–224.

Watkins, B.R. (1972). The development of evolution of a transductive learning technique for the treatment of social incompetence. *Dissertation Abstracts International, 33*, 2361.

Weiner, L., Becker, A., & Friedman, T.T. (1967). *Home treatment.* Pittsburgh: University of Pittsburgh Press.

Werner, J.S., Minkin, N., Minkin, B.L., Fixsen, D.L., Phillips, E.L., & Wolf, N.N. (1975). Intervention packages: An analysis to prepare juvenile delinquents for encounters with police officers. *Criminal Justice and Behavior, 2*, 55–84.

Whalen, C. (1969). Effects of a model and instructions on group verbal behavior. *Journal of Consulting and Clinical Psychology, 3*, 509–521.

Whitaker, C.A., Malone, T.P., & Warkentin, J. (1956). Multiple therapy and psychotherapy. In F. Fromm-Ruchmann & M. Moreno (Eds.), *Progress in psychotherapy* (pp. 210–216). New York: Grune & Stratton.

Wolberg, L.R. (1954). *The technique of psychotherapy.* New York: Grune & Stratton.

Wood, M. (1977). *Adolescent acquisition and transfer of assertiveness through the use of structured learning therapy.* Unpublished doctoral dissertation, Syracuse University, Syracuse, NY.

Zimmerman, D. (1984). *Enhancing perspective-taking and moral reasoning via structured learning therapy and moral education with aggressive adolescents.* Unpublished master's thesis, Syracuse University, Syracuse, NY.

7

School Violence and Vandalism

Berj Harootunian

Student pranks and misbehavior have long been an aspect of the folklore connected with America's schools. School violence and vandalism have become major problems confronting education, because what was once merely student mischief has in recent years escalated to aggravated assault with lethal weapons and property damage with malicious intent.

The basic thesis of this chapter is that the continuing dilemma of aggression in schools is attributable in large part to inadequate perspective and faulty conceptualization of the problem. Currently there is no lack of proponents for various aggression controls, models, and prevention techniques. Most of these approaches have been reported in the literature and have worked at some time or in some place, but they have been applied in a fractionated, if not haphazard, manner.

In too many instances, the problem of school violence is perceived as someone else's responsibility or fault. As McPartland and McDill (1977) emphasize, finger-pointing and scapegoating are often the result of such perceptions, and the involved participants—teachers, students, administrators, parents, boards of education, and society—end up blaming one another.

The idea that aggression in school involves complex and multiple variables and cannot be dealt with effectively without similarly complex and multiple interventions has been only recently spelled out in detail (Harootunian & Apter, 1983; Goldstein, Apter, & Harootunian, 1984; Zwier & Vaughan, 1984). For example, Zwier and Vaughan argue that the selection of a strategy to deal effectively with school vandalism is largely a function of the ideological congruence of the interested participants—teachers, parents, students, and principal. They contend, moreover, that the choice of which variable to study or strategy to employ regarding school vandalism depends on the ideological orientation of the investigator. This point will be elaborated later.

Apter, Goldstein, and Harootunian in their various writings, view the problem of school violence from an ecological, interactionist, or systems perspective. They maintain that aggression in school will be countered most readily when the interventions simultaneously consider the involved youngsters, their teachers, the school's administrators, and such out-of-school influences as parents and community. (See Apter's chapter in this volume for a more complete consideration of the ecological perspective.)

This chapter attempts to remove some of the murkiness enveloping the various approaches to school aggression by drawing upon the perspectives of the individuals noted earlier. But before considering their work, the background and context of school violence need to be reviewed. Also, some of the issues and arguments over disruptive school behavior such as the nature and scope of the problem, the role of the school vis-à-vis school violence, and some of the classificatory schemes of various measures to control school aggression need to be considered.

BACKGROUND AND CONTEXT OF SCHOOL VIOLENCE

Aggressive behavior in school has increased in a manner that parallels the rapid rise of crime in general in the period from 1960 to 1975. Since the mid-1970s, the data show a leveling or stabilizing of the crime rate at a relatively high level. Some part of this increase is attributable to the increase in the school-age population that resulted from the post–World War II baby boom. To attribute aggression in school entirely to this increase would be folly. Between 1950 and 1975, the number of students grew by 86%, but school arson, for example, increased by a remarkable 859%, or ten times as much (Rubel, 1977). Other types of disruptive school behavior similarly exceed the population changes. There were 15,000 assaults on teachers reported in 1955; 41,000 in 1971; 63,800 in 1975; and 110,000 in 1979.

The vast majority of aggressive incidents are directed toward other students. Slightly more than three of four personal victimizations in school (assaults, rapes, robberies, larcenies) were against students (McDermott, 1979). The majority of these attacks involve victims and attackers of the same race.

Aside from the human cost, the waste due to school vandalism is considerable. Estimates to repair the effects of school vandals are reported to be about $200 million annually (National Institute of Education, 1977).

The data just presented exemplify the extent of aggressive behavior in and toward America's schools. The problem is a real one and may be even more severe than the data reveal. School violence and vandalism are often imprecisely defined or reported. Moreover, administrators, teachers, and even communities may avoid volunteering information that will reflect adversely on themselves. Some students of aggression have estimated that the levels of school aggression may actually be 50% higher than the data indicate (Ban & Ciminillo, 1977).

THE RELATIONSHIP BETWEEN THE SCHOOL AND AGGRESSION

There is some disagreement about whether the school causes or reflects violent behavior. Those individuals who see the school as the source of aggression argue that the school in one setting fosters all of the necessary conditions for violence and vandalism (Elliott & Voss, 1974; Gold, 1978). According to this view, the school controls major psychological and social forces that provoke delinquent behavior. The school labels various students as failures and by making their failures obvious to themselves and to others, forces youngsters toward aggression as a face-saving response.

Others hold the school responsible for the violence that occurs (Frease, 1973; Kelly, 1975; Polk & Schafer, 1972), but explain the linkage in terms of the organizational structure of the school such as tracking or other systems for segregating students. Individuals holding this perspective would argue that the school is the principal cause of aggression because it labels youngsters as "losers" almost upon their entrance to school. These youngsters, in turn, then fulfill the negative expectations of their teachers and principals.

The ultimate point in the argument by those individuals who see the school as the source of aggressive behavior becomes manifest when the school or its agents resort to physical or corporal punishment. Hyman (1979) observed that the public response to misbehavior has demanded more punitive action and has resulted in the institutional acceptability of hitting or paddling children. An editorial in the *New York Times* (1980) titled "Regents Buckle on Spanking" succinctly summarized the relevant issues by noting that a policy of corporal punishment would do little to protect the teacher's rights to self-defense. Moreover, the victims of such a policy, as studies have shown, are almost never muscular, undisciplined adolescents; rather, they tend to be young children.

There is another, somewhat less sanguine, position regarding the connection between violence and the school. The holders of this perspective maintain that the school is an important factor contributing to school aggression, but it is not the principal source (McPartland & McDill, 1977). The research carried out by Feldhusen and his associates supports this contention (Feldhusen, Aversano, & Thurston, 1976; Feldhusen, Roeser, & Thurston, 1977; Feldhusen, Thurston, & Benning, 1973). By testing, interviewing, and measuring behavior over an 11-year period on a group of about 1,500 children, they found that family variables were more important than school-related factors in predicting the prosocial or disruptive behavior of these children.

The school is also seen as the victim of aggression rather than its provoker. Gangs use schools as their base of operations for recruiting, drug sales, extortion, robberies, meetings, and other activities. (Bayh, 1977). The school, especially in large cities, may become an extension of street-corner norms and behavior (Foster, 1974; McPartland & McDill, 1977).

One additional perspective needs to be noted. According to Wenk (1975), the increase in disruptive behavior in schools reflects a mismatch between school and society. He maintains that the current level of school violence manifests the disparity between today's more complex, unstable society and the maintenance of school programs targeted and designed for a simpler, more predictable state of affairs.

It is obvious that the answer to the question, "Why does aggressive behavior occur in school?" will vary according to the particular perspective a respondent chooses to adopt. One can blame the student, the nature of the school, its structure, the family, the peer group and gang, or society, depending on one's theoretical, ideological, or value perspective. Simply stated, if the source of the disruption is viewed in terms of the disruptive student, then appropriate treatments are aimed at the student. On the other hand, if the reason for violence and vandalism is defined by what the school is or does, then the remedies that are posited and researched focus on a different set of variables.

But as noted earlier, unidimensional studies of school violence and vandalism are all too numerous. At least 126 attempted solutions have been identified and categorized under the following nine headings: student oriented, teacher oriented, curriculum, administrative, physical school alterations, parent oriented, security personnel, community oriented, and state and federal oriented (Goldstein, et al. 1984). Marvin and associates (Marvin, McCann, Connolly, Temkin, & Henning, 1977) used four categories to classify 137 programs designed to combat disruptive school behavior as follows: security systems, counseling services, curricular/instructional programs, and organizational changes. They found that these programs tended to be idiosyncratic, varied, were usually successful in reducing violence and vandalism, and often required cooperation among school personnel, outside community agencies, parents, students, and the larger community.

It would seem that the various solutions proposed to reduce aggression in schools exceed the proposed causes or sources. In sum, the dilemma facing the school-aggression problem is that it is usually posed as one about which there is disagreement concerning both its origins and its solutions. As it has usually been conceptualized, the one generalization that may be drawn from the hundreds of programs that have been implemented is that explicit recognition of a violent-behavior problem in a school is in itself a first step in reducing its incidence. Let us examine some of the results of some attempts to understand aggression in schools and then consider the school-violence problem from a multidimensional perspective.

AN OVERVIEW OF SCHOOL AGGRESSION LITERATURE

As just noted, attempts to cope with or solve the school aggression problem are many, varied, and usually reported as successes. Of what use, then, would another compilation of evidence variously categorized serve? There are at least three reasons that provide answers to this question. First, if the categories applied are conceptually different from previous ones, they may furnish adequate reason for another look at the evidence. Second, the classification scheme itself may serve as a heuristic for understanding and providing insight about the extensive literature. And third, such an overview of various school violence and vandalism issues and findings at this juncture sets the stage for looking at the problem from more than one dimension.

The various approaches that have been applied toward the reduction of aggression in school can be conceptualized and classified in terms of Kurt Lewin's now classic formula $B = f(P, E)$, which translates as behavior is the result of the combined function of the person and environment. Looking at school aggression under the headings of Behavior, Person, and Environment will help bring into clearer focus the issues involved and the extant knowledge about each of these categories and will, as well, allow the identification of those studies that have attempted to take into account the joint or interactive consequences of behavior, person, and/or environment. Space does not allow a detailed description of the different studies and programs that have been reported. Moreover, the citations under each heading are not intended as a comprehensive review of the literature, but only as illustrative of the various issues involved.

Behavior

Earlier in this chapter, data were cited to indicate the extent to which the problem of school aggression has become a pervasive aspect of our culture. David Hunt (1971) has argued that an essential first step in the training of training agents (e.g., teachers, principals, social workers, etc.) is the development of their skills in discriminating among different behaviors. These front-line personnel have to have a clear conception about violent and vandalistic behavior as distinct from other types of school crime. However, McPartland and McDill (1977) note that "there is no well-established classification system for grouping student offenses into categories that have empirical scientific or practical meaning" (p. 4). They state that school crimes are too restrictively defined and consequently present an inadequate portrayal of the saliency and intensity of the problem. The categories often include a "mixed bag" of violent and nonviolent behaviors. McPartland and McDill have identified four types of behaviors based on their analysis of survey data and suggest the following four categories: (a) School attacks, thefts, and withdrawals; (b) drug and alcohol abuse; (c) student protests and demonstrations: and (d) racial and ethnic group tensions (pp. 5–6).

The primary focus of this chapter is on the first of the categories by McPartland and McDill, because it includes vandalism of school property, stealing from students and staff, as well as physical attacks on school members. All of these behaviors are "hostility directed"

(Thaw, 1980) and intentional. But whether a particular act is perceived and reported as an aggressive one is not context free. In other words, whether the behavior is seen as violent or vandalistic is a function of the actor and the environment. The leaving of one's name or initials on a desk or on a wall may be viewed as traditional wear and tear (Zwier & Vaughan, 1984), and an episode of violent student behavior in certain instances will go unreported because of a "boys-will-be-boys" attitude. Foster (1974) makes the important point that what may be perceived by the teacher as threatening and illegitimate violence by lower class students frequently is only a test of the teacher's capability to control and set limits. The recognition of this problem is exemplified by the efforts of Brodinsky (1981), who has set up guidelines by which school administrators can provide more uniform reporting systems on violence and vandalism.

As Zwier and Vaughan (1984) emphasize, the question of which behaviors define school aggression will affect the response strategies that are employed. In their words,

> If a certain behavior were regarded as "fairly normal," it would be sensible to concentrate on changes in the environment (e.g., by replacing glass by Lexan, a hard-to-break glass substitute), rather than attempt a change in pupil behaviour (e.g., by using behavior modification techniques). (p. 266)

Duke's (1978) survey of 100 randomly selected New York high schools and 100 in California is relevant about the behavior that gets labeled as disruptive. Administrators of urban and nonurban high schools identified their three most severe discipline problems as skipping class, truancy, and lateness to class. For teachers, the highest priority problems were classroom disruption, fighting, and disrespect for their authority. Interestingly, the administrators viewed fighting, disruption, drug use, and profanity among the least important problems. Duke believes that students would rank theft and fighting as the most serious and states:

> If my speculations concerning teacher and student perceptions of the most pressing discipline problems are accurate, it becomes somewhat more understandable why a "crisis" in school discipline seems to exist. *Each of the three major role groups involved in high schools is concerned primarily about a different set of discipline problems.* Self interest dictates priorities. (Duke, 1978, p. 326)

It is important to note that the incidence of aggressive behavior in itself requires multilevel explanations and approaches (Goldstein & Keller, 1983). Violence and vandalism in school can be reported in various ways, and each way carries with it some degree of ambiguity. Goldstein and Keller (1983) point out that the measurement or incidence of aggressive behavior needs to be conceptualized not only by its motoric acts, which are publicly observable, but as well by its cognitive and physiological concomitants. The choice of the behavior that is reported as aggressive, then, is itself more than a matter of simple reporting and counting. How and by whom the reporting, counting, and measuring of behavior is done may all contribute to the variation in the information yield on aggression. As the behavior that describes and circumscribes violence and vandalism in school comes into sharper focus, not only will the problems be more fully acknowledged, but even more research findings will be available. Perhaps then school violence will receive more than two incidental listings in the *Encyclopedia of Educational Research, Fifth Edition* (Mitzel, 1982), and vandalism, which is nowhere to be found in the index, may even be listed.

Person

What can be said about the student who commits an aggressive act against school persons or property? The answer to this question lies in how well answers can be found to a series of questions adapted from Ossorio (1973):

- Who is the aggressive student? (identity)
- What does this person want? (intention)
- What does this person know? (knowledge)
- What does this person know how to do? (competence)
- What is the person trying to do? (action)

Not all of these questions can be answered quite adequately or completely, or without some controversy. There is, however, enough research evidence to provide at least a rough sketch of the individual who is likely to be responsible for acts of school violence and vandalism.

According to McPartland and McDill (1977), several generalizations can be made about youth who commit crimes. These youth are usually male, economically and educationally disadvantaged, members of racial or ethnic minorities, and are in adolescence. But as these writers point out, the vast majority of individuals who fit these descriptors do not commit crimes.

To explain these generalizations, McPartland and McDill (1977) have identified five major themes or hypotheses in theories of youth crime as follows:

1. Restricted opportunity. Young people must overcome various hurdles or barriers to attain the good jobs, material possessions and status that represent the American dream. The school is the most readily identifiable element of the system that holds young people back, and criminal acts represent their response to such frustration.
2. Subcultural differences in values and attitudes. Middle class values and aspirations are rejected by members of some subcultures, and crime and violence are a fact of life.
3. Prolonged adolescent dependence. Students are in effect in a holding pattern until they can become eligible for adult jobs. Individuals with time on their hands or wishing to demonstrate their independence often engage in delinquent behavior.
4. Seriously damaged personality. Violent and disruptive behaviors are the result of mental and emotional disorders. The individual is unable to control aggressive and antisocial acts.
5. Labeling and stereotyping. The youngster perceives and internalizes negative self-images which the school and other authorities provide and reinforce. Aggressive behavior by such youth exemplifies a self-fulfilling prophecy.

McPartland and McDill point out that the first three themes above (restricted opportunity, subcultural differences, and prolonged adolescence) are drawn from sociology, while the last two themes (seriously damaged personalities and labeling and stereotyping) are from psychology. Each of these themes suggests a number of interventions that might be applied by the school to counter school violence, and, as noted earlier in this chapter, a wide variety have been applied. For the most part, however, schools have responded to aggression by assigning the youngster to a special class, a special school, suspension, and in some instances counseling and behavioral change strategies.

While McPartland and McDill have presented the problem of the violent student in general terms and themes, others have provided a more detailed picture. Feldhusen and colleagues (Feldhusen et al., 1973, 1976, 1977) have carried out longitudinal and complex statistical analyses of over 1,500 children in Grades 3, 6, and 9 who have been identified as exhibiting either consistent prosocial or disruptive behavior. The students were subjected to considerable testing, their parents were interviewed, and they were followed in school over 11 years with various kinds of data collection. Several notable differences were found. Aggressive children tended to have families in which there was no cohesion; fathers were either too strict, too lax, or inconsistent in discipline; mothers were inadequate in their supervision; physical punishment was used; parents lost their temper and were indifferent or hostile to the child; parents felt they had little control on the development of their child; and parents were less educated and, if employed, were in low-status occupations.

The school-related variables yield a number of important differences between prosocial and disruptive youths. The latter were 9 points lower in mean IQ, lower in reading and mathematics achievement-test scores, more likely to drop out of school, had lower class standing among the graduates, and were rated lower by their teachers in personality and social characteristics. None of the school-related findings is particularly surprising, and they are consistent with the general portrait depicted earlier by McPartland and McDill (1977). What is noteworthy is that Feldhusen and associates (1976, 1977) were able to predict delinquency with considerable accuracy (up to 79%) over the long term, and among the best predictors is the teacher's original identification of the youngster with behavior problems.

Lefkowitz and colleagues (Lefkowitz, Eron, Walder, & Heusmann, 1973, 1977) also studied and reported on a group of boys and girls over a period of years. They identified 875 children in third grade and followed up 10 years later. Aggression at age 8 was found to predict later aggression. Parental rejection, low IQ, and low identification with mother were all significantly related to aggression in both boys and girls. Long-term predictors of violence for boys were parental mobility, reluctance to confess misbehavior to parents, and preference for watching violent programs on TV. For girls, long-term predictors include negative identification with father and parents' low church attendance. The best single predictor of aggressive school behavior over the 10-year period was low IQ for both boys and girls, and for both sexes there was a negative correlation between school achievement and aggression. The learning of socially acceptable behavior in school may thus be limited by the low IQ of the child which, in turn, may set off a chain of events involving low achievement, frustration, and aggression. This chain will be discussed in more specific terms later.

Elliott and Voss (1974), from the results of their longitudinal research on school behavior, would argue for the inclusion of two additional descriptors of the delinquent or disruptive youngster. They confirmed that while real or anticipated school failure contributed to hostile behavior, so did a youngster's normlessness or alienation, as well as his or her exposure to other norm-violating youth. "Normlessness in the school is the best predictor of delinquency for both sexes" (p. 170). It is the combination of failure with normlessness that leads to delinquency.

The specific studies cited thus far are not inconsistent with McPartland and McDill's earlier cited generalizations, and they even seem to have validity across different populations. Duke (1976), for example, investigated rural high school students who caused disciplinary problems. He suggested that their misbehavior could be explained by their low IQs and by third grade, their lack of success in reading, language, study skills, and mathematics. Problem children were more frequently labeled "lazy," "aggressive," "disruptive," and "selfish." Duke has proposed that intervention should occur early in a student's academic life if it is to ameliorate later aggression.

Jessor and Jessor (1977), on the basis of their 4-year longitudinal study of junior high, high school, and college youth, claim strong support for a "syndrome" of problem behavior. The interrelated variables that describe this syndrome in an adolescent include the low value placed on academic achievement, the expectation of poor academic performance, the concern for independence, a problematic perspective of society, and low interest in institutions such as church and school. But as Jessor and Jessor point out, this syndrome is characteristic of most adolescents and may reflect essentially that "the normal course of developmental change in adolescence is in the direction of greater problem-proneness" (p. 238).

It is important to keep this last observation in mind. Again, there are more youngsters who can be characterized by the variables that describe aggressive youngsters who do *not* engage in violent or vandalistic behavior. More noteworthy are the findings that aggression by persons in schools is preventable or can be countered in some way. For example, Goldstein and Pentz (1984) present evidence that the social-psychological skill deficiencies of aggressive youngsters such as interpersonal behaviors, planning, aggression management, and the like may be amenable to training. These findings are consistent with those of Fremont and Wallbrown (1979) who believe that disruptive students may lack the ability to perceive the subtleties of teacher and student behaviors, moods, and attitudes. Let us consider now some of the treatments or environments that have been applied.

Environment

Programs addressing the problem of aggression in schools are, in effect, environments designed to counter or reduce violence and vandalism. Earlier in this chapter, we cited two attempts as classifying some of the many and varied programs that have been implemented (Goldstein et al., 1984; Marvin et al., 1977). Marvin and associates found 23 of their 137 programs focused on the development of security systems to protect the school and its members from personal and property assaults; 30 programs provided counseling services of various kinds to disruptive students and/or their families; 36 programs developed curriculum or instructional options that helped students acquire basic skills, personal management skills, conflict resolution skills as well as courses in such areas as law and law enforcement; 39 were nongraded schools, contracting with students, dividing the school into smaller schools, etc.; and 9 schools were classified as other. Of the 137 changes in programs or environments, 129 were rated as helpful by the participants. While only 40 of the programs were formally evaluated, the others provided support of their effectiveness by supplying evidence of three principal types—attitudinal change, reduction of criminal acts, and/or reduction of educational disruptions. Perhaps most interesting and noteworthy from the perspective of this chapter is that all of the programs were implemented at school district (86) or building (51) level. The investigators "were unable to identify any program confined to a singles classroom" (Marvin et al., 1977, p. 53). This lack of focus on the classroom level may be an explanation for the recent conclusion that changes in school organization have not been matched by improvements in students' and educators' behaviors (Duke & Jones, 1983).

The number and variety of program interventions reflect considerable imagination and creativity. Specific examples that have been applied to solve the problem are listed in Table 7.1. The items in Table 7.1 range from very specific solutions, such as installation of better lighting and use of Plexiglas windows, to more complex ones, like Adopt-a-School and less restrictive child-labor laws. Nearly all of the solutions or interventions in Table 7.1 are self-explanatory, but a few may not be well-known. Adopt-A-School programs are one way of bringing together the school and community. Businesses, organizations, and industries adopt schools and contribute money, people, or services to the school. Helping Hand programs are best understood by their symbol, a red handprint, which is placed in a window of a place where children can go to and from school to seek any necessary help.

Table 7.1. Attempted Solutions to School Violence and Vandalism

I. *Student Oriented*
Diagnostic learning centers
Regional occupational centers
Part-time programs
Academic-support services
Group counseling
Student advisory committee
Student patrols (interracial)
Behavior modification: contingency management
Behavior modification: time-out
Behavior modification: response cost
Behavior modification: contracting
Financial accountability
School transfer
Interpersonal skill training
Problem-solving training
Moral education
Value clarification
Individual counseling
More achievable reward criteria
Identification cards
Peer counseling
Participation in grievance resolution
Security advisory council
School-safety committee

II. *Teacher Oriented*
Aggression-management training for teachers
Increased teacher–student nonclass contact
Teacher–student–administration group discussions
Low teacher–pupil ratio
Firm, fair, consistent teacher discipline
Self-defense training
Carrying of weapons by teachers
Legalization of teacher use of force
Compensation for aggression-related expenses
Individualized teaching strategies
Enhanced teacher knowledge of student ethnic milieu
Increased teacher–parent interaction

III. *Curriculum*
Art and music courses
Law courses
Police courses

Courses dealing with practical aspects of adult life
Prescriptively tailored course sequences
Work–study programs
Equivalency diplomas
Schools without walls
Schools within schools
Learning centers (magnet schools, educational parks)
Continuation centers (street academies, evening high schools)
Minischools
Self-paced instruction
Idiographic grading

IV. *Administrative*
Use of skilled conflict negotiators
Twenty-four-hour custodial service
Clear lines of responsibility and authority among administrators
School-safety committee
School administration–police coordination
Legal-rights handbook
School-procedures manual
Written codes of rights and responsibilities
Aggression-management training for administrators
Democratized school governance
Human relations courses
Effective intelligence network
Principal visibility and availability
Relaxation of arbitrary rules (re smoking, dressing, absences, etc.)

V. *Physical School Alterations*
Extensive lighting program
Blackout of all lighting
Reduction of school size
Reduction of class size
Close off isolated areas
Increase staff supervision
Implement rapid repair of vandalism targets
Electronic monitoring for weapons detection
Safety corridors (school to street)
Removal of tempting vandalism targets
Recess fixtures where possible
Install graffiti boards

Table 7.1. (*Continued*)

Encourage student drawn murals
Paint lockers bright colors
Use ceramic type, hard-surface paints
Sponsor clean-up, pick-up, fix-up days
Pave or asphalt graveled parking areas
Use Plexiglas or polycarbon windows
Install decorative grillwork over windows
Mark all school property for identification
Use intruder detectors (microwave, ultrasonic, infrared, audio, video, mechanical)
Employ personal alarm systems
Alter isolated areas to attract people traffic

VI. Parent Oriented
Telephone campaigns to encourage PTA attendance
Antitruancy committee (parent, counselor, student)
Parenting skills training
Parents as guest speakers
Parents as apprenticeship resources
Parents as work–study contacts
Increased parent legal responsibility for their children's behavior
Family education centers

VII. Security Personnel
Police K-9 patrol units
Police helicopter surveillance
Use of security personnel for patrol
Use of security personnel for crowd control
Use of security personnel for intelligence gathering
Use of security personnel for record keeping

Use of security personnel for teaching (e.g., law)
Use of security personnel for counseling
Use of security personnel for home visits
Development of school security manuals

VIII. Community Oriented
Helping Hand programs
Restitution programs
Adopt-a-School programs
Vandalism prevention education
Mass-media publication of cost of vandalism
Open school to community use after hours
Improved school–juvenile court liaison
Family back-to-school week
Neighborhood day
Vandalism watch on or near school grounds via mobile homes
Encourage reporting by citizen band radio users of observed vandalism
Community education programs
More and better programs for disruptive/disturbed youngsters

IX. State and Federal Oriented
Establish uniform violence and vandalism reporting system
Establish state antiviolence advisory committee
Stronger gun control legislation
Enhanced national moral leadership
Better coordination of relevant federal, state, community agencies
Stronger antitrespass legislation
More prosocial television programs
Less restrictive child labor laws

Note. From *School Violence* by A.P. Goldstein, S.J. Apter, and B. Harootunian, 1984, Englewood Cliffs, NJ: Prentice-Hall.   Copyright 1984 by Prentice-Hall. Reprinted by permission.

There is obviously no lack of suggested solutions to the problem of school aggression. As noted earlier, most of the interventions that have been reported claim some degree of success in coping with the problem, even though the solutions or environments may be very different in concept and/or application. A few examples that have appeared in the recent literature aimed at public school personnel are sufficient to underscore this point.

Many of the solutions focus on security measures or changes in the physical structure of the school. Rascon (1981) would use security officers to reduce aggressive actions. Harris (1981) suggests that the installation of a computer system to monitor fire, burglary, and vandalism would not only reduce crime, but energy costs as well. Falk and Coletti (1982) report on reduced vandalism by the addition of low-pressure sodium lighting. Smith (1982) presents a number of strategies for stronger school security including restricted access to keys, an after-hours alarm system, and full prosecution of vandals. Lewis (1982) cites silent alarm systems, visits to the school at odd hours by the principal, quick repair of broken equipment, and other suggestions as ways of reducing vandalism. Mancuso (1983) presents a similar list of steps that can be taken by schools.

A number of behavioral approaches have been described and recommended as ways of curbing school-based aggression. DeJames (1981), McCormack (1981), White and Fallis (1981), and Bullock (1983) all describe various programs that focus on the use of rewards or such behavior change strategies as response cost and time-out. Some of these programs are aimed at elementary as well as the usual secondary school students.

In contrast, other writers have explicity emphasized various alternatives to "behaviorist" or "behavioral" interventions. Van Avery (1975) describes a "humanitarian" approach, while Medick (1982) espouses love and understanding, and Ohanian (1983) stresses teaching style and competence as the essentials for handling disruptive students. For Huey (1983), aggression in the adolescent can be reduced through group assertiveness training.

It is not the purpose here to attempt a review of all of the various approaches that have been applied toward the reduction of school violence and vandalism. The examples that have been presented in this section, however, are sufficient to illustrate that such interventions that have occurred have come from a number of sources, but generally have focused on one specific facet of the school aggression problem. Which of these proposed solutions is the appropriate one? How does a teacher, school, district, or community decide? The answers to these questions require consideration of the environment or solution in conjunction with such factors as the type of aggressive behavior, the nature of the disruptive individual, and a host of other factors. In sum, school violence and vandalism are likely not going to be dispelled with simple nostrums and will require more complex considerations, if they are to be better understood.

AGGRESSION IN SCHOOL: MULTIPLE PERSPECTIVES

A corollary to the view that school aggression is a complex phenomenon is that the understanding and explanation of this phenomenon requires, in turn, the study and unravelling of a complex set of variables. This multidimensional perspective requires the involvement of several disciplines; various theories; interventions at different levels; goals of the interventions; the ideologies and values of teachers, administrators, communities, and researchers; alternative solutions; and other similar variables. The many facets of school violence require an understanding of both its many antecedents and consequences.

A violent or disruptive incident may be thought of as the concluding event of a possible chain of events that led to it. But there are several alternative hypothetical explanatory chains that may be linked together for any specific act. In Figure 7.1, four such causal chains are proposed, each suggesting not only a different attribution for the violent act, but each also indicating different targets or levels of intervention within each chain. The problem can be conceptualized at an even more complex level when each of the four depicted chains is thought of as part of some larger system of linkages. What follows is an attempt at bringing together three different, but overlapping, conceptual approaches for grasping the problem of aggressive school behavior. Each of these depictions is an attempt at a proposed solution to school violence or vandalism by providing a matrix through which the different dimensions of the problem are brought into focus; in sum, where the behavior, person, and environment can be looked at simultaneously.

In Table 7.2, the major dimensions are conceptualized in terms of the level at which the intervention or solution is implemented and the goal of the intervention. The meaning of

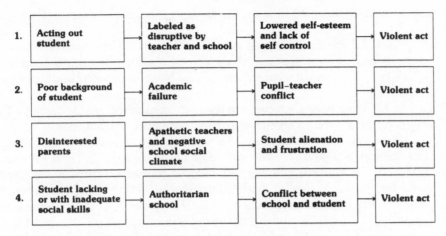

Figure 7.1. Examples of Possible Chains of Causation Resulting in a Violent Act.

the level of student, teacher, school, or community is straightforward. Level simply refers to the target of the intervention to reduce or control aggression. The target may be directed specifically at the disruptive student; it may provide the teacher with new skills or knowledge; it may require changes in the school curriculum; or it may involve the community in the way it supports education. What may not be clear from Table 7.2 is the idea that any effort at one level is only a partial solution; a problem approach at several levels is more likely to yield positive results.

The goal of the intervention in Table 7.2 needs some additional explanation. Various actions taken against aggression are initiated to prevent or discourage hostile acts directed against persons or school property. Such measures as 24-hour custodial service and better lighting are designed to prevent aggression. The use of Plexiglas windows may not prevent aggressive acts, but it will certainly compensate against the incidence of broken windows. Compensatory interventions do not in themselves change aggressive or disruptive students, but they do offset the consequences of their actions. Remedial interventions, on the other hand, are aimed at changing students, not simply providing them with ways of circumventing their aggressive acts. In Table 7.2, this remediation is exemplified as prescriptively tailored courses, which at the student level may be implemented by specific applications of behavior

Table 7.2. A Multilevel, Multigoal Solution Approach to School Violence

Level of Intervention	Goal of Intervention		
	Prevention	Compensatory	Remediation
Community	Adopt-a-School	Less restrictive child labor laws	Family support services Short-term treatment centers
School	24-Hour custodial service	Use of Plexiglas windows	Prescriptively tailored courses
Teacher	Programs to enhance knowledge of ethnic and minority milieu	Lower teacher/pupil ratio	Acquisition of new training techniques in psychological skills, e.g., structured learning
Student	Identification cards	School transfer Part-time programs	Interpersonal training Behavior modification

modification or courses designed to teach the students the basic interpersonal skills they lack.

The key in Table 7.2 and the tables that follow is not a specific intervention at a specific level, but rather seeing or looking at the whole table as a systematic or total approach to school aggression. The proposed solution can then be better understood both in its intent and consequences.

In Table 7.3, the dimensions characterizing levels of intervention are the same as Table 7.2. What is different are the categories describing the horizontal variables or modes of intervention. These intervention modes may be psychological, educational, administrative, legal, and/or physical. It should be noted that some of the solutions in Table 7.2 also are listed in Table 7.3. For example, prescriptively tailored courses are listed at the juncture of School and Educational in Table 7.3, while interpersonal skills training can be found at the intersection of Psychological and Student. Table 7.3 provides another systematic basis for conceptualizing the solutions to the problems of school aggression. Actually, the classification categories in Tables 7.2 and 7.3 can be combined. The consequences of such a combination are depicted in Figure 7.2.

The three-dimensional classification of intervention strategies for school violence and vandalism, at first glance, might suggest an overly complex response to the problem. But as previously reviewed approaches have reported, any one strategy in isolation often results in confusing, if not contradictory, findings. Figure 7.2 makes it possible to determine where a suggested approach falls and how it may influence or be influenced by adjacent solutions. By providing a larger, more comprehensive view, Figure 7.2 also helps reveal gaps and overloads in the system. For example, Zwier and Vaughan (1984) report that almost one half of the literature on school vandalism focuses on the physical dimension of the school— better lighting, design of buildings, and so on. In sum, most current efforts focus largely on prevention or "vandal-proofing" the school environment.

What Figure 7.2 suggests is that while school violence can be depicted in terms of the linear chains that were presented in Figure 7.1, the strategies or approaches for the resolution of the problem need to be conceptualized more in terms of a mosaic that represents the total ecology of school aggression. The categories and classification depicted in Figure 7.2 serve as a heuristic for understanding the nature of this mosaic. As research and experience accumulate to clarify the various cells, school violence will likely begin to shed some of its murkiness. One additional facet needs to be considered, and it is presented in Table 7.4.

Table 7.4 is somewhat different in that neither of its dimensions is exactly like any of the ones in the previous two tables. What is noteworthy about Table 7.4 is the inclusion of ideological orientation, which Zwier and Vaughan (1984) view as an essential dimension. They stress that, "we must remember that the identification of the cause of a social problem is tantamount to the discovery of its solution" (p. 270).

The assumptions underlying the conservative, liberal, and radical ideologies, as defined by Zwier and Vaughan (1984), reflect the issues discussed earlier in this chapter about the relationship between the school and aggressive behavior. The particular solution most congruent with a specific ideology should also be noted. In sum, what Table 7.4 indicates is that individuals with a conservative orientation are likely to favor or propose measures such as better lighting, alarm systems, and so on; those with a liberal orientation would first change the school curriculum; and radicals would focus primarily on changes in the society or community in which the school exists.

The linkage between ideology and the various attempts at solving problems of school aggression can be seen by viewing the various cells depicted in Figure 7.2 and determining which of these cells are assigned priority by individuals espousing the different ideological

Table 7.3. A Multidimensional Intervention Strategy For School Violence

Level of Intervention	Mode of Intervention				
	Psychological	Educational	Administrative	Legal	Physical
Community	Programs for disturbed children	Prosocial TV programs	Adopt-a-School programs	Gun control legislation	Near school, mobile home vandalism watch
School	Use of skilled conflict negotiators	Prescriptively tailored course sequences	Reduction of class size	Legal-rights handbook	Lighting, painting, paving programs
Teacher	Aggression management training	Enhanced knowledge of student ethnic milieu	Low teacher–pupil ratio	Compensation for aggression related expenses	Personal alarm systems
Student	Interpersonal skills training	Moral education	School transfer	Use of security personnel	Student murals, graffiti boards

Note. From Goldstein, personal communication, 1984.

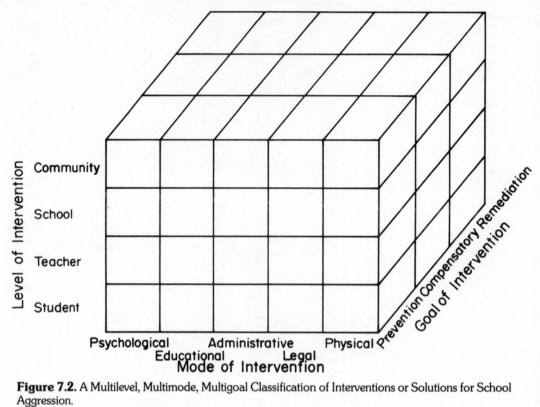

Figure 7.2. A Multilevel, Multimode, Multigoal Classification of Interventions or Solutions for School Aggression.

orientations. For a particular solution or intervention to be feasible, the values it elicits must to some extent overlap with the values of those who are asked to accept and participate in its implementation. In all probability, the greater the degree of congruence of values between the proposed course of action and the actors, the more likely the espoused goals will be successfully attained.

In sum, this section has attempted to conceptualize the various approaches to counter school aggression in terms of four dimensions—goals, levels, modes, and ideological orientations. These four dimensions are dynamic, interact with one another, and need to be understood better to unravel many of the murky complexities surrounding school violence and vandalism.

IMPLICATIONS FOR RESEARCH AND PRACTICE

One problem is very straightforward for research on aggression. The ideological orientations of the participants in the research effort become an important variable in any conclusions. The choice of methodology will in itself mirror ideological considerations and priorities. Moreover, the cells or sections of Figure 7.2 that gain attention will also reflect the ideological lens through which the problem is viewed.

The multidimensional framework this chapter has described will accommodate a number of research paradigms. Reliable knowledge about school aggression will accumulate through no one dominant strategy, but will necessitate a wide range of traditional and innovative

Table 7.4. The Relationship Between Ideological Orientation, Assumption Concerning the Cause of School Vandalism, and Type of Solution Offered

Ideological Orientation and Assumption of Cause	Type of Solution		
	Specific Physical Environment	School System	Diffuse Community at Large
Conservative Vandals are deviant. They must be caught and punished.	Protection of school and school grounds, employment of security officers and caretakers[a]	Encouragement and enforcement of school rules, use of contingency contracts	Involvement of community in anti-vandalism patrols and (parent) restitution programs, dependence on judicial system
Liberal The school system is malfunctioning. Vandals capitalize on this.	(Superficial) improvement of the design, appearance, and layout of the school grounds	Modifications in school climate, curriculum, and use of special conflict management programs[a]	Extension of recreational activities, use of school after hours for health and social services
Radical The school system is debilitating. Vandalism is a response of normal individuals to abnormal conditions.	Promotion of radical changes in the structure and appearance of the school, approval of policy to decrease the size of large schools, and maintain small schools	Provision of student involvement in decision-making process, adoption of changes in assessment procedures, and exploration of alternative schooling methods	Involvement of the whole community in school affairs, installment of community education programs, improvement of social situation in society at large[a]

Note. From "Three Ideological Orientations in School Vandalism," by G. Zwier and G.M. Vaughan, 1984, *Review of Educational Research, 54*, p. 269. Copyright 1984 by American Education Research Association, 1230 17th St. NW, Washington, DC, 20036.
[a]The solution considered most favorably by the particular ideological orientation.

procedures. Goldstein and Keller (1983) have suggested that these procedures need eventually to result in complex prescriptive strategies for the prevention and control of aggression and will require research designs or interventions that will simultaneously involve multiple levels, processes, accessibility channels, and disciplines.

Zwier and Vaughan (1984) believe that the study of aggression in school is too dynamic to be studied by traditional means. Knowledge about it can be obtained over time only by conditional hypotheses and action research in which the investigator is actively involved in the implementation of change. Oja (1984) recently has presented some evidence supporting the more direct participation of the researcher as a collaborator in the investigative process. A panoply of other research paradigms and tools can be brought to bear upon the complex issues of violence and vandalism. Case studies, ethnography, and even tools like multivariate statistical analysis all will have their appropriate uses. It should be clear here that what is proposed is an enhancement of research paradigms rather than the abandonment of traditional statistical analysis.

This chapter has attempted to present a view of school aggression that will yield a clearer picture of the problem than previous, isolated, hit-and-run studies. Whether the picture is an accurate one that will persist under the light of examination, only time will reveal. What is likely is that the picture will change as school violence and vandalism change. Aggression is a multidimensional school problem and changes in any one dimension will affect the ecology of the other dimensions. But as long as researchers insist on maintaining the "myth of general effects" (Hunt, 1975), the babel will persist. That there is no one correct research paradigm for the problems confronting schools is exemplified by the growing number of quantitatively oriented methodologists who have espoused alternative approaches: anthropology (Campbell, 1974), humanistic aspects (Glass, 1975), and clinical inquiry (Berliner, 1980). Cronbach (1975) has aptly expressed the reasoning behind such thinking:

> The special task of the social scientist in each generation is to pin down the contemporary facts. Beyond that, he shares with the humanistic scholar and the artist in the effort to gain insight into contemporary relationships, and to realign the culture's view of man with present realities. To know man as he is is no mean aspiration. (p. 126)

In their discussion of difficulties encountered in the implementation of a program in a natural setting like a school, Reppucci and Saunders (1974) have identified the "problem of two populations" (p. 654). Their first population refers to the training agents who will put the program into practice, while the second population refers to the recipients of the training. Both theory and practice have generally focused on the second population and have neglected the importance of the first. According to Hunt (1976), this neglect occurs because our models for research designs come from the natural sciences, which emphasize manipulation and control of the independent variable. As presented in previous sections, the issues encompassing school violence and vandalism require that the "problem of two populations" be expanded and redefined in terms of multiple populations—students, teachers, schools, communities, and the larger society. Implicit in this redefinition is the idea that research and practice will more likely yield successful results if the appropriate multiple populations are considered and involved from the start. Polyani (1958) expresses what the problem has been in these words:

> We cannot comprehend a whole without seeing its parts, but we can see the parts without comprehending the whole . . . . By looking very closely at several parts of a whole, we may succeed in diverting our attention from the whole and even lose sight of it altogether. (p. 29)

Sarason (1976) has stated a similar concern:

. . . how you approach and deal with the part is influenced mightily by where you see it in relationship to the whole, that is what you hope to do and the ways in which you go about it are consequences of how you think it is imbedded in the larger picture. (pp. 323–324)

The thesis of this chapter from the start has been the idea that many of the research findings and intervention attempts regarding school aggression have emphasized the "parts" at the expense of the "whole." If future such endeavors are to pay off, it would appear that paradigms that look at the "whole" might be more productive. The strategies laid out in this chapter suggest one such course of action. There are likely to be others. Irrespective of whichever method, strategy, or paradigm is chosen, the task will not be easy. Who said it would?

REFERENCES

Ban, J.R., & Ciminillo, L.M. (1977). *Violence and vandalism in public education.* Danville, IL: The Interstate Printers & Publishers, Inc.

Bayh, B. (1977). (Chairman) *Challenge for the third century: Education in a safe environment—Final report on the nature and prevention of school violence and vandalism.* Washington, DC: U.S. Government Printing Office.

Berliner, D. (1980). Studying instruction in the elementary classroom. In R. Dreeben & J.A. Thomas (Eds.), *The analysis of educational productivity; Volume I: Issues in microanalysis* (pp. 191–222). Cambridge, MA: Ballinger.

Brodinsky, M. (1981). *Reporting violence, vandalism and other incidents in schools.* Washington, DC: Office of Juvenile Justice and Delinquency Prevention.

Bullock, L. (1983). School violence and what teachers can do about it. *Contemporary Education, 55,* 40–44.

Campbell, D.T. (1974). *Qualitative knowing in action research.* Kurt Lewin Memorial Address to the American Psychological Association, New Orleans.

Cronbach, L.J. (1975). Beyond the two disciplines of scientific psychology. *American Psychologist, 30,* 116–127.

DeJames, P.L. (1981). Effective parent/teacher/child relationships. *Education, 102,* 34–36.

Duke, D.L. (1976). Challenge to bureaucracy: The contemporary alternative school. *Journal of Educational Thought, 10,* 34–38.

Duke, D.L. (1978). How administrators view the crisis in school discipline. *Phi Delta Kappan, 59,* 325–330.

Duke, D.L., & Jones, V.F. (1983). *Assessing recent efforts to reduce student behavior problems.* Paper presented at the meeting of the American Educational Research Association, Montreal, Canada.

Elliott, D.S., & Voss, H.L. (1974). *Delinquency and dropout.* Lexington, MA: Lexington Books.

Falk, N., & Coletti, R.F. (1982). Better vandalism protection at less cost. *American School and University, 54,* 52–54.

Feldhusen, J.F., Aversano, F.M., & Thurston, J.R. (1976). Prediction of youth contacts with law enforcement agencies. *Criminal Justice and Behavior, 3,* 235–253.

Feldhusen, J.F., Roeser, T.D., & Thurston, J.R. (1977). Prediction of social adjustment over a period of six or nine years. *Journal of Special Education, 11,* 29–36.

Feldhusen, J.F., Thurston, J.R., & Benning, J.J. (1973). A longitudinal study of delinquency and other aspects of children's behavior. *International Journal of Criminology and Penology, 1,* 341–351.

Foster, H.L. (1974). *Ribbin', jivin', and playin' the dozens.* Cambridge, MA: Ballinger Publishing Co.

Frease, D.E. (1973). Schools and delinquency: Some intervening processes. *Pacific Sociological Review, 16,* 426–448.

Freemont, T.S., & Wallbrown, F.H. (1979, Spring). Types of behavior problems that may be encountered in the classroom. *Journal of Education, 5*–24.

Glass, G.V. (1975). A paradox about excellence of schools and the people in them. *Educational Researcher, 4,* 9–13.

Gold M. (1978). Scholastic experiences, self-esteem, and delinquent behavior: A theory for alternative schools. *Crime and Delinquency, 24,* 290–294.

Goldstein, A.P., Apter, S.J., & Harootunian, B. (1984). *School violence.* Englewood Cliffs, NJ: Prentice-Hall.

Goldstein, A.P., & Keller, H.R. (1983). Aggression prevention and control: Multitargeted, multichannel, multiprocess, multidisciplinary. In. A.P. Goldstein (Ed.), *Prevention and control of aggression* (pp. 338–350). New York: Pergamon Press.

Goldstein, A.P., & Pentz, M.A. (1984). Psychological skill-training and' the aggressive adolescent. *School Psychology Review, 33,* 311–323.

Harootunian, B., & Apter, S.J. (1983). Violence in school. In A.P. Goldstein (Ed.), *Prevention and control of aggression* (pp. 66–83). New York: Pergamon Press.

Harris, J.W. (1981). Cramping your arsonist's style and cutting energy costs—All by computer. *Thrust for Educational Leadership, 11,* 18–19.

Huey, W.C. (1983). Reducing adolescent aggression through group assertiveness training. *School Counselor, 30,* 193–203.

Hunt, D.E. (1971). *Matching models in education.* Toronto: Ontario Institute for Studies in Education.

Hunt, D.E. (1975). Person-environment interaction: A challenge found wanting before it was tried. *Review of Educational Research, 45,* 209–230.

Hunt, D.E. (1976). Teachers are psychologists too: On the application of psychology to education. *Canadian Psychological Review, 17,* 210–218.

Hyman, I.A. (1979). Psychology, education and schooling: Social policy implications in the lives of children and youth. *American Psychologist, 34,* 1024–1029.

Jessor, R.J., & Jessor, S.L. (1977). *Problem behavior and psychological development.* New York: Academic Press.

Kelly, D.H. (1975). Status origins, track positions, and delinquent involvement. *Sociological Quarterly, 12,* 65–85.

Lefkowitz, M.M., Eron, L., Walder, L., & Heusmann, L. (1973). Environmental variables as predictors of aggressive behavior. *International Journal of Group Tensions, 3,* 30–47.

Lefkowitz, M., Eron, L., Walder, L., & Heusmann, L. (1977). *Growing up to be violent.* New York: Pergamon Press.

Lewis, B. (1982). Tips on school security. *School Administrator, 30,* 12.

Mancuso, W.A. (1983). Take these steps to keep schools safe and secure. *Executive Educator, 5,* 24–25, 27.

Marvin, M., McCann, R., Connolly J., Temkin, S., & Henning, P. (1977). *Current activities in school.* In J.M. McPartland & E.L. McDill (Eds.), *Violence in schools* (pp. 53–70). Lexington, MA: Lexington Books.

McCormack, S. (1981). To make discipline work, turn kids into self-managers. *Executive Educator, 3,* 26–27.

McDermott, M.S. (1979). *Criminal victimization in urban schools.* Albany, NY: Criminal Justice Research Center.

McPartland, J.M., & McDill, E.L. (Eds.). (1977). *Violence in schools: Perspectives, programs, and positions.* Lexington, MA: Lexington Books.

Medick, J. (1982). The loving teacher's guide to discipline. *Instructor, 92,* 66–68.

Mitzel, H.E. (Ed.). (1982). *Encyclopedia of educational research (5th ed.).* New York: The Free Press.

National Institute of Education. (1977). *Violent schools—safe schools: The Safe School Study Report to the Congress* (Vol. 1). Washington, DC: U.S. Government Printing Office.

Ohanian, S. (1983). There's only one true technique for good discipline. *Learning, 11,* 16–19.

Oja, S.N. (1984). *Studies of relationship of teacher conceptual level with collaborative action research.* Paper presented at American Educational Research Association, New Orleans.

Ossorio, P. (1973). Never smile at a crocodile. *Journal of Theory of Social Behaviour, 3,* 121–140.

Polk, K., & Schafer, W.E. (1972). *Schools and delinquency.* Englewood Cliffs, NJ: Prentice-Hall.

Polyani, M. (1958). *The study of man.* Chicago: The University of Chicago Press.

Rascon, A., Jr. (1981). Using security agents to enforce the law in your schools. *Thrust for Educational Leadership, 11,* 15–17.

Regents buckle on spanking. (1980, March 15). *New York Times,* p. 28.

Reppucci, N.D., & Saunders, J.T. (1974). Social psychology of behavior modification. *American Psychologist, 29,* 649–660.

Rubel, R.J. (1977). *Unruly school: Disorders, disruptions and crimes.* Lexington, MA: D.C. Heath.

Sarason, S.B. (1976). Community psychology networks, and Mr. Everyman. *American Psychologist, 31,* 317–324.

Smith, C. (1982). Use these strategies for stronger school security. *Executive Educator, 4,* 21–22.

Thaw R.F. (1980). Preventable property damage: Vandalism and beyond. In K. Baker & R.J. Rubel (Eds.), *School crime and violence: Theoretical perspectives* (pp. 66–83). Lexington, MA: D.C. Heath.

Van Avery, D. (1975). The humanitarian approach. *Phi Delta Kappan, 57,* 177–178.

Wenk, E.A. (1975, August). Juvenile justice and the public schools; mutual benefit through educational reform. *Juvenile Justice,* 7–14.

White, J., & Fallis, A. (1981). *Vandalism prevention programs: A case study approach.* Toronto, Canada: Ontario Government Bookstore.

Zwier G., & Vaughan, G.M. (1984). Three ideological orientations in school vandalism research. *Review of Educational Research, 54,* 263–292.

8

Ecological Perspectives on Youth Violence

Steven J. Apter
Cathy A. Propper

The problem of youth violence and crime is seemingly omnipresent; we are confronted with it in our newspapers, magazines, and television newscasts on a daily basis. Many of us are also confronted with it personally as it is increasingly the case that people have either been the victims or know the victims of violence perpetrated by youngsters. Recently, Surgeon General C. Everett Koop described violence by young people as an extensive and chronic epidemic in American society. Citing statistics that documented a dramatic rise in violent fatalities for 15- to 24-year-olds in three categories (homicides, suicides, and motor vehicle deaths), Koop called for a major effort to stop the escalating violence and prevent the destruction of so many young lives. Koop's speech is one of many recent examples of American concern about the problem of youth violence. Many social scientists, educators, government officials, and interested citizens have also written and spoken about one or another aspect of America's serious level of youth violence in recent years.

One of the most frequently discussed topics in this area has to do with youth crime. Bullock and Reilly (1979), for example, reviewed the professional literature on adjudicated adolescents and found that while only 16% of arrests made in the United States in 1947 involved persons under 21 years of age, arrests of persons 21 and younger comprised nearly 60% of all arrests made in 1976.

Additional examples include the following representative statistics:

1. Between 1960 and 1973, juvenile arrests increased 138%. Arrests of persons over 18 during that same time period increased 16 percent.
2. This increase was most dramatic in arrests for serious offenses; juvenile arrests for murder, rape, robbery, and aggravated assault increased 254% between 1960 and 1973.
3. In 1960, 2% of the nation's juvenile population appeared before a juvenile court. By 1975, that figure had doubled to 4%.
4. The popular press is typically filled with stories about violent teenagers. Recent examples include 1983 descriptions of adolescent murderers in the *New York Times* in which one 14 year-old-girl is said to have written in her diary that she and a friend had "lots of fun" killing an old woman.
5. Finally, it should be noted that juveniles are victims as well as perpetrators of violence. In 1978, for example, 5.1% of all deaths among youngsters from age 1 through 17

years were attributed to homicide, while only 1% of deaths of 18-year-olds and over were the result of murder.

6. In 1979 alone, homicides of youngsters under 18 accounted for 90,000 person years of lost life.
7. Between 1976 and 1979, 9% of homicide victims reported to the FBI were under 18 years old.

Youth violence finds broad expression not only in the streets, but also in America's schools. In a typical recent year there were 110,000 assaults on teachers, 9,000 rapes, $600 million in damage to school property from vandalism, 20 million thefts, and 400,000 acts of property destruction. From 1950 to 1975, the number of students in America's schools increased by 86%, while school arson grew by 859% (Goldstein, Apter, & Harootunian, 1984).

Our response to the problem of youth violence has been, on the whole, inadequate. Piecemeal strategies have been brought to bear on a problem that demands a much more comprehensive approach. Our resources in each of the many systems that bear some responsibility for youth violence have already been cut dramatically and may well continue to diminish in the coming years. Schools, police, family courts, and social services are each overwhelmed by the problem of violence in young people. The need for effective, comprehensive, and coordinated approaches to the problems of violent youth has never been greater. It seems clear that a holistic and ecological perspective is a required basis for understanding and ultimately stopping youth violence.

During the 1970s, as the incidence of juvenile crime escalated to new heights, the public's growing alarm encouraged a more systematic investigation of both the factors contributing to youth crime as well as the programs developed to affect violent youth (McCord & Sanchez, 1983). The findings of these investigations have resulted in a resurgence of interest in the social systems that encompass troubled youth (including families, schools, neighborhoods, the community, and the broader political arena). Youth who commit crimes and acts of aggression are inextricably bound to a particular social context within which these acts occur and the important role of context in youth violence is being increasingly recognized.

This interest in the social forces affecting youth in society today has spread to a more detailed analysis of the variables that seem to promote positive development in the individual and those variables that inhibit such growth. One variable that is receiving considerable attention involves the notion of social support. According to Cobb (1976), social support refers to ". . . information leading the subject to believe that he is cared for and loved, esteemed and valued, and a member of a network of communication and mutual obligation" (p. 300).

In this chapter, we will examine the role of social support in both the etiology of youth violence and in efforts to develop effective intervention programs with youngsters involved in violent activities. Social support may be profitably viewed as one element of the broader ecological or systems perspective on disordered behavior. In the next section, we provide an overview of this developing point of view that can also serve as the basis for our discussion of social support issues in the remainder of the chapter.

ECOLOGICAL PERSPECTIVE

The ecological orientation to human behavior is based on the notion that all actions are determined by the *interaction* of individual and environmental characteristics. Such a perspective acknowledges the continual presence of both supportive and restrictive forces in all systems and views the role of intervention as helping to maintain harmony or balance between the individual and the environment.

Instead of focusing only on individuals then, ecologists are more interested in examining ecosystems: interaction systems comprised of living things and the nonliving environment. In order to do this, ecologists engage in naturalistic research in an attempt to understand human behavior in its natural setting. Ecologists typically do not consider disordered behavior to be a physical disease located solely within a child, but prefer to look at a disturbed ecosystem, in which disturbance can more profitably be viewed as a "failure to match."

The ecological orientation is based on the assumption that each child must be viewed as a complete entity surrounded by a unique "mini" social system or ecosystem. When the various aspects of a child's system are working together harmoniously, ecologists say that the ecosystem is congruent or balanced, and the child's behaviors appear to be "normal." On the other hand, when such congruence does not exist, the child is likely to be considered deviant (out of harmony with social norms) or incompetent (unable to perform purposefully in the unchanged setting). When this is the case, ecologists say that the system is not balanced; that particular elements are in conflict with one another. Such conflicts are termed "points of discordance" for example, specific places where there is a "failure to match" between the child and his/her ecosystem. According to ecologists, the search for solutions to the problem of inappropriate behavior must focus on these points of discordance and the resulting failure to match. When systems function harmoniously, a state of balance exists, and the stage is set for positive behavior, competent functioning, and increasing psychological growth and development.

The words *ecological orientation* carry a number of meanings, depending upon the perspective and viewpoint of the persons involved. In its most general sense, ecology can be defined as the biologist saw it, "the study of living things in their natural habitat." More relevant to our concern in this chapter, the ecological viewpoint stresses the need to go beyond narrow visions of behavior and development and to find ways to focus on the *interactions* of children and youth with critical aspects of their environments. We must increase our knowledge of the actual conditions in which children live, according to the ecologists, before we can use what we learn from such experiences as the basis for our intervention programs. Without such comprehensive knowledge, it could not be reasonable to expect our efforts to have an impact on children within the context of their systems.

It may be helpful to review some of the major assumptions made by persons who develop intervention programs based upon ecological principles.

1. Each child is an inseparable part of a small social system. Just as every child is considered to be unique, so is every ecosystem. When there is too much discordance for the ecosystem to function harmoniously, the system is considered to be troubled (although the youngster will probably be identified as the disturbed party). Efforts to help "troubled children" then should be addressed to the problem of "troubled systems," with the goal of making the system work in the interests of the child.
2. Disturbance is not viewed as a disease located within the body of the child, but rather as discordance (a lack of balance) in the system.
3. Discordance may be defined as a disparity between an individual's abilities and the demands or expectations of the environment— "failure to match" between child and system.
4. The goal of any intervention is to make the system work; and to make it work, ultimately, without the intervention.

5. Improvement in any part of the system can benefit the entire system.
6. This broader view of disturbance gives rise to three major areas for intervention:
   (a) Changing the child.
   (b) Changing the environment.
   (c) Changing attitudes and expectations.

At those times when the ecological system is disrupted (points of discordance), intervention is called for. The ecological viewpoint allows a variety of interventions, but demands that all interventions be examined with regard to potential effects on the entire ecosystem. Interventions must strive to be as comprehensive, coordinated, and functional as possible. Such a perspective raises a number of important implications, some of which are listed here:

1. Disordered behavior must be viewed, at least in part, as culturally relative. Behavior that is "normal" in one environment may be viewed as deviant in a different behavior setting.
2. Interventions must focus on all elements of given ecosystems—not only on the identified child.
3. Interventions must focus on the realities existent in a given ecosystem. While it is obviously difficult to change the environmental conditions that surround many of the youngsters involved in violent activities, ignoring those conditions is not likely to reduce the level of youth violence.
4. Especially in schools where the focus for so long has been on changing the child to fit the system, this perspective advocates considerable change in program planning. For example, the following is a list of interventions that might be developed in response to a troubled system. Clearly, targeting intervention on the identified child is just one of many strategies.
   (a) Work with the child.
   - Build new competencies.
   - Change priorities.
   - Obtain necessary resources.
   - Find more appropriate environments.
   (b) Work with the adults.
   - Alter perceptions.
   - Raise or lower expectations.
   - Increase understanding or knowledge.
   - Restructure activities.
   (c) Work with the community
   - Bring more resources in to school.
   - Allow more entry into community.
   - Develop coordinating ties.
   (d) Develop new roles
   - Resource teacher.
   - Diagnostic-prescriptive teacher.
   - "Linking" person.
   (e) Develop new program models
   - Community education/schools.
   - Outdoor education.
   - Alternative public schools.

- Focus on prevention.
  - —Teach "mental health."
  - —Preventive mainstreaming.

5. Finally, one major implication of an ecological orientation is that we must give up our search for a magical answer to the problems presented by violent children and youth. Instead, we must learn to think in terms of troubled systems and increase our understanding of the reciprocal person–environment interaction patterns. The rationale for thinking ecologically about the problem of youth violence may be seen in the following points:

   (a) On the whole, we must realize that traditional children's mental health, educational, and judicial programs have not been successful in reducing the problem of youth violence. The ecological orientation proposes that this failure may be due to the narrowness of previous efforts.

   (b) A systems viewpoint seems to be essential in examining the problem of adolescent aggression. Even in the case of severely troubled youngsters, it seems clear from a reading of the current literature that the targeted child is seldom, if *ever*, *the whole problem*.

   (c) Everyone has needs and we must pay attention to them. The ecological orientation stresses the importance of looking at the entire system surrounding each child. Our own experiences and the documentation of efforts by many others indicates the importance of understanding and responding to the needs and concerns of significant others (parents, teachers, friends, etc.) in each child's environment. Focusing all our attention on the child while ignoring the family, school, and community that surround him/her is not likely to be an effective strategy.

   (d) Building strong ecosystems should be the ultimate goal of intervention with troubled children. Linkages between various aspects of each child's world are seen as critical elements (not "fringe extras" to be considered if time allows) in the development of successful programs. Increasingly, research (Lewis, 1982) indicates that the single most important determinant of success for troubled adolescents is the quality of linkages between the intervention program and community supports.

   (e) Ecological interventions can use numerous resources ignored by other approaches. Children live and learn within the context of their own environments. Parents, siblings, neighborhood peer groups, church, school, and playground are all potential elements of a particular child's world and each may play an important role in intervention planning.

   (f) Ecological interventions can have a broad positive impact benefitting others as well as the "target" child. The implications of an ecological perspective for the *prevention* of youth violence are enormous.

ECOLOGICAL PERSPECTIVE AND YOUTH VIOLENCE

As shown in the preceding paragraphs, it is not always possible to understand youth violence by focusing on individual youngsters. The ecological view emphasizes the importance of *interactions*; which individuals at what particular points in time in which physical and psychological environments are prone to violence? Consequently, the ecological perspective can also emphasize a variety of targets for intervention that is setting-focused as well as individual-focused.

There is some evidence for this interactionist point of view. Chess, Thomas, Rutter, and Birch (1963), for example, have studied the interaction of youngsters' temperament and environment in the production of behavioral disturbances. They concluded that temperament alone could not account for behavioral disturbances.

> Rather, it appears that behavioral disturbance as well as behavioral normality is the result of the interaction between the child with a given patterning of temperament and significant features of his developmental environment. Among these environmental features, intrafamilial as well as extra-familial circumstances such as school and peer-group, are influential. (p. 147)

Parke (1979), in a discussion of emerging themes in the study of social-emotional development, agrees with the interactionist view and with the conclusions reached by Chess et al. (1963). Parke (1979) points out that social-emotional development must be seen as having multiple causes and multiple sources of influence.

> The child is embedded in a variety of social systems and settings in which various agents shape the child's social-emotional development. These range from smaller immediate settings and systems such as the family or peer group, in which the child has considerable influence, to larger or more remote systems such as the school, the community, or the wider culture, over which the child has less control. (pp. 930–931)

The interaction (or lack thereof) between home and school may be an especially significant factor in youth violence. For example, Walberg (1972) has noted that "a general propensity to be a delinquent and to be apprehended is negatively associated with: frequency of school talks with parents, frequency of family outings, and the amount of scheduled study time" (p. 295).

Finally, we could not conclude this introduction without some discussion of the relationship between youth violence and broader societal conditions. McPartland and McDill (1977) have noted that there "appears to be a significant negative association between the health of the economy or the availability of jobs and the level of youth crime. . ." (pp. 7–8).

There is then, from the ecological view, some connection between youth violence and the contexts or systems that surround such behavior. The important question for those who wish to understand and ultimately intervene in the chain of events that lead to violent activity in young people may be: "What are the mediating structures through which environments have an impact on individuals?"

We know that intervention programs based in any of the major human service systems (education, mental health, juvenile justice, social welfare) have frequently failed to incorporate ecological factors into their planning and program development efforts. While, Apter (1977, 1982), Hobbs (1966, 1975, 1982), Rhodes (1976, 1970), Swap (1974, 1978), and others have pointed to the need for comprehensive ecological approaches to the problems of troubled children, service delivery agencies have frequently persisted in their efforts to apply simplistic solutions to complex problems.

We also know that attempts to intervene with behavior disordered adolescents can often be accurately viewed as a case of "too little, too late." In fact, the intractability of adolescent problems causes many mental health and education personnel to wonder why more wasn't done for these youngsters before they reached this point. Many special education teachers, for example, feel that by the time troubled adolescents reach junior high school, their skills and motivation to succeed are both so low that it is nearly impossible to find ways to reverse this long-standing pattern. Unfortunately, school itself may exacerbate this problem. Morse (1978) has reminded us that for all too many youngsters, feelings of adequacy and competence *decrease* directly with time in school. The same pattern may hold true for youngsters involved with juvenile justice and social service systems.

One emerging area of research interest that seems to show great potential for application to the problem of youth violence centers around the concept of psychosocial support. As we shall see in the next section, support in a variety of forms seems to be a critical factor in the determination of individual behavior patterns. With reference to youth who commit or are at high risk for committing violent acts, there seem to be two critical questions:

1. What exactly constitutes support?
2. How does one gain access to appropriate sources of support?

The remainder of this chapter will investigate the concept of psychosocial support as it applies to the problem that concerns us in this volume: the reduction and prevention of youth violence. The ecological perspective, based as it is on the inseparable interaction of person and environment, seems to be a most appropriate vehicle for analysis of this complex and critical area.

YOUTH VIOLENCE AND PSYCHOSOCIAL SUPPORT

People have a variety of specific needs that demand satisfaction through enduring interpersonal relationships, such as for love and affection, for intimacy that provides the freedom to express feelings easily and unself-consciously, for validation of personal identity and worth, for satisfaction of nurturance and dependency, for help with tasks, and for support in handling emotion and controlling impulses. Most people develop and maintain a sense of well-being by involving themselves in a range of relationships in their lives that in total satisfy these specific needs, such as: marriage, parenthood, other forms of loving and intimate ties, friendships, relationships with colleagues at work, membership in religious congregations and in social, cultural, political and recreational associations, and acquaintanceships with neighbors, shopkeepers, and providers of services; intermittent relationships of help-seeking from professional caregivers such as doctors, nurses, lawyers and social workers; and continuing dependence for education and guidance on teachers, clergymen, intellectuals, and community leaders, and men of authority and influence. (Caplan, 1974, p. 5)

The above quotation from Caplan's book on *Support Systems and Community Mental Health* describes the importance of interpersonal relationships to each of our lives. Caplan goes on to detail how such relationships can become the center of support systems that serve to enable individuals to live their lives productively in spite of the stress involved in daily functioning. The concept of *support system*, according to Caplan (1974), "implies an enduring pattern of continuous or intermittent ties, that play a significant part in maintaining the psychological and physical integrity of the individual over time" (p. 7). Further, support systems are characterized by three essential elements: help in mobilizing psychological resources and dealing with stress, sharing of tasks, and the provision of material and psychological resources.

Support systems can both guide individuals to appropriate decisions and actions and also provide safety and comfort at times of particularly intense stress. And yet, Caplan notes that support systems may be least readily available or accessible to those who may need them most; persons who for a variety of reasons need assistance to uncover or utilize individual strengths and abilities to respond to environmental stresses, but for whom neither natural (family, friends) nor formal (helping services) support systems or networks seem available.

Hawkins and Fraser (1983) have summarized the results of research on the etiology of delinquency as they relate to the issue of social support. They noted that the evidence indicated that young people who are not attached or "bonded" to their families, schools, and communities are more likely to associate with delinquent peers, and are more likely to engage in delinquent behavior. Thus, efforts at delinquency prevention, according to Hawkins and Fraser, must focus on the development of individual–societal attachments and on the replacement of negative social networks with positive ones. Such bonding occurs when families, schools, and communities provide youngsters with opportunities for meaningful involvement, with the skills necessary to fulfill their responsibilities, and with rewards for work well done.

When these attachments don't form, Hawkins and Fraser (1983) note that the resulting increase in youth crime is due at least in part to society's failure to provide youngsters with the involvements, skills, and rewards necessary for strong social bonding. Instead of preventing youth crime through strong social bonding, society then must try to intervene by providing direct services to juvenile offenders. The fact that such services are often ineffective is, according to Hawkins and Fraser (1983), not hard to understand:

> If the families, schools, and communities in which juvenile offenders have been socialized have not bonded these youngsters in a manner capable of preventing their delinquent behavior, it is unlikely that they will have the capacity to control subsequent delinquency unless these social units themselves are altered. (p. 335)

Instead, these authors suggest that indirect service approaches, the provision of assistance to those significant others (family members, friends, teachers) who can strengthen the social support of "at risk" youth may be more effective. Toward that end, Hawkins and Fraser have described a social support centered approach to the prevention and reduction of juvenile crime. Three strategies are emphasized: the provision of social supports to families, the development of supportive relationships for identified youngsters, and the strengthening of home–school linkages.

Gottlieb (1983) has discussed more generally the role of social support in the prevention of disordered behavior. Gottlieb points out that the Community Mental Health movement of the 1960s and 1970s was a response to the following "discoveries" of that time:

1. The realization that most people seek help for emotional problems within the context of their own systems of family and friends and "informal" helpers.
2. The implication of stressful life events in the onset of physical and psychological disorder.
3. The notion that social support could serve to moderate the effects of psychosocial stressors.

The Community Mental Health movement was initiated then, at least in part, as a way to shift the locus of intervention from artificial and formal settings (i.e., mental hospitals) to the natural environment (local communities and neighborhoods). A developing body of ecological research documented the relationships between community conditions and psychological disturbance and, as Gottlieb (1983) says, ". . . converged on a common theme, namely the importance of access to informal social support . . ." (p. 279). Today, the emphasis on developing interventions in the natural environment is even stronger and many such efforts focus on a variety of formats for mobilizing support systems that are available to a range of clients.

Barth (1983) notes that while adolescents and their families seem to be increasingly in need of helping services, such services, for a variety of reasons, may be unavailable or ineffective. The recent increased emphasis on social support networks therefore may provide a much needed and better matched core of services to troubled adolescents and their families.

Barth cites the wealth of research that documents both how families use social supports to buffer stress and also that families isolated from such supports seem vulnerable to medical and psychological difficulty. The support that families may gain from social networks can in turn be passed on to troubled adolescent family members. As Barth says, ". . . social supports inoculate families emotionally and materially against stress and give them the strength needed to help their young people during transitional crisis" (p. 301).

Sandler (1980) conducted a study that bears on the family support issue raised by Barth. Sandler investigated the effects of three social support elements (older sibling vs. no older sibling, one-parent vs. two-parent families, and ethnic congruence vs. noncongruence in the community) on the relationship between stress and maladjustment in young school children. Sandler's results indicated that the presence of older siblings and two parents in the family each reduced the negative effects of stress on his young subjects. The effectiveness of two-parent families in moderating stress seemed to be particularly evident when specific aversive events were taking place. Sandler suggested that further research in this area would, it is hoped, produce a more comprehensive picture of youngsters' social support systems and of the particular aspects of those systems that are most helpful in moderating the effects of stressful situations.

Monahan and Klassen (1982) have done a comprehensive review of recent environmental analyses of violent behavior and have identified what they consider to be the most likely (at this stage of research) environmental correlates of violent activity. Three of these elements, the family environment, the peer group, and the work environment, have been grouped together by Monahan and Klassen and identified as both the source of life stress and the repository of support systems to deal with those stressors.

In the family environment, factors such as number of children, financial resources, residential mobility, crowding, and the presence or absence of supportive others seem to have an impact on violent behavior. Overall, Monahan and Klassen note that the quality of relationships within a family represents both stresses and supports and may be directly related to the likelihood of violent behavior. Thus, persons concerned with developing interventions for violent youth would do well to initiate a comprehensive assessment of the identified youngster's current living situation.

Peers can be both models for violent behavior as well as valued sources of social support for nonviolent lifestyles. They can also be victims of youth violence. Research does not yet provide definitive answers to the question of under what conditions peers play this variety of roles. By examining factors such as the number, quality, and duration of peer relationships; the structure and content of peer group activities; and the effects of disruption of peer relationships, it should be possible to gain a further understanding of the ways in which peers can become even a stronger source of social support for potentially violent youth.

Stress associated with unemployment or difficult work situations can also provide an impetus to violent behavior. This is particularly relevant to the problem of youth violence because adolescents, particularly those who represent minority groups, are frequently cited as the most-likely-to-be-unemployed group in the country. Factors such as frequency of job changes, duration of unemployment, dissatisfaction with work and/or colleagues, and perceived adequacy of pay may all be related to the potential for violent behavior. On the other hand, a factor such as steady job holding may be critical in the provision of sufficient social support to prevent violent behavior.

While there are additional situational factors such as the availability of victims, weapons, and alcohol, it seems clear that families, peers, and work (or for those youngsters still involved, school) represent three critical sources of both life stress and social support to cope with stress in nonviolent ways. Monahan and Klassen (1982) suggest that further research into situational determinates of violent behavior might profitably focus on four issues: the definition of "situation," the size of environmental units, perceived or actual situations, and the ways in which individuals and situations interact.

With regard to this last factor, the ways in which individuals and situations interact, Mitchell (1982) has examined the differences in social networks between psychiatric clients and members of clients' families. Building on research that indicated the likelihood that ". . . psychiatric patients have social networks characterized by fewer linkages overall, fewer intimate relationships, greater asymmetrical relationships, and lower scores on indices of perceived support" (p. 388), Mitchell set out to examine the process by which social networks are influenced by both individual and environmental characteristics.

Mitchell found that size of network is both influenced by and, in turn, influences the interpersonal problem-solving style of the individual. In other words, clients may need to improve their interpersonal skills in order to take better advantage of the opportunities for social support available in their own environments. This is an important finding for violent youth, as it suggests that such youngsters may need to learn more appropriate interpersonal skills in order to utilize the supports that may be available to them.

Cobb (1976), in his discussion of social support as a moderator of life stress, has cited voluminous documentation of the finding that social support is protective of individuals facing physical and/or psychological distress. The question that remains, according to Cobb, is what are the mechanisms through which this sort of protection occurs? Cobb suggests "coping" (which he defines as "manipulation of the environment in the service of self") and "adaptation" ("change in the self to improve person–environment fit") as two likely pathways through which social support makes its impact felt (pp. 311–312). Cobb wondered if it wouldn't be possible to teach all patients how to both give and receive social support.

In a related study, Cauce, Felner, and Primavera (1982) examined the structure of social support and its relationship to the adjustment of adolescents characterized by low-income, high-stress, inner-city backgrounds. Their analysis revealed three major structures for the provision of support: families, formal supports (including counselors, teachers, and clergy), and informal supports (including friends and other adults).

Cauce et al. (1982) were also interested in examining the *perceived helpfulness* of each source of support as related to specific adolescent characteristics. Their findings revealed some interesting age, sex, and ethnic background differences including the following:

1. Blacks viewed family members as significantly more helpful than did whites or hispanics.
2. Older adolescents viewed formal supports more highly than did younger adolescents.
3. Females viewed informal supports more highly in terms of helpfulness than did males.

Cauce et al. point to these findings and others as evidence for their belief that social support can be divided into clearly identifiable elements and that the perceived helpfulness of one or another element will vary with individual adolescent characteristics. They point out, for example, that certain subgroups of their population (black males, for example) rate particular support structures (formal supports in this case) at a level of perceived helpfulness that might surprise professionals. One implication of such a finding is that black males might be responsive to formal programs of social support developed, for example, by school personnel.

Cauce et al. (1982) also point out the sometimes negative relation between social support and adolescent adjustment. For example, in this study, adolescents with higher levels of informal (peer) support showed *poorer* academic adjustment (but higher ratings on peer self-concept). While these sometimes seemingly contradictory findings may be understandable according to the authors, they argue "that vague and global conceptualizations of support systems both structurally and emotionally, may be, at best, not very informative and at worst, lead to poorly designed and damaging interventions" (p. 426). Instead, Cauce et al. note, we need better investigations of the relationships between perceived helpfulness and actual degree of use of available supports. And of course, with regard to our focus in this chapter, we need similar investigations with already violent youth.

While we do not have much in the way of research in this area as yet, there are two examples that can be cited here. Bry (1982) developed a comprehensive prevention–intervention program that included teachers, parents, and other professionals that was successful in reducing delinquency problems over a 5-year time period. In an effort to build a pervasive, cohesive, supportive environment, it became clear to Bry and her colleagues that all concerned adults had to be involved. A program built on formal weekly progress reports and group meetings developed into the desired environment and yielded very positive effects.

> These environmental and family factors were of greater relevance to an antisocial outcome than the nature of the psychiatric symptomatology or diagnosis . . . . .
>
> Comprehensive treatment programs must therefore give attention not only to the children's psychiatric problems, but to their family and social environment . . . .
>
> How are youth services today meeting these needs? We have developed a multiplicity of community alternatives for the relatively nonviolent emotionally disturbed child . . . . With few exceptions, this cannot be said for the disturbed and violent child. (p. 452)

The remainder of this chapter will examine the operations of a variety of efforts to provide social supports to youngsters involved in violent activities.

Social support may be delivered through formal helping institutions (e.g., psychiatric hospitals and community-based services) or through informal means (e.g., families and peer groups). In the absence of informal support systems, a phenomenon that may be increasingly prevalent, the burden of responsibility lies with the formal agencies that have been established to provide both direct and indirect care.

The primary objective of the following discussion is to present and analyze findings relating to the effectiveness of various helping organizations, beginning with more formal program structures, including psychiatric and juvenile detention facilities, working through formal alternatives to residential treatment, and concluding with an examination of more informal support systems. Our focus throughout will be on the isolation and discussion of those variables that emerge consistently in reports of program effectiveness. At the same time, attention needs to be directed toward the interpretation and understanding of those factors that have inhibited the attainment of program goals. The importance of a social-ecological approach to violent and aggressive youth, that is, the need to address the individual's difficulties from a system's perspective, will become readily apparent.

FORMAL SUPPORT SERVICES

Psychiatric Settings

A group of 66 boys and girls, ages 12 through 15, were among the admissions to the children's unit of Creedmoor State Hospital[1] in 1960 (cf. Faretra, 1981). Their histories included one or more of the following: serious assult including homicide; sexual attack; attacks or threats with deadly weapons; dangerous fire-settings; and serious suicidal attempts or threats. In all cases, the acts either resulted in serious injury or had great destructive potential.

The length of the hospitalization ranged from under 1 month to 55 months, with an average stay of about 6 months. Although regular, extended-care visits either at the unit or in a special community-based clinic were made available to all patients following discharge, few appeared.

The results of an extensive effort to follow these former patients through a 15-year period revealed continuing patterns of antisocial behavior, accompanied by frequent psychiatric problems, for a majority of individuals. In brief, 20% followed a course of constant mental hygiene contacts, whether in the community or in residential services; 36% had periodic and persistent contacts with courts and correctional facilities; and 33% were involved intermittently with both psychiatric and correctional agencies. For most of these individuals, subsequent psychiatric contacts occurred early in the follow-up period, while later contacts became almost exclusively court and correctional.

What factors may have contributed to the perceived failure of this psychiatric treatment program? Faretra (1981) reports that those children engaging in the most extensive and ongoing antisocial behavior shared certain characteristics. The original symptoms leading to their initial hospital admission appeared to have behavioral roots, rather than a purely psychiatric origin. Therefore, psychiatric treatment may have provided few benefits for these children. Unfortunately, many professionals continue to expound on the link between violence and mental health, although recent evidence suggests the absence of a relationship (Cocozza, Hartstone, & Braff, 1981). In addition, their family backgrounds were replete with knowledge of antisocial tendencies and one-parent homes in deprived and disadvantaged areas to which the majority returned after discharge. It is likely that these environmental and family variables restricted the overall effectiveness of this program, serving as evidence against those programs that are limited in scope and in the types of support services provided.

The potential impact of the community on the continued success of various treatments has largely been ignored. It is assumed that troubled youths can singularly overcome the negative social forces of their deviant peers, dysfunctional families, and repeated experiences of school failure upon their reintegration into community settings. Yet the literature is replete with accounts of the behavioral deterioration that occurs when an individual is faced with the same social and economic alternatives that existed prior to admission into a treatment program (cf. Coates, Miller, & Ohlin, 1978). Increasingly apparent, then, is the

---

[1] A research unit established in 1956 in New York City by the State Department of Mental Hygiene. Children came primarily from Queens and Brooklyn. In 1970, it merged into Queens Children's Psychiatric Center.

need to examine the social contexts in which youth live and to incorporate, rather than exclude, family members into the treatment process.

Reform Schools

McCord and Sanchez (1983) conducted a 25-year follow-up study on the effects of two different treatment orientations on the subsequent social adjustment of comparable groups of boys. The Wiltwyck School of New York and the Lyman School of Massachusetts are the settings under investigation.

The Wiltwyck School endorses milieu therapy. It has provided "psychiatric treatment, psychological counseling, and social work services in a residential setting to severely disturbed boys who have been referred by the New York courts. . ." (p. 239). The school operated according to the philosophy of "disciplined love," and encouraged children to assume responsibility for their actions in this setting characterized as "safe" and "nonpunitive."

The program at the Lyman School, the first reform school in America, had a more punitive orientation. Physical punishment of the children was not only tolerated, but encouraged. The Lyman officials saw no need for psychological treatments or the enhancement of interpersonal skills.

The results of this follow-up comparative study are somewhat confusing. In terms of commitments for serious offenses, Wiltwyck graduates had a significantly lower recidivism rate than did Lyman graduates during the first 5 years after their release. The recidivism rate of Lyman graduates was originally quite high, but declined as they grew older. The rates of criminal activity among Wiltwyck graduates, however, increased steadily with age. Moreover, the more deprived ethnic groups in each population had a higher rate of recidivism at each age level. In addition, neither Wiltwyck nor Lyman had an appreciable effect upon the adult rates of emotional disturbance or alcoholism among their graduates.

While Wiltwyck may boast of its positive impact on the younger age groups, and Lyman may account for some successful outcomes for older age groups, neither program can be considered especially beneficial. One massive shortcoming, characteristic of both programs, is the lack of adequate reintegration of these individuals into the mainstream. In most instances, these individuals returned to the community without an established network of social support and having to singularly overcome their dysfunctional family systems. Provisions were not made for regular outpatient visits to a community agency.

Another serious limitation entails the lack of contact with or involvement of families. Many of the children referred to the Wiltwyck and Lyman schools emerged from families disrupted by divorce or parental desertion. Their parents, particularly the fathers, often had ongoing records of deviant behavior. One immediately recognizes the futility of narrow child-focused-only rehabilitative efforts with children of parents who are encouraging socially deviant behavior.

Community Programs

In his article on the Southwest Denver Community Mental Health program, Polak (1978) discusses the advantages of a system of treatment that places primary emphasis on intervening directly in social systems disturbances in the real-life setting of the client. Psychiatric hospitalizations are prevented through the use of regular home visits from qualified professionals and social systems intervention. The Denver program has a backup system of small, community-based social settings (private homes) used for situations where brief separation from the real-life setting is deemed appropriate. While this mental health program initially was designed for troubled adults, its therapeutic components can be viewed easily in terms of their potential application to disturbed youth.

Before the initial home-based interview takes place, several phone contacts are made with key members of the social system to determine who should participate in the first meeting. Thus, from the beginning, an individual's problems are considered to be the shared responsibility of important persons in the individual's life, not just the individual. The therapeutic approach emphasizes whole systems and the need to reestablish a healthy equilibrium by intervening at a systems level.

In a study comparing the effectiveness of the Southwest Denver home-based treatment program with more traditional psychiatric hospital treatment, the clients who participated in the Denver program reportedly had more successful treatment outcomes, expressed greater satisfaction with their treatment, and attained more goals than their psychiatric hospital counterparts. These findings were consistent with those reported during a follow-up investigation 4 to 5 months later. Clearly, clients serviced in the community mental health program fared better than those receiving psychiatric services.

The model of service delivery proposed by the Southwest Denver Community Mental Health Center emphasizes a comprehensive approach to an individual's presenting problem. All aspects of an individual's life are explored, as the disturbance is viewed as an interaction between the individual and one or more social systems. Intervention is aimed at the juncture(s) in the system where the disturbance appears to have developed.

In contrast to the Denver program, psychiatric treatment models generally focus on the individual as the sole owner of the disturbance as well as the sole agent of change. There are few attempts to elicit the participation of key members of the individual's family or work environments and therapy is conducted within the isolated, sterile hospital setting.

Another alternative to mental hospital treatment, described by Stein and Test (1978), is the Training in Community Living Program (TCL). This program is predicated on the belief that healthy adjustment in the community depends on the following factors:

1. Access to material resources, e.g., food, clothing, medical care.
2. Development of coping skills to meet the demands of community life.
3. Motivation to persevere and remain involved with life.
4. Freedom from pathological dependent relationships, and
5. A supportive system that actively helps the individual with the above-mentioned needs.

The treatment prescribed by the Training in Community Living Program necessarily requires the patient to participate in a full schedule of daily living activities. Where such assistance is needed, staff members visit patients in their homes and neighborhoods, offering training in daily living skills, such as shopping, cooking, budgeting, and so on. In addition, efforts are made to locate jobs or sheltered workshop placements with continual contact between staff and the patient and employer to ensure optimal adjustment to the job situation. Furthermore, patients are encouraged to participate in social and recreational activities with or without staff support and to develop effective and appropriate social skills.

The staff calls on family members for their support and understanding. Where dysfunctional families exist, contact between the patient and his or her family is discouraged until the family equilibrium is restored either naturally or through clinical intervention. Commitments from community members, for example, apartment landlords, to aid in the development of the individual's independent, community living skills, are secured in order to facilitate successful adjustment to the demands of community life.

Although the TCL program was designed as an alternative to hospitalization, and every effort was made to minimize its use, the hospital setting provided benefits to some patients for short periods of time. Patients were hospitalized only when they expressed homicidal or suicidal feelings or required medication for severe psychotic episodes. Following discharge, they were officially admitted into the TCL program.

An important role assumed by staff in the Training for Community Living Program involves that of linking the troubled individuals with appropriate community mental health agencies as well as employment and housing opportunities. Staff continue their contact with the participating community supports as well as their supervision of the client. They ultimately facilitate the creation of a satisfying network of social support systems, enabling the individual client to feel as if he or she belongs "somewhere" in society and that he or she can contribute to society in a meaningful and valuable way.

What relevance do community mental health programs such as those illustrated here have for having a specific impact upon violent and aggressive youth? One widely promulgated assumption about violent, behaviorally deviant children is that in addition to exhibiting socially maladaptive behavior, these children suffer from some form of mental illness (Cocozza et al., 1981). Psychiatric hospitalization, therefore, has become the primary mode of treatment. Cocozza and colleagues demonstrated that few children who are referred on the basis of their behavior also have accompanying symptoms of a psychiatric origin. They conclude that while the placement of violent juveniles in psychiatric settings may be an appropriate and effective intervention for a small number of youths, the majority of juveniles may not benefit from the services provided in a psychiatric milieu because they are not clinically disturbed. The key issue here may be that youngsters who display violent behavior in the community may profit more from intervention programs based in the community than from institutionalization.

The alternative, then, to hospitalization appears to rest with programs structured to provide a comprehensive service delivery package. Children engaging in violent behavior often are responding to negative home or school environments and the absence of support. Staff from the community agencies illustrated earlier would investigate the small systems that surround the child and extend treatment to all key persons in these systems who may be having a detrimental effect on the child's development. Disturbance is not viewed as belonging to the child, but as an interaction between child and setting characteristics in situations where the violent behavior occurs. Moreover, community mental health agencies are prepared to offer support and supportive services to families of behaviorally disturbed children as well as aid in the establishment of a network of solid, social support.

INFORMAL SUPPORT SYSTEMS

The relationship between violent youth and their concomitant isolation or detachment from peers and family has been well-documented (Hirschi, 1969; Weis et al., 1981). The aggressive adolescent spontaneously severs those ties within the community that may have offered refuge and support, and becomes the responsibility of an often unsympathetic legal system. Society's response to juvenile offenders typically has been to provide direct services through the efforts of social workers, juvenile probation and parole officers, and so on. Evident, too, however, has been the relative ineffectiveness of these service providers in combatting and preventing youth violence. The failure of our more formal support structures to eliminate or reduce youth crime does not negate the value of their programs. Instead, it confirms our beliefs that: (a) treatment goals need to extend beyond the individual in distress into the family, school, and community-at-large, and (b) formal service delivery systems cannot supplant permanently those informal support systems necessary for one's daily survival and general well-being. Given the difficulty that exists in our delivery of direct services and their inherent limitations, it is time to consider the potential role of more informal types of support.

Families

Berleman (1980) has pointed out that troubled youngsters often display a lack of commitment to or "bonding" with family members. These youngsters exclude themselves from that network of support, that is, the family, which is vital to the development of social skills and moral values. It is difficult to determine the exact cause of a youngster's detachment from family members, but often it is related to economic and social factors that are impinging upon the family's ability to function in a supportive and productive fashion.

It has been argued that families require social support very much as individuals do and, in fact, families who have direct access to various support resources, for example, close neighbors and friends, are better prepared to offer support to individual family members (see Barth, 1983). The types of support that may be exchanged mutually between families include child-rearing suggestions, babysitting services, serving as positive role models for parents and children alike, and offering material and emotional aid, all of which are directed toward reducing the intolerable stress that can beset families for indefinite periods of time. An extreme example of the manner in which families demonstrate this notion of support is the raising of funds for families who are plagued by devastating fires or chronic illnesses. The reduction of financial burdens may then allow victimized families to direct their emotional energies to rebuilding their homes or caring for their ill.

Parents

Gulotta and Adams (1982) present an overview of the historical and theoretical factors associated with adolescent substance abuse and programs aimed at prevention. Of particular interest is their description of an organization known as "Parent Power" (Prevention Resources, 1979), a group of ordinary citizens in a Georgia town who banded together to combat drug use in their community. The program, established by Parent Power, uses group support to improve parenting skills, for instance, facilitating effective communication with children; distributes knowledge and information about various drug effects; and strives to develop a common set of guidelines that present a "unified parental front." Groups such as Parent Power are struggling to understand the myriad of forces motivating children to behave in socially undesirable ways and to overcome their fear of these negative forces as well as feelings of failure as parents. Certainly, this form of parent support could be elicited in any neighborhood of any city and could address the issues of youth violence and aggression. Yet how do we encourage parents to become involved in a group of this nature?

The neighborhood is a somewhat neglected, but nevertheless powerful socializing force. Families in particular neighborhoods have a specific array of needs, dependent not only on individual characteristics, but based on the enduring social context as well. The neighborhood is a familiar place with familiar faces, thus serving as a comfortable setting or "safety zone." It is proposed that our neighborhoods become the forum through which the issues of aggressive youth are discussed. Neighborhoods that have succeeded in attaining control over incidents of aggression can then join forces with other neighborhoods battling similar problems.

Families in jeopardy are often too hesitant or too fearful to acknowledge their difficulties privately, let alone in any public forum. Great care needs to be taken to respect the need for privacy while simultaneously offering support and assistance. The notion of neighborhood groups as opposed to school- or community-based groups is advocated here because its size and structure intuitively promote a sense of cohesiveness, homogeneity, and trust.

Neighborhood parent groups can settle upon a specific course of action. The participants may perceive a need to provide greater opportunities for recreation and positive social interaction. Certain group members may be willing to offer employment opportunities or to serve as recreation supervisors (Barth, 1983). Other members may consider respite care services, for example, inviting the troubled youth to accompany them on a weekend camping trip or to stay overnight. The group also may strive to become more informed about services provided by agencies, both direct and indirect, or better acquainted with the legal ramifications of problematic behavior. Regardless, the most rewarding consequence of any group structure is the emotional support that inevitably is exchanged among its members.

Peers–School

A second form of naturally occuring self-help organizations involves peer mobilization. "Project Pride" in Florida relies on a peer delivery system. Selected young people undergo an intensive 9-week training program designed to foster "communication skills, active listening, empathy, honesty, and confrontation." These youth are then prepared to offer empathy and support to other young people experiencing personal difficulties (Resnick, 1978; Wall, Hawskins, Lishner, & Fraser, 1980). The Teen Involvement Program, located in the schools of Fort Jackson, South Carolina, also concentrates on training youths to help other youngsters in crisis (NIAAA, 1980).

Peer groups clearly present an important source of support for young people. Unlike adults, peers are rarely accused of "not understanding" the problem or "not caring" about the individual in distress. Delinquent behavior, however, has been associated with pressures exerted by peer groups (Eisenthal & Udin, 1972); hence, care needs to be taken to encourage only those peer interactions that are socially-appropriate.

Cross-age tutoring programs are easily implemented in schools and nicely serve to enhance the tutor's self-esteem, self-confidence, and purposeful activity in the school setting. Those children identified as "troublemakers" by teachers, administrators, and other students may, indeed, demonstrate skill in an academic or nonacademic area that another student lacks. Not only will the privilege of displaying one's talents provide the troubled student with a sense of pride or success, but it will lead the student to believe that he or she is a valued member of the school community.

A "buddy" system, much like Big Brother, Big Sister programs, could be established in schools nationwide. Cross-aged or same-aged students could be paired during the early weeks of school in the hopes of creating a permanent and satisfying friendship. A variety of activities could be introduced in the school building to stimulate the "buddy" system partnerships, including athletic events, fund-raising endeavors, academic pursuits, and so on. Although all students would benefit from this type of intervention, troubled youngsters who may have great difficulty forming peer relationships are blessed with companionship and opportunities for positive social interaction.

Peer groups including older youngsters who have been adjudicated and have successfully undergone treatment may provide valuable role models for other children following similar routes. High-risk youngsters and those already involved in minor delinquent acts can learn about the consequences of criminal involvement from the personal experiences described by "reformed" delinquents. A peer contact and support system could be established whereby youngsters trying to resist the temptation to engage in delinquent behavior telephone a sponsor, that is, someone who can identify with the youngster, but who also can offer more positive behavioral alternatives as well as praise and encourage the youngster for inhibiting the delinquent response.

Hawkins and Fraser (1983) review a number of school-based peer support programs aimed at preventing delinquency. Their findings reinforce the importance of programs such as Positive Peer Culture (Malcolm & Young, 1978) and peer culture development (Boehm & Larson, 1978) in reducing the incidence of delinquent behavior. Central to the success of these programs has been the integration of both troubled youngsters and youngsters exhibiting positive social and academic development into one group striving toward similar goals. Moreover, group members consist of those youths identified as "born leaders" by their teachers and peers, that is, influential representatives of a particular clique or organized group in the school setting. These recruited "leaders" discuss problems and issues relevant to the school, community, or a single individual and generate possible solutions under the supervision of an adult facilitator. The rationale guiding the recruitment of peer leaders involves the hope that these leaders will learn to advocate only socially appropriate behaviors and similarly influence their followers. Further, in becoming a member of a peer culture group, each member necessarily assumes responsibility for his or her actions as well as the actions of the clique with whom he or she affiliates. Thus, greater pressure to conform may be exerted by the leader on his or her particular peer group.

The potential of "informal helping networks" in preventing or eradicating delinquent behavior has not been well-studied. Preliminary results indicate, however, that social support positively affects parent and adolescent relationships (Burke & Weir, 1978) and mediates the stress encountered in daily living (Albee, 1980). Parents are better able to provide emotional support to children, and children develop a greater commitment to the family unit and the values adopted by family members.

The peer group represents another important avenue through which social support is exchanged. While suggestions for stimulating positive peer interactions are included in this chapter, they symbolize only a fraction of the myriad of possible interventions. Groups such as Positive Peer Culture (Malcom & Young, 1978) report significant decreases in adolescents' self-reports of delinquent behavior, but more information is needed to substantiate these findings.

It is not our intent to advocate that informal helping systems be created in isolation from the more formal services presently offered. Rather, we emphasize the need to coordinate professional support and the support of those individuals involved in troubled youngsters' lives such that treatment effects can be maintained once the youngsters return to their homes and communities. However, the potential of the informal support network, in and of itself, in preventing youth violence and delinquency, should become a primary focus of research.

REFERENCES

Albee, G.W. (1980). Primary prevention and social problems. In G. Gerbner, C.J. Ross, & E. Zigler (Eds.), *Child Abuse: An agenda for action* (pp. 106–107). New York: Oxford University Press.

Apter, S.J. (1977). Applications of ecological theory: Towards a community special education model for troubled children. *Exceptional Children, 43*, 366–373.

Apter, S. (1982). *Troubled children/troubled systems*. New York: Pergamon Press.

Barth, R. (1983). Social support networks for adolescents and their families. In J. Whittaker & J.

Garbarino (Eds.), *Social support networks: Informal helping in the human services* (pp. 299–331). New York: Aldine Publishing Company.

Berleman, W. (1980). *Juvenile delinquency prevention experiments: A review and analysis*. National Institute for Juvenile Justice and Delinquency Prevention, Office of Juvenile Justice and Delinquency Prevention, Law Enforcement Assistance Administration, U.S. Department of Justice, Washington, DC: U.S. Government Printing Office.

Boehm, R.G., & Larsen, R.D. (1978). *An evaluation of peer group counseling in Berrien County, Michigan*. Berrien County, MI: Berrien County Probate and Juvenile Court Services.

Bry, B.H. (1982). Reducing the incidence of adolescent problems through preventive intervention: One and five-year follow-up. *American Journal of Community Psychology, 10*, 265–275.

Bullock, L.M., & Reilly, T.F. (1979). In R. Rutherford & A. Prieto (Eds.), *Severe behavior disorders of children and youth* (pp. 79–104). Reston, VA: Council for Exceptional Children.

Burke, R.J., & Weir, T. (1978). Benefits to adolescents of informal helping relationships with their parents and peers. *Psychological Reports, 42*, 1175–1184.

Caplan, G. (1974). *Support systems and community mental health*. New York: Behavioral Publications.

Cauce, I.M., Felner, R.D., & Primavera, J. (1982). Social support in high-risk adolescents: Structural components and adaptive impact. *American Journal of Community Psychology, 10*, 417–427.

Chess, S., Thomas, A., Rutter, M., & Birch, H. (1963). Interaction of temperament and environment in the production of behavioral disturbances in children. *American Journal of Psychiatry, 120*, 142–147.

Coates, R.B., Miller, A.D., & Ohlin, L.E. (1978). Diversity in youth correctional system: Handling delinquents in Massachusetts. Cambridge, MA: Ballinger.

Cobb, S. (1976). Social support as a moderator of life stress. *Psychosomatic Medicine, 38*, 300–312.

Cocozza, J., Hartstone, E., & Braff, J. (1981). Mental health treatment of violent juveniles: An assessment of need. *Crime and Delinquency, 27*, 487–496.

Eisenthal, S., & Udin, H. (1972). Psychological factors associated with drug and alcohol usage among neighborhood youth corps enrollees. *Developmental Psychology, 1*, 119–123.

Faretra, G. (1981). A profile of aggression from adolescence to adulthood: An 18-year follow-up of psychiatrically disturbed and violent adolescents. *American Journal of Orthopsychiatry, 51*, 439–453.

Goldstein, A.P., Apter, S.J., & Harootunian, B. (1984). *School violence*. Englewood Cliffs, NJ: Prentice-Hall.

Gottlieb, B.H. (1983). Social support as a focus for integrative research in psychology. *American Psychologist, 38*, 278–287.

Gulotta, T., & Adams, G. (1982). Substance abuse minimization: Conceptualizing prevention in adolescent and youth programs. *Journal of Youth and Adolescence, 11*, 409–423.

Hawkins, J.D., & Fraser, M.W. (1983). Social support networks in delinquency prevention and treatment. In J.K. Whittaker, J. Garbarino, & Associates (Eds.), *Social support networks: Informal helping in the human services* (pp. 333–352). New York: Aldine Publishing Co.

Hirschi, T. (1969). *Courses of delinquency*. Berkeley, CA: University of California Press.

Hobbs, N. (1966). Helping disturbed children: Psychological and ecological strategies. *American Psychologist, 21*, 1105–1115.

Hobbs, N. (1975). *The futures of children*. San Francisco: Jossey-Bass.

Hobbs, N. (1982). *The troubled and troubling child*. San Francisco: Jossey-Bass.

Lewis, W.W. (1982). Ecological factors in successful residential treatment. *Behavioral Disorders, 7* (3), 149–156.

Malcolm, P., & Young, I. (1978). *Evaluation: Positive peer culture, instructional research report #1977-3*. Omaha, NE: Omaha Public Schools.

McCord, W., & Sanchez, J. (1983). The treatment of deviant children: A twenty-five year follow-up study. *Crime and Delinquency, 29*, 238–253.

McPartland, J.M., & McDill, E.L. (1977). *Violence in schools: Perspectives, programs and positions*. Lexington, MA: Lexington Books.

Mitchell, R. (1982). Social networks and psychiatric clients: The personal and environmental context. *American Journal of Community Psychology, 10*, 387–401.

Monahan, J., & Klassen, D. (1982). Situational approaches to understanding and predicting individual violent behavior. In M.E. Wolfgang & N.A. Weiner (Eds.), *Criminal violence* (pp. 292–319). Beverly Hill, CA: Sage.

Morse, W.C. (1978). Children and youth with socio-emotional impairments: Implications for prevention in the public schools. In S.J. Apter (Ed.), *Focus on prevention: The education of children labeled emotionally disturbed* (pp. 19–44). Syracuse, NY: Publication in Education.

National Institute of Alcohol Abuse and Alcoholism (NIAAA). (1980). Children of military prevention focus. *Information and Feature Service, 5*.

Parke, R.D. (1979). Emerging themes of social-emotional development. *American Psychologist, 34*, 930–931.

Polak, P.R. (1978). A comprehensive system of alternatives to psychiatric hospitalization. In L.I. Stein & M.A. Test (Eds.), *Alternatives to mental hospital treatment* (pp. 115–137). New York: Plenum.

Prevention Resources. (1979). *Celebrating parent power in Georgia* (DHEW Publication No. ADM 79–827). Washington, DC: U.S. Superintendent of Documents.

Resnick, H.S. (1978). *It starts with people: Experiences in drug abuse prevention* (DHEW Publication No. 78–590). Washington, DC: U.S. Superintendent of Documents.

Rhodes, W.C. (1970). A community participation analysis of emotional disturbance. *Exceptional Children, 37*, 309–314.

Rhodes, W.C. (1976). The disturbing child: A problem of ecological management. *Exceptional Children, 33*, 449–455.

Sandler, I.N. (1980). Social support resources, stress, and maladjustment of poor children. *American Journal of Community Psychology, 8* (1), 41–51.

Stein, L.I., & Test, M.A. (1978). An alternative to mental hospital treatment. In L.I. Stein & M.A. Test (Eds.), *Alternatives to mental hospital treatment* (pp. 43–55). New York: Plenum Press.

Swap, S.M. (1974). Disturbing classroom behaviors: A developmental and ecological view. *Exceptional Children, 41*, 163–172.

Swap, S.M. (1978). The ecological model of emotional disturbances in children: A status report and proposed synthesis. *Behavioral Disorders, 3*(3), 186–196.

Walberg, H.J. (1972). Urban Schooling and delinquency: Toward an integrative theory. *American Educational Research Journal, 9*, 285–300.

Wall, J., Hawskins, J., Lishner, D., & Fraser (1980). *Juvenile delinquency prevention: A compendium of thirty-six program models*. Seattle, WA: National Center for the Assessment of Delinquent Behavior and Its Prevention.

Weis, J., Hall, J., Henney, J., Selderstrom, J., Worsley, K., & Zeiss, C. (1981). *Peer influence and delinquency: An evaluation of theory and practice, Parts I and II*. National Institute for Juvenile Justice and Delinquency Prevention, Law Enforcement Assistance Administration, U.S. Department of Justice. Washington, DC: U.S. Government Printing Office.

9

Social Competence, Coping Skills, and Youth Crime: A Pragmatic and Theory-Based Approach*

Richard J. Gable

Youth violence is a phenomenon that has intrigued social scientists, frightened citizens, and resulted in relatively constant movement in government policy since the turn of the century. In recent times, the quantity and, perhaps more important, the quality of violent acts by youth have become a major focus of the media and the public at large. This concern is indeed warranted!

In a recent monograph, Snyder (1984) indicated that the number of arrests of youth for violent crimes had increased 160% between 1964 and 1982. While this increase is, in fact, less than the adult increase during the same period, it is still of major significance. There is little question that the past 2 decades have seen a steady growth in arrests of juveniles for violent crimes which has been largely unimpeded by new program and policy initiatives.

Perhaps the most puzzling aspect of youth violence is the finding by a number of investigators (Farrington, 1981; Wolfgang, 1977) that, with scarce exceptions, there are very few youth who "specialize" in violent activities. This finding is often explained by the extremely high rate of generalized delinquent activity attributed to this group of violent offenders. Violent acts by youth appear to be almost randomly interspersed among other nonviolent crimes. Farrington has described this phenomenon as "a small amount of specificity superimposed on a large amount of generality" (p. 26). The task of understanding and successfully intervening in youth violence may, therefore, be best pursued through a more general understanding of the causes and maintenance of delinquency and antisocial behavior. Of particular importance in this pursuit is the determination of remediable behaviors that can stand the test of theoretical significance and can be modified by clinical or official court intervention.

With this as a primary objective, the current chapter explores the concepts of coping and social competence. This relatively new and largely unexplored approach to the understanding of delinquency causation has the potential for both theoretical rigor and honest "down-to-earth" application. It is our intent to lay the historical and theoretical foundations that suggest a fertile area of investigation and to present preliminary findings from a recently completed survey that may serve to propel subsequent study.

*Research presented in this chapter was supported by a grant from the William T. Grant Foundation, New York City.

It should be noted that early social competence work conducted by the author and colleagues at the National Center for Juvenile Justice became known in the practitioner community as the "What Went Right" project. It is with that optimism for the future that this chapter is presented.

SOCIAL COMPETENCE AND DELINQUENCY—EMPIRICAL SUPPORT

The etiology of delinquent behavior in children has been of primary concern to social science researchers for over 40 years. From the earliest writings of Aichorn in 1935 to more current investigations (Gove, 1975), the specific antecedents of delinquency have shown themselves to be elusive and without considerable generalizability. What has emerged over nearly 4 decades of investigation in this area is a "patchwork quilt" of factors loosely joined to provide a preliminary, if not satisfyingly complete, picture of the life and times of a predelinquent youngster. Further, research has suggested that those indices that are related to the onset of antisocial behavior may be quite different from those that are associated with its maintenance over time (Robins, 1974). Perhaps the only point upon which all investigators might agree is that both etiology and maintenance of the behavior is multideterminant, with little specificity of cause and effect.

Within the past few years, increasing attention has focused on the requisite skills that a child should acquire in order to perform adequately in his or her environment. Interest has developed in many areas and is motivated by mounting evidence gleaned from both empirical investigation and clinical perception. The major thrust of this line of inquiry is in the direction of determining if, in fact, antisocial (or, for that matter, a wide range of disturbed) children manifest a deficit in their skill levels that puts them at a severe disadvantage for healthy development. Such disadvantage has been clearly linked with emergent and continuing delinquency. While much of the research has been consistent with this generalized notion, the specific areas of study have come from a widely divergent array and are not well synthesized. Various researchers examining delinquency causation have differentially emphasized the importance of skills associated with school performance (Frease, 1973; Offord, 1978), peer relations (Gesten et al., 1979; Hartup, 1979), adult relations (Rutter, 1979; Shure & Spivack, 1979), family interactions (Jacob, 1975), and nonacademic achievement (Kelly & Baer, 1971), to name but a few. Still others have underscored the importance of conceptual skill areas such as problem solving (Sigel, 1979), adaptability (Murphy & Moriarity, 1976), and self-maintained responsibility (Kohlberg, 1974). Finally, much excitement has been generated by findings that document specific skill deficits in a population of disturbed children (i.e., learning disability [Berstein & Rulo, 1976], reading retardation [Rutter & Yule, 1973; Sturge, 1972], lack of social comprehension [Bandura, 1976], etc.). It is quite clear that each of the factors cited has some role in the successful transition from infancy to adulthood. Such revelations are neither surprising nor novel. The point remains, however, that, to date, a theoretical/empirical structure has not been devised that can accurately assess and make use of information from such a wide variety of factors.

Social competence, a term coined by Robert White 2 decades ago (1959), has recently been resurrected in an attempt to provide a theoretical umbrella under which most of the factors mentioned above can find refuge (White, 1978). The term, however, has become a theoretical construct, with ambiguities no more certain than those encountered when attempting to understand the term "personality." Social competence, as it is currently used, can be taken to mean that set of skills *and* attributes of a child which are required for successful interaction with the environment. The components that make up the general construct of social competence are not well difined. Particularly, those areas that are not associated with school achievement (and therefore have fewer reliable numeric indices) have not been adequately addressed. Three noteworthy examples include the paucity of measures for areas such as nonschool achievement, peer relations, and adult-child interactions.

While social competence provides a point around which particular measures of skills and attributes can rally, much work is needed in understanding and defining the importance and interrelationship of the wide range of factors associated with the child's development of the preferred social adaptation. The motivation for understanding the development of social competence in children has resulted from more than the necessity to provide a theoretical framework for the melding of individual skill areas. Clinical observation and decades of research have left their mark. Antisocial youngsters have been identified as at least one group for whom socially adaptive behaviors are in short supply. The value of social competence as a unifying construct in understanding these deficits provides a much needed link between observation and theory. Its central role in the thesis of this chapter requires a careful examination of its tenets and historical development.

A Brief Historical Perspective: Social Competence

Robert White's paper (1959), describing his newly formulated notions regarding the motivational aspect of competency and effectance, signaled a new area of research and theory. Prior to that work, most of human psychology was dominated by behavioral and psychoanalytic schools which shared a belief in intrinsic drives as the primary source of human motivation. The aegis of the drives differed between groups, with the behaviorists identifying hunger as the predominant drive and the psychoanalysts emphasizing the importance of a erotic instinctual drive.

White observed that there were many human behaviors that were inadequately explained by the predominant drive theories of the time. Included were children's common exploratory behaviors and their apparent intrinsic pleasure at mastering new problems. He was further influenced by the writings of Jean Piaget who described the joy a 3-month-old could derive from self-initiated play with crib toys. White surmised that these behaviors must be motivated by yet another drive, one which had mastery as its primary objective.

In his early writings, White described this motivation as an "urge toward competence" (White, 1959). Since that time, he has expanded the concept and has vacillated in his terminology. In a later paper (White, 1960), he began using the phrase "effectance motivation," the intrinsic desire to have an *effect* on one's surroundings and to be *effective* in dealing with the environment. This descriptor has stood as the primary phrase of White's work until recently, when competence, once again, has been primarily associated with his writings.

Whether effectance motivation or urge toward competence, the phenomenon White described in 1959 was not novel in psychology. Ironically, however, it was much less associated with human psychology than it was with the experimental psychologists who were attempting to define the parameters of laboratory animal behavior. Animal psychologists had begun in the 1950s to speak of an exploratory drive, even a drive to activity. Some investigators had used similar notions to describe human activities, including Mittelman (1954) who had postulated a motility urge and Bettelheim (1960) who had emphasized self-initiated activity which he named autonomy. As White said in a reminiscent paper in 1979:

Was this a new idea? Looking for footprints in the sand, I found they were plentiful! . . . I was talking about something that was hardly more than common sense, something that everybody knew about; everybody, that is, except the behaviorists and strict Freudians who at that time dominated psychological theory. (p. 23)

In part because the notion of effectance motivation was relatively simple, little attention was paid to it by empirical psychology during the period 1960 through 1974. Although the concept had obvious heuristic value for the study of the developing child, White's idea had little explanatory value due to the very breadth of behaviors he subsumed under its rubric. In fact, the terms effectance motivation and competence motivation had become so muddled in the past 2 decades that there was, in the psychological literature, almost no convergence of opinion as to their meaning. Competence had come to mean being successful at almost anything, while effectance motivation had fallen out of common usage altogether. In short, the motivational aspects of White's original paper had given way to a rather inglorious explanation for any investigator's finding that one group of children were superior to another on any psychometric or observational measure of behavior. While developmental psychologists, like Anna Freud in London and Louis Murphy in the United States, continued to examine the coping mechanisms of youngsters in their struggle through normal development, little attempt was made to operationalize White's effectance motivation construct and, therefore, make it subject to empirical scrutiny.

Vulnerability Research

In the mid-1960s, a new area of research set the stage for the re-emergence of White's ideas about competence and effectance motivation. Within schools of psychiatry and psychology, traditional notions of intrapsychic disruption were being questioned by those interested in the etiology of mental illness. Largely centered on schizophrenia research, the exploration began for pre-determinant factors that made one vulnerable to mental illness. This area of research has spread in many directions, examining biological, constitutional, and environmental factors. Among the most notable early contributors to this exciting new research enterprise were Anthony in St. Louis (1974), Garmezy in Minnesota (1974), Mednick and Schulsinger in the Scandinavian countries (1974), and Rutter in London (1977).

The most universal research paradigm among the various "vulnerability" groups called for longitudinal or anterospective follow-up of children deemed to be at high risk for schizophrenia. Based largely on the findings of Erlenmeyer-Kimling (1975) and Kety, Rosenthal, Wender, Schulsinger, and Jacobson (1975), the high-risk researchers assumed that genetic loading in offspring of schizophrenic parents (mostly mothers) would produce an increased incidence of schizophrenia as the children reached adolescence and adulthood. By following these children and meticulously observing a variety of potentially meaningful biological and social functions, it was hoped that the developmental pattern of schizophrenia might be tracked.

The assumptions about increased incidence appear to have been well founded. Mednick and Schulsinger (1974) suggest that, by the end of the risk period at age 45, perhaps 12 to 14% of their experimental sample will have suffered some form of schizophrenic disorder; a rate nearly 20 times that in a normal population. What is more, an additional 35% or so will likely manifest some other form of mental disorder, varying from relatively mild depression to fairly severe character disorder. Similar findings have been reported by all of the high-risk researchers. Unfortunately, the hope once held for definitively tracking the course of a schizophrenic disorder has been less well sustained.

Perhaps more exciting and valuable than the primary findings for the vulnerability research has been the attention those studies have focused on the high-risk population that did not develop any form of observable disorder. Looking again at Mednick and Schulsinger's predictions, it is clear that 50% of their high-risk population will develop in a normal way with no mental disorder developing at any point in time. It was this finding, replicated almost simultaneously by vulnerability researchers throughout the world, that began to refocus the spotlight on the competence and effectance motivation constructs proposed by White some 15 years before.

Invulnerability

Norman Garmezy at the University of Minnesota was, perhaps, the first to portray the significance of the large percentage of high-risk subjects who appeared mentally well. In part because of the disappointment with the specificity of findings concerning the vulnerables and because of the optimism that accompanies the study of those who succeed, Garmezy heralded the call for the study of factors associated with "invulnerability," a term he chose to describe the healthy population (Garmezy, 1970). In reviewing the sparse writings that did attempt to describe this population, he was struck by the continuity of findings. Not only did the invulnerables appear to be free of serious mental illness, but at least one investigator (Heston, 1966) had offered a qualitative impression which suggested that they might, in fact, be better adjusted or, at least, more creative than the control population.

Indeed, in reporting the results of his high-risk subjects who were reared in foster care from birth, Heston noted the following:

> One further result deserves special emphasis. The twenty-one (21) experimental subjects who exhibited no significant psycho-social impairment were not only successful adults but in comparison to the control group were more spontaneous when interviewed and had more colorful life histories. They had held the more creative jobs: musician, teacher, home designer; and followed the more imaginative hobbies: oil painting, music, antique aircraft. It must be emphasized that the finding of what may be especially adaptive personality traits among persons in the experimental groups was noticed only in retrospect as the material compiled on each person was being reviewed. Such traits were not systematically investigated. . . We wish to report a strong *impression* that within the experimental group there was much more variability of personality and behavior but more evidence is required before this can be regarded as confirmed. (p. 371)

As Garmezy rightly points out (1974), the conclusion that creativity and emotional disorder are somehow related is far beyond reason for the impressionistic data presented in these studies. Of greater significance, however, is the suggestion that there are, in fact, personal traits and environmental circumstances that may protect or "insulate" an individual against the predicted onset of mental disease.

Primary Prevention

At the same time that the high-risk researchers were beginning to explore the notion of invulnerability, the field of primary prevention in mental health was reawakening in academic spheres. Although the community mental health movement of the mid-60s was well underway, it wasn't until 1973 that George Albee and his colleagues at the University of Vermont began to focus an empirical spotlight on the prevention enterprise. Beginning with a review article (Kessler & Albee, 1977), the Vermont group established an annual conference addressing the major issues in primary prevention. In format, it was not unlike the Nebraska Symposia of the 50s and 60s.

The public health notions of primary prevention challenged the methods, and even the language, of the vast majority of psychopathology research. Prevention, by definition, required that deleterious influences in the genetic, constitutional, or environmental makeup of an individual be revised or somehow compensated for. Primary prevention research could not continue simply to display the precursors to emotional disorder but, rather, needed to address the mediators of those precursors as well.

With a few notable exceptions, the worlds of psychological and psychiatric research represented a "problem" literature, a body of findings that discovered and replicated individual and societal deficits that were seen to be associated with emotional disorder. There was no mutually agreed definition of mental health, nor was there much attention to the strengths and adaptive skills necessary for normal development. One outstanding observer who perceived this shortcoming was Lois Murphy:

> It is something of a paradox that a nation which has exulted in its rapid expansion and its scientific technological achievements should have developed in its studies of childhood so vast a "problem" literature; a literature often expressing adjustment difficulties, social failures, blocked potential and defeat . . . . In applying our clinical ways of thinking formulated out of experience with broken adults, we were slow to see how the language of inadequacy to meet life's challenges could become the subject matter of psychological science. Thus, there are thousands of studies of maladjustment for each one that deals directly with the ways of marrying life's problems with personal strength and adequacy . . . . We know that there are devices for correcting, bypassing or overcoming threats, but for the most part these have not been directly studied. (1962, p. 186)

In the 1950s and early 60s, Murphy and Grace Heider were among the few researchers in the country who paid primary attention to coping skills and competence in youngsters. The Coping Project of the Menninger Foundation had decided to follow the infants of the former Escalona-Leitch study in Topeka, Kansas. At the time the Coping Project began, these youngsters were between 3 and 5 years of age. The longitudinal study envisioned by Murphy and Heider was intended to identify the behaviors and attributes of the youngsters that were significant in their ability to cope with the stresses of growing up. Rather than examine normative development, the study specifically addressed the skills that assisted in overcoming adversity. Such a study approach was novel at the time of its inception and remained unique for nearly 2 decades.

It was the emergence of the emphasis on an empirical approach to primary prevention in mental health that brought the Kansas studies into the forefront. By definition, the study of primary prevention of psychopathology must address those factors that mediate against the onset of mental disorder. As such, the independent variables in a study design must include the strengths of an individual, in essence, the coping skills that prevent the disorder.

The research regarding primary prevention of psychopathology was still in its infancy at the opening of the 1970s. With little guidance from earlier psychopathology research, and little success in translating basic public health principles to the study of psychopathology, the field was left with a void of measures, assumptions, hypotheses, and study designs. Mental health research simply had not developed the tools with which to adequately examine the role of primary prevention.

As is often the case, the "void" was soon filled with a plethora of ideas, a full complement of "best guesses" by experts around the country as to those influences that appeared most salient in the study of primary prevention. As has been pointed out by Cowen and Zax

(1968), the search for leads in the investigation of primary prevention can include virtually anything. Kessler and Albee (1977), in their Annual Review chapter, expressed it as follows:

> During the past year we found ourselves constantly writing references and ideas on scraps of paper and emptying our pockets each day of notes on the primary prevention relevance of children's group homes, titanium paint, parent-effectiveness training, consciousness raising, Zoom, Sesame Street, the guaranteed annual wage, legalized abortion, school integration, limits on international cartels, unpolished rice, free prenatal clinics, anti-pollution laws, a yoghurt and vegetable diet, free VD clinics, and a host of other topics. Nearly everything, it appears, has implications for primary prevention, for reducing emotional disturbance, for strengthening and fostering mental health. (p. 560)

The investigatory path was paved for a reemergence of competence and coping skills as a primary areas of focus. Its explanatory value, although limited, opened further doors of intellectual curiosity. With attention still focused on "normal" development and psychopathology research, the recognition of the value of understanding coping skills in a delinquent population was soon to follow.

COMPETENCE REVISITED—NEW OPTIONS FOR RESEARCH AND INTERVENTION

Until 1974, the original work of White (1959), although forming the basis for competence as a construct to explain a youngster's successful interaction with his environment, had not been examined with regard to the motivational component originally proposed; specifically, White's early interest in the motivational drive.

Works by Harter and Zigler (1974) and later of Harter (1978) have attempted to reexamine and expand upon White's earlier theoretical notions. In addition, Harter recognized that adequate measures were not available which could begin to give empirical dimension to the construct.

Harter's work (1978) is a reclassification of White's model for competence and effectance motivation. As represented in Figure 9.1, White's model proposes that the successful completion of a mastery attempt will result in feelings of intrinsic pleasure, which in turn support effectance motivation.

Harter, although recognizing the value of such a scheme, points out a number of deficiencies that have not been addressed by White or others since his original paper. Specifically, Harter (1978, p. 34) underscores the following issues as necessary to broaden the explanatory value of the concept and its amenability to empirical scrutiny:

1. Effectance motivation must not be considered as a unitary construct. Rather the components of the scheme must be examined in a developmental context;

2. The effect of failure as well as success must be examined as components of the motivational system;

3. The notion of intrinsic pleasure as a component of the motivational system must be qualified. The degree of intrinsic pleasure should be related to the degree of challenge presented by the mastery attempt;

4. The role of socializing agents as they relate to the functions of reward for an individual are important in determining the motivational aspects of successful mastery;

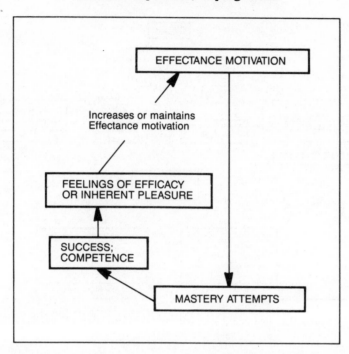

Figure 9.1. White's Model of Competence and Effectance Motivation*. *Note.* Figures 9.1 and 9.2 are from "Effectance Motivation Reconsidered: Toward a Developmental Model" by S. Harter, 1978, *Human Development, 1,* p. 36–38. Copyright 1978 by Karger Publishing Co. Reprinted by permission.

5. Over time, the internalization of reinforcement should lead to a self-reward system and a set of individual mastery goals;

6. The motivational system must take into account both intrinsic and extrinsic reward systems and the developmental process describing the relative strength of each; and

7. Correlates such as perceived competence and perception of control must be examined in relation to the overall motivational system.

In attempting to incorporate the above issues into a expanded theory of effectance motivation and to provide a model that could be subject to empirical scrutiny, Harter developed the expanded scheme shown graphically in Figure 9.2.

This new model proposed by Harter takes, as its starting point, White's original conception of an intrinsic motive force that impels the organism toward competent adaptive behavior. The expansion, however, provides the opportunity for measurement of correlates to the central motivational system. It further defines the expected parallel system that is associated with failure in mastery attempts, in effect, the negative motivational scheme.

While the formulation presented above is relatively recent, Harter has been able to document data that appear to support the model. Harter and Zigler (1974) examined the correlation among measurable indices of a child's behavior in four components of the system: (a) response variation—the impetus to change one's behavior to produce differences; (b) curiosity for novel stimuli; (c) mastery for the sake of competence--with no external reinforcement; and (d) preference for challenging tasks. Since the four correlative components in the model should be positively associated, Harter and Zigler's finding that there

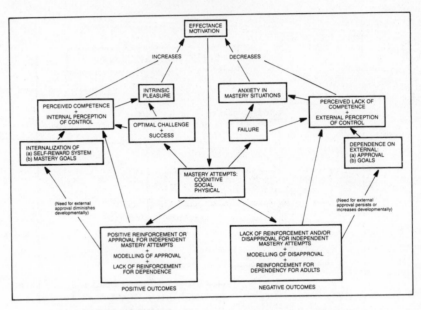

Figure 9.2. Harter's Expanded Model of Effectance Motivation.

was a weak, but statistically significant, positive relationship between components provides some encouragement for the model.

Subsequent work has demonstrated, at least in correlational analyses, that other segments of the model appear to be properly constituted. Harter (personal communication, October, 1979) found a positive linear relationship between pleasure, as measured in smiling, and task difficulty. A further refinement, however, suggests that, rather than a linear relationship, pleasure and perceived difficulty may better be represented as a curvilinear, inverted-U relationship (Harter, personal communication, October, 1979). That is, smiling behaviors increase with level of perceived difficulty to a point and then decrease with the perception of a very difficult challenge. Interestingly, this finding was consistent, whether or not the child was successful in completing the task.

More recent work (Harter, personal communication, October, 1979) has examined the relationship of perceived competence and motivational orientation. The model predicts that competence should be positively related to intrinsic motivational orientation. That is, the more a child perceives his ability to be successful, the more he will be internally motivated to attempt new challenges. Examining the results of two newly constructed questionnaires given to a sample of 800 school children, Harter found that children who are intrinsically motivated to master, to be curious, to seek challenge do, in fact, perceive themselves to be more competent. It is interesting that the test items on the motivational orientation subscales make reference to liking or preferring challenge; that is, they tap the affective components hypothesized by the model. Two other subscales that do not tap affective dimensions, "independent judgment and internal criteria," are not significantly related to perceived competence.

While Harter and her students continue to attempt to provide a solid empirical link between theoretical components in the model, work to date is encouraging. The Harter model of effectance motivation provides a valuable structure not only for the increased understanding of the motivational system but also as a departure point for meaningful investigation of predicted clinical correlates.

The Measurement of Competence

Much of the theoretical work presented in the previous section was derived without the availability of adequate measures to begin to establish empirical links. Harter and her colleagues recognized that the process of theory testing and nomological "net-weaving" required the development of sound measures. Although popular measures such as the Coopersmith (1967) self-esteem inventory and the Piers-Harris (1964) self-concept scale were available, they were rejected on both practical and theoretical grounds.

Harter (1977) observed that a major difficulty in the development of scales purporting to tap self-concept or competency domains was the nonexistence of a clear conceptual definition of constructs. Given this shortfall, the global concept, such as self-esteem, has questionable value when operationalized. In beginning the process of scale construction, Harter's approach was to specify the possible components of the construct. Perceived competence was not viewed as a global trait. Rather, it was decided that a profile of a child's perception of competence across different domains would lead to more conceptual clarity and precise operationalization of the construct.

A number of practical considerations also governed the development of the new scale material. A preliminary study of the Coopersmith scale (1967) indicated that there was a significant correlation between the self-esteem score and the lie scale embedded in the measure. Further, scores were positively and significantly correlated with the Children's Social Desireability Scale (Crandall, Crandall, & Katkousky, 1965). Such a pattern of findings suggested that children's responses could, indeed, be more idealized than actual. Further problems in administration of both the Coopersmith and Piers-Harris instruments argued for the development of a new measure.

The Perceived Competence Scale for Children, first described in 1978, identifies three general areas of competence seen as important during the school years: (a) cognitive competence which emphasizes academic performance; (b) social competence which examines a child's relationships with peers; and (c) physical competence which focuses on games, sports, and nonacademic achievement. The measure includes a separate subscale for each of these competence domains. Independent of the work being conducted by Harter, another scale, the Achenbach Child Behavior Checklist (Achenbach, 1979), was developed and introduced in 1979. This inventory, which is divided into two sections, focuses both on competencies and behavioral manifestations of problems. Although the scales differ in construction, it is interesting to note that the competence domains addressed in the Achenbach scale overlap almost entirely with those developed by Harter. Individual subscale scores in the Achenbach are available for: (a) school competence which reflects school performance and achievement; (b) social competence which taps involvement in social relationships; and (c) activities competence which measures the amount and quality of involvement in sports, hobbies, chores, and nonschool activities.

The major difference between the two measurement devices involves the structure of the individual test items. The Harter inventory is a relatively straightforward self-report questionnaire which is structured in a forced-choice format to reduce the pull of social desirability. The content of individual items requires a child to make a qualitative judgment regarding his or her competence in a variety of areas. The Achenbach measure, on the other hand, was first developed as a parent-report form. As such, it is more open-ended and requires the respondent to specify areas of involvement and then to make a judgment regarding amount of involvement and quality of involvement. Recently, Achenbach has developed and tested a child self-report form of his original inventory. Preliminary data from that trial indicate that the psychometric properties of the instrument are more stable with children as "self" respondents than with parents as "other" respondents (Achenbach, personal communication, January, 1980).

The similarity of the two measures with regard to content area and subscale division provide a fascinating and, until recently, untried opportunity for comparison. The validation process of both the measures and the original theoretical construct could significantly benefit from the attempt.

PERCEIVED COMPETENCE STUDY—AN INITIAL STEP

In order to determine if the theoretical construct of social competence was, in fact, worthy of pursuit in understanding youth violence and delinquency, an explanatory survey was conducted at the National Center for Juvenile Justice. This project, sponsored by the William T. Grant Foundation of New York City, was conducted over an 18-month period.

The method employed in this survey consisted primarily of the administration of a self-report inventory to measure multiple indices of perceived social competence. This instrument, the Combined Social Competence Inventory, was a hybrid containing both the Harter and Achenbach subscales. The inventory was administered to approximately 1,200 delinquents nationwide and to approximately 450 nondelinquents. Pretests were conducted in Allegheny County, Pennsylvania, for both delinquent and nondelinquent populations. Demographic data were gathered for the entire subject pool, and a limited amount of court data were collected for the delinquent population.

In that this study was an epidemiological analysis of social competence in a delinquent population, it was important that the subject pool be representative of the delinquent population in the United States. Drawing on the previous work of the National Center for Juvenile Justice (Snyder, Finnegan, & Hutzler 1980), a subject pool was derived that mirrored the activity of juvenile courts nationwide. The 10 courts chosen represent a diversity of population and geography ranging from the rural area of Cedar Falls, Iowa, to the bedroom community of Somerville, New Jersey, to the dense urban setting of Chicago, Illinois. Together, these courts process slightly less than 5% of the total nationwide juvenile court caseload.

Our original intent was that every child for whom an intake appointment at the court was scheduled during a 1-month period would complete the Social Competence survey. In each of the courts, an intake interview is scheduled in approximately 80% of all cases referred to the courts. The manner in which the intake appointments were conducted varied greatly, however. In each jurisdiction, time was devoted to establishing a procedure that would insure that all youth completed the survey instrument.

Slightly more than 1,200 completed forms were collected by the project staff over a 7-month period. Approximately 16% of the forms were rejected for being improperly completed, resulting in a total delinquency sample of 1,004. The youngest child surveyed was 8; 80% were 14 or older. Of the delinquents, 80% were male, half were white, 44% black, and 5% Spanish. Nearly half (45%) of the youth were referred to court for burglary or theft; 17% were referred for crimes against persons, mostly robbery or assault, although two youths were referred for rape and one for homicide. Half of the juveniles had not been previously referred to court; another 20% had been seen once before. This profile of prior referrals should not be construed to mean that 70% of the surveyed delinquent youth had never or only rarely before been in trouble. An informal adjustment at the police level is common in many of the jurisdictions. In Chicago, for example, a youth may be arrested by the police, warned and released for five or six separate instances before he is brought to the juvenile court.

Subjects for the control sample were drawn from two high schools in Allegheny County, Pennsylvania. The control sample questionnaire was identical to that used for the delinquent sample except for an additional question: "Have you ever been taken to juvenile court?" Approximately 5% of the sample answered affirmatively and were excluded from the study. Students were also asked to indicate their age, sex, and race. The survey forms were distributed in a classroom setting by teachers who read standard instructions to the students. A slightly higher percentage of the control group's forms were eliminated for being incorrectly completed.

The final control sample was 372 nondelinquent youth. Of these, 70% were ages 16 or 17. The population was fairly evenly divided between male and female, almost all were white.

The results of the survey, presented in Figures 9.3–9.8, are encouraging. As can be seen from the graphic representations, the individual scale scores for the Harter and Achenbach portions of the Combined Social Competence Inventory do indicate a small but statistically significant and consistent difference between delinquents and their nondelinquent peers. Perhaps of more interest are the individual profiles of subscales within the two groups.

The Harter subscale "Self," which consists of a number of items addressing general perceptions of well-being, most clearly differentiated the two groups. This finding is largely in keeping with the notions of diminished self-esteem in a delinquent population. In all of the subscales except the Harter "Sport," nondelinquent youngsters judged their own competence to be greater than that of the delinquent sample.

A further analysis examined only the delinquent sample to determine if the measure differentiated between types of offenders. In the first comparison, the delinquent sample was divided into those youngsters referred for serious offenses, defined by the FBI Uniform Crime Reports' Violent Crimes (homicide, rape, robbery, aggravated assault), and those youngsters referred for less serious offenses. This comparison produced 153 serious offenders and 851 nonserious offenders.

The Combined Social Competence Inventory measures did not adequately differentiate these two groups. In fact, the Harter subscales showed a consistent pattern of higher scores for the serious delinquent sample. This finding was, at first, somewhat discouraging. It would appear that a youngster's perception of competence is not related to the specific behavior that ultimately results in his arrest and referral to court.

The theoretical model presented above would not, however, suggest that competence is related to types of behavior, and is consistent with the finding. It is not surprising, therefore, that serious or violent offenders do not perceive their competence to be less than that of their less seriously offending counterparts.

A second comparison was conducted examining another dimension of "serious" delinquency. In this instance, the delinquent group was divided into those with relatively long court histories (more than three prior referrals) and those with less previous delinquency activity. This produced a sample with 128 high-prior delinquents and 876 low-prior delinquents.

In this comparison, every subscale of the Combined Social Competence Inventory differentiated between groups. In fact, the differences between these subgroups were almost equal to those in the original delinquent-control comparison.

This finding is consistent with the theoretical model which suggests that perceived competence is a factor in a *motivational* drive toward success. The delinquent who has a

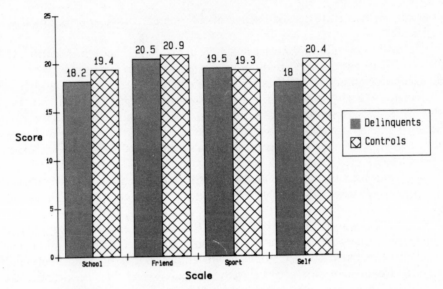

Figure 9.3. Perceived Competence of Delinquents and Controls, Harter Scale.

sustained history of arrests and court appearances has not only failed in a number of environmental settings, but has failed in his avoidance of apprehension. This series of failures would reduce perceptions of competence and would, in turn, diminish effectance motivation.

The data presented are the result of the first analyses in an ongoing research effort. While certainly not overwhelming, the consistency of differences across subscales and the variability of findings between comparison groups gives ample impetus to continue. The measurement of internal attributes is always difficult, rarely fully satisfying, and only valuable when viewed in a larger theoretical/empirical context. In this regard, the study of social

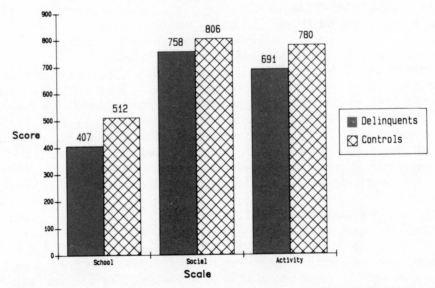

Figure 9.4. Perceived Competence of Delinquents and Controls, Achenbach Scale.

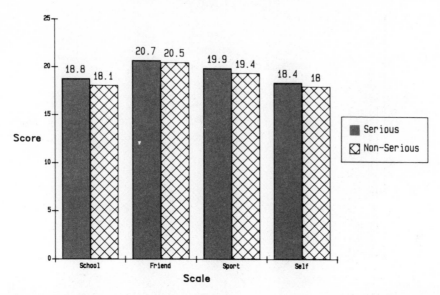

Figure 9.5. Perceived Competence of Serious and Nonserious Offenders, Harter Scale.

competence in a delinquent population will become more useful as the full developmental notion of effectance motivation is explored. If youth criminality can be diminished by a change in perceived competence through skill development, the entire motivational theory can hold hope for maintenance of those gains. Future work planned in this area includes a follow-up of the delinquent youth identified in this survey to determine if perceived competence at one point in time predicts the cause of youthful criminality. It is also our intent to compare measurements of perceived competence over time to better understand the developmental pattern and its relationship to delinquency recidivism or devolution. It is, as has so often been said before, a first step.

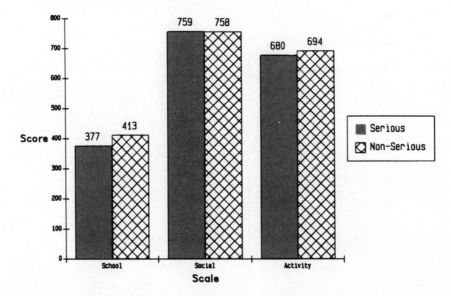

Figure 9.6. Perceived Competence of Serious and Nonserious Offenders, Achenbach.

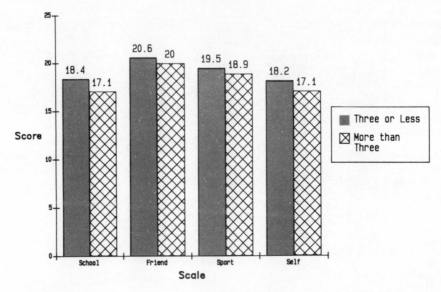

Figure 9.7. Perceived Competence by Number of Prior Referrals, Harter Scale.

CONCLUSION

The study of social competence and coping skills in a delinquent population is a relatively new and unexplored area of social science research. Its value to the investigator is that it allows for research that is based on a theoretical matrix within which a number of key elements have prior empirical support.

More important, however, is the utility of social competence and coping skill development for the practitioner. Rather than the complex and intangible notions of "self-esteem," "personality development," and "ego-strength," the concept of social competence provides a

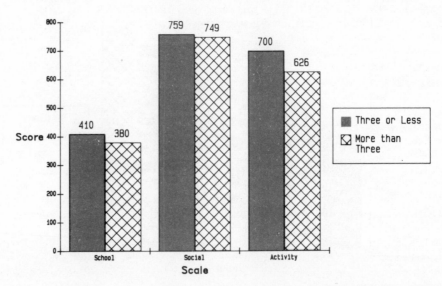

Figure 9.8. Perceived Competence by Number of Prior Referrals, Achenbach Scale.

crisp and understandable point of intervention. For the probation officer, judge, or juvenile corrections worker, the process of skill development becomes a clear agenda with definable goals and measurable progress. What is more, it is a concept that is not alien to those untrained in the nuances of clinical intervention. As a pragmatist, such clarity is vitally needed both in the treatment and prevention of youth crime.

It is unlikely that a wholesale shift in emphasis towards skill development will occur within the policy and program worlds of juvenile justice. On an individual basis, however, in the personal interaction between worker and delinquent, this is often precisely what is occurring. Until recently, there was little theoretical, and even less empirical, support for such activity. The social sciences have finally arrived at the same point and, with continued diligence, may help to refine the utility of those efforts and prescribe more effective interventions with this difficult and troublesome population.

REFERENCES

Achenbach, T.M. (1979). The child behavior profile: An empirically based system for assessing children's behavioral problems and competencies. *International Journal of Mental Health, 7* (3–4), 24–42.

Aichhorn, A. (1935). *Wayward youth.* New York: Viking Press.

Anthony, E.J. (1974). The syndrome of the psychosocially invulnerable child. In E. J. Anthony & C. Koupernik (Eds.), *The child in his family: Vol. 3. Children at psychiatric risk (pp. 529–544).* New York: Wiley.

Bandura, A. (1976). Social learning analysis of aggression. In E. Ribes-Estes & A. Bandura (Eds.), *Analysis of delinquency and aggression* (pp. 18–34). Hillside, NJ: LEA Press.

Bettleheim, B. (1960). *The informed heart.* New York: Free Press.

Berstein, S., & Rulo, J. H. (1976). Learning disabilities and learning problems: Their implications for the juvenile justice system. *Juvenile Justice, 27,* 43–47.

Coopersmith, S. (1967). *The antecedents of self-esteem.* San Francisco: W. H. Freeman.

Cowen, E.L., & Zax, M. (1968). Early detection and prevention of emotional disorder: Conceptualization and programs. In J. W. Carter (Ed.), *Research contribution from psychology to community mental health* (pp. 46–59). New York: Behavioral Publications.

Crandall, V.C., Crandall, V. J., & Katkousky, W. (1965). A children's social desirability questionnaire. *Journal of Consulting Psychology, 29,* 27–36.

Erlenmeyer-Kimling, L. A. (1975). A prospective study of children at risk for schizophrenia: Methodological considerations and some preliminary findings. In R. D. Wirt, G. Winokur, & M. Roff (Eds.), *Life history research in psychopathology* (Vol. 4, pp. 263–281). Minneapolis: University of Minnesota Press.

Farrington, D.P. (1981). *Delinquency from 10 to 25.* Paper presented at the Society for Life History Research Meeting, Monterey, CA.

Frease, D.C. (1973). Delinquency, social class and the schools. *Sociology and Social Review, 57,* 443–449.

Garmezy, N. (1970). Process and reactive schizophrenia: Some conceptions and issues. *Schizophrenia Bulletin,* Issue 2, 30–74.

Garmezy, N. (1974). The study of competence in children at risk for severe psychopathology. In E. J. Anthony & C. Koupernik (Eds.), *The child in his family: Vol. 3. Children at psychiatric risk* (pp. 77–98). New York: Wiley.

Gesten, E.L., Flores de Apodaca, R., Rains, M., Weissberg, R.P., & Cowen, E.L. (1979). Promoting peer-related social competence in schools. In M.W. Kent & J.E. Rolf (Eds.), *Primary prevention of psychopathology: Vol. 3. Social competence in children.* (pp. 245–273) Hanover, NH: University Press of New England.

Gove, W.R. (1975). *Labelling of deviance: Evaluating a perspective.* New York: Wiley.

Harter, S. (1977). *The perceived competence scale for children: A new measure.* Paper presented at the Rocky Mountain Psychological Association Convention, Albuquerque, NM.

Harter, S. (1978). Effectance motivation reconsidered: Toward a developmental model. *Human Development, 1,* 34–64.

Harter, S., & Zigler, D. (1974). The assessment of effectance motivation in normal and retarded children. *Developmental psychology, 10,* 169–180.

Hartup, W.W. (1979). Peer relations and the growth of social competence. In M.W. Kent & J.E. Rolf (Eds.), *Primary prevention of psychopathology: Vol. 3. Social competence in children.* Hanover, NH: University Press of New England.

Heston, L.L. (1966). Psychiatric disorders in foster home-reared children of schizophrenic mothers. *British Journal of Psychiatry, 112,* 819–825.

Jacob, T. (1975). Family interaction in disturbed and normal families: A methodological and substantive review. *Psychological Bulletin, 82,* 33–65.

Kelly, F.J., & Baer, D.J. (1971). Physical challenge as a treatment for delinquency. *Crime and Delinquency, 17,* 432–437.

Kessler, M., & Albee, G. (1977). An overview of the literature of primary prevention. In G. Albee & J. Joffe (Eds.), *Primary prevention of psychopathology: Vol. 1. The Issues* (pp. 351–399). Hanover, NH; University Press of New England.

Kety, S., Rosenthal, D., Wender, P.H., Schulsinger, R., & Jacobsen, B. (1975). Mental illness in the biological and adoptive families of adopted individuals who have become schizophrenic: A preliminary report based on psychiatric interviews. In R. R. Fieve, D. Rosenthal, & H. Brill (Eds.), *Genetic research in schizophrenia* (pp. 112–163). Baltimore: The Johns Hopkins University Press.

Kohlberg, L. (1974). *Research in moralization: The cognitive-development approach.* New York: Holt, Rinehart & Winston.

Mednick, S. A., & Schulsinger, F. (1974). Studies of children at high risk for schizophrenia. In S. Mednick et al. (Eds.), *Genetics, environment, and psychopathology* (pp. 101–140). Amsterdam: North Holland.

Mittelman, B. (1954). Motility in infants, children, and adults. *Psychoanalytic Study of the Child, 9,* 142–177.

Murphy, L.B., & Moriarity, A.E. (1976). *Vulnerability, coping and growth from infancy to adolescence.* New Haven: Yale University Press.

Murphy, L.B., and associates. (1962). *The widening world of childhood: Paths toward mastery.* New York: Basic Books.

Offord, D.R. (1978). School performance, I. Q., and delinquency. *British Journal of Criminology, 18,* 67–79.

Piers, E.V., & Harris, D.B. (1964). Age and other correlates of self-concept in children. *Journal of Educational Psychology, 55,* 91–95.

Robins, L.N. (1974). Anti-social behavior disturbances of childhood. In E. J. Anthony & C. Koupernik (Eds.), *The child in his family: Vol. 3. Children at psychiatric risk* (pp. 222–241). New York: Wiley.

Rutter, M. (1977). Early sources of security and competence. In J.S. Bruner & A. Garton (Eds.), *Human growth and development* (pp. 212–222). London: Oxford University Press.

Rutter, M. (1979). Protective factors in children's responses to stress and disadvantage. In M. W. Kent & J. E. Rolf (Eds.), *Primary prevention of psychopathology: Vol. 3. Social competence in children* (pp. 79–92). Hanover, NH: University Press of New England.

Rutter, M., & Yule, W. (1973). Specific reading retardation. In L. Mann & D. Sabatino (Eds.), *The first review of special education* (pp. 520–533). NJ: Buttonwood Farms.

Shure, M.B., & Spivack, G. (1979). Interpersonal problem-solving, thinking, and adjustment in the mother-child dyad. In M.W. Kent & J.E. Rolf (Eds.), *Primary prevention of psychopathology: Vol. 3. Social competence in children* (pp. 93–118). Hanover, NH: University Press of New England.

Sigel, I.E. (1979). Consciousness-raising of individual competence in problem-solving. In M.W. Kent & J.E. Rolf (Eds.), *Primary prevention of psychopathology: Social competence in children* (pp. 119–127). Hanover, NH: University Press of New England.

Snyder, H.N. (1984). In *The juvenile court and serious offenders.* Reno: National Council of Juvenile and Family Court Judges.

Snyder, H.N., Finnegan, T. & Hutzler, J. (1982). *Delinquency 1979: A description of delinquency cases processed by courts with juvenile jurisdiction.* Pittsburgh: National Center for Juvenile Justice.

Sturge, C. (1972). *Reading retardation and anti-social behavior.* Unpublished manuscript, University of London.

White, R.W. (1959). Motivation reconsidered: The concept of competence. *Psychological Review, 66,* 297–333.

White, R.W. (1960). Competence and the psychosexual states of development. In M.R. Jones (Ed.), *Nebraska symposium on motivation* (pp. 112–124). Lincoln: University of Nebraska Press.

White, R.W. (1978). Competence as an aspect of personal growth. In M.W. Kent & J.E. Rolf (Eds.), *Primary prevention of psychopathology: Vol. 3. Social competence in children* (pp. 6–19). Hanover, NH: University Press of New England.

Wolfgang, M.E. (1977). From boy to man—from delinquency to crime. In *The serious juvenile offender: Proceedings of a national symposium* (pp. 85–98).

10
Television and Film Violence
George Comstock

Television and film violence have been the subject of most of the empirical investigations of the effects of media violence. The principal effects studied have been aggressiveness and antisocial behavior of a more disruptive than destructive cast, although in a few instances seriously harmful antisocial and criminal behavior have been the focus. Television and films merit such attention because of the preeminence of violence in their content and because of their popularity among young persons; even adolescents, who are far below children and adults in average television viewing, view an average of about 20 hours of television a week and are a principal component of the theater movie audience (Comstock, Chaffee, Katzman, McCombs, & Roberts, 1978). These media also merit attention because of the forcefulness of such audio-visual stimuli as influences analogous to those of direct, real-life experience on learning and behavior (Bandura, 1973). The broader topic of inquiry, however, remains media violence; and the evidence on television and film violence is instructive as to what can be plausibly speculated about the effects of violence in television news, newspapers, comic books, cartoon drawings, fiction in books and magazines, rock performances, and "Music Television."

Three major scientific issues must be confronted in evaluating the empirical evidence on the influence of television and film violence on the antisocial behavior of adolescents and young adults. They are:

1. The *external validity* of the many experiments that document unambiguously that, within the experimental setting, subsequent to exposure to violent television or film portrayals, subjects of college age behave in ways categorized by the experimenters as aggressive or antisocial at levels or frequencies higher than subjects not so exposed.
2. The *implications* for the behavior of those older persons of the many experiments that document unambiguously that, within the experimental setting, subjects of nursery school age subsequent to exposure to violent television or film portrayals behave in ways categorized by the experimenters as aggressive or antisocial at levels or frequencies higher than subjects not so exposed.
3. The *size of the effect*, if any; that is, the degree to which levels or frequencies of behavior categorized as antisocial or aggressive are altered by exposure to media violence.

Fundamental in each of these instances is the question of the *character*, or qualitative nature, of the behavior under scrutiny—criminal, seriously harmful, disruptive, or acknowledgedly antisocial and aggressive but of minor significance.

SINCE 1963: THE EVOLUTION OF THE EMPIRICAL EVIDENCE BEARING ON TELEVISION AND FILM VIOLENCE

In 1963, the first two experiments demonstrating that exposure in such circumstances to violent television and film portrayals increased aggressiveness were published in the *Journal of Abnormal and Social Psychology* (Bandura, Ross, & Ross, 1963a; Berkowitz & Rawlings, 1963). Since then, there have been seven important developments in the accumulation and evolution of empirical evidence bearing on the possible contribution of television and film violence to aggressive and antisocial behavior (Comstock, 1983a):

1. *The decline of the catharsis hypothesis.* Many psychologists once believed that the vicarious experience of violence in television and film would purge viewers of aggressive impulses. However, one of those two 1963 experiments (Berkowitz & Rawlings, 1963) demonstrated that the previously documented reduction in expressed hostility as a consequence of exposure to media violence (Feshbach, 1961) was more plausibly interpretable as the inhibition of aggressive impulses than as the catharsis of those impulses, and that a violent portrayal that did not heighten such inhibitions could increase aggressiveness.

2. *The development of three theoretical explanations for an influence of violent television and film entertainment on aggressive behavior.* Since the publication of those two early experiments in 1963, three theoretical explanations have been devised to account for the occurrence of such phenomena. They are: (a) Social learning theory (Bandura, 1973, 1978) which holds that humans learn ways of behaving, the circumstances in which the behavior in question is appropriate, and the likely efficacy of such behavior from observing the behavior of others both in real life and through the mass media; (b) disinhibition and cue theory (Berkowitz, 1962, 1964, 1973) which holds that television and film portrayals can alter the restraint associated with an internal state, such as anger, as well as the response likely to be evoked by an external stimulus; and (c) arousal theory (Tannenbaum & Zillman, 1975) which holds that the excitement induced by portrayals stimulating to their viewers may transfer to subsequent behavior, driving it beyond its normal threshold.

3. *The introduction of evidence from a variety of methods, each with its own advantages and disadvantages.* Experiments conducted in laboratory settings, such as those of 1963, are the foundations of psychology as a science because they permit causal inference and the investigation of questions not amenable to exploration by other means. In the case of aggression and the media, however, they are open to skepticism on such grounds as the artificiality of the circumstances, the absence of the possibility of retaliation by a victim, the brevity of the television exposure, and the immediacy of the measurement of effect. The introduction of new data from surveys in the Surgeon General's 1972 inquiry into television violence (Comstock & Rubinstein, 1972a, 1972b; Comstock, Rubinstein, & Murray, 1972; Murray, Rubinstein, & Comstock, 1972; Rubinstein, Comstock, & Murray, 1972; Surgeon General's Scientific Advisory Committee on Television and Social Behavior, 1972) was important, because such data, while problematic for causal inference, represent everyday viewing and everyday aggression.

4. *A progressive increase in the ecological validity of manipulations and measures.* One of those 1963 experiments (Bandura, Ross, & Ross, 1963a), using nursery school children as subjects, employed a specially made portrayal of young adults as a stimulus and attacks by children on a Bobo doll as a measure of aggression. The other (Berkowitz & Rawlings, 1963), using college students as subjects, employed a brief boxing sequence from a popular film as a stimulus and criticism of the experimenter's assistant as a measure of aggression. The literature today, embracing surveys and field experiments as well as experiments performed in laboratory settings, includes manipulations and measures less contrived—for example, episodes from commercial television programs; whole programs and films; be-

havior during play and social interaction; *everyday* television viewing; the delivery of noxious noise or electric shock to another person; peer- and self-reports of interpersonal aggression, troublemaking, and criminal acts; and crime rate statistics—which allow the question of the dependence of the results on manipulations and measures that lack ecological validity to be addressed empirically.

5. *Sufficient maturation of the scientific literature to permit the use of meta-analyses.* Meta-analysis is a quantitative assessment of a scientific literature in which the findings of individual studies become the data, with each study assigned a role analogous to that of a respondent in a survey and the findings aggregated to determine quantitatively the average or direction of the results (Glass, McGaw, & Smith, 1981). Two such analyses of the evidence on television and film violence are available. One covers 67 laboratory experiments, field experiments, and surveys involving about 30,000 persons (Andison, 1977). The other covers 230 such studies and involves approximately 100,000 persons (Hearold, in press).

6. *The identification of psychological processes on which effects are contingent.* Because of their sensitivity for exploring cause-and-effect relationships, the laboratory experiments have produced a catalogue of circumstances that increase the probability of an effect. These circumstances fall into four broad dimensions: The *efficacy, normativeness,* and *pertinence* ascribed by the media and perceived by the viewer in regard to the behavior in question, and the *susceptibility* of the viewer.

7. *The inclusion of measures that represent criminal acts or harmful antisocial behavior.* The threshold of harm is arguably most fairly placed in the eye of the victim, and from that viewpoint the mildest of incursions against person or property might be judged as excessive. The scientific record, however, does contain instances in which the behavior under scrutiny has clearly exceeded the threshold of "acceptable" aggressive or antisocial behavior.

The resulting literature on violence and its effects—approximately 650 items published between 1955 and 1980, including reviews and commentaries (Murray, 1980)—gives considerable empirical support to the overarching hypothesis that exposure to television and film violence increases the likelihood of subsequent aggressive or antisocial behavior. For example, the meta-analyses support these three conclusions (Andison, 1977; Hearold, in press):

1. A large majority of studies record a positive association between exposure to television and film violence and aggressive and antisocial behavior, and although there are decided differences in the size of this majority, there is no type of design, no variety of measure, and no category of persons for which there is not a majority of positive findings.
2. The increasing of ecological validity does not reduce to null the average magnitude of the recorded association between exposure and behavior, although it does reduce its size.
3. Exposure to violent and antisocial portrayals is associated with higher levels of such behavior and lower levels of constructive, positive, or altruistic behavior; exposure to portrayals of constructive, positive, or altruistic behavior is associated with lower levels of aggressive and antisocial behavior and higher levels of such prosocial behavior.

The literature as a whole gives little comfort to those who assert that the findings are evenly divided, that the association of exposure to media violence with aggressive and antisocial behavior is a product of ecologically inferior studies, or that violent television and film portrayals in some circumstances do not influence behavior. Nevertheless, different issues arise, and differing qualifications and emphases are required depending on the age of the population in question.

YOUNG CHILDREN

In that pioneer 1963 experiment, Bandura, Ross, and Ross (1963a) observed the behavior of nursery school children in a playroom with a Bobo doll and other toys after they had seen either (a) no behavior involving a Bobo doll or the Bobo doll attacked verbally and physically by (b) a live model, (c) the same model in a film sequence, or (d) a female attired in a cat costume such as might appear in children's entertainment. Prior to the manipulated experience, in order to heighten the likelihood of aggressive behavior, the children were mildly frustrated by being taken away from a room full of attractive toys. The result was that children in all three treatment groups (b, c, and d) displayed more aggressive behavior than those in the control condition. Nonimitative as well as imitative aggressive behavior was affected, although the effect was most prominent for imitative acts. Although the children exposed to the cat lady exhibited decidedly less aggression than those seeing the live model, they were definitely more aggressive than those in the control condition.

In their next experiment, Bandura, Ross, and Ross (1963b) manipulated the exposure of children of nursery school age to film sequences involving young adults identified as "Rocky" and "Johnny." In one version, Rocky successfully takes Johnny's toys away and is rewarded. In the other, Johnny successfully defends himself against Rocky, and Rocky, in effect, is punished. The children imitated Rocky's play with the toys when he was rewarded and made derogatory comments about Johnny, although they also were highly critical of Rocky. Those who saw Rocky punished were critical of Rocky, but did not criticize Johnny, the target of his attack. In the first experiment, behavior is a function of observation; in the second, of perceived efficacy.

These experiments are typical of the several dozen subsequent experiments by Bandura and others testing propositions derived from social learning theory in regard to the influence of violent television and film portrayals on the aggressiveness of young children. When the question of external validity is raised, the answer varies with the age of the population in question. For adolescents, young adults, and older persons, the implications for current behavior are clouded by (a) the gulf in ages, (b) the distance between attacks against an inflated toy and adult aggression of any kind, (c) the departure of the television viewing from the commercial entertainment typically viewed by adults in lengthy blocks of time, and (d) the measurement of effects immediately after exposure in a situation in which the physical stimuli present are similar or identical to those in the portrayal. Contrarily, it must also be acknowledged that such experiments arguably explore processes basic to human learning, with children the proper subjects as *tabulae rasae*. (Certainly, the child is closer to the man than the rat omnipresent in learning experiments is to the human.)

For young children, the situation is quite different. The experiments closely approximate childhood experience—adults in charge, mild frustration involving toys, a little television, an opportunity to play. Play is certainly the context of much childhood aggressiveness (and much of that on the part of older persons as well). For the everyday play of children of nursery school age, these experiments have a clear claim to external validity and therefore a similar claim to the development of aggressive patterns traceable to early childhood play experience.

Parallelism between the experimental setting and everyday life is not, of course, the sole factor on which external validity depends. External validity in the present case also draws support from the fact that experimental results have not become null or inverse with increases in the ecological validity of the manipulations and measures, as exemplified by Steuer, Applefield, and Smith (1971). In this experiment, children who viewed ordinary violent television programs for children during a break from the nursery school routine became more aggressive in everyday playground interaction than children who were comparable in pre-exposure playground aggressiveness but viewed nonviolent programs (Figure 10-1). Such experiments, in which the subjects are children of nursery school age, remind us that whenever real life approximates the circumstances of an experiment, however rarely, the challenge of external validity is vanquished; external validity varies with circumstance. In the case of children's play, it has been unambiguously demonstrated repeatedly that the viewing of violent television and film portrayals increases aggressive behavior.

ADOLESCENTS AND YOUNG ADULTS

In that other 1963 experiment, Berkowitz and Rawlings employed the ratings by the college student subjects of the experimenter's assistant as a measure of hostility. The experiment was designed to test their interpretation of the earlier results reported by Feshbach (1961) in which angered subjects exposed to a violent film episode expressed less hostility than those exposed to a neutral film. They attributed the lower level of hostility among Feshbach's subjects to the inhibition of aggressive responses as a consequence of exposure to violence instead of the lowering of aggressive drive specified by the catharsis formulation; sensitized to their impulses, the subjects suppressed them.

In the crucial comparison, Berkowitz and Rawlings examined aggressiveness scores for subjects who had seen the same episode from the movie *Champion,* in which the character played by Kirk Douglas is brutally beaten in the boxing ring, after having been told that the beating was (a) unjustified by the victim's prior behavior or (b) justified as punishment for that behavior. Before viewing the episode, subjects were provoked by the experimenter's assistant who made insulting and harassing comments while they attempted to complete an alleged IQ test; this gave them some reason to feel hostile toward the assistant.

The subjects in the crucial comparison were kept alike in regard to provocation, exposure to a violent film episode, and opportunity to express hostility toward the person who had harassed and insulted them. Berkowitz and Rawlings varied the degree to which the inhibitions about behaving aggressively were aroused by the episode by depicting the beating as justified in one condition and unjustified in the other. Presumably, such inhibitions would be reduced by seeing an example of socially approved (by way of the experimenter's description) retribution. Those for whom the retribution was depicted as justified did in fact express a higher degree of hostility toward the experimenter's assistant.

In subsequent experiments, Berkowitz and Geen (1966, 1967) manipulated the degree to which the experimenter's assistant was linked to the film by identifying him as either "Bob" or "Kirk" (the actor in the film). Anger was encouraged by the assistant giving the subjects the maximum number of possible electric shocks as the evaluation of their solution to a problem. Aggression was measured by the number of electric shocks delivered to the assistant by the subject in a reversal of the original problem-solving situation. Aggression was greater among those subjects for whom the assistant was linked to the film by the identicality of names.

Berkowitz and Alioto (1973) and Geen and Stonner (1972), in later experiments employing the same paradigm, manipulated the motives ascribed to those engaged in the portrayed behavior. In two instances, boxers were described as either engaged in a professional encounter or in a grudge match in which their goal was injury; in another, football teams were so distinguished. Subjects who were told that the behavior was motivated by an intent to injure engaged in higher levels of aggressiveness.

These findings exemplify the dimensions of normativeness and pertinence, in contrast to that of efficacy exemplified in the Rocky and Johnny experiment. Normativeness of

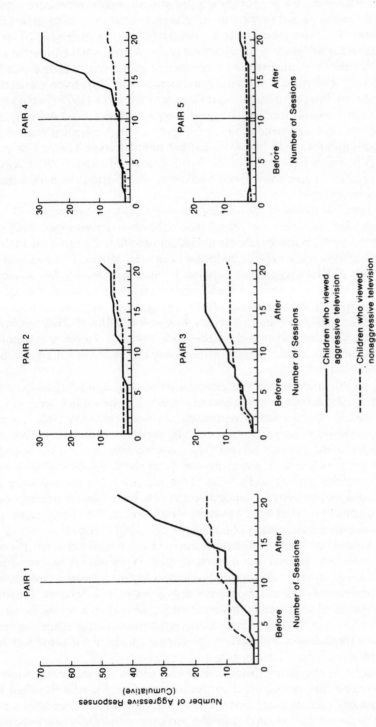

Figure 10.1. Aggressive Responses During Play of Preschool Children and Exposure to Violent Programs. *Note.* From *Television and Human Behavior* (p. 243) by G. Comstock, S. Chaffee, N. Katzman, M. McCombs, and D. Roberts, 1978, New York: Columbia University Press. Copyright 1978 by Rand Corporation. Reprinted by permission.

183

aggressive and hostile behavior is strongly implied when sports events are described as involving merited vengeance and retribution and the motive on the part of participants as injury to each other. Pertinence represents the degree to which a portrayal is linked by a viewer to real life and is achieved by the matching of the names of the film victim and the target of the electric shocks in the real life experiment. Susceptibility, of course, was heightened by the anger induced in the first phase of the experiments. That there are subtle links between the factors involved is apparent from Geen and Stonner's (1972) finding that the relationship between vengeful motive and greater aggressiveness occurred only among angered subjects; among nonangered subjects, the "professional" condition evoked greater aggression. Anger apparently was necessary for the normativeness imputed to vengeful violence by the portrayal to have an influence; in the absence of anger, such behavior may have been dismissed as inappropriate. Thus, pertinence would appear to have a pervasive role in linking these concepts.

These experiments are typical of the several dozen testing varied propositions, derived from disinhibition, cue (of which the "Kirk" manipulation is an example), and arousal formulations, regarding the influence of violent television and film portrayals on adolescents and young adults. Effects occur repeatedly in the laboratory setting. The apparent ability of violent portrayals to inhibit aggressive impulses is far from common, for, as the meta-analyses record, a very large majority of these experiments document heightened aggressiveness as a consequence either of exposure to a violent as compared to a nonviolent portrayal or of exposure to one or another version of a violent portrayal. They are, however, far from immune to skepticism in regard to external validity. They imply that exposure of adolescents and young adults to violent entertainment causes increased aggression and antisocial behavior.

Quite apart from the artificiality of the experimental setting, which arguably could encourage a certain playful deviance on the part of subjects that would not occur in real life in response to the stimuli supposedly represented in the laboratory, there are several ambiguities. The measures of aggression are typically the administering of electric shocks; these undeniably represent a hurtful act, yet they are administered under the approval of the experimenter in a context in which some degree of shock must be administered to provide feedback on the puzzle-solving tasks. They are not quite the voluntary act of aggression that is of social concern. Certainly they do not in these experiments approximate seriously harmful antisocial or criminal behavior. Retaliation by the victim, surely in real life a major deterrent to the expression of hostility, is not likely to have been perceived by the subjects as probable or even possible. The audio-visual stimuli are taken from commercial entertainment, but are brief, out of context, and are not viewed as a small part of the larger experience of viewing television at home or a film in a theater. The passage of time between exposure and measured hostility is only a few minutes, and the experiments guarantee the presence of an arguably deserving target, as well as a means by which to inflict punishment. The punishment is particularly appropriate to the injury—a lowered performance rating for rudeness and incivility, or electric shocks of the same sort administered earlier by the experimenter's assistant to the subject.

These experiments do not all approximate everyday adolescent and young adult experience. They document that effects occur in the laboratory setting and therefore would occur when laboratory circumstances occur in real life; they do not themselves make a strong case that exposure to television and film violence in everyday life increases the aggressive and antisocial behavior of adolescents and young adults.

The seemingly most plausible solution to the problem of external validity is the field experiment. Field experiments contrive to produce the factors on which causal inference in experimentation depend in naturalistic surroundings not challengeable for failing to approximate everyday experience for the subjects. These factors are comparability among groups and the manipulation of experience; if groups are comparable, subsequent differences between them can be attributed to differences in the experiences under the control of the experimenter.

In the laboratory setting, comparability is achieved (a) by making every subject's experience identical in every way except for the manipulations whose effects are to be examined and (b) by randomly assigning subjects to conditions so that the makeup of the control and one or more treatment groups varies only within the boundaries of chance. The statistical analysis applied to results then estimates the probability that differences reflect variation attributable to the vagaries of random assignment, and differences are said to be significant when the obtained probability falls below some criterion set by the experimenter.

Unfortunately, comparability and the manipulation of experience are not easily achieved outside the laboratory setting. Random assignment is often impossible; experience may be difficult to control or manipulate. The consequence is that the external validity ostensibly gained by the increase in the naturalism of the experimental circumstances very often has a high price—a decided loss in the confidence with which differences in behavior can be attributed to the intended and purposeful manipulations of the experimenter.

The several field experiments involving adolescents or adults (Feshbach & Singer, 1971; Leyens & Camino, 1974; Leyens, Camino, Parke, & Berkowitz, 1975; Loye, Gorney, & Steele, 1977; Milgram & Shotland, 1973; Wells, 1973) are not only mixed in outcome, but because of the ambiguities courted by field experiments do not encourage one to attempt to discriminate between the more and less convincing outcomes. While one meta-analysis (Andison, 1977) certainly records that a majority of field experiments (a collection that would include some with younger subjects) report aggressiveness or antisocial behavior increased by exposure to television or film violence, the other (Hearold, in press) reports that the average effect size among such studies is very close to zero. Valid though the outcomes may be, one cannot extend a full measure of credibility to a "no-TV violence" manipulation that must be diluted with violent programming in order to quell the complaints of the adolescents who are subjects (Feshbach & Singer, 1971)—an event that hints at frustration as an unintended manipulation—or to a design that requires subjects to commit a crime a week after viewing a television program for the medium to be recorded as having some influence on behavior (Milgram & Shotland, 1973). Lesser or more proximate effects are thereby ignored, although in the latter case the data appear to support the proposition derived from the research of Bandura and Berkowitz and their colleagues that antisocial behavior on the part of provoked subjects will be inhibited by exposure to a portrayal in which such behavior is punished (Comstock, 1983a). This was not, however, so interpreted by Milgram and Shotland. Cook, Kendzierski, and Thomas (1982) are correct to conclude in their analysis, commissioned by the National Academy of Sciences, that the field experiments so far available do not contribute much to the evidence on the influence of television and film violence on aggressive and antisocial behavior.

The remaining recourse is to seek evidence that reflects everyday events from a source other than field experiments. Such evidence is available from a series of surveys that began to influence conclusions about the effects of television and film violence with their publication as part of the research sponsored by the Surgeon General's 1972 inquiry (Chaffee, 1972; Comstock 1983a; Comstock et. al., 1978). They divide into five groups: (a) the large national and Maryland samples in the Surgeon General's inquiry (McIntyre & Teevan, 1972; Robinson & Bachman, 1972); (b) the Maryland and Wisconsin samples in the Surgeon General's inquiry (McLeod, Atkin, & Chaffee, 1972a, 1972b); (c) a series of studies by

Eron, Lefkowitz, and colleagues in which data are obtained from the sample over periods as distant from one another as a decade (Lefkowitz, Eron, Walder, & Huesmann, 1977), as well as over briefer spans of time (Huesmann, Lagerspetz, & Eron, 1982); (d) a survey of 1,500 London male teenagers by Belson (Belson, 1978); and (e) a panel survey spanning 3½ years in the lives of several hundred boys and girls (Milavsky, Kessler, Stipp, & Rubens, 1982a, 1982b).

The large national and Maryland surveys in the Surgeon General's inquiry (Chaffee, 1972; Comstock 1983a; Comstock et. al., 1978) examined associations between a preference for violent television programs and a variety of aggressive and antisocial behaviors. The national sample (Rubinson & Bochman, 1972) consisted of 1,559 19-year-old males; several television items were inserted in the final wave of a multi-wave panel study of American males that had begun several years earlier with a probability sample of 2,299 drawn from 87 high schools scattered over the United States. The Maryland sample (McIntyre & Teevan, 1972) consisted of 2,270 males and females from five senior and eight junior high schools. In both surveys, preference for violent programs was measured by asking the respondents to list their four favorite programs and by weighting the choices by program violence ratings obtained from a panel of judges. Aggressive and antisocial behaviors were measured by self-report.

The major findings were:

1. In the national survey, preference for violent programs was positively associated with interpersonal aggression among those who were initially higher in such aggression. When seriousness of delinquency was examined, such preference was positively associated with certain more serious acts, such as major theft, but not with less serious delinquency, such as petty theft, shoplifting, or drinking.
2. In the Maryland survey, preference for violent programs was positively associated with aggressive and violent acts, petty delinquency, defiance of parents, political protest, and serious delinquency, defined as involving conflict with the law. These associations remained positive when age, sex, socioeconomic status, and participation in social relationships were taken into account and were strongest for serious delinquency.
3. In the Maryland survey, conventional levels of statistical significance were achieved for all the associations (significance was not calculated for the national sample), but the associations were very modest, ranging from .06 (political protests) to .16 (serious delinquency).

These data suggest an association between preference for violent programs and aggressive and antisocial behavior. Arguably, preference would be positively associated with exposure and therefore be a surrogate for a measure of exposure; other surveys, however, have documented that the two are not synonymous (Chaffee, 1972; McLeod et al., 1972a, 1972b). Whether the reported associations are underestimates of the actual associations within these particular samples between exposure and behavior because of the weakness of the preference measure is moot, because there is no way empirically to discover the answer. These surveys can only be said to examine preference, not exposure.

The Wisconsin and Maryland surveys (McLeod et al., 1972a, 1972b) examined associations between aggressive and antisocial behavior, as reported by the respondents themselves and by peers and others, and the regular viewing of violent television programs. The Wisconsin sample consisted of about 600 junior and senior high school boys and girls. Exposure to violent programming was measured by obtaining from each respondent a score as to the frequency with which he or she regularly viewed all the major programs regularly broadcast in the area; frequency of viewing each program was then weighted by a program violence score obtained by having all the programs rated as to typical violence by a panel of viewers. For each respondent, the sum of these weighted scores represented the quantity (albeit crudely) of recent exposure to television violence. The Wisconsin measures of aggression and antisocial behavior included both reports from the respondents themselves and ratings of the respondents' behavior by classmates, teachers, and parents; the emphasis was on interpersonal aggression, verbal and physical. A variety of other data were also collected. They included a measure of the respondents' preference for (as contrasted with actual viewing of) particular programs (obtained by asking for each respondent's favorite programs). There were several important results:

1. Consistent positive associations were found between prior exposure to violent television programming and aggressive and antisocial behavior. Correlations were moderate ($r = .30$ is typical of the strongest), and the peer and self-report measures were responsible for the consistent pattern of positive associations.

2. A plausible explanation for the findings that would absolve the viewing of violent programming of any causal contribution is that young persons who are more aggressive and antisocial in behavior prefer violent programming and thus are, on the average, higher in its consumption. In such an interpretation of the data, the behavior and its antecedents would explain the media exposure, rather than the media exposure explaining, to some degree, the behavior. The data on program preferences offer an empirical test. If the preference for violent entertainment of young persons higher in antisocial and aggressive behavior is responsible for the positive associations between such behavior and the viewing of violent programs, the expressed preference for violent programs should correlate at least as strongly with antisocial and aggressive behavior as does the viewing of such programs; preference should explain the association with exposure. The explanation was proven to be invalid. In this instance, the correlations between preference and behavior were irregular and much more modest than those between exposure and behavior.

3. The associations between exposure to violent programs and aggressive and antisocial behavior were not reduced to null when a variety of variables in addition to program preference were taken into account. These variables included intelligence and scholastic achievement, socioeconomic status, age, and sex. Each offered an opportunity to test empirically both (a) the universality of the association and (b) the plausibility of the proposition implied by the experimental literature—that television had a causal role. The discovery that the associations in a larger sample were attributable to a subgroup would not eliminate the possibility that television was causally implicated for that subgroup, but would merely qualify the circumstances under which such a possibility could be entertained. In fact, in no instance did the controlling for another variable identify a subgroup for which the exposure and behavior association did not hold. On the other hand, controlling for these variables did eliminate several threats to the plausibility of the proposition implied by the experimental literature. Young people lower in intellectual performance do typically watch more television (California Assessment Program, 1980), and they might behave on the average more aggressively and antisocially because of economic and social frustration and less restrictive norms. Neither, however, reduced the associations to null.

4. When the data are arrayed by both sex and school grade, the direction of correlations remains consistently positive, although, as would be expected when the initial correlations are modest, not all remain statistically significant. Thus, the associations in the larger sample are not largely attributable to the deviant but inexplicable television viewing and aggressive and antisocial behavior of some single segment of the sample.

5. When it was possible, the associations between current aggressive and antisocial

behavior and exposure to violent television programs, both recently and at an earlier age, were examined. The correlations were at least as strong with exposure at an earlier age. Since such a retrospective measure of exposure to television programs would almost certainly be less reliable than a measure of recent exposure, this suggests a stronger association of the behavior with earlier than with recent viewing and would be consistent with the interpretation that earlier exposure to violent television programs has contributed to recent aggressive and antisocial behavior.

Survey data such as these supply what laboratory experiments cannot by their very nature provide and what field experiments may fail to provide because of the difficulties inherent in attempting to equal the inferential prowess of the laboratory experiment in real life. Survey data provide evidence that a phenomenon (in this case, aggressive and antisocial behavior) that in the laboratory has been demonstrated to be caused to some degree by an experience (in this case, exposure to violent television or film portrayals) is in everyday life associated with the everyday experience ostensibly simulated in the laboratory.

Surveys are highly problematic for causal inference; this is not solely a function of the inability of the cross-sectional survey to establish unambiguously time-order (a phenomenon that follows another can hardly be its cause), but also of the complexities of the possible interrelationships among variables measured and between measured and unmeasured variables (the latter of which might be responsible for the observed association between measured variables) when antecedent experience has not been manipulated and other factors assiduously controlled, as is possible in the laboratory setting. Surveys, however, are far from being without implications for causal inference. As in the present instance, they can establish whether an association implied by experimentation occurs in everyday life. Also as in the present instance, they can heighten or diminish the likelihood that a causal sequence demonstrated experimentally applies to the real world by examining, when such an association occurs in the real world, the plausibility of alternative explanations and the consistency of the data as a whole with the causal interpretation under scrutiny. The major early study by Eron, Lefkowitz, & colleagues (1963, 1971) involves data collected from the same sample in a rural upstate New York county spanning a 10-year period. The second collection was sponsored by the Surgeon General's inquiry (Lefkowitz, Eron, Walder, & Huesmann, 1972), although the fullest account is *Growing Up To Be Violent* (Lefkowitz et. al., 1977). At the time of the first collection, the respondents were in the third grade. Ten years later, data could be obtained from about half (211 males and 216 females) of the original number of subjects. The study is extraordinary in regard to media influence on child development because of the length of time covered; only the inclusion of questions about television exposure in the first wave, in what was conceived as an examination of the correlates of aggression with no particular attention to the media, made it possible (Eron, Walder, & Lefkowitz, 1971). It has provoked much comment and controversy (Howitt, 1972; Huesmann, Eron, Lefkowitz, & Walder, 1973; Kaplan, 1972; Kay, 1972; Kenny, 1972; Neale, 1972), principally because the authors interpret the data as identifying greater exposure to television programs in the third grade as the "probable cause" of increased aggressiveness a decade later.

The principal measure of aggressive behavior was peer-ratings, in which everyone who said they knew a respondent rated that person. The 10-item scale covered such behavior as starting fights, pushing and shoving, taking things, getting into trouble, bothering others, telling lies, and making unfriendly gestures. In effect, third grade ratings represented the average judgement of those in the same classroom; later ratings represented the average judgement of those who said that they knew the person. The third grade measure of exposure to violent television programs was based on children's three favorite programs, as reported by their mothers; the later measure was based on the respondent's report of his or her four favorites. The investigators' conclusion, based on the pattern of intercorrelations among variables synchronously as well as over time, applied only to the males.

The decline in recent years in the credibility placed in the analytic model, cross-lagged correlation, encourages rejection of this conclusion (Cook & Campbell, 1979; Rogosa, 1980). There are also reasons to question the suitability of the data for this model (Chaffee, 1972; Comstock, 1978). Rejection of an author's conclusion as stated, however, does not necessarily imply lack of merit, value, or interpretability of the data. In fact, these data significantly increase the credence that can be extended to the proposition that exposure to television violence increases aggressiveness in real life. They do so by adding to the positive synchronous correlations of the cross-sectional surveys a positive correlation between exposure and behavior across a number of years—a correlation that is not only larger than the early synchronous correlation among this sample, but also that is not reduced to null by eliminating from the television-behavior relationship the influence of aggression in the third grade and thereby almost certainly the influence of any factors affecting third grade aggressiveness. That the mode of later measurement of aggression does not precisely date the occasion as a decade after the first measurement, but some vague period in the mind of the rater, hardly invalidates the data as representing behavior a number of years subsequent. That a mother's report of a child's three favorite programs is acknowledgedly not a highly accurate index of exposure does not consign such data to irrelevance; norms would hardly call for a mother to inflate her child's preference for violence. A mother also would not yet have become indifferent to or ignorant of her child's television viewing, and so the data is this case probably do distinguish, if crudely, between greater and lesser exposure to violent programs. Hitting and shoving, starting fights, lying, troublemaking, and the like indisputably are aggressive and, in the teenage society in which they occur, antisocial. Although like the measures in the cross-sectional surveys they fall short of the criminal, they, as do the cross-sectional measures, unmistakably border on the seriously harmful. These data thus make their significant contribution by the notable over-time correlation that exceeds the same-time correlation for the two variables and is dependent on the level of aggressive behavior at the time of initial measurement.

The Belson (1978) survey is the most substantial to date on the topic of television violence and aggressive and antisocial behavior. The sample of 1,565 London males between the ages of 12 and 17 is large, in fact the largest of a single sex in any of the surveys measuring exposure to violent programs; and its representativeness is exemplary, since probability methods were used. This stands in contrast to the surveys discussed so far, which, while employing methods to preclude any bias in selection, could not be said at the same time to be a representative sample of any particular larger group. Hypotheses were elaborated with diligence, leading to 22 major and 150 minor hypotheses. Exposure to violent programs and aggressive and antisocial behavior were measured with meticulous sensitivity. As in other surveys, judges were employed to score programs for violence; the resulting measures not only weight frequency of exposure but also distinguish between exposure to 13 different types of violence such as "realistic fiction," "gruesome," "horrific," and 'in a good cause' in addition to such program genres as cartoon, wrestling and boxing, other sports, science fiction, and slapstick. Judges were also used to score hypothetical acts for the degree to which they represent aggressive and antisocial behavior; thus, higher scores can be said to represent with validity behavior thought to be aggressive and antisocial by ordinary mortals. The scales also include behavior that is unambiguously criminal and harmful, such as attempted rape, burning someone with a cigarette while others hold him down, attacking someone with a tire iron, firing a revolver at another person, falsely reporting bomb plantings to the police, beating pets, striking someone with a broken bottle, and telling someone that his or her mother has just been killed in an auto accident.

Belson, by statistically matching his respondents on all variables except those of principal interest and by weighting the likelihood of the various plausible interpretations by statistical manipulations, concluded that:

> The evidence gathered through this investigation is very strongly supportive of the hypothesis that high exposure to television violence increases the degree to which boys engage in serious violence. Thus for serious violence by boys: (i) heavier viewers of television violence commit a great deal more serious violence than do lighter viewers of television violence who have been closely equated to the heavier viewers in terms of a wide array of empirically derived matching variables; (ii) the reverse form of this hypothesis is *not* supported by the evidence. (Belson, 1978, p. 15)

It is not necessary to place such an inferential burden on these data to assign them some importance. The validity of such a causal inference depends on the ability of Belson to overcome the fundamental limitations of (a) measures obtained essentially within the same time span, for which time order cannot reasonable be established, and (b) the possibility of an alternative explanation for the observed concordance. Few studies, experimental or survey in design, fully and conclusively satisfy all the objections that can be raised about internal and external validity. The issue is not acceptance or dismissal of an author's interpretation(s), but the probabilities that should be assigned to the various possible interpretations and the precise meaning that it is reasonable to attach to the outcome. In the present instance, the data pose far fewer ambiguities for interpretation when they are assessed in terms of association (in contrast to causation) and of the degree to which the pattern of associations is consistent with a causal role for exposure to violent television programs. From this perspective, the major findings are:

1. Male teenagers who had viewed a substantially greater quantity of violent television programs than males otherwise like them in measured characteristics and attributes committed a markedly greater number of seriously harmful antisocial and criminal acts. As with the Maryland and Wisconsin data (McLeod et al., 1972a, 1972b), there was little to suggest that this association could be attributed to the seeking out of more violent entertainment as a consequence of such behavior.

2. Each of three less serious categories of aggressive and antisocial behavior also were positively associated with greater exposure to television violence. Although the seeking out of more violent entertainment as a consequence of such behavior could not be said to explain these associations, such an explanation could not be dismissed with as much confidence as in the case of seriously harmful antisocial and criminal behavior.

3. Exposure to violence in newspapers, comic books, and theater films was also positively associated with aggressive and antisocial behavior less serious than seriously harmful antisocial and criminal behavior, and exposure to violence in comic books and theater films was associated with seriously harmful antisocial and criminal behavior. The seeking out of more violent communications stimuli as a consequence of such behavior could not be said to explain these associations, but neither could such an explanation be dismissed with as much confidence as in the case of the association between exposure to television violence and seriously harmful antisocial and criminal behavior.

4. Two specific forms of antisocial and aggressive behavior, (a) aggressiveness in sports and play and (b) swearing and the use of bad language, were associated with exposure to television violence. There was some possibility that these associations could be explained by the seeking out of such entertainment as a consequence of the behavior in question, but the indication is that such a circumstance was not likely.

5. Associations for behavioral and cognitive variables were not symmetrical, as no notable associations were recorded between exposure to television violence and attitudes favoring or accepting of violence, such as preoccupation with such behavior, expressed willingness to engage in such behavior, belief that such behavior is a way to solve problems, or perceiving such behavior as human nature.

The Belson data add importantly to the evidence gained from surveys of a positive association between exposure to television violence and aggressive and antisocial behavior by documenting, for the sample under study, a positive association between such exposure and seriously harmful and criminal behavior, as well as positive associations between exposure and less serious levels of such behavior. It extends the findings of the Wisconsin and Maryland samples (McLeod et al., 1972a, 1972b) to more serious misbehavior; the borders of the seriously harmful and criminal behavior, on which the former lay, have here been crossed.

The survey by Milavsky et al. (1982a, 1982b) spans 3 years in the lives of children and teenagers in a southwestern and a midwestern American city. In total, data were obtained from about 2,400 boys and girls in the second through sixth grades and from about 800 male teenagers in Fort Worth and Minneapolis. Measures of aggressive and antisocial behavior and television exposure were obtained six times from the elementary school sample and five times from the teenage sample. Other data were collected from school records, parents, and the respondents. The elementary school measure of aggression was peer report by classmates and emphasized interpersonal aggression; both the method of collection and the character and seriousness of the aggression paralleled those of the 10-year survey by Lefkowitz et al. (1977). Teenage aggression was measured by the replies of the respondents to four distinct scales—"personal," "property," "teacher," and "delinquency"—because the absence of the elementary school practice of pupils remaining in the same classroom for the entire day made classroom peer reports impractical. The character and seriousness of the aggression measured by the "personal" scale resembles that measured among the elementary school sample. The measure of television exposure involved the same procedure as that employed in the Maryland and Wisconsin surveys (McLeod et al., 1972a, 1972b): frequency of exposure to individual programs as reported by the respondents weighted by the violence ratings of the programs obtained from judges.

Respondents entered and left the sample, depending on whether they were available on the day of data collection (a family's moving away obviously eliminated their child), and respondents in some waves were added. The attrition results in a varying number of respondents in each wave of measurement, with substantially fewer in each wave than in the total from whom data were collected over the 3 years. Over time, the number from whom data were collected at two points in time decreases markedly as the span of time lengthens; for example, among elementary school males with 3 months between measurements, $n = 497$; 9 months, 356; 2 years, 211; 3 years, 112.

The consequence is a body of data resembling in some respects the Wisconsin and Maryland surveys of McLeod et al. (exposure measures, peer reports, interpersonal aggression), the survey by Lefkowitz et al. (measurement of the same sample over a span of time, peer reports), and the Belson survey (measurement of antisocial behavior serious enough to qualify as "delinquency"). It combines the superior exposure measure of the first with the over-time measurement of the second; and although the delinquency measured cannot be said to approach the Belson study in thoroughness or range, it qualifies as seriously harmful or criminal behavior (knife fights, mugging, car thefts, gang fights, arrest, being beaten up). The sample, while much smaller than that of Belson and without claim to representing statistically a larger population (as was also the case with the Wisconsin and

Maryland and the Lefkowitz et al. [1977] data), is sizable and does permit examination of associations both synchronously and between waves. The major findings were:

1. For both elementary school boys and girls and for the teenage males, there were low positive correlations between exposure to television violence and interpersonal aggression that achieved statistical significance in each wave of measurement. After the attempted elimination of the contribution to this association of other variables, such as socioeconomic status and race, the associations remained consistently positive but often fell below the level of conventional statistical significance.

2. When the synchronous associations are deserted for those over time, positive associations remain more frequent, but, to a marked degree, only among the elementary school boys (Tables 10.1 and 10.2) and the teenage males. Among the elementary school boys, the associations were uniformly positive and noticeably larger in size for the 5 of the 15 wave pairings that represent the longest spans of time between measurement—2 years or more. The shorter time spans (3 months is the minimum) of course had substantially greater number of respondents (sometimes by severalfold), and several of the correlations for these lengthier spans are larger in magnitude than those that achieved significance when the spans were shorter and the numbers of respondents were much larger. The implication is that the number of correlations said to be significant would have been greater had not attrition so sharply reduced sample size for the lengthier spans of time between waves. Among the teenage males, the pattern of increasing association with the passage of time occurs only with personal aggression, the self-report measure that approximates the peer reports of interpersonal aggression. Of the four aggression measures, this measure was the one with the strongest modest synchronous correlation with exposure to violent television entertainment.

3. When the over-time associations in the elementary school sample of boys were examined among 95 subgroups formed on the basis of 43 social and personal attributes, a majority were positive and 9% achieved statistical significance; similar results occurred for the girls.

4. The analytic model employed for the over-time correlations largely eliminates the influence of other variables from the association of prior exposure to violence with later aggression (by controlling for prior aggression and thereby all variables up to that time contributing to aggression); thus, positive correlations encourage attributing any observed association to the causal influence of exposure. When the investigators impose on the various over-time analyses criteria for the number of significant positive correlations that would lead them to accept such an inference (a step made necessary by the lack of independence between the various pairings of waves, so that an anomaly would affect more than one pairing, as well as by the possibility that some could be attributable to sampling variation), they regularly find that the number is at the border of their criteria.

5. When the data are arrayed by the length of span between waves and the various coefficients of association for each span are averaged, the increasing degree of association with lengthening of span observed for 5 of the 15 lengthiest spans among the elementary school boys appears to hold generally, and for both boys and girls (Figure 10.2), except for spans of middling length, which represent an anomaly (Cook, Kendzierski, & Thomas, 1983).

6. The likelihood that the increasing association with the passage of time between exposure to violent television programming and aggressive behavior is attributable to such behavior among males of lower socioeconomic status is diminished by the data for middle class girls—about 70% of the entire female sample—which display a pattern similar to, if less pronounced than, that of the males (Table 10.2; Figure 10.2).

Table 10.1. Basic Model Regression Coefficients for Over-time Associations Between Earlier Exposure to Violent Television Programs and Earlier Aggressive Behavior and Later Aggressive Behavior[†] (without controls for intervening TV variables)

Wave Pair	Duration	Earlier Aggression Coefficients		Earlier TV Violence Exposure Coefficients		
		b	beta	b	beta	n
Elementary School Boys						
III–IV	3 months	.921*	.857	.167*	.063	497
II–III	4 months	.852*	.844	.091	.038	413
I–II	5 months	.713*	.686	−.070	−.026	364
II–IV	7 months	.844*	.771	.244*	.094	409
I–III	9 months	.710*	.671	−.016	−.006	356
I–IV	1 year	.699*	.632	.065	.023	349
IV–V	1 year	.723*	.734	−.070	−.026	301
V–VI	1 year	.688*	.723	.154	.058	188
III–V	1 yr./3 mos.	.727*	.734	.016	.007	291
II–V	1 yr./7 mos.	.737*	.665	.038	.016	240
I–IV	2 years	.685*	.594	.176	.067	211
IV–VI	2 years	.673*	.708	.125	.049	161
III–VI	2 yrs./3 mos.	.620*	.642	.281(*)	.121	147
II–VI	2 yrs./7 mos.	.765*	.677	.152	.065	121
I–VI	3 years	.644*	.543	.306	.113	112
Elementary School Girls						
III–IV	3 months	.891*	.784	.138*	.081	491
II–III	4 months	.754*	.762	.082	.060	426
I–II	5 months	.616*	.676	−.062	−.037	391
II–IV	7 months	.766*	.662	.168*	.105	408
I–III	9 months	.555*	.634	−.008	−.005	384
I–IV	1 year	.612*	.636	.036	.020	369
IV–V	1 year	.504*	.501	.120	.062	296
V–VI	1 year	.499*	.585	.153	.101	153
III–V	1 yr./3 mos.	.694*	.614	−.043	−.028	292
II–V	1 yr./7 mos.	.672*	.602	.005	.004	245
I–V	2 years	.437*	.484	.103	.062	236
IV–VI	2 years	.573*	.679	−.017	−.011	134
III–VI	2 yrs./3 mos.	.659*	.616	.135	.094	133
II–VI	2 yrs./7 mos.	.622*	.606	.215*	.157	123
I–VI	3 years	.541*	.596	−.049	−.029	113

*Coefficients approach or exceed twice their standard errors.
**"b" refers to *metric* partial regression coefficients; "beta" refers to *standardized* partial regression coefficients.
(*) Coefficient = 1.94 its standard error.
[†] Adapted from Milavsky et al., 1982a, pp. 147, 149.

7. For teenage boys, the over-time analyses of the more serious measures of aggression —"property," "teacher," and "delinquency"—do not indicate any regular pattern of association whether the criterion is statistical significance or the frequency of positive vs. negative signs among the measures of association.

Milavsky et al. (1982a, 1982b) interpret these data as inconsistent with the view that exposure to violent television programming increases the likelihood of subsequent greater aggressive or antisocial behavior. They conclude that there is no evidence in their data of

Table 10.2. Lisrel Analyses of Over-time Associations Between Earlier
Exposure to Violent Television Programs and Later Aggressive Behavior
(Elementary School Sample)

Wave Pair	Duration	N (Boys/Girls)	A(t-1) Beta (Boys/Girls)	TV(t-1) Beta (Boys/Girls)	TV(t-1) Beta[a] (Middle-Class Girls)
I–II	5 months	364/391	.724/.749	−.046/−.090	−.004
I–III	9 months	356/384	.714/.691	−.018/−.024	.013
I–IV	1 year	349/369	.668/.682	.038/.008	.051
I–V	2 years	211/236	.624/.496	.096/.078	.032
I–VI	3 years	112/113	.571/.651	.160/−.024	.137
II–III	4 months	413/426	.876/.801	.046/.087*	.058
II–IV	7 months	409/408	.792/.676	.124*/.132*	.092*
II–V	1 yr./7 mos.	240/245	.694/.638	.014/−.006	.015*
II–VI	2 yrs./7 mos.	121/123	.699/.601	.070/.213	.144
III–IV	3 months	497/491	.885/.801	.078*/.068*	.041
III–V	1 yr./3 mos.	291/292	.753/.657	.015/−.043	.022
III–VI	2 yrs./3 mos.	147/133	.663/.610	.133*/.141	.200*
IV–V	1 year	301/296	.759/513	−.043/.074	.088
IV–VI	2 years	161/134	.721/.723	.059/−.022	.082
V–VI	1 year	188/153	.750/.650	.075/.109	.109

Note. From "The Implicit Assumptions of Television Research: An Analysis of the 1982 NIMH Report on Television and Behavior" by T.D. Cook, D.A. Kendzierski, and S.V. Thomas, 1983, *Public Opinion Quarterly*, 47, p. 184. Copyright 1983 by the University of Chicago Press. Used with permission.
* p < .05; all aggression coefficients are significant.
[a] Coefficients in this column are from OLS, not LISREL, analyses.

a causal relationship on the grounds that: (a) The synchronous correlations, although all positive and significant, are not amenable to causal inference, because synchronous data collection is problematic for the establishment of time order—a crucial matter in causal inference (experience at time$_2$ can hardly be expected to influence behavior at time$_1$); (b) the various over-time analyses fail in the number of positive correlations meeting the conventional levels of statistical significance applied by the investigators to exceed the number they estimate could occur as a result of sampling variation; and (c) significance in all cases is highly sensitive to the introduction of socioeconomic status as a control variable.

Three independent reviewers (Cook et al., 1983; Huesmann, 1984; Kenny, 1984) have reached quite different conclusions. Cook et al., for example, pointed out that the data on socioeconomic status introduced into the analysis are thoroughly inadequate in both sensitivity and uniform availability for all respondents to bear the inferential weight of diminishing the frequency of significant positive associations. They furthermore faulted Milavsky et al. in the case of the teenagers in their sample for failing to adjudicate among the different waves on the basis of quality of the data.

When Cook et al. isolated the data of highest quality for this portion of the sample, they found: (a) for "personal" aggression, nonnegative coefficients that increase with the span of time between waves (2, above); (b) for "teacher" aggression, nonnegative coefficients unrelated in size with the time spanned; (c) for "property" aggression, inconsistent results; and (d) for "delinquency" aggression, nonnegative coefficients that increase with the span of time between waves. They also argued that the dismissal of the possibility of decided evidence of effects among some subgroups is cavalier and that the analytic model employed tends to minimize the likelihood of obtaining evidence of an effect by ignoring truly cu-

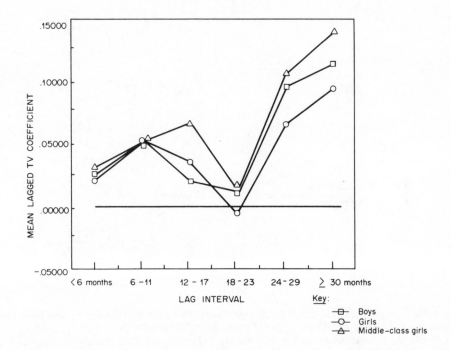

Figure 10.2. Over-Time (Lagged) Television Coefficients and Delay between Waves, Elementary School Sample. *Note.* From "The Implicit Assumptions of Television Research: An Analysis of the 1982 NIMH Report on Television and Behavior" by T. D. Cook, D.A. Kendzierski, and S. V. Thomas, 1983, *Public Opinion Quarterly, 47,* p. 185. Copyright 1983 University of Chicago Press. Reprinted by permission.

mulative influences of earlier television viewing on earlier aggression—heightened aggression that itself could contribute to later aggression with no direct influence of the earlier television exposure on the later aggression (Figure 10.3). Finally, they introduced data from recent over-time surveys of American and Finnish elementary school boys and girls undertaken by several of the investigators involved in the earlier 10-year survey by Eron, Lefkowitz, and colleagues (Huesmann, Lagerspetz, & Eron, in press), using the viewing weighted by program violence measure as the exposure measure and peer ratings as the aggression measure, with the exposure measure reflecting cumulative exposure to violent programming over a 2-year period rather than the briefer period implied by the techniques used in all prior surveys (Table 10.3). Cook et al. observed that the results "were similar to Milavsky et al. in direction, magnitude, and the low frequency of statistical significance" (p. 191) and that Huesmann, Lagerspetz, and Eron (in press) interpret their data as "evidence of an effect."

The data collected by Milavsky et al. add importantly to the evidence about the effects of exposure to television violence on the aggressive and antisocial behavior of adolescents and young adults. They unambiguously confirm the earlier findings of the Wisconsin and Maryland surveys (McLeod et al., 1972a, 1972b) of a positive association between exposure in everyday life to violent television programs and everyday behavior that is aggressive and antisocial. They do so impressively, because of the comparatively large number of respond-

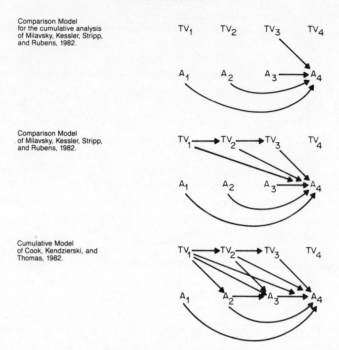

Figure 10.3. Alternative Models for Analysis of Cumulative Effects. *Note.* From *Television Research for Science and Policy: An Alien Perspective on the NIMH Report on Television and Behavior* by T. D. Cook, D. A. Kendzierski, and S. V. Thomas, 1982. Unpublished manuscript prepared for the Committee on Research and Law Enforcement and the Administration of Justice of the National Research Council on the National Academy of Sciences. Reprinted by permission.

ents, the repeated replication in wave after wave, and its presence for both sexes at all ages. These data are the strongest documentation of an association between the exposure and behavior in question to date. That this confirmed association may be attributable to the influence of one or more other variables, without television in fact heightening the behavior, is certainly possible, but the search for such variables in the Wisconsin and Maryland data and in all the other surveys was unsuccessful. Milavsky et al. are themselves

Table 10.3. Cumulative Exposure to Violent Programs in 1976 and 1977 and Aggressive Behavior in 1978 (Standardized Regression Coefficients—Elementary School Sample, Grades 1–5)

Boys	Girls
U.S. Sample	
.079	.135[*]
(n = 191)	(n = 221)
Finnish Sample	
.110	.012
(n = 80)	(n = 85)

Note. From "The Implicit Assumptions of Television Research: An Analysis of the 1982 NIMH Report on Television and Behavior" by T.D. Cook, D.A. Kendzierski, and S.V. Thomas, 1983, *Public Opinion Quarterly, 47*, p. 191. Copyright 1983 by Columbia University Press. Reprinted with permission.
[*]$p < .05$.

not more successful because of the problematic character of their measures of socioeconomic status.

Like the Lefkowitz et al. (1977) 10-year survey, Milavsky et al. document positive associations over time, although such a conclusion must ignore the criteria employed by the investigators. It rests not on exceeding an arbitrary threshold in the frequency of coefficients said to be significant, but on the decided pattern of coefficients: A majority are positive, the average is clearly positive, they increase among the lengthier time spans to levels that often would achieve the investigator's significance were it not for the sharp attrition in numbers of respondents, and the frequency of coefficients that achieve the required level is in fact at the border of the required threshold. The correspondence of their data with that of Huesmann et al. (1982) adds credibility to this interpretation. Because of the use by Milavsky et al. of an analytic model that would encourage causally attributing the greater aggressive and antisocial behavior to the higher prior exposure to violent television programs, this pattern supports such an inference.

In regard to implications for causation, Milavsky et al. put their emphasis very strongly on their over-time analysis. They are certainly correct to do so, because the availability of repeated over-time measurement is the particular strength of their data. They are wrong, however, not to give some role to the synchronous associations in assessing the likelihood that everyday exposure to violent television programs increases everyday aggressive and antisocial behavior. This is particularly so because of their anemic measurement of socioeconomic status; without its introduction, the coefficients achieving significance are undeniably abundant. Even if one unreasonably accedes to the diminished number remaining after its introduction, the coefficients remains on the average positive. These data in fact further enhance the external validity (in regard to the behavior of adolescents and young adults) of the laboratory experiments whose subjects were college students by the repeated documentation of a positive association between exposure to violent television programs and aggressive and antisocial behavior among teenage males.

The associational evidence is certainly strongest for the synchronous correlations (because of the near-universal achievement of the applied criterion for statistical significance at all waves among all three samples—elementary school boys and girls and teenage males—prior to the introduction of the inadequate measure of socioeconomic status). It is also strongest for interpersonal aggression since, among the four measures of teenage aggression, it is this one that displays the strongest synchronous correlation with exposure to television violence, thereby paralleling the data for the elementary school samples.

The over-time associational evidence nevertheless is far from null. Among the elementary school samples, the modest positive average associations and the increase over time to levels that would meet the criteria statistical significance without the sharp attrition (for example, the number of males in the two most distant wave pairings is less than one fourth those in the two most adjacent) are apparent.

The evidence is least strong in regard to the more serious forms of teenage aggressive and antisocial behavior—"property," "teacher," and "delinquency." These only begin to resemble the data for lesser misbehavior when Cook et al. (1983) confine the analysis to waves with the ostensibly most valid data. Nevertheless, Cook et al. (1982, 1983) do find increasing association over lengthening spans of time among these selected data for the most serious misbehavior, "delinquency."

On the whole, then, the data of Milavsky et al. are consistent with and add to the support given by the data from surveys for the proposition that greater exposure to violent television entertainment heightens subsequent aggressive and antisocial behavior. They give only the scantest conceivable support, however, to the major finding of the Belson survey—that the association in question extends to seriously harmful and criminal behavior.

The five groups of survey evidence progressively strengthen the external or everyday validity among adolescents and young adults of the causal sequence demonstrated in the laboratory experiments. In regard to aggressive and antisocial behavior, they document:

1. Small positive synchronous correlations with a weak and ambiguous measure of exposure (number of violent programs among stated favorites);
2. Modest positive synchronous correlations with a valid measure of exposure (frequency of viewing weighted by program violence) for interpersonal aggression;
3. Modest over-time correlations involving the same valid exposure measure and interpersonal aggression;
4. Repeated instances in which such exposure and behavioral associations synchronously and over time have been found;
5. No persistent or compelling demonstration that these associations are wholly explained by a set of variables that does not include a causal contribution by television exposure;
6. Interpersonal aggression as the type of behavior most convincingly associated with exposure, as it has been measured repeatedly and correlations have regularly ranged from small to modest positive, both synchronously and over time; and,
7. In the two instances in which measured behavior exceeded the threshold of seriously harmful behavior, (a) a marked positive correlation between exposure to violent television programs and seriously harmful and criminal behavior and (b) marginal evidence of a positive correlation increasing over time.

IMPLICATIONS OF THE EXPERIMENTS

The associational evidence over time implies a developmental process, with earlier television experience affecting later behavior. It does so because of the absence of any alternative explanation within the data for the consistently increasing degree of association with the passage of time. The experiments in which the subjects were very young children, usually of nursery school age, thus come to have implications for the behavior of adolescents and young adults in two respects. First, they identify the circumstances on which the influence of exposure to violent television and film portrayals on the aggressive and antisocial behavior of young children are contingent. That is, they define the early experiences involving television that have implications for later behavior through their immediate effects. Second, by investigating what are most probably basic human age-indifferent influences by which behavior is shaped, these experiments also identify those circumstances for adolescents and young adults. In effect, they define continuing experiences involving television likely to have implications for present and future behavior regardless of age.

The first of these, of course, on the surface is the most compelling because the generalizations about immediate behavior extend to the population of the same age as the subjects. The second, however, has in its support social learning theory, which is well and thoughtfully developed (Bandura, 1969, 1971, 1973, 1978), has extensive support from both experiments and events drawn from everyday behavior, and has been applied with success in explaining and predicting behavior varying widely in type, including aggression, altruism, pathological and self-defeating behavior, and coping (Comstock, 1983b; Farquhar et al., 1977; Rushton, 1980). The principal caveat to such dual application is that it cannot be applied indiscriminately in reverse with regard to the age of subjects; that is, manipulations on which effects among subjects of college age are contingent may not have implications for very young viewers, because the concepts involved, such as justified vs. unjustified or malicious vs. nonmalicious violence, may have little or no meaning for them. Among these circumstances are:

1. Reward or lack of punishment for the portrayed perpetrator of violence (Bandura, 1965; Bandura et al., 1963b; Rosekrans & Hartup, 1967).

2. Portrayal of the violence as justified (Berkowitz & Rawlings, 1963; Meyer, 1972).

3. Association with violence of cues in the portrayal that resemble those likely to be encountered in real life, such as a victim in the portrayal with the same name or characteristics as someone towards whom the viewer holds animosity (Berkowitz & Geen, 1966, 1967; Donnerstein & Berkowitz, 1981; Geen & Berkowitz, 1967).

4. Portrayal of the perpetrator of violence as similar to the viewer (Rosekrans, 1967; Lieberman Research, 1975).

5. Depiction of behavior ambiguous to the viewer solely on the basis of the behavior itself as motivated by the desire to inflict harm or injury—in effect, perception of behavior that might be ascribed to other motives as motivated by malicious intent, such as perceiving a football game as a grudge match with injury to the opponent as important as scoring (Berkowitz & Alioto, 1973; Geen & Stonner, 1972).

6. Violence portrayed so that its consequences do not stir distaste or arouse inhibitions over such behavior, such as violence without pain, suffering, or prolonged hurt on the part of the victim, sorrow among friends and lovers, or remorse by the perpetrator (Berkowitz & Rawlings, 1963).

7. Violence portrayed as representing real events rather than events concocted for a fictional film (Feshbach, 1972).

8. Portrayed violence that is not the subject of critical or disparaging commentary (Lefcourt, Barnes, Parke, & Schwartz, 1966).

9. Portrayals of violence whose commission particularly pleases the viewer (Ekman et al., 1972; Slife & Rychiak, 1982).

10. Portrayals in which the violence is not interrupted by violence in a light or humorous vein (Lieberman Research, 1975).

11. Portrayed abuse that includes physical violence and aggression instead of or in addition to verbal abuse (Lieberman Research, 1975).

12. Physical aggression against a female by a male engaged in sexual conquest when a likely real-life target is a similar female (Donnerstein & Barrett, 1978; Donnerstein & Hallan, 1978).

13. Physical aggression against a female by a male engaged in sexual conquest in which the victim is portrayed as eventually relishing the assault and a likely real-life target is a similar female (Donnerstein & Berkowitz, 1981).

14. Portrayals, violent or otherwise, that leave the viewer in a state of unresolved excitement (Zillman, 1971; Zillman, Johnson, & Hanrahan, 1973).

15. Viewers who are in a state of anger or provocation before seeing a violent portrayal (Berkowitz & Geen, 1966; Donnerstein & Berkowitz, 1981; Geen, 1968).

16. Viewers who are in a state of frustration after viewing a violent portrayal (Geen, 1968; Geen & Berkowitz, 1967; Worchel, Hardy, & Hurley, 1976).

Those that most clearly apply to younger children involve reward or punishment, similarity of viewer and perpetrator, perceived reality, gratification received, humorous violence, and such emotionally and physically facilitated factors as excitement, anger, or provocation. These latter circumstances appear to be particularly forceful in regard to children; as the meta-analysis (Hearold, in press) records, the average effect size for exposure to antisocial television stimuli when the dependent variable is a physiological response—an unambiguous indicator of arousal or excitation—is more than three times greater for children between the ages of 5 and 11 than for persons of college age.

The wide applicability of the factors examined in the experiments has been questioned because of the frequent presence of prior provocation or frustration. The argument is that such a state approaches a necessary condition and that effects would be rare. Quite apart from the fact that the provocations and frustrations present in the experiments are the peccadilloes encountered daily—rudeness and minor deprivation—Hearold's meta-analysis (in press) documents that while such a state will heighten the likelihood of an effect, the effects recorded in the experiments are not an artifact of frustration or provocation but are attributable to differences in the television and film stimuli experienced by the subjects. When subjects are dealt with in such a manner only in the treatment condition, the average effect size is substantially greater than when they are so dealt with in both the control and treatment conditions; the effect size in the latter instance, however, remains substantial. There are also individual experiments in which effects are reported in which no frustration or provocation has occurred (for example, Steuer et al., 1971). In short, applicability is not threatened by the frequent presence of frustration or provocation.

Variation by sex was prominent in the early experiments by Bandura and colleagues (Bandura, 1973; Bandura et al., 1963a, 1963b). Girls invariably displayed a lower level of aggressive behavior, leading to the widespread impression that they were less affected than boys by television and film violence. What was overlooked is that although the levels of aggressive behavior for girls in the treatment group might be markedly below those for boys in the treatment group, so too was the level of aggression by girls in the control group compared to that of boys in the control group. Hearold (in press) finds that the effect size associated with exposure to antisocial portrayals is about the same for very young boys and girls, both when the dependent variables include all measures of antisocial behavior and when they are confined to physical aggression. At this age, the data come entirely from experiments. At later ages, when the data in the meta-analysis begin to aggregate that from surveys and experiments, the sexes diverge in effect size, with the effect size for males beyond elementary school increasing with age over that recorded for very young boys and the effect size for females declining with age over that for very young girls. This divergence is emphatically more extreme for physical aggression alone than for all antisocial behavior, of which physical aggression is a major component. The surveys, on the whole, record somewhat stronger patterns of association, both synchronously and over-time, between exposure to violent television programs and aggressive or antisocial behavior for males than for females, but this is not universally so, and the patterns for the females on the whole resemble those for the males. Thus, the divergence in effect size implies a more limited, but not null, association of exposure and behavior for females.

The experimental findings, in fact, lead precisely to such an expectation. They record that sex of model and viewer interact (Bandura, 1965, 1973; Bandura et al., 1961, 1963a, 1963b). Among boys, males are more effective than females as models; among girls, males and females are about equally effective, with the pairing least likely to alter behavior the female model and male subject. Apparently, status, which would favor the male, and appropriateness of behavior, which in the case of aggression would also favor the male, take precedence over the experimentally demonstrated influence of similarity between model and viewer. The expectation, then, would be that females would be less frequently or less strongly influenced than males by violent television and film entertainment because of the preponderance of males among aggressive models. Nevertheless, these male models would not be without their influence on females and that influence of violent entertainment on females would increase with two important social changes—the increasing number of aggressive female models in entertainment and the increasing degree to which male behavior is perceived as unisexual.

Belson's (1978) data also enrich the body of circumstances that plausibly figure in any effect. By weighting the programs viewed by his respondents not only for degree of violence but type of violence, he was able to identify those types most likely to be involved. They are:

1. Protagonists displaying great strength and power who defeat essentially weak villains;
2. Violence with numerous victims, such as mass killings;
3. Violence that erupts among friends, allies, or gang members;
4. Violence that is extreme compared to the events leading up to it;
5. "Violence of a nasty kind [that] appears to be sanctioned by showing it being done in a good cause with seeming legality" (p. 18);
6. Dramas that encourage identification with the aggressor;
7. Violence not easily dismissible as fiction because of its great realism.

Such a "most likely" list derived from survey data cannot identify types of violent entertainment associated with heightened aggressive and antisocial behavior as precisely as experimentation in the laboratory. There is likely to be a high degree of intercorrelation among such exposure measures that thereby casts a pall on the confidence with which each can be construed to have an independent effect, as does the very nature of survey data on the attribution of a causal sequence to these associations.

Nevertheless, it is striking that these findings are so in accord with the American laboratory experiments and the four broad dimensions to which their findings lead: (a) *efficacy* (reward or lack of punishment; an eventually grateful victim); (b) *normativeness* (justified, consequenceless, intentionally hurtful, physical violence); (c) *pertinence* (commonality of cues, similarity to the viewer, absence of humorous violence); and (d) *susceptibility* (pleasure, anger, frustration, absence of criticism). Whatever heightens these four conditions—the first three of which are beliefs or perceptions and the fourth of which is the internal state of the viewer—within a portrayal, or in real life in regard to a way of behaving, increases the likelihood that this experience will contribute to behaving in such a way in the future.

For both groups and individuals, some variation in television and film effects would be expected as the stimuli achieve a better or worse fit in respect to these factors. Belson, for example, did not find any association between any type of aggressive and antisocial behavior and exposure to television sports and cartoons. These two findings increase the credibility of the associations he does report, because they discriminate among media exposure, demonstrating that the reported associations do not reflect some anomaly in which any television exposure is positively associated with the behavior under examination. They also make good sense in developmental and psychological terms; sports exposure would be unlikely to affect a male teenager on the three belief and perception dimensions because what he sees is what he would expect, and no alternation in beliefs or perceptions would be expected to occur. Similarly, for a teenage sample, cartoons would be low on all dimensions. It would be an error to expect this finding to apply to very young children.

The Belson London teenage data are suggestive of other developmental factors as well. He did not find associations between exposure to violent television programs and attitudes approving of violence, favoring its use, or expressing callousness. He similarly did not find associations between exposure and violence committed with other boys and between exposure and being irritating, annoying, or argumentative. The type of aggressive and antisocial behavior most clearly and regularly associated with exposure were acts of an unplanned and spontaneous nature that plausibly could be attributed to the emulation of what had been seen. The behavioral data corroborate what would be expected from the experiments in terms of the close relationship between real-life situational factors and cues and examples presented by television, but the attitudinal data suggest that basic consciously held beliefs and values in regard to violence in general are formed earlier and what television influences is the status of the four dimensions for the particular kind of behavior in question.

The developmental factor is further elaborated by the data of Huesmann, Eron, Lefkowitz, and Walder (in press) which add another decade to the data on aggressive behavior from the same sample as in the 10-year survey (Lefkowitz et al., 1977). Measures of aggressive behavior among the males, now at the modal age of 29, were associated positively to a modest degree that achieved conventional standards of statistical significance with earlier levels of aggressive behavior in both the initial measurement 20 years earlier and the measurement 10 years previously. In regard to the possible influence of television, the males are of special interest, because it was only among the male sample that the earlier positive significant correlations over time were recorded; early exposure to television violence had a consistently positive association with aggressive behavior 20 years as well as 10 years later. Thus, the data support the two-stage model: (a) synchronous contributions by exposure to violent programs from childhood into adolescence and young adulthood and (b) over-time contributions that are attributable to early exposure to violent programs.

It is important, however, not to overlook changes in the maturing individual that are likely to affect his or her response to television and film portrayals. These principally involve increases in reasoning ability and experience and habituation in regard to stimuli encountered in the media. For example, Himmelweit, Oppenheim, and Vince (1958), in their wide-ranging examination of the influence of the introduction of television on British children, found that the ritualistic, stereotypic, and familiar violence of the then-popular westerns did not particularly frighten young viewers. Instead, they were most frightened by violence that endangered someone they identified or valued, such as a child or an adult in a parenting role, or in which dangerous but ever-present household items were employed, such as knives or scissors. Westerns typically would contribute little to arousal, a particularly significant factor with younger children. It should also be obvious that as a child matures he or she becomes increasingly better able to understand the motivations of the characters, the consequences for them and others of their behavior, and the plot and theme.

The precise implications of this for the operation of the four basic dimensions would depend on the particular drama in question, as well as on the individual viewer. Certainly, superior comprehension of the adverse consequences of aggressive and antisocial behavior would be an inhibiting factor; however, it must be remembered that much in popular entertainment runs counter to this theme, with the glorification of criminal behavior, ruthlessness, retribution, and bravado in pulling off a caper. The demonstrated influence of justified aggression (Berkowitz & Rawlings, 1963) certainly provides no comfort over the frequent television and film dramas with vigilante themes. The same must be said of those with themes involving the harassment and victimization of women, given the role of cues (Berkowitz & Geen, 1966, 1967; Geen & Berkowitz, 1967); and particularly when, as is so often the case, there is an erotic undertone to the pursuit, given the demonstrated facilitation of aggression against women by portrayals in which males abuse females in a sexual context (Donnerstein, 1980; Donnerstein & Barrett, 1978; Donnerstein & Berkowitz, 1981; Donnerstein & Hallan, 1978; Malamuth, Feshbach, & Jaffe, 1977). There is also the familiar ascendancy of immediate over delayed consequences in their influence on behavior.

Whatever the eventual outcome, television and film dramas supply numerous instances in which aggressive and antisocial behavior is rewarding in the short term, with both the characters portrayed and the viewer highly gratified, of which the caper is an example. It is likely then that often viewers disassemble the plot the theme, recasting certain elements so that when punishment is eventual, the behavior for which it is imposed is set free; after all, the mistake, the miscue, the accident, or the flaw that brought ruin was not inevitable.

Finally, it should be remembered that the experiments, regardless of the age of the subjects, investigate the circumstances on which effects are contingent, even if those effects are rare. By sensitively examining factors difficult to disentangle in the everyday flow of experience, and by doing so in a way that permits causal inference, they provide an incipient empirical psychology of response to the mass media in regard to aggressive and antisocial behavior. This psychology would still explain effects involving seriously harmful and criminal behavior, even if they occurred so rarely as to make no visible difference in any recorded national crime statistic. The odd sniping, the exotic (but perhaps unintended) suicide, the emulated crime, the random terrorizing, brutality as play—when these are contiguous with similar behavior portrayed in television or film drama, and coincidence is not at work, what has occurred is neither more nor less than ordinary human behavior in response to external stimuli under conditions that extended atypical power to those stimuli. Thus, the criterion for external validity of regularity of occurrence is suspended in the case of the psychological dynamics demonstrated, and the important confirmation by the survey data of everyday behavior consistent with what the experiments imply is unnecessary for the experimental findings to be informative about media effects.

SIZE OF EFFECT

The most unusual instance in which an estimate of size of effect is obtained is the archival examination by Hennigan and colleagues of shifts in crime statistics associated with the introduction of television in the United States in the early 1950s (Hennigan, Heath, Wharton, Del Rosario, Cook, & Calder, 1982). These investigators took advantage of an immense natural experiment unintentionally designed by the federal government when it temporarily halted television station licensing in the early 1950s to assess various technical problems. The consequence was that between 1951 and 1954 there were substantial portions of the country with and without television. The result is a research design labelled by Cook (the senior investigator for this project) and Campbell (1979) as an "interrupted time series with switching replications." They write:

> Imagine two nonequivalent samples, each of which receives the treatment at different times so that when one group receives the treatment the other serves as a control, and when the control group later receives the treatment the original treatment group serves as the control . . . The power of the design derives from its control for most threats to internal validity and from its potential in extending external and construct validity. External validity is enhanced because an effect can be demonstrated with two populations in at least two settings at different moments in history. Moreover, there are likely to be different irrelevancies associated with the application of each treatment and, if measures are unobtrusive, there need be no fear of the treatment's interacting with testing. (p. 223)

The diffusion of television in the second period was extraordinarily rapid (Figure 10.4), so there was no difficulty in establishing the point in time at which a population could be said to have television, there being no other household technological innovation with such rapid and thorough diffusion, including the swivel-handled potato and vegetable peeler. In

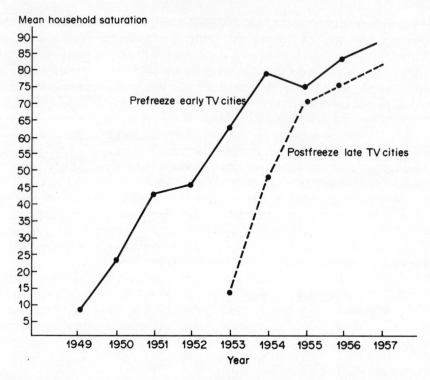

Figure 10.4. Diffusion of Television for Prefreeze and Postfreeze Cities. *Note.* From *Quasi-experimentation: Design & Analysis Issues for Field Settings* (p. 226) by T. D. Cook and D. T. Campbell, 1979, Chicago: Rand McNally. Copyright 1979 by Houghton Mifflin Co. Reprinted by permission.

this case, the design involves comparing the television with the nontelevision population at the first point in time, and the late television with the early television population at the second point in time. In each instance, the latter serves as a control condition in which behavior cannot be said to have been affected by the introduction of television into the geographical site.

Hennigan et al. extended the design to encompass data from two distinct pools, cities and states. That is, they were able to identify states as well as cities that, on the basis of the degree of television set diffusion at the first point in time, could be said to be early or late television sites. Statistics for reported crimes of four types were then examined: (a) crimes involving violence, whatever else may have been involved; (b) larceny theft; (c) auto theft; and (d) burglary. Larceny theft is defined as:

> The unlawful taking, carrying, leading, or riding away of property from the possession or constructive possession of another. Thefts of bicycles, automobile accessories, shoplifting, pocket-picking, or any stealing of property or article which is not taken by force and violence or by fraud. Excluded embezzlement, "con" games, forgery, worthless checks, etc. (Hennigan et al., 1982, p. 465)

Burglary is distinguished from larceny by the involvement of breaking and entering.

The results are striking (Table 10.4, Figure 10.5). No significant shifts were found for violent crimes or burglary. Two significant positive shifts were found for auto thefts—both for the sites acquiring television before the licensing freeze. For larceny theft, all four shifts are significant and positive. The data for the prefreeze cities, the prefreeze states, the postfreeze cities, and the postfreeze states display the identical pattern.

Table 10.4. Changes in Crime Rates Among Prefreeze and Postfreeze Cities and States Associated with the Introduction of Television

Crime and sample	Estimated change in the level of crime (I_y)			Estimated Magnitude of Significant and Consistent Changes	
	ωo	$t(df)$	$\delta 1$[a]	$(e^{\theta} + \omega_o - e^{\theta} o)$	
Violent crime index				Series	
Prefreeze cities	.0275	.32 (35)	—	Prefreeze cities	13.31%
Postfreeze cities	.2023	1.27 (37)	—	Postfreeze cities	5.45%
Prefreeze states	.1780	1.34 (35)	—	Prefreeze states	14.08%
Postfreeze states	.0333	.32 (35)	—	Postfreeze states	18.01%
Larceny theft					
Prefreeze cities	.1229	3.00 (30)**	−.3306		
Postfreeze cities	.0804	6.03 (30)**	.9599		
Prefreeze cities	.1328	2.20 (36)*	.3955		
Postfreeze cities	.1672	2.89 (37)**	.1541		
Auto theft					
Prefreeze cities	.2011	2.71 (35)*	.6324		
Postfreeze cities	.1030	1.31 (35)	.8648		
Prefreeze states	.2956	3.03 (34)**	−.0636		
Postfreeze states	.1243	1.00 (37)	—		
Burglary					
Prefreeze cities	−.0184	.35 (31)	—		
Postfreeze cities	−.0494	.90 (33)	—		
Prefreeze states	.0379	.70 (36)	.9794		
Postfreeze states	.1467	1.46 (37)	—		

Note. Adapted from Hennigan et al., 1982, pp. 470, 473.

[a] δ_1 was removed from the model when its estimate was outside the bounds of system stability and there did not appear to be a relevant change in slope. δ_1 was removed from the violent crime analyses in an attempt to increase power; the results for violent crime lead to the same conclusion with or without δ_1.

* $p < .05$
** $p < .01$

Because of the failure of the postfreeze to match the prefreeze data for auto thefts, the Hennigan et al. are disinclined to attribute the increases in auto thefts to the introduction of television. Because of the replication at both points in time and for both city and state data, they do attribute the increases in larceny theft to the introduction of television.

The investigators question whether the shifts in larceny theft can be explained by social learning theory or emulation, because of the great deal of violent crime in television drama at the time (Head, 1954; Remmers, 1954; Smythe, 1954). If so, they wonder why violent crime did not display a similar pattern of increase. Instead, they attribute the increases in larceny theft to the strong emphasis on material well-being in television commercials and in much of television drama as well. Television, they suggest, may have created a state of widespread relative deprivation that some attempted to redress by theft.

These data are pertinent to the present inquiry because of the substantial proportion of such offenses committed by youths and young adults, particularly males. The explanation offered by Hennigan et al. is highly plausible, and certainly the emphasis on material success in drama—an emphasis achieved not only in the motivations and goals of the principal characters but also in their possessions and the circumstances and places in which they live—would be inextricably bound up in any effect explained by social learning theory. Nevertheless, a principle documented as implicit in the violence of early television drama is that antisocial and illegal means are effective in achieving goals (Larsen, Gray, & Fortis,

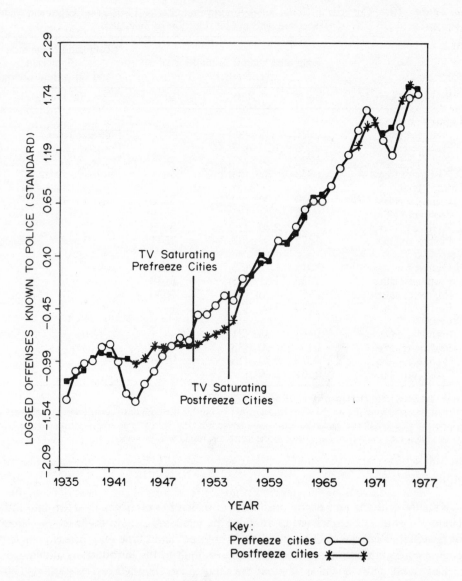

Figure 10.5. Larceny Theft Rates in Prefreeze and Postfreeze Cities, 1936 – 1976. *Note.* From "Impact of the Introduction of Television on Crime in the United States: Empirical Findings and Theoretical Implications" by K. M. Hennigan, L. Heath, J. D. Wharton, M. L. Del Rosario, T. D. Cook, and B. J. Calder, 1982, *Journal of Personality and Social Psychology, 42,* p. 471. Copyright 1982 by The American Psychological Association, Inc. Reprinted by permission.

1963). This suggests a conclusion somewhat different from that of Hennigan et al.: The emulation of television was indeed at least partially responsible for the increases in larceny theft, but at a level at which application was most likely to bring gain and least likely to result in apprehension or, if apprehended, in punishment of much severity.

The investigators are strict constructionists in their refusal to attribute the increases in auto theft in the prefreeze sites to television, because the strength of "interrupted time series with switching replications" lies in the fact of replication with a different population at a different time. Admittedly, the observed increases are not as pronounced as those for larceny theft (one at $p < .05$ and one at $p < .01$ versus one at $p < .05$ and three at $p < .01$). Nevertheless, they may be too conservative, because this is an instance in which the different points in time may figure prominently. The more adjacent to World War II, the more salient and valued the auto would be as redress for relative deprivation. Thus, the failure to replicate for the two time periods in this case is not as severe a threat to inference as would be the failure to replicate at the earlier point in time across the city and state data. An effect on auto theft thus has a claim to, if decidedly lower, validity.

When the investigators estimate the size of the effects on larceny theft, they range from 5.5 to 18% (Table 10.4), with an average of 12.7%. A conservative (if arbitrary) approach would be to accept the smallest estimate as the lower limit and take the average of the remaining three as the upper limit, leading to a range of 5.5–15.1, with a midpoint of 10.3%. Given the fact that these represent reported crimes, they are substantial figures. The logic of experimental design implies that they are present today, but unobservable because of the ubiquity of television. That may be so, but there are very good reasons for discounting somewhat the likelihood of television having as powerful an influence today on criminal behavior.

When television was introduced, it brought a sharply higher emphasis on material goods, aggressive and antisocial behavior, and the use of the latter to obtain the former into American homes. This would have been particularly so for adolescents and young adults, as well as children, for whom the limitations of age and geography had not been overcome by experience. The argument in behalf of a present effect of the same size rests on the assumption that the baseline for relative deprivation is the real-life circumstances of the viewers. If so, a present effect of similar magnitude may exist.

It is equally plausible that the source of relative deprivation was not disparity with the environment, but with prior entertainment and advertising. From this perspective, the crucial unfavorable comparison between television and the environment would depend on the escalation of the stimuli in question in entertainment and advertising and would be confined to the period of the introduction of television.

In addition, there is the possible influence of television as a coveted device rather than as a disseminator of content. As the rapidity of its diffusion testifies, it is hard to think of another common family or personal possession that so quickly became catalogued as a necessity. The only products that rivaled the attention it drew from sidewalk crowds and shoppers when placed on display were the new model automobiles manufactured at the end of World War II. Because it was less expensive, television was more accessible to consumers than a new car, but because it was unique, people could not continue to get along with an older model. The introduction of television brought a visible and compelling lesson to the nation in what being a "have not" versus a "have" meant. From this perspective, the relative deprivation would hinge on the novelty of television, a factor surely not current.

On the other hand, the violence in television drama has not remained at the same level or character that it was in the early 1950s (Baker, 1969; Catton, 1969). It increased markedly in quantity between then and the early 1960s as the action-adventure series became established as a television staple, and the violence has undeniably increased in graphicness, particularly when theater films shown on television are taken into account. Violence today is also more frequent in the theater films shown on television, because violence as a central plot element has become more frequent in movies made for theaters since the advent of television (Clark & Blankenburg, 1972), certainly in part a consequence of the competition with television for the audience. If the associations detected by Hennigan et al. were contingent on the quantity of violence in television entertainment, their figures could be underestimates of the current contribution of the medium to seriously harmful and criminal behavior.

The other estimates of size of the effect vary in regard to the aggressive and antisocial behavior under scrutiny (Table 10.5). Those reflecting interpersonal aggression, which borders on the seriously harmful, suggest that television, exclusive of other influences, including prior aggressiveness when the correlation is over time, explains—in the statistical sense of being predictive of a degree of association—between about 4 and 10% of the variance; that is, between 4 and 10 % of the differences among the aggression scores of the individuals in the sample are predicted by exposure to violent television programs. The explanation of variance for girls is less consistent, and on the whole the explained variance is somewhat smaller. The United States sample (Milavsky et al., 1982a, 1982b) in which measures of both interpersonal aggression and such more serious behavior as "teacher," "property," and "delinquency" aggression were employed suggests a smaller figure, especially among teenage males.

One tempting inference is to attribute less explained variance to television for more serious than for less serious aggressive and antisocial behavior. Unfortunately, for such an inference, the size of the association within the teenage male sample for "personal" aggression—the teenage self-report approximation of the elementary school peer-rated measure of interpersonal aggression—is not markedly greater than for the more serious "teacher" and "delinquency" measures. The inference that the data support is that the developmental influence of television within a 3-year time span is greater among elementary school males than among teenage males. The size of the association over the span of the 10-year survey does not encourage discarding the 4 to 10% range for smaller figures. It implies, in fact, that the association for "personal" aggression for the teenage males in the multi-wave 3-year survey would have been greater had a longer span of time been involved and thus hints that the associations for the more serious types of misbehavior might similarly increase.

Certainly, the London teenage data do not suggest that the association of exposure to violent television programs with the most serious conceivable aggressive and antisocial behavior is insignificant or in any meaningful way less substantial in social importance than that for the three lesser levels of such behavior measured. In these data, the association with exposure to violent programs is proportionately much greater for the most serious than for less serious behavior (49% versus 13% and 11%, in descending order of seriousness of behavior). In regard to the number of acts represented, the pattern is different: The high-television-violence group exceeds the matched low-exposure group in acts committed over the previous 6 months by an average of 1.42 for the most serious behavior, and by 13.25 and 29.07 when behavior increasingly less serious is included. The reason is that the most serious aggressive and antisocial behavior is, fortunately, not common among young males. The frequency of such acts over the previous 6 months for the low-television-violence group was very low (5.02), while it was much higher when the increasingly less serious behavior was included (100.85 and 265.03).

These data make it clear that the association of exposure to violent programs with antisocial and aggressive behavior in this sample is greater in terms of quantity for the less serious behavior. The least serious behavior is typified by:

"I wrote in big letters on the side of a building,"
"I threatened to give a boy a hiding," and
"I played my hi-fi equipment loudly to annoy the neighbors."

Table 10.5. Selected Estimates of Size of Association Between Exposure to Violent Programs and Aggressive and Antisocial Behavior

Source	Behavior Measure	Association	Time Span	Other Variables Controlled	Sample
Wisconsin and Maryland surveys (McLeod, Atkin, & Chaffee, 1972a, 1972b)	Self-reported interpersonal aggression	$r = .30^{**}$	Synchronous	None	68 seventh grade males and 83 tenth grade males and females (N = 151); Wisconsin sample
	Self-reported interpersonal aggression	$r = .32^{**}$	Synchronous	None	248 seventh and 243 tenth grade males and females (N = 473); Maryland sample
	Self-reported interpersonal aggression	$r = .24^{**}$a	Synchronous	Total television viewing time	68 seventh grade males and 83 tenth grade males and females (N = 151); Wisconsin sample
	Self-reported interpersonal aggression	$r = .28^{**}$a	Synchronous	Total television viewing time	248 seventh and 243 tenth grade males and females (N = 473); Maryland sample
10-year Survey (Lefkowitz, Eron, Walder, & Huesmann, 1977)	Peer-rated interpersonal aggression	$r = .21^{**}$	Synchronous	None	184 males, modal age = 9
	Peer-rated interpersonal aggression	$r = .31^{***}$	10 years	None	184 males, modal age = 19
	Peer-rated interpersonal aggression	$r = .25^{**}$	10 years	Peer-rated interpersonal aggression at initial wave of measurement 10 years earlier	184 males, modal age = 19
London survey (Belson, 1978)	Seriously harmful antisocial and criminal behavior	49%, or an average of 1.42 more acts by treatment than control population during preceding 6 months*	Synchronous	All major correlates with aggressive and antisocial behavior	1,565 males, ages 12-17
	All aggressive and antisocial behavior measured except the most trivial	13%, or an average of 13.25 more acts by treatment than control population during preceding 6 months*	Synchronous	All major correlates with aggressive and antisocial behavior	1,565 males, ages 12-17

Table 10.5. Selected Estimates of Size of Association Between Exposure to Violent Programs and Aggressive and Antisocial Behavior *(continued)*

Study	Measure	Effect	Time span	Controls	Sample
	All aggressive and antisocial behavior measured, including most trivial	11%, or an average of 29.07, more acts by treatment than control population during preceding 6 months[*]	Synchronous	All major correlates with aggressive and antisocial behavior	1,565 males, ages 12-17
Three-year multi-wave survey (Milavsky, Kessler, Stipp, & Rubens, 1982)	Peer-rated interpersonal aggression	Unweighted average for six individual waves of measurement, $r = .173$[*,b]	Synchronous	None	553, 428, 510, 546, 406, and 236 elementary school males and females per wave, in order of date of measurement[c]
	Peer-rated interpersonal aggression	Unweighted average for five wave pairs with longest time spans, $\underline{b} = .208$[d] $\underline{B} = .083$[e]	2-3 years	Aggression at time of pair's initial wave	211, 161, 147, 121, and 112 elementary school males per wave, in order of increasing span of time between waves
	Peer-rated interpersonal aggression	Unweighted average for five wave pairs with longest time spans, $\underline{b} = .077$ $\underline{B} = .055$	2-3 years	Aggression at time of the pair's initial wave	236, 134, 133, 123, and 113 elementary school females per wave, in order of increasing span of time between waves
	Self-reported interpersonal aggression	Average for five individual waves, $r = .13$[f]	Synchronous	None	389, 561, 561, 672, and 636 teenage males per wave in order of date of measurement
	Self-reported interpersonal aggression	$\underline{b} = .016$[*] $\underline{B} = .094$	19 months; longest span of survey	All prior measures aggression; all prior television measures; association between the television measure and the aggression measure in the preceding wave	285 teenage males
	Self-reported teacher aggression	$\underline{b} = .009$ $\underline{B} = .051$	Average for waves of 5, 7, and 19 months[g]		272 teenage males

	Seriously harmful and criminal behavior	P = probability of committing such an act for percentile standing in prior television exposure	25 months	Prior seriously harmful and criminal behavior	172 teenage males
		Percentile P 5th .212* 10th .229* 50th .304* 90th .436* 95th .508*			
Interrupted time series with switching replications (Hennigan, Heath, Wharton, Del Rosario, Cook, & Calder, 1982)	Larceny thefts reported to police	5.5 - 11.4%*	Shifts associated introduction of television	Time-specific social and historical events; crime trends	Prefreeze and post-freeze cities; prefreeze and postfreeze states
Meta-analysis (Hearold, in press)	Antisocial behavior as measured by investigators	.30 effect size[i]	Varied	—	528 comparisons from all genres of method
	Antisocial behavior as measured by investigators	.20 effect size	Varied		159 comparisons, studies rated highest in quality of methodology
	Antisocial behavior as measured by investigators	.34 effect size	Mostly immediate		290 comparisons from all laboratory experiments
	Antisocial behavior as measured by investigators	.32 effect size	Mostly synchronous		165 comparisons from all surveys

[a] Partial correlations.

[b] Corrected for unreliability of measurement; $p < .05$ for all six waves.

[c] Valid data only; children reporting viewing an unusually large number of nonexistent television programs excluded.

[d] $\underline{b}$ refers to metric partial regression coefficients.

[e] $\underline{B}$ (beta) refers to standardized partial regression coefficients.

[f] $p < .05$ for four of the five waves.

[g] Coefficients for longest time spans are reported for interpersonal aggression and seriously harmful and criminal behavior, because the coefficients increased with time span; average is reported for teacher aggression because the pattern was positive, but no increase over time occurred.

[h] Minimum estimate plus average of three higher estimates.

[i] Effect size = average difference in scores between treatment and control populations expressed as a proportion of the standard deviation for the control population.

* $p < .05$.

** $p < .01$.

*** $p < .001$.

At the next level, the least serious included:

> "I hit a boy with bare fists in a fight,"
> "I deliberately smashed a school window," and
> "I told a teacher to get stuffed."

At the highest level, the least serious are (in ascending order of seriousness):

> "I twisted a boy's arm until he yelled with pain,"
> "I slashed the tires of some cars,"
> "I broke into a house and smashed everything I could find,"
> "I stabbed another boy," and
> "I threw the cat into the fire."

While the above are not equal in imposed distress to the measure of the most serious behavior, these less serious acts are hardly benign in their implications for others. The association of the most serious behavior with exposure to violent programs is the most impressive on three grounds: (a) It extends the evidence of association to behavior more serious than generally has been examined; (b) the association is substantial; and (c) within the sample there is the lowest likelihood that any of the television and behavior associations is attributable to anything other than the causal influence of television.

Andison (1977) in his meta-analysis recorded that a majority of published survey data displayed a positive association between exposure to television violence and aggressive and antisocial behavior, while Hearold (in press) recorded an average survey effect size of .32 for published and unpublished studies, or about one third of a standard deviation. The Hearold effect size for laboratory experiments is almost identical, .34. The aggregation of several hundred comparisons thus does not support the popular and intuitively pleasing view that the experiments exaggerate effects. Quite the contrary, the reduction in effect size that occurs when a variable that emphasizes the characteristics of the ideal experiment is introduced ("study quality") suggests that experiments underestimate the actual association. This smaller association within experiments, which encompass only immediate effects and effects that are additive to the experience the subjects bring to the laboratory, again is suggestive of a developmental as well as continuing contemporary contribution of television to the behavior in question.

The various estimates do not converge to a single figure. The amount of aggressive and antisocial behavior involved is small, but certainly enough to qualify for social significance if even the lower limit of the probable range is taken as the best estimate. The measures of interpersonal aggression qualify as representing behavior unpleasant, unwelcome, and disruptive for others. Measures more definitively above the threshold of seriously harmful and criminal behavior do not display a pattern markedly or consistently different than those for interpersonal aggression.

There are two reasons to suspect that the measures of association underestimate the actual degree of relationship between exposure to violent television programs and aggressive and antisocial behavior. The first is the statistical axiom that unreliability of measurement reduces the association that will be found among variables. In this, the measures of television exposure and of behavior indisputably are not perfectly reliable; thus, if the fact of association indicated by the data is true and not attributable to sampling variability, the degree of actual association is certain to be larger than that recorded. The second is the ubiquity and prominence of television, which means that in effect persons comparatively "low" in measured exposure typically have had a substantial degree of exposure to television and are knowledgeable of the violence in its entertainment. The associations reflect a very restricted range of television exposure and conceivably would be larger in magnitude if persons with zero exposure rather than only those with comparatively low prior and current exposure were included in substantial numbers in the samples. Thus, the central tendency implied for the effect of exposure to violent television programs on aggressive and antisocial behavior is positive, probably modest or small, not exclusive of seriously harmful and criminal behavior, certainly inclusive of behavior unwelcome by others, socially significant, and possibly greater in magnitude than the figures obtained.

IMPLICATIONS

Huesmann, Eron, Klein, Brice, and Fischer (1983) have demonstrated that a calculated, forceful, and quite explicit indoctrination program on the character and possible effects of television violence can reduce peer-rated aggression among first and third grade children. The indoctrination emphasized the lack of reality of television violence and the undesirability of imitating it and involved the children in such self-persuasion and role-playing as writing brief essays on these themes. In effect, they lowered the capacity of violent television entertainment to operate through the four major dimensions by which effects occur: efficacy, normativeness, pertinence, and susceptibility. McLeod et al. (1972a, 1972b) found that the correlations between exposure to television violence and aggressiveness were markedly lower when parents disapproved of such behavior for resolving conflicts. There are three implications:

1. The apparent effect of exposure to television violence on aggressive and antisocial behavior is amenable to intervention and remedy.
2. Effective interventions may focus either on (a) increasing the undesirability of the behavior or (b) increasing skepticism and knowledge about the medium.
3. The key to effective intervention lies in raising or lowering the likelihood that a young viewer will attribute efficacy, normativeness, or pertinence to the portrayed behavior, and altering the degree to which he or she is rendered more or less susceptible by a particular experience.

Education and training, by parents and through schools and other organizations, are the only plausible recourse, as no major steps to reduce the violence available to viewers can be expected from either the federal government or the entertainment industry. In the five decades since the passage of its original authorizing legislation, the Communications Act of 1934, the Federal Communications Commission has shown scant interest in attempting to shape programming content other than through its fairness doctrine (which required broadcasters to give "reasonable" time to controversial, important issues and to allow opposing views on those issues to be heard) and the equal-time provision of the Communications Act (which stipulates that candidates for public office must have equal access to broadcast time, complimentary or paid, outside of bonafide news coverage). Congressional legislation or FCC regulation banning violence or involving its prior review by some official body on a program-by-program basis would almost certainly be rejected in the courts when challenged on First Amendment grounds (Krattenmaker & Powe, 1978), although the FCC might well be able to enforce standards incompatible with at least some kinds of violent entertainment, such as more programming for children and families (Albert, 1978). In addition, technology is eroding the range of home entertainment subject to federal regulation; cable television is exempt, and in-home playback is beyond the legal boundaries of federal intervention. Little help can be expected from the federal government, nor should it be. It is difficult to imagine a less effective operation, concerned with appearances rather than consequences, than a federal program of review and censorship of entertainment. The entertainment industry has economic incentive to continue to produce violent programs and films. The three networks invoke codes and maintain departments of broadcast standards and practices that place a restraining brake on the quantity and graphicness of violence; the in-house arbiters of acceptability definitely reduce the amount of violence that otherwise would be broadcast, but they diminish, not restrain, the tide.

Competition among the media ensures that violence in television, as well as in film drama, in the future will not be lower in quantity than today, and for the same reason it may become greater in graphicness and ferocity. Remedy and intervention thereby necessarily fall to the home, the school, and the community.

REFERENCES

Albert, J.A. (1978). Constitutional regulation of televised violence. *Virginia Law Review, 64*(8), 1299–1345.

Andison, F.S. (1977). TV violence and viewer aggressiveness: A cumulation of study results, 1956–1976. *Public Opinion Quarterly, 41*(3), 314–331.

Baker, R.K. (1969). The views, standards, and practices of the television industry. In R.K. Baker & S.J. Ball (Eds.), *Violence and the media. A staff report to the National Commission on the Causes and Prevention of Violence* (pp. 593–614). Washington, DC: U.S. Government Printing Office.

Bandura, A. (1965). Influence of models' reinforcement contingencies on the acquisition of imitative responses. *Journal of Personality and Social Psychology, 1,* 589–595.

Bandura, A. (1969). *Principles of behavior modification.* New York: Holt, Rinehart & Winston.

Bandura, A. (1971). *Social learning theory.* New York: General Learning Press.

Bandura, A. (1973). *Aggression: A social learning analysis.* Englewood Cliffs, NJ: Prentice-Hall.

Bandura, A. (1978). Social learning theory of aggression. *Journal of Communication, 38*(3), 12–29.

Bandura, A., Ross, D., & Ross, S.A. (1961). Transmission of aggression through imitation of aggressive models. *Journal of Abnormal and Social Psychology, 63,* 575–582.

Bandura, A., Ross, D., & Ross, S.A. (1963a). Imitation of film-mediated aggressive models. *Journal of Abnormal and Social Psychology, 66,* 3–11.

Bandura, A., Ross, D., & Ross, S.A. (1963b). Vicarious reinforcement and imitative learning. *Journal of Abnormal and Social Psychology, 67,* 601–607.

Belson, W.A. (1978). *Television violence and the adolescent boy.* London: Saxon House, Teakfield Limited.

Berkowitz, L. (1962). *Aggression: A social psychological analysis.* New York: McGraw-Hill.

Berkowitz, L. (1964). The effects of observing violence. *Scientific American, 21*(2), 35–41.

Berkowitz, L. (1973). Words and symbols as stimuli to aggressive responses. In J.F. Knutson (Ed), *Control of aggression: Implications from basic research* (pp. 112–143). Chicago, IL: Aldine-Atherton.

Berkowitz, L., & Alioto, J.T. (1973). The meaning of an observed event as a determinant of its aggressive consequences. *Journal of Personality and Social Psychology, 28,* 206–217.

Berkowitz, L., & Geen, R.G. (1966). Violence and the cue properties of available targets. *Journal of Personality and Social Psychology, 3,* 525–530.

Berkowitz, L., & Geen, R.G. (1967). Stimulus qualities of the target of aggression: A further study. *Journal of Personality and Social Psychology, 5,* 364–368.

Berkowitz, L., & Rawlings, E. (1963). Effects of film violence on inhibitions against subsequent aggression. *Journal of Abnormal and Social Psychology, 66,* 405–412.

California Assessment Program. (1980). *Student achievement in California schools. 1979–80 annual report: Television and student achievement.* Sacramento, CA: California State Department of Education.

Catton, W.R. (1969). The content and context of violence in the mass media. In R.K. Baker & S.J. Ball (Eds.), *Violence and the media. A staff report to the National Commission on the Causes and Prevention of Violence* (pp. 473–486). Washington, DC: U.S. Government Printing Office, 1969.

Chaffee, S.H. (1972). Television and adolescent aggressiveness (overview). In G.A. Comstock & E.A. Rubinstein (Eds.), *Television and social behavior: Vol. 3. Television and adolescent aggressiveness* (pp. 1–34). Washington, DC: U.S. Government Printing Office.

Clark, D.G., & Blankenberg, W.B. (1972). Trends in violent content in selected media. In G.A. Comstock & E.A. Rubinstein (Eds.), *Television and social behavior: Vol. 1. Media content and control* (pp. 188–243). Washington, DC: U.S. Government Printing Office.

Comstock, G. (1978). A contribution beyond controversy. *Contemporary Psychology, 23*(11), 807–809.

Comstock, G. (1983a). Media influences on aggression. In A. Goldstein (Ed.), *Prevention and control of aggression* (pp. 241–242). New York: Pergamon Press.

Comstock, G. (1983b). The mass media and social change. In E. Seidman (Ed.), *Handbook of social intervention* (pp. 268–288). Beverly Hills, CA: Sage.

Comstock, G., Chaffee, S., Katzman, N., McCombs, M., & Roberts, D. (1978). *Television and human behavior.* New York: Columbia University Press.

Comstock, G.A., & Rubinstein, E.A. (Eds.). (1972a). *Television and social behavior: Vol. 1. Media content and control.* Washington, DC: U.S. Government Printing Office.

Comstock, G.A., & Rubinstein, E.A. (Eds.). (1972b). *Television and social behavior: Vol. 3. Television and adolescent aggressiveness.* Washington, DC: U.S. Government Printing Office.

Comstock, G.A., Rubinstein, E.A., & Murray, J.P. (Eds.). (1972). *Television and social behavior: Vol. 5. Television's effects: Further explorations.* Washington, DC: U.S. Government Printing Office.

Cook, T.D., & Campbell, D.T. (1979). *Quasi-experimentation: Design & analysis issues for field settings.* Chicago, IL: Houghton Mifflin Co.

Cook, T.D., Kendzierski, D.A., & Thomas, S.V. (1982). Television research for science and policy: An alien perspective on the NIMH Report on Television and Behavior. Unpublished manuscript (prepared for the Committee on Research and Law Enforcement and the Administration of Justice of the National Research Council of the National Academy of Sciences), Northwestern University, Evanston, IL.

Cook, T.D., Kendzierski, D.A., & Thomas, S.V. (1983). The implicit assumptions of television research: An analysis of the 1982 NIMH Report on *Television and Behavior. Public Opinion Quarterly, 47,* 161–201.

Donnerstein, E. (1980). Pornography and violence against women: Experimental studies. In F. Wright, D. Bahn, & R.W. Rieber (Eds.), *Annals of the New York Academy of Sciences: Vol. 347. Forensic psychology and psychiatry* (pp. 277–288). New York: The New York Academy of Sciences.

Donnerstein, E., & Barrett, G. (1978). The effects of erotic stimuli on male aggression toward females. *Journal of Personality and Social Psychology, 36,* 180–188.

Donnerstein, E., & Berkowitz, L. (1981). Victim reactions in aggressive erotic films as a factor in violence against women. *Journal of Personality and Social Psychology, 41*(4), 710–724.

Donnerstein, E., & Hallam, J. (1978). The facilitating effects of erotica on aggression toward females. *Journal of Personality and Social Psychology, 36,* 1270–1277.

Ekman, R., Liebert, R.M., Friesen, W.V., Harrison, R., Zlatchin, C., Malstrom, E.J., & Baron, R.A. (1972). Facial expressions of emotion while watching televised violence as predictors of subsequent aggression. In G.A. Comstock, E.A. Rubinstein, & J.P. Murray (Eds.), *Television and social behavior: Vol. 5. Television's effects: Further explorations* (pp. 22–58). Washington, DC: U.S. Government Printing Office.

Eron, L.D. (1963). Relationship of TV viewing habits and aggressive behavior in children. *Journal of Abnormal and Social Psychology, 67,* 193–196.

Eron, L.D., Walder, L.O., & Lefkowitz, M.M. (1971). *Learning of aggression in children.* Boston: Little, Brown.

Farquhar, J.W., Maccoby, N., Wood, P.D., Alexander, J.K., Breitrose, H., Brown, B.W., Jr., Haskell, W.L., McAlister, A.L., Meyer, A.J., Nash, J.D., & Stern, M.P. (1911). Community education for cardiovascular health. *Lancet, 1,* 1192–1195.

Feshbach, S. (1961). The stimulating versus cathartic effects of a vicarious aggressive activity. *Journal of Abnormal and Social Psychology, 63*, 381–385.

Feshbach, S. (1972). Reality and fantasy in filmed violence. In J.P. Murray, E.A. Rubinstein, & G.A. Comstock (Eds.), *Television and social behavior: Vol. 2. Television and social learning* (pp. 318–345). Washington, DC: U.S. Government Printing Office.

Feshbach, S., & Singer, R.D. (1971). *Television and aggression: An experimental field study.* San Francisco: Jossey-Bass.

Geen, R.G. (1968). Effects of frustration, attack, and prior training in aggressiveness upon aggressive behavior. *Journal of Personality and Social Psychology, 9*, 316–321.

Geen, R.G., & Berkowitz, L. (1967). Some conditions facilitating the occurrence of aggression after the observation of violence. *Journal of Personality, 35*, 666–676.

Geen, R.G., & Stonner, D. (1972). Context effects in observed violence. *Journal of Personality and Social Psychology, 25*, 145–150.

Glass, G.V., McGaw, B., & Smith, M.L. (1981). Meta-analysis in social research. Beverly Hills, CA: Sage.

Head, S.W. (1954). Content analysis of television drama programs. *Quarterly Journal of Film, Radio and Television, 9*, 175–194.

Hearold, S.L. (in press). A synthesis of 1045 effects of television on social behavior. In G. Comstock (Ed.), *Public communication and behavior* (Vol. 1). New York: Academic Press.

Hennigan, K.M., Heath, L., Wharton, J.D., Del Rosario, M.L., Cook, T.D., & Calder, B.J. (1982). Impact of the introduction of television on crime in the United States: Empirical findings and theoretical implications. *Journal of Personality and Social Psychology, 42*(3), 461–477.

Himmelweit, H.T., Oppenheim, A.N., & Vince, P. (1958). *Television and the child: An empirical study of the effects of television on the young.* London: Oxford University Press.

Howitt, D. (1972). Television and aggression: A counter argument. *American Psychologist, 27*, 969-970.

Huesmann, L.R. (1984). Television: Ally or enemy? A review of Milavsky et. al. *Contemporary Psychology, 29*(4), 283–285.

Huesmann, L.R., Eron, L.D., Klein, R., Brice, P., & Fischer, P. (1983). Mitigating the imitation of aggressive behaviors by changing children's attitudes about media violence. *Journal of Personality and Social Psychology, 44*(5), 899–910.

Huesmann, L.R., Eron, L.D., Lefkowitz, M.M., & Walder, L.O. (in press). The stability of aggression over time and generations. *Developmental Psychology.*

Huesmann, L.R., Eron, L.D., Lefkowitz, M.M., & Walder, L.O. (1973). Television violence and aggression: The causal effect remains. *American Psychologist, 28*, 617–620.

Huesmann, L.R., Lagerspetz, K., & Eron, L.D. (1982). Intervening variables in the television violence-aggression relation: A binational study. Unpublished manuscript, University of Illinois at Chicago Circle.

Huesmann, L.R., Lagerspetz, K., & Eron, L.D. (in press). Intervening variables in the television violence-aggression relation: A binational study. *Developmental Psychology.*

Kaplan, R.M. (1972). On television as a cause of aggression. *American Psychologist, 27*, 968–969.

Kay, H. (1972). Weaknesses in the television-causes-aggression analysis. *American Psychologist, 27*, 970–973.

Kenny, D.A. (1972). Threats to the interval validity of cross-lagged panel inference, as related to "Television violence and child aggression: A follow-up study." In G.A. Comstock & E.A. Rubinstein (Eds.), *Television and social behavior: Vol. 3. Television and adolescent aggressiveness* (pp. 136–140). Washington, DC: U.S. Government Printing Office.

Kenny, D.A. (1984). The NBC study and television violence: A review (with comment by Milavsky et. al., and response by Kenny). *Journal of Communication, 34*(1), 176–188.

Krattenmaker, T.G., & Powe, L.A., Jr. (1978). Televised violence: First amendment principles and social science theory. *Virginia Law Review, 64*(8), 1123–1197.

Larsen, O.N., Gray, L.N., & Fortis, J.G. (1963). Goals and goal-achievement in television content: Models for anomie. *Sociological Inquiry, 33*, 180–196.

Lefcourt, H.M., Barnes, K., Parke, R., & Schwartz, F. (1966). Anticipated social censure and aggression-conflict as mediators of response to aggression induction. *Journal of Social Psychology, 10,* 251–263.

Lefkowitz, M.M., Eron, L.D., Walder, L.O., & Huesmann, L.R. (1972). Television violence and child aggression: A follow-up study. In G.A. Comstock & E.A. Rubinstein (Eds.) *Television and social behavior: Vol. 3. Television and adolescent aggressiveness.* Washington, DC: U.S. Government Printing Office.

Lefkowitz, M., Eron, L., Walder, L., & Huesmann. (1977). *Growing up to be violent.* New York: Pergamon Press.

Leyens, J.P., & Camino, L. (1974). The effects of repeated exposure to film violence on aggressiveness and social structures. In J. DeWit & W.W. Hartup (Eds.), *Determinants and origins of aggressive behavior.* The Hague: Mouton.

Leyens, J.P., Camino, L., Parke, R.D., & Berkowitz, L. (1975). Effects of movie violence on aggression in a field setting as a function of group dominance and cohesion. *Journal of Personality and Social Psychology, 32*(2), 346–360.

Lieberman Research. (1975). *Children's reactions to violent material on television* (Report to the American Broadcasting Company). New York: Author.

Loye, D., Gorney, R., & Steele, G. (1977). Effects of television: An experimental field study. *Journal of Communication, 27,* 206–216.

Malamuth, N.M., Feshbach, S., & Jaffe, Y. (1977). Sexual arousal and aggression: Recent experiments and theoretical issues. *Journal of Social Issues, 33*(2), 110–133.

McIntyre, J.J., & Teevan, J.J., Jr. (1972). Television violence and deviant behavior. In G.A. Comstock, & E.A. Rubinstein (Eds.), *Television and social behavior. Vol. 3. Television and adolescent aggressiveness.* Washington, DC: U.S. Government Printing Office.

McLeod, J.M., Atkin, C.K., & Chaffee, S.H. (1972a). Adolescents, parents and television use: Adolescents self-support measures from Maryland and Wisconsin samples. In G.A. Comstock and E.A. Rubinstein (Eds.), *Television and social behavior: Vol. 3. Television and adolescent aggressiveness* (pp. 173–238). Washington, DC: U.S. Government Printing Office.

McLeod, J.M., Atkin, C.K., & Chaffee, S.H. (1972b). Adolescents, parents, and television use: Self-report and other-report measures from the Wisconsin sample. In G.A. Comstock and E.A. Rubinstein (Eds.), *Television and social behavior: Vol. 3. Television and adolescent aggressiveness* (pp. 239–313). Washington, DC: U.S. Government Printing Office.

Meyer, T.P. (1972). Effects of viewing justified and unjustified real film violence on aggressive behavior. *Journal of Personality and Social Psychology, 23,* 21–29.

Milavsky, J.R., Kessler, R., Stipp, H.H., & Rubens, W.S. (1982a). Television and aggression: Results of a panel study. In D. Pearl, L. Bouthilet, & J. Lazar (Eds.), *Television and behavior: Ten years of scientific progress and implications for the eighties: Vol. 2. Technical reviews* (pp. 138–157). Washington, DC: U.S. Government Printing Office.

Milavsky, J.R., Kessler, R., Stipp, H.H., & Rubens, W.S. (1982b) *Television and aggression: A panel study.* New York: Academic Press.

Milgram, S., & Shotland, R.L. (1973). *Television and antisocial behavior: A field experiment.* New York: Academic Press.

Murray, J.P. (1980). *Television and youth: 25 years of research and controversy.* Boys Town, NB: Boys Town Center for the study of Youth Development.

Murray, J.P., Rubinstein, E.A., & Comstock, G.A. (Eds.) (1972). *Telelvision and social behavior: Vol. 2. Television and social learning.* Washington, DC: U.S. Government Printing Office.

Neale, J.M. (1972). Comment on "Television violence and child aggression: A follow-up study." In G.A. Comstock & E.A. Rubinstein (Eds.), *Television and social behavior: Vol. 3. Television and adolescent aggressiveness* (pp. 141–148). Washington, DC: U.S. Government Printing Office.

Remmers, H.H. (1954). *Four years of New York television.* Urbana, IL: The National Association of Educational Broadcasters.

Robinson, J.P., & Bachman, J.G. (1972). Television viewing habits and aggression. In G.A. Comstock & E.A. Rubinstein (Eds.), *Television and social behavior: Vol. 3. Telelvision and adolescent aggressiveness* (pp. 372–382). Washington, DC: U.S. Government Printing Office.

Rogosa, D. (1980). A critique of cross-lagged correlation. *Psychological Bulletin, 88,* 145–158.

Rosekrans, M.A. (1967). Imitation in children as a function of perceived similarities to a social model of vicarious reinforcement. *Journal of Personality and Social Psychology, 7,* 307–315.

Rosekrans, M.A., & Hartup, W.W. (1967). Imitative influences of consistent and inconsistent response consequences to a model on aggressive behavior in children. *Journal of Personality and Social Psychology, 7,* 429–434.

Rubinstein, E.A., Comstock, G.A., & Murray, J.P. (Eds.). (1972). *Television and social behavior: Vol. 4. Television in day-to-day life: Patterns of use.* Washington, DC: U.S. Government Printing Office.

Rushton, J.P. (1980). *Altruism, socialization, and society.* Englewood Cliffs, NJ: Prentice-Hall.

Slife, B.C., & Rychiak, J.F. (1982). Role of affective assessment in modeling aggressive behavior. *Journal of Personality and Social Psychology, 43*(4), 861–868.

Smythe, D.W. (1954). Reality as presented by television. *Public Opinion Quarterly, 18,* 143–156.

Steuer, F.B., Applefield, J.M., & Smith, R. (1971). Televised aggression and interpersonal aggression of preschool children. *Journal of Experimental Child Psychology, 11,* 442–447.

Surgeon General's Scientific Advisory Committee on Television and Social Behavior. (1972). *Television and growing up: The impact of televised violence* (Report to the Surgeon General, United States Public Health Service). Washington, DC: U.S. Government Printing Office.

Tannenbaum, P.H., & Zillmann, D. (1975). Emotional arousal in the facilitation of aggression through communication. In L. Berkowitz (Ed.), *Advances in Experimental Social Psychology* (pp. 150–193) (Vol. 8). New York: Academic Press.

Wells, W.D. (1973). Television and aggression: Replication of an experimental field study. Unpublished manuscript, Graduate School of Business, University of Chicago.

Worchel, S., Hardy, T.W., & Hurley, R. (1976). The effects of commercial interruption of violent and nonviolent films on viewers' subsequent aggression. *Journal of Experimental Psychology, 2,* 220–232.

Zillmann, D. (1971). Excitation transfer in communication-mediated aggressive behavior. *Journal of Experimental Social Psychology, 7,* 419–434.

Zillmann, D., Johnson, R.C., & Hanrahan, J. (1973). Pacifying effect of happy ending communication involving aggression. *Psychological Reports, 32,* 967–970.

11

Programming for Juvenile Delinquents: An Administrative Perspective

Barry Glick

The administration of programs for juvenile delinquents is both complex and challenging. Partly this is due to the nature of the population served by such programs and partly to the complexity of the juvenile justice system in the United States. Within the past half decade, the juvenile justice system has grown to enormous proportions. More than 1.3 million cases were heard in juvenile courts throughout the United States during *each* of the years of 1980–1984. The impact of this caseload upon the number of youth placed in either community programs or residential programs, both in the public and private sectors, is great. It is this vast system of youth services, fueled by the myriad of statutes, regulations, court decisions, and advocacy groups that provides the challenges to those who are charged with the responsibilites of administering quality youth programs and services.

It should be noted from the very outset that the organization and administration of youth programs for juvenile delinquents is both an art and a science that has evolved into a technological discipline. The professional administrator, who may be trained in a variety of academic backgrounds, such as social work, psychology, counseling, education, or public administration, must nevertheless integrate the wealth of history and development within the child-care industry in order to successfully administer rehabilitation programs for delinquents. The successful administrator must know the development of child-care services and the history of how the juvenile justice system evolved, as well as possess considerable sensitivity to the nature of the adolescent who must survive in the latter part of the twentieth century. Only then can the administrator be in a position to comprehend the nature, strengths, and weaknesses of the administrative models that have seemed to work within juvenile institutions, as well as to address the administrative issues and challenges that confront each administrator whether the task is the operation of a seven-bed group home in a community, a youth camp in the rural countryside, or a larger secure institution for juvenile felons.

By and large, in North America, the juvenile justice system is organized at the state or provincial levels of government. Most juvenile justice systems are organized so that there exists a governmental agency that sets standards through established policies and procedures. The functions of budget planning, fiscal control, personnel, program initiatives, and monitoring quality of care are usually centralized within the agency, whether it be an office whose chief administrative officer is a supervisor, a division whose head is a director, or a department whose executive is a commissioner. Each is responsible to the public in order to provide communities that are safe and a system of programs and services to youth placed in custody.

The juvenile justice system evolved from the child-care institutions of the late 19th and early 20th centuries. As early as 1825, there was a growing concern with the undisciplined behaviors of boys, especially those who were neglected by their families. In 1877, the Charity Organization Society, the Associations for Improving the Condition of the Poor, and other church-affiliated groups began to support larger refuge houses and institutions to care for those children who were without family support or in trouble in their communities. Also, the Society for the Prevention of Pauperism established a house of refuge for these types of youth, an intervention approach subsequently replicated in several urban areas. There was no formal system of rehabilitation or control for delinquency that was empowered to send children to institutions until the first juvenile court was established in Chicago in 1899.

Once juvenile courts were established in order to protect the health and welfare of children, voluntary child-care agencies grew throughout the United States in order to deal with the delinquents incapable of living at home. By 1925, the training school, a large institution that was self sufficient and housed delinquent youth from ages 7 to 21, was prominent throughout the northeast and south. These institutions often developed into repositories for youth and relied on rigid regimentation and corporal punishment in order to control acting-out behaviors, all in the name of rehabilitation.

By 1940, many youth advocacy groups, including the American Law Institute, became so concerned with the failures of institutional placements for juveniles, that it was recommended there be established Youth Correction Authorities throughout the United States. The states of California, Massachusettes, Minnesota, Texas, and Wisconsin were the first to heed the recommendation and form some sort of youth authority. The purpose of these youth authorities was to establish a board responsible to consider the special needs of youth and order the commitment of youth for whom it appeared necessary to the most appropriate institutions available. By 1945, states such as New York had formalized their youth commissions into state agencies responsible for youth services and programs.

Thus, the juvenile justice system evolved from a rather informal structure motivated by church people to provide services to the unwanted and the destitute to a multi-billion dollar industry that employs thousands of people to provide services to juvenile delinquents, some of whom have committed the most heinous of crimes. The juvenile justice system of the 1980's relies upon the public and private sectors in order to provide services to youth. These programs represent an array of community-and non-community-based residential facilities that are available to local family courts as they dispose of juvenile cases. The administrators of these programs and services are faced with challenges to rehabilitate youth placed in their care and return them to communities as productive, effective, contributing citizens.

ADMINISTRATIVE MODELS

Until recently, little systematic effort was made to understand the operations of residential facilities. Often, attempts to structure the administrative and managerial processes within child-care institutions were resisted as being "academic" or nonpractical. It was not surprising to find chief executive officers of these residential child-care facilities who were not formally trained in administration and who often managed by their intuitive processes, commonly referred to as "seat-of-the pants" management. With the advent of technological advances, as well as sociological changes, it is no longer permissible to allow managers to be untrained, inefficient, or ineffective. Indeed, the nature of the youth, who require sophisticated interventions for their rehabilitation, require competent managers.

To fully comprehend the magnitude of the tasks involved in order to operate a childcare facility, one first must understand that since the mid-1970s, institutions have been asked to program more using less money. The principle of "doing more with less" first began to evolve during the Nixon administration and continued with every federal administration including Reagan's. The federal budget, which supports the childcare functions (institutional placements, foster home care, community based residences), has been reduced by almost 40% since Nixon's first budget proposals. Additionally, federal legislation, such as the Child Welfare Reform Act, which transfers the burden of programming for youth including juvenile delinquents from the federal government to state governments, further exacerbates the problems for administrators. During this same time period, child-care institutions have closed, providing less beds to youth in need of services. State budgets have also been capped so that public sector juvenile services have been reduced or eliminated as well. All of this has placed more stress on the juvenile justice administrator to be as well trained, competent, efficient, and effective as possible.

Within juvenile justice institutions, there are two types of processes relative to organization and administration. There is the formal process that include the written statements for the Agency's mission, goals, and objectives, as well as organizational charts, policies and procedures, and financial plan. This formal structure is meant to set the parameters of the organization. All involved are usually aware of these processes and typically are able to negotiate their needs within the established structure. A second process is an informal one. This structure is not committed to paper, nor is it part of a new employee's training and orientation. Yet, it is the informal processes that define much of the activity within the institution, create much of the conditions for the facility's successful (or unsuccessful) operations, and serve as the bases upon which staff interpret the institution's more formal, written documents. The management literature is replete with organizational models and theories that support the notion of both the formal and informal structures (Galbraith, 1977).

Although the first historical notes about organizational and administrative principles date back to 165 BC in China where officials were chosen by examination, there are similarities found between the appointments process and its administrative implementation in the modern civil service systems as well. It was not until after the French Revolution in 1789, when Max Weber first posited the ideal organization and coined the term "bureaucracy," that organizational processes were actually formalized. Weber identified five principles integral in any bureaucracy. These included: (a) division of tasks; (b) hierarchical structures; (c) formal set of rules; (d) impersonality between superiors, subordinates, and their clients; and (e) employment for life with promotion by merit. Based upon these principles, others (Fayol, 1949; Gullick, 1943; Taylor, 1975; Urwick, 1955, 1961) added significantly to the management and administration literature. With little deviation, most students of administration and management would agree that to be a successful manager within a juvenile justice facility, one must attend to the following: budget and finance, personnel, program development, administration, and public and community relations. In addition, if the institution is private, the chief administrator needs to attend to the Board of Directors; if it is public, the accountability mechanism is through the legislative and executive branch of government to the citizen taxpayer.

Within the child-care institutions, and the juvenile justice facilities in particular, three management and administrative theoretical clusters have evolved.

Chain-of-Command Theories

Those facilities that endorse this group of management theories structure their organization in a hierarchical fashion. The formal authority, as well as communications, flows from the top of the organization to the bottom. Decision making within the organization is made by those at or near the top of the administrative structure, and those at or near the bottom of the administrative structure are expected to implement the decisions made.

Advantages in using chain-of-command management systems include: (a) the ability to make decisions quickly without much need for consultation and collaboration; (b) the ability to make decisions and mandate actions with little debate and resistance; and (c) the ability to enforce decisions that require one-way communication. However, a great deal of control over the environment is required in this area. In fact, it is assumed that the chief administrative officer is in charge because he or she is the most competent.

Thus, what happens most often in chain-of-command organizations is that personnel spend a great deal of time and effort exercising control over those below them in the hierarchical structure. They also spend an equal or greater amount of time protecting themselves from those above them in the same chain-of-command structure. Informal organizations often evolve and proliferate in this type of organization. In human services institutions, since children are the clients, they often are perceived, and in reality are, at the bottom of the hierarchy, with the least formal power and authority. In actuality, they require the most effort to control. Besides the control issue, there is a second disadvantage in that the chain-of-command organization requires limited and specific roles and functions of its personnel. Thus, the division of responsibility among staff often leads to a truncated view of the child and a disjointed treatment plan operation.

Parent-Child Management Theories

A second group of theories has evolved within the child-care industry in which the chief executive officer of the institution is perceived and behaves as the parent, while the staff within the facility are perceived and behave as the children. A few agencies, such as Bruno Bettelheim's Orthogenic School and Daddy George's George Junior Republic, are examples of this type of organizational structure. The struggle between the parent figure as director with the staff as children is central to the growth and development of the programs and services within the facility.

The administrative model reflects the same pattern that exists between the staff and the youth they serve. Staff and youth are viewed as growing and developing through stages already described in the psychology literature by Freud and Erikson. It is assumed that if the parent figure is of excellent quality, then the organizational structure will produce mature, fully functioning human beings. Institutions that endorse administrative organizations in this model assume that everyone—children, staff, administrators—is human with essentially the same feelings, needs, and interpersonal actions; all are on a continuum of development and growth. Thus, the administrator of this type of organization would emphasize human interactions rather than organizational functions.

Developmental-Community Theories

The administrator who endorses theories within the developmental-community area assumes social interaction is an integral part of the operation of the agency and advocates for the creation of an environment that supports personal and professional growth. Within these theories, there is a direct positive relationship between the level to which the individual within the organization feels protected, emotionally supported, recognized, and valued and the individual's ability to function as part of an integrated social group that increases the competence of the structure to plan, solve problems, and make decisions. Thus, the organizational structure for the theories within the developmental-community area is a human support system that is capable of responding to the individuals within it, as well as accomplishing the mission, goals, and objectives of the institution.

The theories clustered within this area assume that all participants in the facility grow and develop within a generic human process, but acknowledge that each is an individual with his or her own unique motives, actions, and perceptions. Further, each is presumed to be a multifaceted individual, whose various attributes have extensive implication for the institution.

Reported in Table 11.1 is a comparison of generic management issues as depicted within each of the three theoretical clusters. The purpose of this overview is to clarify as well as highlight the philosophical similarities and differences among the three cluster areas. Individuals may find descriptions of management issues in one area more compatible with their own management styles and philosophical position than in another. Naturally, the closer one identifies with a particular theoretical cluster, the easier it is to adapt to specific management style and the more concrete the administrative system.

Of the three types of theoretical clusters, chain-of-command, parent-child management, and developmental-community, it is the latter that has had the most popularity and recent implementation within the Juvenile Justice System. The developmental-community theoretical cluster seems to be most amenable to the philosophies adopted within the juvenile justice system. The objectives that include youth (re)habilitation, a controlled environment to enhance safety and security for staff and youth, and a value for human interaction, as well as a holistic educational, social, living milieu are all relevant factors integral for the successful administration of a juvenile justice agency. They are also addressed best by the developmental-community administrative theories. Another factor is the more recent development of systems management.

Churchman (1968) first defined the systems approach as "a set of parts to accomplish a set of goals" (p. 17). He identifies the following components of a system that need to be assessed within any organization:

1. The total system objectives and, more specifically, the performance measures of the whole system;
2. The environment of the system—the fixed constraints;
3. The resources of the system;
4. The components of the system, their activities, goals, and measures of performance;
5. The management of the system.

Churchman's analysis of each factor accounts for the system's objectives, environment, and resources, as each relates to the total integrated community.

No matter which cluster of theories is used to manage an institutional setting within the juvenile justice system, it is clear that the burden of program implementation and success falls to the core of administrators charged with the responsibility for the youth's rehabilitation. The issue is not how comfortable a chief executive officer may be with a particular administrative model, but rather how refined a theory of management may be so that it can be internalized within an organization and readily available for implementation. Thus, any administrative theory is only useful to the manager if it can be easily implemented,

Table 11.1. A Comparison of Management Issues Across
Theoretical Clusters

Management Issues	Chain-of Command	Parent/Child	Developmental/Community
Organizational (authority)	Hierarchical	Hierarchical	Horizontal
Structure (power)	Pyramid	Vertical	Interactional
Problem identification	Department/ Unit head	Chief executive officer	All decision centers/support groups
Problem resolution	Staff within Department/Unit	Workers in the agency	Decision centers/ Support groups determined by delegated roles/ functions
Locus of control	External to Staff; external to organizational structure	External to Staff; internal to organization-al structure	internal to staff; internal to organizational structure
Task performance	Assigned to different depart-ments; staff work within work/day, work/ week parameters	Workers assume task and comp-lete as required both on and off the job	Assignments divided and monitored by each decision center
Delegated authority	Department/head Unit/head	Chief executive officer	Decision center manager/support group facilitator
Supervisor/ subordinate line of authority	Staff subordinate to superior	Supervisor limited by staff autonomy	Supervisor retains sphere of influence through decision centers
Decision making authority	Agency/ institutional policies	Permission delegated to underlings	Functional within each decision center

trained, refined, and replicated. Indeed, within the child-care industry, and especially within the juvenile justice system of institutions, there exists a paucity of management theories that provide a clearly defined set of principles for the facility superintendent, director, or agency commissioner. Thus, the models that follow are offered as examples of theories that have proven beneficial to juvenile justice administrators, albeit only in a limited number of institutions or settings.

Situational Leadership

In 1977, Hersey and Blanchard posited a theory of leadership that many believe is especially helpful to managers. Ever since McClelland's theory of achievement motivation, much has been written about the styles of management that administrators use in order to maximize worker productivity. It was not until the publication of *Management of Organizational Behavior: Utilizing Human Resources* (Hersey & Blanchard, 1977), however, that managers were actually able to assess and diagnose the particular attributes of a given situation in order to choose the most appropriate management style to foster worker productivity and growth. The manager who adopts situational leadership theory to administer programs and services within a juvenile institution is afforded the opportunity to determine the amount of task behavior (direction) and the amount of relationship behavior (socio-emotional support) necessary to provide staff, given the situation and the level of "maturity" of the staff.

The concepts of task behavior and relationship behavior in management theory are not new. Indeed, these two dimensions have been an important part of the management and administration literature for decades. Such labels are employee-oriented and production-oriented, or autocratic and democratic, or administration-centered and labor-centered, have long been used and are common terms in most facilities. These ideas, though, were always referred to as either/or styles of leadership.

Hersey and Blanchard, after observing the behaviors of leaders in a wide variety of situations posited that task behaviors and relationship behaviors on the part of managers need not be orthogonal. In fact, they suggest that these two styles may actually be complimentary. They define each as follows:

Task Behavior is the extent to which a leader engages in one-way communication by explaining what each follower is to do as well as when, where, and how tasks are to be accomplished; and *Relationship Behavior* is the extent to which a leader engages in two-way communication by providing socio-emotional support, "psychological strokes," and facilitating behaviors.

According to Hersey and Blanchard, then, a manager's style may be plotted on a two-dimensional axis, and leadership style may be depicted in one of four ways as reported in Figure 11.1. Thus, situational leadership may be considered an interaction among the amount of task behavior and relationship behavior a manager displays toward a worker in a given situation and the worker's maturity level exhibited on certain tasks. Maturity level of a worker is a combination of the ability to take responsibility, willingness to take responsibility, education, experience, and the capacity to set high and achievable goals.

Hersey and Blanchard state that as the level of maturity of the worker increases, given a specific task, the manager needs to reduce the amount of *task behavior* and increase the amount of *relationship behavior* exhibited. As the worker develops beyond the average level of maturity and is able to function more independently, given a task, the manager needs to decrease both task behaviors and relationship behaviors relative to leadership styles. As the worker is able to provide his or her own socio-emotional support, the manager needs to reinforce this type of behavior and dependency with decreasing frequency. Thus, there is less supervision and greater delegation of responsibility, given a specific situation. It is the appropriate leadership styles of the manager, given the maturity of the worker in any given task situation, that makes situational leadership a most potent tool for the juvenile justice administrator.

As depicted in Figure 11.1, a manager's style is dependent on the maturity level of the worker, that is, the amount of direction the worker requires and the amount of socio-emotional support the manager must thus provide. Generally speaking, those workers who are low in Maturity (M1), given a specific task, have the highest probability of success in that task if their supervisor provides high-task and low-relationship managerial behaviors (S1). Those workers who are low to moderate in their maturity levels (M2) will experience the highest degree of success if their supervisors demonstrate high-task and high-relationship behaviors in their management style (S2). Those workers who are moderate to high in maturity level (M3), will benefit most from managers who provide high-relationship and low-task supervisory behaviors (S3). Finally, workers who are of the highest maturity level, (M4), given a particular task, require managers who provide low-task and low-relationship

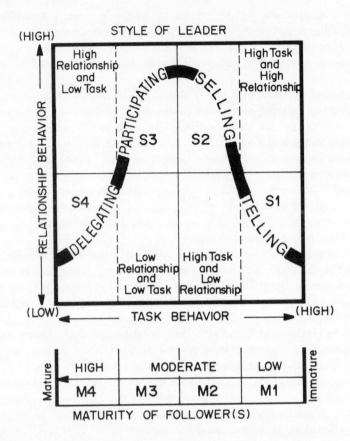

Figure 11.1. Situational Leadership. Note. From *Management of Organizational Behaviors: Utilizing Human Resources* (p. 152) by P. Hersey and K. Blanchard, 1977, Englewood Cliffs, NJ: Prentice-Hall. Copyright 1977 by Prentice-Hall. Used with permission.

behaviors. (S4). Thus, four leadership styles emerge from situational leadership theory:

1. Telling is high-task, low-relationship behavior and is characterized by one-way communication. The manager defines the role of the worker and tells each what tasks to perform, how to perform the task, and when to perform it.
2. Selling is high-task, high-relationship behavior and is characterized by the supervisor still directing much of the worker's role. The manager attempts to use two-way communication and socio-emotional support systems to get the worker to support decisions that are made.
3. Participating is low-task, high-relationship behavior and is characterized by two-way communication between the manager and the worker. Both share in the decision-making process, although the manager still provides supportive behavior and acknowledges that the worker has the ability and the knowledge to complete the given task.
4. Delegating is low-task, low-relationship behavior and is characterized by the worker acting independently of the manager. The workers are willing and able to take responsibility to manage their own behavior, given a particular task, and are able to consult appropriately with the manager as necessary.

Situational Leadership has wide applicability for the juvenile justice system. It is easily administered within a given facility, no matter what the size of the organization. There is technology available and instrumentation developed to help the manager assess the leadership styles of all personnel, for example, self-assessments for managers and subordinates and charts and graphs to plot self reports. It is a useful and promising tool.

The Michigan Model

The Michigan Association of Children's Agencies posited an administrative model that has had widespread implementation within the juvenile justice, child-care industry. Such Michigan agencies as the Donald M. Whaley Center in Flint, Barat Human Services in Detroit, Boysville of Michigan in Clinton, and Good Will Farm in Houghton first piloted the Michigan Community Developmental Model of Administration. Later the same model was adapted to the Elmcrest Children's Center in Syracuse, New York (1975), Auburn Special Residential Center in Auburn, New York (1978), and the Annsville Youth Center in Taberg, New York (1984).

In the initial work of the Michigan project, the primary objective was to design a managerial system that would integrate the various components of a child-care agency. Such programs and services as residential child care and parenting, education, vocational and occupational programs, recreation, behavioral management, and counseling, as well as administration and case management, were often discreet entities within the institution with little or no coordination. It was in fact often an administrative nightmare to manage. The Michigan Model not only developed a management system but also began to integrate the supervisory and treatment components operating within the child-care agencies.

The model allows for a variety of assumptions to be made and actions to be taken. It is basically people-oriented; thus, it assumes that people are basically good and desire to perform successfully at their jobs. Central to the model is the assertion that participatory management within the child-care institution is preferable to decisions made by one or a few. It also declares that responsibility may be delegated to mature workers with the authority to accomplish tasks and the accountability mechanisms to insure successful accomplishments. Finally, the theory allows for the planning, decision-making process to occur using individuals within the organization to support each other in meeting problems, identifying issues, and deciding actions.

Within the framework of the Michigan Model of Administration, however, some definition of terms need to be put forth. A *manager* is one who creates the environment for staff to grow and develop, both personally and professionally. A *supervisor* is one who monitors staff tasks, sets standards for work to be accomplished, provides feedback to employees to help them alter their behaviors and learn new ones, trains staff on skills required to accomplish their tasks, and, most of all, is an advocate for the employee. Thus, it is incumbent upon the manager and the supervisor to maximize staff potential. Only then can the various components of the juvenile justice institution be integrated into a holistic unit that is perceived by residents as organized, consistent, safe, and predictable.

A basic structure within the community developmental model of administration is the *decision center*. The decision center is a support group composed of individuals with similar functions or roles in the organization. These decision centers are chaired by a manager who acts as the linking pin with the other managers of the facility. There are as many decision centers as there are major functions within the institution. Depending on the size of the institution, some functions may be merged into one decision center. At a 60-bed juvenile facility, for example, it is conceivable to have decision centers for education, program, physical plant, health and food services, fiscal and clerical operations, as well as administration. Each decision center would be managed by the most senior person available within that particular discipline. There is, however, a wide spectrum of salary grades, educational levels, and competencies in any one decision center. The product is a cross-section of workers participating together in the administration, decision making, planning, training, and implementation of the total program. While the one disadvantage to this model is that it requires a rather confident and trusting chief executive officer, the advantages that accrue, given the mission and goals of the child-care industry, are far reaching. Figure 11.2 represents an organizational structure that depicts a community-developmental administrative model.

Notice that the organization is not hierarchical, but rather horizontal. It is important to realize that each manager of a decision center has neither more nor less authority than another when it comes to the decision-making process or managing delegated responsibilities. This includes the chief executive officer of the facility as well. Although the chief administrator is responsible for the facility or organization, many of the decision-making processes are delegated to the decision centers and in turn use the interactional system already described. There are few administrative issues, such as contractual agreements or agency policies, that contradict the operation of this model. Practically, it requires relearning on the part of employees under this managerial system, to behave and respond not to a central authority figure, but to many. In a similar vein, the decisions that are made are shared rather than unilateral. Managers of decision centers are not merely representatives of their particular cohesive interest group, but more importantly a composite of the entire institution. Thus, as decision centers deliberate their problems, tasks, and issues, each become more aware of the other's mission, goals, and objectives. Decisions evolve and develop, broadened by the interactions between decision centers, influenced by the dynamics of the institutional community, and refined by the shared information that is fostered by the process.

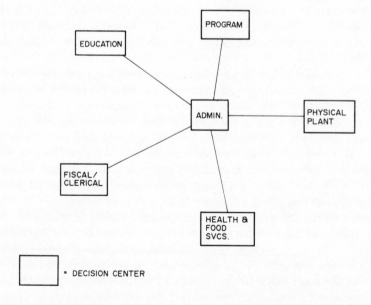

Figure 11.2. Organizational Chart for Decision Center Model of Administration.

In juvenile justice facilities, where integration of roles and functions is so critical, so too is the notion that administrative models and management theories need to be as well. As one reviews the two models presented, given the administrative issues that face the juvenile justice manager, it is quickly apparent that they are not incompatible, but may be used in tandem. It is this very concept that makes the situational leadership and Michigan models so enticing for the administrator of juvenile justice systems. Both allow the manager to develop institutional policies and procedures, develop rehabilitation services, coordinate staff, plan, detail budget, evaluate programs and services, and direct and train supervisors, as well as provide professional leadership to the field. Both models, when successfully integrated and applied, provide juvenile justice administrators with a unique and potent management tool to assess the current state of their administrative system, as well as plan for the future.

ADMINISTRATIVE ISSUES

Budget and Finance

Ever since the beginning of the 1980s, particulary within the human services, and specifically for the juvenile justice system, the total amount of dollars available has been dwindling. Juvenile justice administrators have become accustomed to the budget message of "doing more with less", i.e., retaining or even expanding programs with the same or less amounts of money. The early 1980s quickly became known as the years of the "politics of finance." The juvenile justice manager learned that it was not enough to merely justify program needs and youth services.

In the public sector, the taxpayers were even less interested in supporting rehabilitation programs, but rather, as economic times became harder, demanded that communities be safe and streets ridded of the delinquent. In the private sector, many residential facilities for delinquent youth were forced to close, unable to keep up with growing inflation rates and skyrocketing interest. The result was fewer beds for the delinquent and a more focused approach to which a child was to be placed and for how long. To make matters even worse, state legistatures began to pass more stringent laws that began to treat the more violent juvenile as an adult and that resulted in some youngsters being incarcerated longer. The impact again was fewer beds, more expensive operations, with less emphasis on rehabilitation. The juvenile justice system began to outprice itself for the reasonable care and retention of the delinquent youth.

Currently, for example, New York State spends approximately $65,000 per year to incarcerate a juvenile offender in one of its (maximum) Secure Centers. Given the inflation rate of 4% per year, and that is conservative, one would expect that by the year 2000, the annual cost for a youngster in New York State's Secure Center will be about $121,743. Such a cost level presents the juvenile justice administrator in the area of budget and finance with a nearly overwhelming problem. Yet, the solutions may well lie within the ingenuity of those creative professionals in the system. Within the community development model of administration lies the notion that the system of budgets and finance should be changed from the traditional object classification and line item structure to that of a process of functional budgeting. This process would require administrators to take charge of the budget process and use the decision center model so that fiscal control becomes an issue for all within the juvenile justice institution, not just the comptroller.

Functional budgeting requires each decision center to plan, organize, and spend a delegated amount of money wisely. The overall fiscal plan would then be the institution's as developed through the community-developmental administrative process. The supervision and administration of the budget process would use the principles of situational leadership to establish the functions between the supervisor and staff.

Personnel

The typical juvenile justice administrator cannot spend enough time dealing with many of the important issues related to personnel that confront the manager regularly. Within the child-care industry, a great deal of attention is devoted to staff, largely because the services rendered and end products are people rather than things. Within the juvenile justice system the human services aspects become even more critical because the youth are placed in institutions involuntarily. Thus, the manager of the system is critically aware that the success of the institution or agency, whether it be program or service, goal or mission, is dependent upon people.

Yet, of all the human services, juvenile justice agencies, when it comes to personnel, are one of the least regulated. Standards for training and qualifications, certifications, licensures, and the other accoutrements reasonably expected as part of a profession are virtually nonexistent within the child-care field. Nevertheless, state legislatures, family courts, and agency executives require staffs within these institutions to provide care to youths *in loco parentis*, even though many of these personnel have no training and are sometimes only required to have a high school diploma.

The juvenile justice administrator is faced with a plethora of personnel issues in order to effectively manage the system and impact upon the agency's mission and goals. Perhaps one of the more obvious demands upon the administrator is to establish a program of staff development that meets the needs of staff members within the system. The outcry across the child-care industry is that not enough training is provided to direct line staff members in order for them to accomplish their tasks. Given the nature of the youth placed within the juvenile institutions, the level of education required of child-care staff, and the array of new statutes and regulations, the petition for more training is justified and necessary. As more training-relevant technology becomes available to the field, as programs become more sophisticated, and as managers demand greater productivitity, training becomes essential. As staff members become better trained, the system benefits in that there is increased productivity within the organization, greater professional identity, pride on the part of the worker, and a higher quality of service to the youth placed in care.

A second important personnel issue for the juvenile justice administrator is that of staff evaluation and performance. For years the level of management skills was secondary to the clinical skills required of the supervisor in the institution. Hence, although a great deal of attention was paid to treatment issues, other issues, such as the management of treatment, the organization of rehabilitation systems, and the supervision of personnel, were not very well addressed. Thus, there evolved a system that was caring, but not highly functional, one that provided services to youth, but was unable to attend to the needs of its staff. The result was greater expenditures, less resources, and at times chaos, not to mention the nonverbal, but very strong, message of uncaring on the part of the administration for the institutional staff.

More recently, a great deal of attention has been paid to the area of staff evaluation and performance. New York State, as one example, undertook a study of its performance evaluation systems for its entire work force. What resulted was a more defined performance evaluation system that required managers to be proactively engaged with their subordinates on a frequent and consistent basis. The system was piloted and in 1982, formally and contractually adopted for all state employees.

Likewise, child-care agencies, and particularly juvenile justice institutions, must revamp their evaluation procedures if quality of services to youth is to be maintained. The message to staff must be clear—Administration cares, is concerned, and wants to assist in staff growth and development, professionally and personally. To accomplish that objective, managers must assure the following:

1. The mission, goals, and objectives of the institution are clearly stated and understood by all staff.
2. Each supervisor meets with staff to define the scope of work for the unit and to describe the job roles and functions within it.
3. Each supervisor meets with individual workers to define the tasks to accomplish the job and the expectations (standards) required to insure the tasks are accomplished.
4. Each supervisor routinely observes and gives staff both informal and formal feedback relative to the staff's performance.
5. The plan for evaluation, as well as the annual or semiannual performance evaluation, is in writing.

Finally, juvenile justice administrators need to set high expectations and standards for staff. There needs to be a constant effort to have staff aim high. That criterion needs to be established first by each staff member for himself or herself. The question to be posed is: What are your career goals, and what steps are you taking to accomplish them? Staff members need to also establish their expectations for themselves as they interact with the administrator and provide adult models for youth to emulate. Lastly, staff members need to set expectations for each other so that they can appropriately facilitate staff relationships, confront staff behaviors, and meet program expectations as professionals.

Program Development

Of all the administrative issues that face the juvenile justice manager, program development is perhaps the most critical and the most challenging. Within the institution the problem is somewhat focused because the population for the facility is defined, as well as the parameters of bed space, assigned staff, and budget resources for services and programs. At the agency or multi-institutional level, however, administrators grapple with more complex questions. Unlike other child-care services, juvenile justice is faced with the twofold problem of insuring safety and security within the institution, as well as designing and implementing a rehabilitation program that insures youth will be returned to their communities as fully functioning citizens.

The juvenile justice administrator knows that a viable program for delinquents must include components such as a system for classification, diagnostics and evaluation, behavior management, and educational, vocational, and health services, as well as the capacity to transition youth who enter and leave the program. There is a paucity of literature that address these program issues, with little research as to what combination of factors is appropriate.

The California Youth Authority did provide the basis for many of the classification systems that have been developed for juveniles. Warren (1971) and Jesness (1972) were pioneers in developing the Interpersonal Level of Maturity Classification system. The system allows youth to be classified according to their perceptions of their world and their behavioral responses to their perceptions. Based upon a youth's classification, a treatment program could be developed in order to target the best interventions and maximize a youth's growth. This is, however, one of the few workable systems available to the juvenile justice administrator in order to classify youth.

When it comes to diagnostic assessments and evaluations of youth, however, there are more instruments and technologies available. Youth placed in juvenile institutions must be provided with adequate education, counseling, health, and vocational programming. Fortunately the state of the art for assessment in these areas is advanced so that a battery of tests may be designed to appropriately place youngsters in a program.

Still left unanswered are the questions for agency policy, as budget is expended for a program. What level of staffing is required in order to establish safety and security within a program? What kinds of classification systems should be adopted? What combination of program components are most desirable in order to effect and maximize youth rehabilitative changes? These are but some of the program dilemmas that face administrators.

Further, should programs be differentiated in treatment modalities, and, if so, how? Is it better to standardize program operations across institutions or to allow treatment to be prescriptive based upon the needs of the population? All of these issues, though relevant, are largely unresolved, partly due to the lack of research available to aid administrators in making the correct policy determination, and partly due to the state of art and technology within the field. Nonetheless, the juvenile justice manager is required to provide a program that meets the needs of youngsters placed and, by and large, is left alone with little guidance to accomplish that task.

A related issue for the juvenile justice manager is that of program accountability. As the program is developed, the administrator becomes accountable for accomplishing the mission and goals of the program, as well as insuring that program and services are provided to youth in an effective and efficient manner. Legislators and taxpayers are interested in more than just the money allocated to program for operations. The administrator must be cognizant of not only how much money is available to deliver the services to youth, but what savings may accrue by the most efficient administration of those funds. In effect, cost containment becomes as important as resource availability.

Yet another hallmark for program accountability is the recidivism rate for juvenile delinquents who leave the system. Again, the research in this area is scarce. Recently, the New York State Division for Youth completed a recidivism study on its institutionalized population. While on average, the study showed that recidivism rates for delinquents leaving institutions were no more or less in the Division than that in other systems, questions were raised as to the aftercare services available and their impact on recidivism. For the administrator of juvenile justice programs, the questions of cost containment, recidivism, program efficiency, readmissions, and rearrests are criteria that determine how well the program accomplishes its mission and, in the long run, criteria for the program's accountability.

Management of Information Systems

There were more than 1.3 million cases heard in juvenile courts last year. Even if only 10% were placed in some type of juvenile justice system of care, there are an estimated 130,000 cases to be documented, detailed, recorded, and filed. The management of information is critical to the efficient operation of a juvenile justice system. The bits of information associated with any given case often fill a 2-inch binder. Yet the manager of the juvenile justice system does not have the technological capacity to deal effectively with this hoard of information. What is most frustrating are the demands placed upon the administrator to cull information in order to justify budgets, request additional staff, embellish programs, or remodel archaic physical plant structures. The mass of information, although there is capability to organize and retrieve it, creates a burden of paperwork for the average juvenile justice manager that the requirement of documentation to accomplish program modifications is rarely met.

How to counteract this vicious cycle requires a tremendous amount of effort on the part of the administrator. First, the advent of computer technology has mandated that the manager become trained in its applications and use. Second, policy makers need to be urged to provide this technology within the field. Third, there needs to be a concerted plan that will train, translate, and transition the manual systems that now exist within the juvenile justice systems into machine.

The advantages and ramifications of appropriately managed information systems yield more efficient use of staff time and the ability to define and assign program tasks more effectively, as well as the capability to respond to accountability issues raised for evaluation and analysis. It behooves the juvenile justice manager to be able to manipulate information, as well as manage the information systems within the institution, so that issues can be defined or resolved.

Advocacy

Historically, there was little activity to protect the rights of youth placed in child-care institutions up until the end of World War II. There was even less interest on the part of the public for those youngsters who were adjudicated juvenile delinquents and removed from their communities either for the protection of the neighborhood or to attempt their rehabilitation.

Not until the early 1960s, with the advent of the New Frontier, was there any effort to protect the rights of juveniles incarcerated for delinquency. It was at that time that lobby groups such as the American Civil Liberties Union began to pressure Congress to legislate standards for the care of youth placed in juvenile justice institutions. Pl 93–415 (The Juvenile Justice and Delinquency Prevention Act of 1974) protected certain youths from being placed in jails and other detention facilities with adults. That law also mandated that those youths who committed status offenses (incorrigible behaviors, truancy), actions that if they were adults were not punishable by imprisonment, be separated from the youngsters who were adjudicated delinquents. Following that major breakthrough, other groups began to take action to further restrict juvenile justice systems from arbitrarily dealing with youth in care. Such actions were either legislated or, more often than not, litigated in the courts. As a result of more recent action, youths are now protected as to their right of treatment (*Rodriquez v. Luger*, 1975, CIV. 199 CBM.) and their right to be placed in a rehabilitation center on a timely basis (*Crespo v. New York State*, 453 NY Supp. 2nd, 392 [1980]; *Ronald W. v. New York State* [1980] Unpublished Court Stipulation, Federal Court, New York City), as well as their restriction from performing menial labor in youth camps without advice and consent or without it being part of an established vocational educational program (*King v. Carey, 1975*, pending Federal Court, Buffalo, N.Y.).

Advocacy, however, is more than just youth-oriented. It is system-oriented as well, and the juvenile justice manager must be prepared to participate in the process to advocate for program and system needs. While this role may be reserved for an institution's Board of Directors within the private sector, there must be a mechanism within the public sector also. The administrator must be skilled at working within the community through lay advisory groups to effect the mission and goals of the institution. Often, the public juvenile justice administrator becomes reactionary to issues rather than proactive and does not develop the skills necessary to be a competent advocate for the system.

Advocacy by the administrator also includes those issues that pertain to staff. As stated before, one of the primary roles of the manager/supervisor is to create a work environment for staff to grow professionally and personally. Thus, a primary administrative function is *employee* advocacy. Such issues as stress on the job or personal problems that interfere with the job need to be assuaged with administrative support. Employee Assistance Programs (EAPs), networking with community mental health centers, and staff training are but a few intervention techniques available to the manager as staff advocate. Additionally, such external pressures as political patronage for jobs, and reduction in work force due to fiscal constraints need to be addressed assertively by the manager in order to protect staff position and status.

There is yet another component of the advocacy issue. There needs to be an independent, objective person who can advocate for the youth's needs and rights. The individual, whether known as an inspector general or ombudsman, must be able to negotiate within the system, but not be supervised by it. The individual must be able to address grievances and bring to the attention of the chief executive officer those concerns that need to be remedied. Advocates in a variety of positions are those who ultimately bring change within the system, refining programs, creating issues, and acting as a catalyst for change.

Planning

The one administrative issue most ignored within the juvenile justice system by a majority of its managers is that of planning. Most managers do not have planning skills, nor is it a priority within the system. Unfortunately, much of the work within the juvenile justice system is crisis management, with little opportunity for data collection, research, analysis, and critical thinking—especially critical thinking and future planning. Thus, many times programs that are developed, services that are provided, and priorities that are established are strategies that on the surface seem admirable, but under closer scrutiny do not address longer term problems. Unfortunately, most juvenile justice administrators are not trained to adequately identify a problem, evaluate its causes, identify system effects, establish normative goals, and ultimately define all possible strategies in order to make an enlightened decision. Most decision making is rather impulsive, with great pressure to identify solutions, whether or not they be feasible and logical. One need only review the state budgets for fiscal year 1984 in the juvenile justice field to recognize the realities and the inadequacies of the planning efforts. Only a few have line items for planning personnel or for resources to support a planning activity.

In order for the juvenile justice system, and particularly the managers within the system, to move beyond the mediocrity of the 1980s, there needs to be established an aggressive program for juvenile justice planning. Indeed, every other area within the human services has received national attention by either a Presidential Commission, White House Conference, or Congressional Task Force, within the past 2 decades, except for the juvenile justice field. Additionally, there need to be more administrators who advocate for planning and are not cowed by the derogatory labels of egghead, academic, esoteric, or nonpractical. Without an assertive planning effort, the juvenile justice administrator will yield whatever progress has been made toward establishing the profession and the level of quality programs that currently exist.

PROFESSIONAL DEVELOPMENT

In order for the manager within the juvenile justice system to continue to grow and develop, there must be a commitment to one's profession and professional identity. Heretofore, administrators have been promoted from within the system, or appointed because of some level of training or proven expertise. For that reason, administrators come from a variety of backgrounds—social work, psychology, education, human service, counseling, and, in a few instances, administration. Thus, very often, the juvenile justice administrator is committed to professional growth within a specific discipline, but not necessarily that of administrator.

Yet, it is critical that the juvenile justice manager identify with a professional organization that will offer appropriate continuing education, establish requirements and standards within the field, offer professional certifications and, if necessary, licensure, provide professional colleagial forums, publish articles and journals, disseminate information relevant to the job function, coordinate networking among administrators, and advocate for its membership, to name but a few. It is incumbent upon the juvenile justice administrator to be in a position to continue learning through professional affiliations and to share information with others, as well as raise professional issues in order to advocate for the profession's growth and development. The following is a list of professional organizations that cater specifically to the administrator who works within the juvenile justice and youth services systems. Information relative to mission, goals, or membership may be obtained by corresponding directly with the following:

American Correctional Association
4321 Hartwick Road
Suite L-208
College Park, MD 20740
(800) ACA-JOIN

Correctional Education Association
Box 40
Huntsville, TX 77340
(409) 291-5130

Council for Exceptional Children
1920 Association Drive
Reston, VA 22091
(703) 620-3660

Council on Children with Behavioral Disorders
Division of Council for Exceptional Children
Same as above

Council of Administrators of Special Education
Division of Council for Exceptional Children
Same as Above

National Association of Juvenile Correctional Agencies
Department for Children and their Families
340 New London Avenue
Cranston, RI 02920
(401) 464-2274

National Council on Crime and Delinquency
760 Market Street, Suite 433
San Francisco, CA 94102
(415) 956-8731

REFERENCES

Churchman, C.W. (1968). *The systems approach*. Quebec: Delta Canada.

Fayol, H. (1949). *General and industrial management*. New York: Pitman.

Galbraith, J.K. (1977). *The age of uncertainty*. New York: Houghton Mifflin.

Gullick, L.F. (1943). *The elements of administration*. New York: Harper and Bros.

Hersey, P., & Blanchard, K. (1977). *Management of organizational behavior: Utilizing human resources* (3rd ed.). Englewood Cliffs, NJ: Prentice Hall.

· Jesness, C.F. (1972). *The Jesness inventory*. Palo Alto, CA: Consulting Psychologists Press.

Taylor, B. (1975). *Management development and training*. London: McGraw Hill.

Urwick, L.F. (1955). The purpose of business. *Dun's Review and Modern Industry, 52*, 103–105.

Urwick, L.F. (1961). Management and human relations. In R. Tannenbaum (Ed.), *Leadership and organization: A behavior science approach* (pp. 118–131). New York: McGraw Hill.

Warren, M.Q. (1971). Classification of offenders as an aid to efficient management and effective treatment. *Journal of Criminal Law, Criminology, and Police Science, 62*, 239–258.

12

Legal Perspectives on Youth Violence

Richard A. Ellison

INTRODUCTION

"The role of the teacher in our society. . . has left for most of us warm memories of our teachers, especially those of the formative years of primary and secondary education."

Justice Lewis J. Powell

"School stunk. I hated school and all its teachers. I hated the crispy look of the teachers and the dragging long hours they took out of my life from nine to three-thirty."

Piri Thomas

"If you think kids are tough now you should have been here in the 1930s."

Anonymous teacher
in the 1950s

We all have different perspectives and expectations of schools that have been influenced by our past experience. Piri Thomas went to school in Spanish Harlem. Justice Lewis Powell, from Virginia, attended school during the time Virginia's schools were racially segregated. The anonymous teacher viewed the issue of school disruption from the perspective of three decades of teaching in New York City. For some, the issue of violence, or inappropriate aggression, in schools is a new phenomenon. For others, schools are not isolated enclaves removed from the turmoil and change of the outside world. Rather, the view of the latter is that our children reflect us, and our children's schools reflect our society—a too violent society. The truth may be closer to this perspective. The secluded, calm, school environment that some experienced also was a reflection, not of a fantasy world, but of a society which excluded many children from full participation.

In selecting a subject for this chapter, juvenile courts and juvenile institutions, because of their obvious involvement with delinquent children, could have been the focus. Alternatively, mental institutions whose population includes violent, aggressive youth, committed because they may be "crazy," could have been chosen as an appropriate subject of the chapter. Schools were chosen as the focus, however, because schools are a microcosm of our community, and because schools are required to respond to most children. Schools have a major role to play in the resolution of conflict. The legal perspective offered is the role of law as an aid, or obstacle, in the resolution of conflict.

The chapter is divided into three sections. The first section concerns the racial and cultural change in schools occasioned by the *Brown v. Board of Education* decision of 1954. This change has unquestioned relevance to the issue of school violence and disruption. The second section deals with discipline, and the role of the courts in regulating this aspect of school life. The final section discusses children with disabilities, and the important Education for all Handicapped Children Act (1975), which has imposed affirmative obligations on the schools, expanding the role of schools in responding to the various needs of children, some of whom are violent and aggressive.

SCHOOLS: THE ISSUE OF RACE

With the arrival of universal compulsory education in the early part of this century, children of certain ages (varying from state to state), were then, as now, required to attend school. Though the legislation generally required that all children receive some education, not all children were intended to be absorbed into the mainstream of the educational system. The state education and labor laws permitted white children who were poor to quit school, and work, at an earlier age than at present.[1] To black children, the segregated society of this period offered, at least in the south by operation of law, segregated schools (*Plessey v. Ferguson*, 1896) (when schools were provided) (*Cumming v. Richmond County Board of Education*, 1899), and a barrier to full participation in those educational opportunities offered white children generally.

The system of segregated schools continued to be constitutionally sanctioned until 1954 when the Supreme Court, in the famous *Brown* opinion, held that the so called "separate but equal" doctrine, which the court only 50 years before had determined was this country's standard of racial equality, could no longer be the law of the land. Notwithstanding this articulation of a new constitutional standard, and the effort by the Court to undo what its previous decisions had helped to perpetuate, the local communities, who were ordered to implement the federal judicial mandate, resisted. A decade later, only a small percentage of black children attended integrated schools (Gewirtz, 1983). This resistance was not limited to the white parent. Both on the federal and the state level, the southern political leadership expressed its strong disapproval of *Brown*, to the point where, in at least one state, the National Guard was called out to *prevent* black children from going to school with white children. Federal marshalls were required to protect these black children from being victimized by violent acts perpetrated by white students and their parents (Woodward, 1974).

We also know that this resistance to integrated schools was not just a regional aberration. In other parts of the country, federal courts were also called upon to respond to the existence of unconstitutionally segregated schools. Neither in the north, nor in the south, were black children welcomed by the local school communities; the invitation to attend integrated schools had to come from outside the communities affected. New terms and expressions even entered our vocabulary such as "white flight" and "tipping." White families did not want too many black families living in the neighborhood, or their children going to school

---

[1] A federal law seeking to regulate child labor was declared unconstitutional in *Hammer v. Dagenhart* (1918). This decision was overruled in *United States v. Darby* (1941).

with black children.[2] White families with the financial means sent children to private schools, or moved from the turmoil of the cities to calmer environs of the suburbs (Gewirtz, 1983). When black children did enter the "integrated" public schools, it was not with the invitation from a gracious host. Rather, their entry occurred often times over the opposition of many of the white children and their parents, who perhaps had viewed them as ignorant children, and perhaps as children to be feared. Moreover, there certainly is no reason to believe that some of the teachers and principals in previously all, or mostly all white schools did not share the majority value toward blacks. So the invitation came from Washington. The hosts, however, were those who did not extend this invitation: the principals, teachers, white children, and their parents.

What happened in this environment? Without the welcome mat, some of the occurrences were not unexpected. Tracking systems or ability groupings were used to sort the new arrivals and, perhaps not surprisingly, intra-school segregation took place. The justification now, however, is not the race of the child, but rather his ability. The prophecy of some was fulfilled. Those who attempted to justify segregation in the pre-*Brown* era as a response to the intellectual inferiority of blacks found "scientific" support, in the post-*Brown* period to segregate a disproportionate number of black children in so called ability groupings. In such tracking systems, black children found themselves placed in classes for children deemed either to have less school ability, or in need of remedial program. In any event, a dispro-portionately large number of black students were quickly labeled as school failures in the eyes of the white students, in the eyes of the white teachers, and most importantly, in their own eyes (Glasser, 1969).[3]

Related to these "second generation" desegregation problems is the disproportionately high rate of suspension of minority students for inappropriate school behavior (Children's Defense Fund, 1975). The failure of minority students to behave in the way that the white students have always been expected to behave has increasingly resulted in their being pushed out of school. When such an event occurs, the focus is almost exclusively on behavior, and not on the poverty, racism, and educational deficiencies which may have contributed to the behavior. Though schools have the right, as well as the obligation, to provide a reasonably safe environment for all students, the pushing out of minority students in such high numbers, coupled with the background of segregation, resistance to integration, and intra-school segregation, suggests the existence of factors other than the misbehavior of minorities and the disciplinary needs of schools: we still have not incorporated the concept of equal educational opportunity articulated in *Brown* more than 30 years ago. The evidence suggests that the new kids, these intruders into the educational mainstream, are still not being welcomed. Their differences are not accepted. The federal courts order the minority children into the front door, but many schools still push them off to the side wings or out the back door (*Hawkins v. Coleman,* 1974).

From a legal perspective one of the difficult questions these "race, students, and school" issues presents is the decision as to which problems are amenable to judicial resolution,

---

[2] In a recent *New York Times* article discussing the effects a decade later of a federal court order directing the busing of public school children to achieve round integration, Gene Maeroff stated that "the biggest change is the racial composition of the student body. The percentage of white students in the school system has dropped by more than half, while the percentage of black students has increased substantially. School officials say so many whites have abandoned the system that not enough are left to provide racial balance" (Maeroff, 1984).

[3] For example, in 1967 a federal court held that the public school tracking system in the District of Columbia was being operated in a racially impermissible manner (*Hobsen v. Hansen,* 1967).

and which problems involve educational policy issues that should be resolved by local and state educational agencies (*Tasby v. Estes,* 1981). The *Brown* case dealt with the ability of schools to deny admission to children for racial (non-educational?) reasons. Part of the Supreme Court's justification for its *Brown* decision was the harm inflicted on the hearts and minds of black children by enforced segregation. The interference by the Brown Court on "educational" policy was minimal—school admission decisions should not be based on the race of the student. When we go beyond the admission decision to punishment and discipline of minority children the issue is more complex, though the rule is still the same.

It is clear that a school cannot discipline a child for racial reasons (*Hawkins v. Coleman,* 1974). It is also clear that a school cannot make educational decisions for racial reasons (*Hobson v. Hanson,* 1967). When we examine the results of school disciplinary decisions however, we see that minority children are apparently being punished and excluded from some school system in statistically disproportionate numbers (*Hawkins v. Coleman,* 1974; Children's Defense Fund, 1975). The reasons may not be overtly racial. Should the courts treat these decisions as "educational" issues if the decisions are based on nonracial factors— even though the results may inflict the same harm to the hearts and minds of the children affected? And, if we found a violation of the Constitution based on result or effect, what is the remedy? It is not a surprise that the first "non-desegregation" education cases to reach the Supreme Court in the post-*Brown* period involved the punishment of students.

Disruption, Discipline, and Due Process

Students' Rights Are Recognized. Beginning in the early 1970s the Supreme Court was called upon to respond to those lawsuits seeking to establish some external limitation on the disciplinary power of those in charge of public schools. In one of the first cases, *Goss v. Lopez* (1975), high school students brought the lawsuit seeking a declaration that their temporary suspensions from school, without being afforded notice of the reasons for the schools' action or an opportunity for some sort of hearing prior to any suspension, denied them due process of law. Before discussing the Supreme Court's response, it may be instructive to consider some of the events that led up to the suspensions.

In 1971 the Columbus, Ohio Board of Education (the defendant in *Goss*) was operating a segregated school system in violation of the Fourteenth Amendment. During the period relevant to the lawsuit, black history week was being observed, racial tensions in the schools were very high, rallies were occurring outside the board of education buildings protesting the racial policies of the district. According to the testimony of Lopez, one of the students who was suspended, two black students had been shot outside the school by white students. We know that in another case concerning the segregation of the Columbus School during this same time period, *Columbus Board of Education v. Penick* (1979), the Supreme Court endorsed the findings of the trial court that the Columbus Board had intentionally caused, and perpetuated, the racial isolation of black students in the district.

Though the *Penick* case was decided after *Goss*, the lower court opinion in *Goss* as well as the record on appeal certainly put the Supreme Court on notice of the racial situation in Columbus at the time of the incident and litigation. Remember, not only did *Brown* consider the right of students but the Supreme Court had also discussed the obligations of school districts. Black students were given an invitation from Washington that school districts, such as Columbus, did not honor. The disruption which occurred and led to the suspension of the black students in *Goss* was *Brown* related. The school district that was being operated in a constitutionally impermissible manner found itself suspending and then litigating against students whose behavior related to the racial tensions and the racial inequality in the schools. Notwithstanding this background, race does not appear to be an articulated factor in the court's decision.

What the *Goss* court did focus on were the procedures utilized by the school in suspending students for a period of up to ten school days. Procedures for longer term suspensions were not in issue. With four members of the court dissenting, the court held that the Fourteenth Amendment did operate as a restraint on the ability of the school to select the procedures for suspending students. What is the restraint?

At the outset the court indicated that students faced with a suspension are to be given "some kind of notice and afforded some kind of hearing" (*Goss v. Lopez*, p. 579). The Court stated that the notice requirement may be an oral or written explanation of what the charges are against the student and should generally precede the removal of the student from school. Regarding the "hearing" the court mandated that the school district provide "at least an informal give and take between student and disciplinarian. . ." which may take place within minutes of the incident. In this "give and take" the student should be given the opportunity to give his version of what happened. Though this process should generally precede any suspension, those "[s]tudents whose presence poses a continuing danger to persons or property or an ongoing threat of disrupting the academic process may be immediately removed from school. In such cases, the necessary notice and rudimentary hearing should follow as soon as practicable. . . ." (*Goss v. Lopez*, pp. 582–583).

Is *Goss* an example of the Court protecting black students from arbitrary suspensions when they were protesting the schools racially illegal setup? Perhaps. But the *Goss* decision was framed in a way that all students "benefit" from the process imposed. Unlike the parent who does not have to give reasons for disciplining his child, removal of the child from the educational system at least requires a reason and some opportunity for a discussion. "Sentence first"? In Wonderland yes, but in Columbus, Ohio and in all other school districts in the United States, no (at least where the punishment is a temporary suspension).

To summarize the Court's opinion, the required hearing may take place immediately after the incident, and may be informal in nature. From the perspective of Justice White who authored the opinion of the court, such a hearing is relatively nondisruptive of the educational process. With respect to the "violent" or severely disruptive student, the school is certainly free to take all necessary steps to protect all the staff and students by, for example, removing him from the premises and holding a post-exclusion hearing. The *Goss* opinion, on the role of the federal constitution in school suspension situations, divided the Supreme Court almost down the middle. Four Justices, in an opinion by Justice Powell, dissented. Why the division?

Unlike Justice White's approach which recognized as constitutionally significant the serious impact that a suspension could have on a students life, Justice Powell concluded that the infringement on the students education is ". . . too speculative, transitory, and insubstantial to justify imposition of a constitutional rule" (*Goss v. Lopez*, p. 586). Citing a study by the Children's Defense Fund, which was contained in their amicus brief to the Court in support of the student's position, Justice Powell noted the increased use of suspensions by various schools. He indicated that school teachers and administrators should be able to maintain use of suspension as one of their disciplinary tools without the need for due process formalism. From Justice Powell's perspective, this decision is an unwarranted intrusion by the federal judiciary into ". . . routine classroom discipline of children and teenagers in the public schools" (*Goss v. Lopez*, p. 585).

In perhaps a nostalgic moment Powell described the pupil–teacher relationship as an on-going one and noted the various roles teachers play such as advisor, friend, and occasional parent substitute, and commented upon the warm memories he had of his primary and secondary school teachers. Justice Powell criticized the majority for trying to change this into an adversary relationship. What is curious in regard to the pupil–teacher relationship envisioned by Justice Powell is his perception of the school disciplinary process as compared to Justice White's. In considering the impact of the decision Justice Powell criticized its interference with the teachers role of protecting students by disciplining disruptive or insubordinate pupils without "frustrating formalities," and for ". . . constitutionalizing routine classroom decisions." His dissent in this regard did not consider the facts in the case before the court which did not involve any direct classroom disruption but rather assumed, I believe incorrectly, that the White opinion would somehow prevent teachers from having disruptive children removed from their classroom without a prior hearing. Justice White focused on the principal, the person in *Goss* as well as most other schools who is empowered to make temporary suspensions and was sensitive to that person's need to act quickly and informally. Furthermore, the dissent in its sanquine view of schools did not make any mention of the racial background of the case nor did it in any way respond to the racial concerns expressed in some of the amicus briefs that minority children in Ohio and in other parts of the country were suspended in disproportionate numbers and that some procedures were necessary in order to reduce arbitrary and discriminatory treatment.

Students' Rights Are Limited. Moving our inquiry south of Columbus to Florida, but during the same school year, the Dade County school system found itself being sued for its practices regarding corporal punishment. Before considering the case a brief racial history of the area may be informative.

Prior to, as well as subsequent to, *Brown* the State of Florida operated segregated public schools. This official segregation of the schools persisted at least through the 1970–71 school year (*Debra P. v. Turlington*, 1981) when the incidents which led to *Ingraham v. Wright* arose. James Ingraham, one of the plaintiffs, attended Drew Junior High School in Dade County. In 1970 there were approximately 1550 black students and no white students in that school. It is instructive to note that, because of the location of Drew Junior High School, the Fifth Circuit Court of Appeals, in another case involving the integration of the schools in Dade County, concluded that ". . .there is no feasible method of desegregating the school" (*Pate v. Dade County School Board,* 1970, p. 1157). Through teacher assignment changes as part of the desegregation plan, however, almost 80% of the teachers in the school were white. Prior to this time, I would assume that this segregated school's teaching staff was 100% black.

In October 1970, James Ingraham, an 8th grade student, was slow to respond to his teachers' instructions and was therefore subjected to more than 20 licks with a paddle while being held over a table in the principal's office. The consequent injury necessitated some medical treatment, and the effects of the beating caused James to miss several days of school. This beating was not an unusual occurrence at Drew. Ingraham, together with another student at the school, brought a lawsuit seeking, among other things, a judgment declaring that the use of corporal punishment was in violation of the cruel and unusual punishment clause of the Eighth Amendment, an injunction preventing its use in the schools, and a judgment declaring that the procedures followed by the school in imposing corporal punishment deprived students of property and liberty in violation of the Fourteenth Amendment.

The Court of Appeals for the Fifth Circuit called the regime at the school a harsh one and stated that "the frequency of the use of corporal punishment suggests real oppressiveness" and that ". . . the punishment meted out at this school was often severe and of a nature likely to cause serious physical and psychological damage" (*Ingraham v. Wright,*

1974, pp. 257–259). Furthermore the Court observed that, in most of the instances of misconduct for which this punishment was inflicted, there was no property damage or physical harm to anyone. Being convinced that the punishment system was ". . . degrading to the children at that institution," the Court concluded that the severity and the system of paddling at Drew violated the Eighth Amendment proscription that punishments not be greatly disproportionate to the offenses charged (*Ingraham v. Wright*, 1974).

As had occurred with the *Goss* decision, the Supreme Court in *Ingraham v. Wright* was divided down the middle. This time however, Justice Powell authors the majority opinion and Justice White the dissent. The difference? Justice Stewart switched sides, joined the majority in both cases, but did not write an opinion in either case. With reference to the issue of the Eighth Amendment, the Powell opinion briefly surveyed corporal punishment, noted that it was practiced and sanctioned in Blackstone's England and that it was still being used today. Notwithstanding this historical excursion, the opinion did not conclude that corporal punishment is compatible with the amendment's proscriptions. Instead the majority concluded that the amendment had no application to non-criminal punishments, regardless of the severity of the school punishment. If students have any redress for severe or excessive corporal punishment, their remedy would have to be found in those state laws which generally prohibit this type of student discipline, and that provide students with the legal basis for bringing a civil suit to recover damages for injuries sustained.[4] Not finding such a limitation in the language of the Eighth Amendment, its purpose, or in prior Court decisions, the dissent argued for an Eighth Amendment limitation on severe forms of punishment, regardless of how the process, or its administering institution, is labeled.

As regards the applicability of the due process clause and the *Goss* decision, the majority concluded that the liberty of the student was implicated when he was punished by the school through restraint, and the infliction of more than *de minimis* physical pain. The majority, nonetheless, refused to extend *Goss'* procedural requirement of "some sort of hearing" prior to the imposition of this punishment because of the availability of the state law remedies for excessive punishment. The Court further concluded that whatever benefit accrued from having prior hearings was outweighed by such hearings ". . . significant intrusion into an area of primary educational responsibility." Justice Powell's approach in *Ingraham* was substantively indistinguishable from his dissent in *Goss*, though he attempts to distinguish, and not overrule, *Goss*.

Justice White dissented on the issue of prior hearings, finding that a possible state lawsuit to recover damages for excessive punishment does not provide adequate process. From White's perspective, the risk of error by the disciplinarian was as great in *Ingraham* as it was in *Goss*, and the burden on the school district of holding some informal hearing prior to the beating is no greater than that imposed by the *Goss* decision. The dissent also took issue with the value choice made by the majority of permitting, in essence, punishment before or even without, trial.

Students' Rights Are Relative. Before considering the role of the Consitution and the Supreme Court in the life of the public school, one further case need be mentioned so as to complete the "schoolhouse" trilogy, and give us a sense of the Court's direction. Unlike

---

[4]In 1978, the European Court of Human Rights, in a case involving judicial corporal punishment arising out of a school fight, found such punishment to be "degrading" and in violation of Article 3 of the Convention for the Protection of Human Rights and Fundamental Freedoms (European Court of Human Rights Tyrer Case). This Article states that "no one shall be subjected to torture or to inhuman or degrading treatment or punishment." In comparison, the Eighth Amendment to the United States Constitution prohibits the infliction of cruel and unusual punishment.

the previous cases, this case (*Board of Curators of the University of Missouri v. Horowitz*, 1978) involves a white medical student who claimed that the procedures used in expelling her from medical school, for unsatisfactory clinical work, were constitutionally inadequate. Specifically, during the many months prior to her dismissal from medical school, Ms. Horowitz had been repeatedly advised of deficiencies in her clinical performance. She was put on probation at one point, and afforded the opportunity to have outside physicians evaluate her work. The dismissal occurred during Horowitz's final year of school.

For the purpose of resolving the *Horowitz* case, the whole court was willing to assume that the student had a liberty or property interest protected by the due process clause of the Fourteenth Amendment. Further, the whole court was in agreement that the procedures afforded the student satisfied the constitutional requirement. Yet five justices wrote opinions. In writing for the majority of the court, Justice Rehnquist said that this case involved a dismissal for academic deficiency which required an expert evaluation of a cumulative record, and, therefore is not adaptable to the process normally followed in administrative or judicial hearings. From this, Rehnquist concluded that due process does not require a hearing when a student is being dismissed for academic reasons. Though the Court did not explicitly state the requirements for due process of law, the Court's focus on the decisionmakers' efforts to continually keep Ms. Horowitz informed of the nature of the problem, and what was required to satisfy the school's standards for awarding a Doctor of Medicine degree, suggests that this approach will satisfy the Amendment's requisites.

Justice White, without mentioning the *Goss* opinion, disagreed with the Court's conclusion about the need for a hearing and asserted that a student is required to be given an opportunity to state her side of the story before the dismissal. Because Ms. Horowitz was afforded this opportunity due process requirements were satisfied.

Horowitz, together with *Ingraham*, signals a none too subtle shift in the Supreme Court's role regarding educational problems and educational institutions. What is it about the nature of academic institutions which produces this reluctance on the part of the Court to be involved?

The Court has relied upon a number of characteristics of educational institutions to justify their approach. One such characteristic is the expertise needed by the institutional decisionmaker in evaluating, examining, and in imposing serious sanctions for, unsatisfactory academic performance. Other characteristics include the specialness of the teacher–student relationship and the tradition of local control over education. Such control presupposes the ability of local school districts to have the tools to respond to their unique problems. These institutional assumptions notwithstanding, the question is whether the characteristics of school administration justify the Court's refusal to require some kind of hearing before serious sanctions are imposed.

A serious sanction imposed for unsatisfactory academic performance is, in essence, the product of a two step procedure analogous to the bifurcated hearing process in juvenile and family courts that would be applicable, for example, in a person in need of supervision proceeding alleging that a student was a habitual truant.[5] The first step is the determination that the student has a serious educational problem (in the family court this would be the fact finding or adjudicatory hearing determination that the student was truant). As regards this part of the process, the Court was certainly correct that the evaluation is made by someone with educational expertise and based on a cumulative record.

The second step in this process is to determine what to do with the student. This is a very critical stage in the student's educational career. The decision, therefore, requires the

---

[5] An example of this proceeding may be found in the New York Family Court Act, Article 7.

thoughtful, deliberate involvement of various persons in the educational institution including teachers, who have to provide insights into the student's strengths and needs; administrators, who are in a position to know what is available in the educational system and who have to make decisions; and the student and his family, who must understand the seriousness of the problem, insofar as its cause and solution are concerned. Their willingness to participate may be essential to any effective resolution of this problem.

The public school may have available a number of alternatives, such as leaving the student back, promoting him, transferring him to a different academic track, program, or school, or perhaps dismissing him from school. In a juvenile proceeding dealing with truancy, the comparable step in the process is referred to as the dispositional hearing (N.Y. Family Court Act §712), a process unique to the juvenile court, and concludes in a judgment as to whether the juvenile needs supervision or treatment. In making such a judgment, the court has the opportunity to inquire into possible causes of the student's educational problems, including whether there are special educational needs, medical needs, psychological needs, or particular family problems that should be addressed. The constitutional guarantee of due process of law, together with statutes in the various states (N.Y. Family Court Act, §741; *in re Ceceilia R.*, 1975), gives juveniles the right to participate in this hearing when it occurs within the juvenile court process.

The Court of Appeals decision (*Board of Curators of the University of Missouri v. Horowitz*, 1976) had directed that there be a formal evidentiary hearing before Ms. Horowitz could be dismissed from medical school. In reversing this decision, the Supreme Court indicated that the educational institution's evaluation process, which provided the student various opportunities over a long period of time ". . . to demonstrate improvement or question the evaluations," was constitutionally sufficient. Though the Court did not require an additional discrete hearing, its approval of the educational process in this case is tantamount to the approval of a quasi-dispositional "hearing without walls."

One of the Supreme Court's obligations is to educate the community about the Constitution, and its requirements, with some degree of clarity. Though the obligation was not clearly met in the *Horowitz* case, I believe that the majority of the Court has concluded that a school that is seeking to dismiss a student, is required to have a fair process. Such a process may take various forms, but must include a clear delineation of the problem, an exploration of various solutions, and the participation by the student and his family. Contrasted with *Goss*, where there was no process before students were suspended (and the Court therefore grafted on to the educational system an additional requirement), in *Horowitz* the institution followed a subsequent *judicially* determined fair participatory process before the dismissal. The Court, therefore, did not have ". . . to further enlarge the judicial presence in the academic community . . ." (*Horowitz*, p. 90) by requiring an additional hearing. Whether out of respect for the expertise of educational decision makers or for the tradition of local control of education that the Court has discussed in other cases, schools have the opportunity to create fair process, so long as they meet the core concerns of the due process clause.

Analysis. The *Horowitz* and *Goss* decisions both impose constitutional procedural restrictions on the ability of a school to push students out the door of the educational system just as *Brown* imposed limitations on the ability of the school to keep black children from coming in the door of the school. But *Ingraham*, which involved a punishment arguably as serious as that inflicted in *Goss* for acts which fell on the non-academic side of the *Horowitz-Goss* line, produces the most deferential opinion. Why?

Unlike the other two decisions, the *Ingraham* decision was dealing with corporal punishment—a non-exclusionary disciplinary sanction. The Court also had before it an *amicus curiae* brief filed by the Dade County teachers' union in support of the school district. In this brief, the teachers discussed the "desegregation years." Within this context, the brief detailed a history of teachers not receiving adequate community support; of the increase in violence in the county schools; of the "combat" conditions in Dade County schools and urban schools generally. The teachers' union argued that, if teachers are going to be asked by society and the courts to educate all the children, the Supreme Court should not restrain them in their ". . . ability to utilize the full panoply of disciplinary methods in working to achieve a safe educational atmosphere" (Brief for United Teachers, 1977, p. 16). Notwithstanding that most of the violence in the school appeared to be the official violence of corporal punishment, the Court affirmatively responded to the concerns of the teachers. *Brown* imposed the affirmative obligation on the schools, and if teachers were making efforts to carry out this mandate the Court was not going to get involved and police the classroom. If a school wished to use corporal punishment, the administration of the sanction was left to school officials' discretion, provided there was some recourse for its abuse. If corporal punishment had been useful to teachers in carrying out their educational function, the Court, sensitive perhaps to the school tensions occasioned by the transition from desegregation to integration, was willing to leave this tool in place.

What is curious about the Court's decision in *Ingraham* is the willingness, not just to leave the disciplinary power in place, but to permit its use without requiring any explanation by the disciplinarian. The Court approached this issue as if it were dealing with parents who were resisting state intrusion into their decisionmaking role of providing for the education and upbringing of their child. Parents have always had broad discretion in raising their children; they can discipline or hit their children for their own family reasons or for no reason. It is only when parents have crossed the vague line constituting abuse or neglect that their family privacy or autonomy shield may be pierced (*Parham v. J.R.*, 1979). If we substitute teachers for parents and excessive corporal punishment laws for child abuse laws, the analogy is clear and the Court seems willing to apply the same rules. We may be at a point in time in our societal development in which the officially sanctioned hitting of children is still thought to have a value in our schools (as well as our homes). Nonetheless schools are not families, and it is therefore difficult to understand why fairness, an important value comprising due process of law, does not require an educational institution *have* a reason, and *convey* that reason, before hitting takes place.

The school teachers' union in Dade County should, of course, be concerned about disruption and violence in the schools. One wonders nevertheless whether the corporal form of punishment, which is not necessarily confined to instances of student violence, will reduce the incidence of disruption and violence, or teach children that physical aggression is wrong. When James Ingraham was paddled for being slow to respond to a teacher's instructions, what did he internalize about the appropriate use of violence?

This willingness by the Court to sanction less stringent constitutional protections for children under the Eighth and Fourteenth Amendments to the Constitution because, in part, of the specialness of the school environment, has recently been extended by the Supreme Court to the Fourth Amendment. In *New Jersey v. T.L.O.* (1985), a student was taken to the school administrator for violating the school's no smoking rule. In the office, the student denied having smoked and further claimed that she never smoked. In response to these denials the administrator searched the student's purse and found, in addition to cigarettes, marihuana, marihuana paraphernalia, and some documents suggesting that she might have been selling marihuana to other students. The drug information was given to the police and subsequently referred to a juvenile court where the student was charged with being a juvenile delinquent. The issue before the court was the legality of the search.

Stating that drug use and violent crime in the schools have become major social problems, and citing *Goss* and *Ingraham* for the propositions that the Court has previously recognized and respected the schools need for flexibility in responding to school disciplinary problems, and in preserving the informality of the teacher–student relationship, Justice White, writing the majority opinion for the Court, held the search to be within the requirements of the Fourth Amendment. However, notwithstanding the application of the Fourth Amendment to school searches, White stated that school authorities acting alone, and not at the behest of, or in conjunction with, outside law enforcement agencies, are not required to obtain a search warrant before searching a student. Furthermore, the school may conduct a search without having probable cause when ". . . there are reasonable grounds for suspecting that the search will turn up evidence that the student has violated or is violating either the law or the rules of the school." Using the standard of reasonableness instead of probable cause, continued the Court, will enable ". . . teachers and school administrators. . . to regulate their conduct according to the dictates of reason and common sense" (*New Jersey v. T.L.O.*, p. 744).

Though the standard of what constitutes "reasonableness" may be vague, the message conveyed by this decision, together with *Ingraham*, *Horowitz*, and even *Goss*, is much clearer: Schools are not going to be restrained by the same rules that restrain other adults and other institutions dealing with children. These decisions suggest that there may be a children's edition of the Constitution that applies to schools: Before adults are searched a search warrant is generally required, but not for children in school; before an adult is searched "probable cause" is required, but "not for children in school where only reasonableness" is required; adults cannot be hit, but children can be beaten provided the school official acts "reasonably." The school's ability to police itself and discipline children will generally not be interfered with by the federal courts except where "reason and common sense" are outraged.

DISABILITY AND DISCIPLINE

Recent studies (Barkley, 1981; Dunivant, 1982; Lewis, Shanok, Balla, & Bard, 1980; Robbins et al., 1983), confirming earlier observations (Glasser, 1969; Rutter, 1975), have suggested that of the children who are delinquent or are violent in school, a statistically significant number have some type of a learning disability that adversely affects their school performance. For example, a 1982 study prepared by the National Commission for State Courts, stated that between 30% and 50% of adjudicated delinquents had a learning disability, and ". . . boys with learning disabilities engaged in more violence, e.g., assault with a dangerous weapon and gang fighting, and experienced more school discipline problems than their non-learning disabled peers" (Dunivant, 1982, p. 16).

Though the causes of this relationship may not be established (Kashani, Husain, Robins, Reid, & Wooderson, 1980), some research suggests there is a direct relationship between learning disability and misconduct because of the personality characteristics possessed by children with learning disabilities (Dunivant, 1982). Such characteristics include lack of impulse control and hyperactivity, making learning disabled children more susceptible to opportunities to engage in misconduct. Other research suggests there is an indirect relationship between learning disability and misconduct arising, for example, because of the frustration, anger, and subsequent aggression occasioned by school failure related to a learning disability (Dunivant, 1982). Still other researchers suggest that learning disability may combine with other various factors—direct and indirect including psychiatric, neurological, social, and economic, to cause inappropriate aggressive or delinquent behavior (Faretra, 1981). In spite of the hypotheses set forth in the various research studies, there seems to be general agreement that a relationship between learning disability and violence exists, and that we should not wait to discover the causal link before intervening with various remedial programs.

The Movement to Secure Equal Education for the Handicapped

In 1927 Justice Holmes, in an opinion for the Supreme Court upholding the power of a state to sterilize mentally retarded persons, stated that:

> It is better for all the world, if instead of waiting to execute degenerate offspring for crime, or to let them starve for their imbecility, society can prevent those who are manifestly unfit from continuing their kind. (*Buck v. Bell*, p. 207)

Because the case at bar neither involved the commission of a criminal act, nor concerned any issue of nutrition or starvation, this dramatic statement by Holmes, though just a gratuitous comment, is probably a reasonable reflection of the then prevalent attitude of the Court and society about disabled people and their place in the community. At the time, not only did this country have laws authorizing the sterilization of mentally retarded persons, to which this case gave constitutional legitimacy, but there also existed large institutions to accommodate the removal and segregation of disabled people from the mainstream of the community (Wolfensberger, 1975). Given this eradicatory or exclusionary approach towards disabled people, it certainly is no surprise that the public schools, during the first half of the 20th century, were largely unavailable to children with physical and mental disabilities.[6]

Shortly after *Brown* was decided in the mid-1950s, parents of disabled children increased political pressure on various legislative bodies to recognize the public schools' obligation to their children. The ripple effect of *Brown's* articulation of new conceptions of equality, the importance of education, and the benefits of integrated education, was starting to be seen and felt.

For example, in 1955 legislation was enacted, with the cautious support of the New York Department of Education,[7] giving local school districts the discretionary authority to provide classes for severely mentally retarded children (N.Y. Laws of 1955). Only 5 years later, this legislation was made mandatory when local school districts demonstrated their unwillingness to set up such classes (N.Y. Laws of 1960). In approving this mandatory legislation in 1960, New York's governor stated that ". . . the facilities of our public school are best adapted to providing the training which these children must have." Additionally,

---

[6] Where *Plessey v. Ferguson* sanctioned separate and inferior schools for black children, *Buck v. Bell* sanctioned the elimination of mentally disabled people. Both groups were constitutionally considered different enough to permit this treatment.

[7] A memorandum to the New York State Education Department concerning this law stated, in part, that ". . . it should be noted as a matter of record that the Department is not at all convinced that the educational authorities of the State should be concerned with training programs for children in this mental age bracket." State Education Department Memorandum, N.Y. Laws 1955, Ch. 795, p. 169.

from a cost viewpoint providing such classes may result in ". . . eventual savings to the people of the State by permitting such children permanently to remain in the community instead of being eventually placed in institutions" (Governor's Memoranda, 1960, p. 571). A memorandum from a joint legislative committee supporting this legislation stated that ". . . the bill will assure the children and their families here involved their constitutional and moral right to a public education which is presently denied them" (Memorandum of Joint Legislative Committee, 1960, p. 184).

During this same time period, regulations of the New York State Education Department required local school districts to locate classes in regular school buildings for educable retarded children, that is, those children whose I.Q. was above 50. In 1960 the legislature passed a bill overruling this regulation by permitting each school district to determine the location of such classes. In vetoing this bill, Governor Rockefeller supported the Education Department's position and stated that ". . . educable retarded children should not be insulated from normal children, because contacts with normal children provide the best opportunity for the full development of such retarded children" (Governor's Memoranda, 1960, p. 609).

In 1964, with respect to children considered emotionally disturbed, the New York Education Department refused to support legislation mandating special education classes for emotionally disturbed children. The New York Education Department was concerned that school districts would use these special classes as a way of excluding those children ". . . whose behavior constitutes a problem to the classroom teacher although such problems may be of a minor behavioral nature and could better be handled in the normal classroom situation" (State Education Department Memorandum, 1964, p. 216). Notwithstanding the department's recommendation that the issue needed further study, the bill was signed by the governor. Such legislative examples from New York suggest that *Brown* not only was the seminal decision regarding equal educational opportunity for children of all races, but had a significant impact on the issue of equal educational opportunity generally.

As with the *Brown* decision, all the prejudices, fears, and devaluation of disabled children by teachers, parents of "normal" children, and the adult society at large, which may have significantly contributed to the unwillingness of the public schools to provide educational programs for disabled children, did not necessarily end with the passage of legislation. Most disabled children were still not provided appropriate public school educational programs. The children were excluded from school because of their disability, exempted from school because of the absence of educational programs, or just simply told no program existed for them. The following excerpt from a letter, received by the parents of a mentally retarded child in 1972 (12 years after mentally retarded children were legislatively provided with the right to an education in New York), does not represent an unusual response:

> Regarding your inquiry about a placement for your daughter. . . . I am sorry to inform you that even though Ann has qualified for placement in a public school program for the past two years, we are unable to assign her because there is no space. Be assured that Ann is on a waiting list and will be taken as soon as an opening occurs. (*Matter of Piontkowski*, 1973)

It was not just mentally retarded children who were denied the opportunity for a public school education. For example, in 1971 in the District of Columbia out of about 16,000 school age handicapped children, including mentally retarded, physically handicapped, and emotionally disturbed children, only 4,000 were receiving educational services (*Mills v. Board of Education*, 1972).

One child so deprived was Duane Blacksheare, who, in 1967, while in the third grade, was excluded from all publicly supported education because he allegedly was a behavior problem. In 1972 he was still not receiving a public education. Another child affected was Steven Gaston, a slightly brain-damaged and hyperactive child. In 1969 Steven was excluded from the first grade because he wandered around the classroom. In 1972 Steven was still not receiving a publicly supported education.

Steven, Duane, and five other children brought *Mills v. Board of Education*, a 1972 class action suit, to require the Board of Education to provide all "exceptional" children with publicly supported adequate education. The defendants did not deny the alleged facts, and conceded the district was under a duty to provide these children with an education. Their only defense was lack of funds. The federal district court rejected this defense and, basing its holding on statutes from the district as well as the due process clause of the Fifth Amendment, directed the defendant to ". . . provide to each child of school age a free and suitable publicly supported education regardless of the degree of the child's. . . disability or impairment (*Mills*, p. 878).

In addition to this directive, the judgement set out detailed procedures and requirements to be followed by the school district that included the following: a presumption in favor of placing all children in integrated or regular school classes; a requirement for a hearing before removing a child from a regular school program; a periodic review of the child's status and the adequacy of educational alternatives; and, a requirement that all children suspended for more than 2 days be provided with their education during the period of any such suspension (*Mills*, p. 880).

Notwithstanding the *Mills* decision, the 1971 *Pennsylvania Association for Retarded Children* (PARC) decision (requiring school districts in Pennsylvania to provide for mentally retarded children what *Mills* essentially required for the whole spectrum of disabled children) and protective legislation in states such as New York, Congress made legislative findings in 1975, that a majority of the more than 8 million handicapped children in the United States were not receiving appropriate educational services that would enable them to have full equality of opportunity. Congress further found that 1 million children were excluded entirely from the public school system, and that many children in regular school programs were not having successful educational experiences because their handicaps had gone undetected (20 U.S.C. §1400). These findings provided part of the justification for the enactment by Congress of the Education for All Handicapped Children Act of 1975 (EAHCA).

In enacting the EAHCA, Congress not only was influenced by the concept of equality and equal educational opportunity articulated in *Brown*, but was also influenced by the reasoning and respective directives contained in the judgments in *Mills* and *PARC*. For example, the *Mills* requirement that the District of Columbia provide all school age children with a free and suitable public education, regardless of the degree of the child's disability or impairment, is reflected in the EAHCA, which requires states to provide all handicapped children with a free appropriate education regardless of the nature and severity of their disability (20 U.S.C. §1412).

Being more specific than *Mills*, the EAHCA defined appropriate education in such a way as to require states to do more than just open the doors of the schoolhouse to all children. In addition to developing and providing educational instruction that meets the unique needs of the handicapped child (20 U.S.C. §1401(18)(19)), appropriate education also means that States are required to provide "related services," defined as "transportation, and such development, corrective, and other supportive services (including speech pathology and audiology, psychological services, physical and occupational therapy, and medical and counseling services, except that such medical services shall be for diagnostic and evaluation purposes only), as may be required to assist a handicapped child to benefit from special education. . ." (20 U.S.C. §1401(17)). This inclusion of related services as part of the definition of appropriate education is not only one of the major substantive requirements of the EAHCA, but this expansive definition also dramatically changes our concept of "education" and the role and obligations of state education agencies.

Furthermore, because of the provision for federal court judicial review of administrative hearing decisions made under the EAHCA (20 U.S.C. §1415(e)), the federal government, primarily through the federal courts, was given a role to play in the delivery of educational services that transcended the overseeing of pupil entrances and exits. However, though a state may be obligated to provide more than just a teacher with a loud voice for a deaf child, the scope of the state's obligation remains unclear, and has been the subject of two recent Supreme Court decisions.

The Supreme Court's Interpretation of the Education for All Handicapped Children Act

Amber Tatro was an 8-year-old girl afflicted with spina bifida. One consequence of this condition was a neurogenic bladder, that prevented her from emptying her bladder voluntarily. To avoid injury to her kidneys, Amber had to be catheterized every 3 or 4 hours by a procedure that can be performed, in a few minutes, by a layperson with less than an hour's training. Though her school was willing to provide Amber with physical and occupational therapy for other impairments related to the spina bifida, the school refused to assume responsibility for the catheterization, even though Amber could not attend school if the procedure was unavailable.

After an unsuccessful pursuit of their administrative remedies, Amber's parents brought a lawsuit in the federal district court seeking, among other things, an injunction directing the school to provide Amber with the procedure because it was a "related service" under the EAHCA. The defendants, as well as the National School Board Association (NSBA) who appeared in the action through an amicus brief in support of the school, did not dispute any of the facts. The issue was the definition of related services, raising the question of the extent of the educational obligation of school districts towards disabled children. This issue eventually reached the Supreme Court.

The defendants' position, as well as that of the NSBA, was that the EAHCA obligated the school to provide only those related services which arose out of the need to educate the child. Since Amber needed the catheterization before, during, and after school hours, it was not a service that arose from the need to educate her. From this perspective, because the child would need catheterization regardless of whether she attended school, or was in a regular or special class, Amber had a health need, as distinguished from an educational need. Therefore, a school, in meeting its obligation to provide a free appropriate education, was not obligated to perform this procedure (Petitioner's Brief for Certiorari at 3, *Irving Independent School District v. Tatro*, 1984).

This narrow definition of education, put forth by the school and the NSBA, was framed in response to their concern that an unfavorable court decision would put school districts inappropriately in the business of providing medical services. The NSBA posed the question whether schools should be forced to take on multiple roles associated with the provision of the health, psychological, respite, and custodial care needs of children. The NSBA's answer was an unequivocal no (Brief for NSBA, p. 13). The American Association of School Administrators also submitted an amicus curiae brief in support of the school, and, on this last point, argued that other state agencies can provide and administer catheterization (Brief for American Association of School Administrators, pp. 8–9).

The position of the school and supporting briefs is reminiscent of Governor Rockefeller's veto of a 1959 bill which sought to mandate public schools classes for the severely mentally retarded. The governor, at that time, indicated that "there is a serious question, however, as to whether our public school system should be charged with this responsibility" (Governor's Memoranda, p. 497). However, not only did the governor reverse himself the following year, and sign this legislation (N.Y. Laws of 1960), but the arguments of the school district had been fought out on the floor of Congress, and subsequently resolved by the enactment of the EAHCA.

The EAHCA definition of a handicapped child includes a child who is "health impaired" (20 U.S.C. §1401 (1)). School districts are required by the EAHCA to provide those supportive or related services that will enable the health impaired child to benefit from the required individually designed instruction. Under the construction of the act urged by the defendants, a school would be required to accept a child who had a health impairment, but could refuse to provide supportive services to meet the child's health needs.

Such a construction is inconsistent with the language as well as the intent of the EAHCA. Prior to the enactment of the EAHCA, children such as Amber, who were not in the appropriate physical condition, were not permitted to attend school. The EAHCA, in part, was designed to correct this situation. If the argument of the defendant was accepted by courts, many children who were finally being served would be excluded again.

It is unfortunate, but perhaps not surprising, that these national organizations joined this particular lawsuit in support of the school district. It is also not surprising that many of the major national organizations, representing persons afflicted with the whole range of disabilities and handicaps covered by the EAHCA, submitted an amicus curiae brief in support of the plaintiff's position. At issue was the nature and scope of the public school's responsibility to handicapped children.

Rather than focusing on Amber's handicap, and then discussing those procedures that may be necessary to aid the child and thus should be considered a related service, the Supreme Court in *Irving Independent School District v. Tatro* (1984) looked to the effect that not providing the service would have on the child. In a previous decision, the Court had emphasized that schools, under the EAHCA, were obligated to do more than just provide access to an educational program (*Board of Education of Hendrick Hudson Central School v. Rowley* 1982). Because the EAHCA gives children the right to an education that will be of benefit to them, the access provided by schools must be meaningful.

The Court in *Tatro* concluded that "meaningful" and "benefit," although rather vague words, provided a legal standard to measure the performance of a school district. Because Amber could not attend school and benefit from the special education to which she was entitled, the Supreme Court, in an opinion authored by the chief justice, held that the catheterization procedure ". . . falls squarely within the definition of a supportive service" (*Irving Independent School District v. Tatro*, p. 3377) and the school district was therefore required to provide it. "A service that enables a handicapped child to remain at school during the day is an important means of providing the child with the meaningful access to education that Congress envisioned" (*Irving Independent School District v. Tatro*, p. 3377). There was no dissent on this issue.

The importance of the *Tatro* case to the plaintiffs, and to the alliance of supportive organizations that submitted an amicus brief, is that the handicapped did not lose that to which they believed they were legally entitled prior to the initiation of the litigation. The Court's construction of the "related services" portion of the EAHCA did not narrow the scope of the requirement mandating that, if the needs of the child relate to the handicapping condition, and if those needs are not met the child will not be able to attend school, the school has responsibility, under the act, to meet those needs.

The *Tatro* Court confirmed the fears of the defendants, and the NSBA, that the plaintiffs' position would require them to go outside their traditional role, and become a multi-functional institution. The Court's opinion did indeed require schools to meet the needs of the child—regardless of whether the needs are labeled as health or education.

To the extent that school administrators also sought some clarification of their future obligations beyond the facts of this case, the *Tatro* Court's construction of the Act did provide some light, at least at the exclusionary end of the continuum. Where exclusion is not in issue, however, the unanimity of the *Tatro* Court's opinion contrasts with a divided Court's unwillingness to override educational administrators in *Board of Education of Hendrick Hudson Central School District v. Rowley* (1982), the first EAHCA case to be decided by the Court.

The Supreme Court's Interpretation of the EAHCA

In *Board of Education of Hendrick Hudson Central School District v. Rowley* the Court was presented with an appeal arising from the refusal of a school to provide a sign-language interpreter in all classes for an elementary school deaf student. Amy Rowley was otherwise receiving "substantial specialized instruction and related services, and was performing above average in the regular classrooms of a public school system" (*Rowley*, p. 202). Finding that, without a sign-language interpreter, the child comprehended less than half of what normal children comprehend, and that sign language may provide a greater degree of educational success, the federal district court reversed the state administrative decisions. The court of appeals affirmed. The Supreme Court, in a decision authored by Justice Rehnquist, reversed these judicial decisions for the following reasons: First, the lower courts had applied an incorrect educational standard in measuring the correctness of the school's decision; and, second, the district court misperceived its own role in reviewing the administrative decision.

With reference to the educational standard, the Supreme Court held that the correct standard to be applied in interpreting the EAHCA is whether the child is being given access to "... specialized instruction and related services which are individually designed to provide educational benefit to the handicapped child" (*Rowley*, p. 201), and not, as the lower court held, whether the services maximize the potential of each handicapped child commensurate with the opportunity provided non-handicapped children.

The difference in the standards lies in the trial court's focus on the fact that the child comprehended 50% less than non-handicapped students. Amy's performance at least at an average level notwithstanding, the lower court held that Amy's unique needs required that she be given the opportunity to comprehend more. Justice Rehnquist, on the other hand, looked at the glass, found it half full, and held, therefore, that the school fulfilled its obligation to the child. Rehnquist's interpretation of the EAHCA was that the school has an affirmative obligation to put something in the child's glass that will be meaningful and nourishing, but does not have to fill the glass to the top. Since, the child was performing at least at average level in her class, and was advancing from grade to grade, and since the school was providing personalized instruction and related services calculated to meet her educational needs, the school satisfied its obligations under the EAHCA.

Analysis

Looking at *Tatro* and *Rowley* together, the approach of the Supreme Court in interpreting the EAHCA becomes somewhat clearer. Going beyond their particular facts, these cases do not stand for the proposition that catheterization is authorized and a sign language interpreter is not authorized under the EAHCA. Rather, the focus in both cases is the impact on the child of withholding supportive services. Thus, for example, if withholding a sign language interpreter would prevent a child from educationally benefiting, or would result in her functional exclusion from school, the school would be obligated to provide that service.

As to the degree of benefit a child is to receive, even though the Court in *Rowley* specifically confined its analysis of the EAHCA to the particular facts of the situation, we know that the Court looked at the total program and the child's progress within that program before concluding that Amy, who was performing at the level of the average student in her class, was receiving her educational entitlement. The requirements of the act were satisfied notwithstanding that Amy was not provided the opportunity to perform at her optimal level.

This approach suggests that the school fulfills its obligation under the EAHCA by admitting a child, and providing a program of instruction and supportive services tailored to the child's needs and aimed at enabling the child to perform at the average level. To the extent that public school programs and expenditures are primarily geared to the needs of the average non-handicapped student, this interpretation of the federal law by the Court, which had previously expressed serious reservations about interfering with local educational institutions, minimizes or reduces the potential federal burden on local school districts by deferring to local educational standards used for measuring all students.

Even though it may be permissible to use similar, or even the same, measuring instruments for handicapped and non-handicapped students, however, it is important to emphasize that the expanded affirmative obligations that the EAHCA had imposed on schools required them to provide a program responsive to the unique needs of the disabled student. For the student who does not have a handicap, the school is under no federal obligation to develop and provide an educational program to respond to his unique needs.

The approach that the Court has taken in interpreting the EAHCA is similar in philosophy and approach to those school cases dealing with the constitutional rights of students. As we discussed earlier, one of the distinctions between *Goss* and *Ingraham* was the willingness of the Court to prescribe procedures for the temporary suspension of students for disciplinary reasons, but not when the school chooses to resolve the problem internally. Further, when the school makes an educational judgment about a student, and has given the student or her or his parents the opportunity to participate in the process, in *Horowitz*, the Court deferred to the expertise of the educational decisionmaker and refused to override the decision to impose a federal constitutional standard on the local institution.

Similarly in *Tatro*, where the result of a refusal to provide catheterization meant that the student could not attend school, the Court overrode the state administrative decision. However, in *Rowley*, where the Court refused to supercede the state administrative decision, the majority characterized the issue as involving the choice of a debated method of educating the deaf when, as here, the student was in school and otherwise benefiting from the program of instruction, and would continue to benefit regardless of the decision.

Violent or Disruptive Behavior: A Unique Need or the Basis for Suspension

The two EAHCA cases discussed above involved the needs of children that were unquestionably related to their handicap. What was placed in issue by the school districts in both cases was the extent of their obligations in meeting the needs of handicapped children and, additionally in *Rowley*, the choice of methods for dealing with a symptom of the disability. In neither case was the relationship between the symptom and the handicap ever questioned. For example, Amy Rowley, because of her deafness, was comprehending less than 50% of what was said in the classroom (*Rowley*, dissent, p. 3053). This diminished comprehension was one "symptom" of her disability. Similarly, for Amber Tatro, her non-functioning bladder was a symptom of her handicap.

What happens, however, if a child who has been assaultive toward other students or teachers, or is disruptive in a class, also happens to be handicapped? Is this student's behavior a "symptom" that may be related to the handicap and must be addressed by the school? Or is this just inappropriate behavior, regardless of whether the student is handicapped, which then provides the school with the basis to suspend or expel the student? This issue has been the subject of recent litigation.[8]

In 1981 in Florida, a number of students who had all been labeled as educable mentally retarded were "expelled" from school for the remainder of the academic year, and the following academic year, for various acts of misconduct, such as insubordination, vandalism, and the use of profane language. Prior to the expulsion, the school district apparently followed the same procedures used when any non-handicapped student is being expelled or suspended. Additionally, the school district complied with the constitutional requirements of procedural due process set forth in *Goss* (*S-1 v. Turlington*, 1981). Notwithstanding this compliance, the students brought a lawsuit in federal court claiming that because they were handicapped, the procedures of the EAHCA and not the state student disciplinary code governed any procedure that could result in a change in their educational placement.

Under the EAHCA, various procedural steps must be followed whenever there is to be a change in the student's educational placement, including the evaluation of the student by the student's teacher, by someone knowledgeable about special educational opportunities, and by the student's parents. In addition, to aid in this evaluation, the parents may be entitled to an independent educational evaluation at public expense. Furthermore, if the parents are unhappy with the result, there is an opportunity for a due process hearing before an independent hearing officer. Provisions are made for an appeal from this decision to the state educational agency, with the opportunity thereafter to bring a civil action in either federal or state court. Pending the outcome of this process, the child has the right to remain in his current educational placement (20 U.S.C. §1415).

In addition to these procedures, one of the substantive guidelines to be followed by the decisionmakers is the doctrine of "Least Restrictive Alternatives." This doctrine holds that to the maximum extent appropriate, handicapped students are to be educated with non-handicapped students and ". . . special classes, separate schooling, or other removal of handicapped children from the regular educational environment occurs only when the nature or severity of the handicap is such that education in regular classes with the use of supplementary aids and services cannot be achieved satisfactorily" (20 U.S.C. §1412(5)). Regardless of the outcome of this process, all that may change is *where* the educational program is to be provided, and *how* the educational program is to be provided. The student is still entitled to a free appropriate education under the continued responsibility of the state educational agency (20 U.S.C. §1412(6)).

One of the first issues for resolution by the court of appeals, therefore, in its review of *S-1 v. Turlington* was the relevance of these EAHCA procedures to the issue of expulsion, and specifically, whether a student could be expelled for misconduct if the underlying

---

[8]For example, see *Doe v. Koger, Kaelin v. Grubbs, S-1 v. Turlington, Sherry v. New York State Education Dep't,* and *Stuart v. Nappi. S-1 v. Turlington* was selected for discussion because it is representative of the approach taken by the courts and because it is the first appellate decision dealing with the issue.

behavior is a manifestation of the handicap itself. On this threshold issue, the defendants conceded there could be no expulsion if the handicap involved was the EAHCA-recognized handicap of "seriously emotionally disturbed." Because the students were mentally retarded and not emotionally disturbed, the defendants argued that the EAHCA had no application to this case (*S-1 v. Turlington*, p. 346).

Though the court's opinion does not set forth the reasons underlying this argument, I would assume the defendants relied on the EAHCA regulation which, in part, defines "seriously emotionally disturbed" as a condition which may have as one of its characteristics "[i]nappropriate types of behavior or feelings under normal circumstances" (34 C.F.R. §300.5(8)(i),(c), 1984). Aside from its definitional vagueness, this handicap is the only EAHCA-recognized disability that focuses on inappropriate behavior as its major characteristic. The court was not persuaded by this argument.

In rejecting the defendants' argument, the court first quoted approvingly from the district court's opinion that stated the defendants' position was ". . .contrary to the emphasis which Congress has placed on individual evaluation and consideration of the problems and needs of handicapped students" (*S-1 v. Turlington*, p. 346). Elaborating on this reasoning, the court, in this very important interpretation of the EAHCA, discussed and was persuaded by the uncontradicted testimony of a psychologist, who testified on behalf of the students, that a connection between the misconduct and the handicaps may have existed. The court quoted from the psychologist's testimony as follows:

> She reasoned that a child with low intellectual functions and perhaps the lessening of control would respond to stress or respond to a threat in the only way that they feel adequate, which may be verbal aggressive behavior. *S-1 v. Turlington*, p. 347

To perhaps further illustrate the non-obvious, though legally relevant, relationship between behavior and disability, the court continued to quote from the psychologist's testimony, this time about an orthopedically handicapped child,

> who would behave in an extremely aggressive way toward other children and provoke fights despite the fact that he was likely to come out very much on the short end of the stick. That this was his way of dealing with stress and dealing with a feeling of physical vulnerability. He would be both aggressive and hope that he would turn off people and as a result provoke an attack on him. *S-1 v. Turlington*, p. 347

The court concluded by holding that these students could not be expelled if the behavior was a manifestation of their disability, regardless of its nature. The court found that the school has the obligation under the EAHCA to provide an appropriate education to all handicapped children; the school has the burden of proving the non-relationship of misbehavior to disability if they wish to expel the student, and the determination must be made within the context of the EAHCA procedures.

Because of our growing knowledge about the relationships linking learning disabilities, school failure, and inappropriate aggressive behavior, the court's conclusion, and especially its willingness to interpret the EAHCA in such a way that a legally recognized relationship may exist between aggressive or violent behavior and "non-behavioral" handicaps, has potential significance regarding both the manner in which schools must respond to inappropriately aggressive or disruptive children, and the extent of their continuing responsibility to such children.

In the excerpt from *S-1* wherein the court quoted approvingly from the testimony of the psychologist about the orthopedically handicapped child, we see that the child's behavior was interpreted as being "indirectly" related to his disability. The psychologist detailed the frustration, anger, and aggressiveness of a young disabled boy who reacted to being different, and was unable to physically compete with other young boys his age. The apparent willingness of the court to accept this relationship as legally relevant under the EAHCA imposes a difficult, but reasonable, burden on those schools that seek to *expel* students for inappropriate behavior. Because of the limitations of our knowledge about learning disabilities generally, and about their relationship to aggressive and violent behavior specifically, the difficulty in demonstrating that a student's behavior is *not* directly or indirectly a manifestation of a disability suggests that, in most cases, *expulsion* will not be available to schools as a disciplinary tool.

The key words however are *exclusion* or *expulsion*. Until the passage of the EAHCA, as we discussed earlier, children with a handicap condition, who were permitted to attend school, were excluded from school when their behavior was inappropriate. Regardless of the nature of the program being offered by the school, the burden was on the student to fit into the Procrustean school bed. Failure to fit meant exclusion.

When any student is expelled, the school, for that period of time, has no obligation to continue the student's education or to exercise any other responsibility to him. The students in *S-1*, for example, were excluded for the remainder of the academic year, and all of the following academic year, without being provided any alternative educational program. In *Mills*, children in the first, second, or third grade of elementary school were excluded for behavioral reasons from all publicly supported education for years, with no one bothering to determine whether there was a relationship between the frustrations of possible school failure and their misconduct. In some states, such as New York, the school's responsibility to provide alternative instruction for a suspended or expelled student ceases when the student reaches the compulsory school age of 16 (N.Y. Education Law §3214).

It is precisely this form of punishment that is affected by the *S-1* decision: the pushing of children out of school; the ceasing of all educational services to the excluded child; and the refusal to assume further educational responsibility for the child. Though this is a significant change in the relationship between schools and students, it is a result consistent with the EAHCA and supporting regulations that require educational authorities to retain their educational responsibility until the handicapped child reaches the age of 21, regardless of where the child is being educated.

Leaving the mandate of the EAHCA aside, what is accomplished by expelling a child from all educational services? One answer is that the permanent removal of a violent child will make the school building a safer place. Recent studies on school violence, however, suggest that some of the more violent behaviors that occur in the school may be caused by young "intruders," who might very well be the same angry, frustrated, hateful, violent children who were pushed out of school and on to the streets, without anyone having further responsibility for them (Toby, 1983). Even if the building is safer, however, the access streets to the school are not necessarily safer for children.

Does the threat of expulsion deter inappropriate behavior? Perhaps with most children it does, but most of these successfully "deterred" children are "wanted" in the school; they have always been part of the mainstream of public education. The children who are suspended for violent, as well as non-violent behavior (most suspensions and expulsions are for non-violent acts) are, in statistically significant numbers, the children who were never part of the mainstream, and who were not wanted in the public school system: black children, Hispanic children, and other handicapped children for whom school has been a source of frustration and failure (Children's Defense Fund, 1975).

Thirty-five years ago, Professors Redl and Wineman discussed the causes of extremely aggressive behaviors in children who may be similar behaviorally to the children whom we are discussing now, stating:

> The Children who hate, we must remember, are the children of neglect. They have been chronically traumatized through repetitive frustration of many of their basic needs. Indeed we might speculate that they suffer from a disease entity directly stemming from neglect itself which, for want of a better term, might be called a "neglect edema." Their frustration swells and festers, as it were, until even frustration which is minor and painless in terms of the "normal" threshold for frustration tolerance becomes for them an intolerable challenge to control which they cannot meet. (Redl & Wineman, p. 258, 1951)

Because of the complex social, economic, and psychological forces at work, these children may not be affected by a school policy threatening expulsion. From their perspective, expulsion may be viewed as just one more kick by a school that has never responded positively to their emotional pain and educational need.

Even though we may try to understand the reasons for disruptive behavior, however, and even though it may be in our society's long-term best interest to keep these angry, unemployed (if not unemployable) adolescents in an appropriate school program, and off the streets and the subways, the challenge for all of us is to develop our educational system so that the needs of these children will be met in a manner that will not prevent anyone from attending a reasonable safe school. *S-1* and the EAHCA, perhaps, give us some guidance.

Although *S-1* may eliminate or significantly reduce the incidence of exclusionary punishment for handicapped students, schools are not prevented from using other forms of discipline for any student guilty of misconduct (*Stuart v. Nappi*, p. 1242, 1978). Nor are schools forbidden to immediately remove a student who is disruptive or violent (*S-1 v. Turlington*, 1981; *Stuart v. Nappi*, 1978). When a student is endangering himself or others, no hearing is required prior to temporarily removing the student from the school environment (*Goss v. Lopez*, 1975). *S-1* prevents the exclusion of children not their discipline. The discretion that *Ingraham* left with the states and local schools to choose appropriate methods of discipline, applies as well to dealing with handicapped children. Physical and verbal punishments, as well as short-term suspension, are still available to the schools. Additionally, if any student commits an act which is in violation of the penal laws of the state, the school certainly has the right to contact the police and have the matter handled through the appropriate juvenile or criminal law procedures.

Furthermore, *S-1* and the EAHCA do not prevent the long-term removal of a handicapped child from the regular school environment to another educational or institutional setting, provided the placement change is pursuant to the procedures of the EAHCA. Such procedures include the development of an appropriate educational program for the child, and the retention of responsiblity by the educational agency for the continued delivery of free appropriate educational services to the child (20 U.S.C. §1412(6); 34 C.F.R. §300.600). However, prior to the changing of the child's educational placement because of aggressive or other inappropriate behavior, the affirmative obligations imposed by the EAHCA require the school to first demonstrate that the behavior continues to exist notwithstanding their efforts to provide appropriate supportive services addressed to the behavior, or the cause of the behavior (*Irving Independent School District v. Tatro*).

The following excerpt is from a letter written prior to the enactment of the EAHCA, but during the time when New York required school districts to provide educational programs for mentally retarded children. The letter, received by the parent of David, a mentally retarded child, illustrates the prior relationship between the school and a disruptive handicapped child, and highlights the impact of the EAHCA and some of the cases we have discussed. The letter stated, in part:

> David was placed with a multi-handicapped group at . . . school because we had no other opening in . . . the city for him. Had he not been placed at Hughes we would not have been able to take him at all. I'm afraid the placement at Hughes has not been satisfactory. David's behavior in that class and during the lunch hour has been extremely disruptive and unpredictable. The principal has been working very hard to maintain him there till the end of the year. (*Matter of Piontkowski*, 1973)

Shortly after this letter was written, David was excluded from school because of his "disruptive" behavior.

Now, the EAHCA, together with the *S-1*, *Rowley*, and *Tatro* decisions, mandates a different approach to resolving David's problem. First, as pointed out in *Rowley*, handicapped students are required to be provided with specialized instruction that is individually designed to provide them with an educational benefit. It appears that David's program was not in any way designed to meet his educational needs; the only reason he was in the particular classroom was there was no other room for him. Without even reaching the *S-1* behavioral issue, in situations where a school has failed to comply with its obligations to a student under the EAHCA, it is unfair as well as inconsistent with the EAHCA to permit a student to be expelled for inappropriate behavior when that behavior arose in an inappropriate school placement. A school should not be permitted to impose any disciplinary sanctions on a handicapped child unless the school has first complied with its educational obligation to the student.

We have made important changes legislatively for a child who has been identified as having a handicapping condition. But what about the child who is not handicapped in the traditional sense? For example, how should we respond to the child who is black, and has not been welcomed at school; who has been placed in a "slower" track, and has failed, who has been stigmatized as being a failure, and is now frustrated, angry, and possibly violent. When he is yet of compulsory school age and misbehaves, do we push him out the door, ending our responsibility? Do we discontinue all services to him because he doesn't have the "right label"?

The giant step taken with the EAHCA only requires states to provide supportive services and continued responsibility to those children who have been given an EAHCA "handicapped" label. The states are certainly free to extend the substance of the EAHCA procedural and substantive requirements to all children regardless of whether they have an appropriate label, however. At this time in our history we should provide appropriate educational services to all children in our community, as well as reasonable supportive services to enable all children to benefit from their educational program. We should not wait until we're hit over the head, figuratively and literally, before we make this commitment.

CONCLUSION

In considering the issues of violence, children and schools, we have focused on legal events that occurred essentially within the last 30 years, since the *Brown* case was decided. *Brown v. Board of Education* and its progeny have had a profound effect on our society generally, and on our schools in particular. Any change can be difficult, but the most difficult is the unwelcome change. Schools during this time period have been asked to accommodate children who had previously been excluded from the mainstream of our public educational life, without perhaps being given adequate financial, social, and political supports to accomplish their difficult task. Especially in our large urban centers, schools have had to provide educational services to a non-homogeneous population, and deal with children having profound problems, manifested, in part, by the increased level of aggression in the schools.

The response of the schools that led to judicial involvement was the effort to exclude many of these children. As we have seen, the Supreme Court has been relatively deferential towards schools, especially when administrators seek to resolve problems within the school system, rather than exclude children.

The most significant educational legislative change during the last decade has been the enactment of the EAHCA. As we have discussed, not only does this law require access to schools for previously excluded handicapped children. The act's affirmative obligations may also have important implications for the future response to aggressive or disruptive children in our schools. The EAHCA is an important step in the process of carrying out the mandate of *Brown v. Board of Education*: All children should be provided with an equal educational opportunity.

I hope that in the next few years we will see an expansion in the application of the EAHCA philosophy to all children. By so doing, we will hopefully abolish banishment or exclusion as a disciplinary tool, and commit ourselves to maintaining responsibility for *all* children.

REFERENCES

Barkley, R. (1981). *Hyperactive children: A handbook for diagnosis and treatment*. New York: Guilford Press.

Board of Curators of University of Missouri v. Horowitz, 435 U.S. 78 (1978).

Board of Curators of the University of Missouri v. Horowitz, 538 F.2d 1317 (1976).

Board of Education of Hendrick Hudson Central School District v. Rowley, 458 U.S. 176 (1982).

Brief for American Association of School Administrators as Amicus Curiae, Irving Independent School District v. Tatro, 104 S. Ct. 3371 (1984).

Brief for National School Board Association as Amicus Curiae, Irving Independent School District v. Tatro, 104 S. Ct. 3371 (1984).

Brief for United Teachers of Dade County, Ingraham v. Wright, 430 U.S. 651 (1977).

Brown v. Board of Education, 347 U.S. 483 (1954).

Buck v. Bell, 274 U.S. 200 (1927).

34 C.F.R. §300.600 (1984).

Children's Defense Fund (1975). *School Suspensions: Are They Helping Children*. Washington, DC: Author.

Columbus Board of Education v. Penick, 443 U.S. 449 (1979).

Cumming v. Richmond County Board of Education, 175 U.S. 528 (1899).

Debra P. v. Turlington, 644 F.2d 397 (5th Cir. 1981).

Doe v. Koger, 480 F. Supp. 225 (N.D. Ind. 1979).

Dunivant, N. (1982) *The Relationship Between Learning Disabilities and Juvenile Delinquency*: Executive Summary. Virginia: National Center for State Courts.

Education for All Handicapped Children Act of 1975, 20 U.S.C. §1400-1461 (1976 & Supp. 1984).

European Court of Human Rights Tyer case, judgment of 25 April 1978, Series A No. 26.

Faretra, G. (1981). A profile of aggression from adolescence to adulthood: An 18-Year follow-up of psychiatrically disturbed and violent adolescents. *American Journal of Orthopsychiatry, 51,* 439–453.

Gewirtz, P. (1983). Remedies and Resistence, 92 Yale L.J. 535.

Glasser, W. (1969). *Schools Without Failure*. New York: Harper & Row.

Goss v. Lopez, 419 U.S. 565 (1975).

Governor's Memoranda on Bills Vetoed, *New York Legislative Annual—1959*, p. 497.

Governor's Memoranda on Bills Signed, *New York Legislative Annual—1960*, p. 571.

Governor's Memoranda on Bills Vetoed, *New York Laws of 1960*, p. 609.

Hammer v. Dagenhart, 247 U.S. 251 (1918).

Hawkins v. Coleman, 376 F. Supp. 1330 (N.D. Tex. 1974).

Hobson v. Hansen, 269 F. Supp. 401 (D.D.C. 1967), *aff'd in part and appeal dismissed in part, sub nom.* Smuck v. Hobson, 408 F.2d 175 (D.C. Cir. 1969).

Ingraham v. Wright, 430 U.S. 651 (1977).

Ingraham v. Wright, 498 F.2d 248 (5th Cir. 1974), *rev'd on rehearing*, 525 F.2d 909 (1976).

In re Cecilia R., 36 N.Y.2d 317, 327 N.E.2d 812, 367 N.Y.S.2d 770 (1975).

Irving Independent School District v. Tatro, 104 S. Ct. 3371 (1984).

Kaelin v. Grubbs, 682 F.2d 595 (6th Cir. 1982).

Kashani, J.H., Husain, A., Robins, A.J., Reid, J.C., & Wooderson, P. C. (1980). Patterns of delinquency in girls and boys. *Journal of the American Academy of Child Psychiatry, 19,* 300–310.

Lewis, D.O., Shanok, S.S., Balla, D.A., & Bard, B. (1980). Psychiatric correlates of severe reading disabilities in an incarcerated delinquent population. *Journal of the American Academy of Child Psychiatry, 19,* 611–622.

Matter of Piontkowski, 12 Ed. Dept. Rep. 202 (N.Y. 1973).

Maeroff, G. (1984, December 28). Boston's decade of discrimination leaves experts disputing effects. *The New York Times*, pp. A1, B8.

Memorandum of Joint Legislative Committee on Mental Rehabilitation, *N.Y. Legislative Annual*, 1960, p. 184.

Mills v. Board of Education of District of Columbia, 348 F. Supp. 866 (D.D.C. 1972).

New Jersey v. T.L.O., 105 S. Ct. 733 (1985).

New York Education Law §3214 (McKinney 1981).

N.Y. Family Court Act §712 (McKinney 1983).

N.Y. Family Court Act §741 (McKinney 1983).

N.Y. Laws of 1955, ch. 795.

N.Y. Laws of 1960, ch. 1028 (Mandatory Law).

N.Y. Law of 1964, ch. 945.

Parham v. J.R., 442 U.S. 584 (1979).

Pate v. Dade County School Board, 434 F.2d 1151 (5th Cir. 1970).

Pennsylvania Association for Retarded Children v. Pennsylvania, 334 F. Supp. 1257 (E.D. Pa. 1971), *modified,* 343 F. Supp. 279 (E.D. Pa. 1972).

Petitioner's Brief for Certiorari, Irving Independent School District v. Tatro, 104 S. Ct. 3371 (1984).

Plessey v. Ferguson, 163 U.S. 537 (1896).

Redl, F. & Wineman, D. (1951). *Children who hate*. New York: Free Press.

Robbins, D.M., Beck, J.C., Pries, R., Jacobs, D. & Smith, C. (1983). Learning disability and neuro-psychological impairment in adjudicated unincarcerated male delinquents. *Journal of the American Academy of Child Psychiatry, 22,* 40–46.

Rutter, M. (1975). *Helping troubled children*. New York & London: Plenum Press.

S-1 v. Turlington, 635 F.2d 342 (5th Cir. 1981).

Sherry, v. New York State Education Dept. 479 F. Supp. 1328 (W.D.N.Y. 1979).

State Education Department Memorandum, *N.Y. Laws of 1964*, p. 216.

Stuart v. Nappi, 443 F. Supp. 1235 (D. Conn. 1978).

Tasby v. Estes, 412 F. Supp. 1192 (N.D. Tex., 1976), Remanded on other grounds, aff'd in part, 572 F.2d 1010 (5th Cir. 1978).

Toby, J. (1983), Violence in school. In M. Tony & N. Morris (Eds.), *Crime & justice: An annual review of research, Vol. 4*. Chicago: University of Chicago Press.

United States v. Darby, 312 U.S. 100 (1941).

20 U.S.C. §1400, 1401, 1412, 1415 (Supp. 1984).

Wolfensberger, W. (1975). *The origin and nature of our institutional models*. New York: Human Policy Press.

Woodward, C.V. (1974). *The strange career of Jim Crow* (3rd rev. ed.). New York: Oxford University Press.

13

Cross-Cultural Perspectives on Youth Violence

Lea Pulkkinen
Marketta Saastamoinen

Conflicts between youth and immediate institutions (e.g., family and school) and social control (police, criminal justice system) are characteristics of all modern societies as Kaiser argues (1981). In several European countries youth (13- to 20-year-olds) make up about 10% of the population but commit almost a third of all offenses. In Sweden, for example, the age range from 15 to 20 years constitutes 7.8% of the population, but in 1977 the proportion of offenses committed by this age group was 31.9% (Nelson, 1981).

Crime reports from several countries reveal an increase in juvenile delinquency, as well as in all offenses over the past decades. In Finland, for instance, the number of all offenses was 131,892 in 1950, and 508,617 in 1981 (Official Statistics of Finland 1982). Offenses committed by 15- to 20-year-olds doubled for thefts, damage to property, and violent offenses from 1960 to 1978, even in proportion to the population in that age group (Joutsen 1980). In a comparison of 1970 and 1981, juvenile crime has — parallel to the general increase in crime — grown in absolute numbers. The growth has especially taken place in the 15- to 17-year-old age bracket; the proportion of the 18- to 20-year-old offenders has decreased, pointing towards a shift in the age structure of young offenders (Criminality in Finland, 1981). In the Federal Republic of Germany, offenses committed by youth and children have also doubled in 25 years (Kreuzer, 1983). Correspondingly, the increase in arrest rates of 15- to 17-year-olds was more than 200% in the United States from 1953 to 1974 (FBI Uniform Crime Report, 1975, cited in Goldstein, Apter, & Harootunian, 1984, p. 6).

Atzesberger (1978) states that juvenile delinquency is much more frequent nowadays than during the world-wide economic crisis in 1928 to 1933. In spite of the general increase in the number of offenses, predisposition to crimes varies from cohort to cohort, at least in Finland (Takala, 1981). High arrest rates for youth under the age of 20 have been found among those individuals who lived their adolescence (a) during the second World War (born 1926 to 1927), (b) during the rapid structural change of the Finnish society (born 1947 to 1948), or (c) immediately after the structural changes of urbanization and industrialization (born 1957 to 1958). Some leveling off in juvenile delinquency can be seen during the past 10 years. Correspondingly, Kreuzer (1983) concludes his survey of the extent and structure of juvenile delinquency by stating that delinquency is slowly, but not dramatically, rising in the Federal Republic of Germany and most comparable countries.

The following characteristics of juvenile delinquency can be found in reports from different countries:

1. Violence has increased more than other crimes. In the United States, the increase of arrest rates of 15- to 17-year-olds was 440% for assaults, but 230% for larceny/theft (Goldstein et al., 1984). In France, Léauté (1981) reports that violence has increased, particularly in large cities. In Germany, the commission of crimes involving dangerous or severe bodily injuries increases with age. The proportion of such offenses committed by boys under 14 years old was 1.7%, 14 to 17, 4.8%, and 18 to 20, 7.7% (Kreuzer, 1983).

McClintock (1981) separated four categories of violence: (a) instrumental violence (e.g., robbery and rape); (b) interpersonal violence (e.g., among family members); (c) ideological and political violence (e.g., terrorism); and (d) destructive violence without a personal motive (e.g., vandalism). McClintock considers that especially the last category is typical of young people who manifest deep personal or social problems. Another category typical of young people is instrumental violence. In London, Manchester, and Glasgow, for instance, two thirds of all robberies in the 1970s were committed by offenders under 21 years of age. Violence is not, however, as frequent in Great Britain as it is in the United States (McClintock, 1981).

2. Offenses committed in groups have increased in the Federal Republic of Germany since 1950 (Atzesberger, 1978). They include burglary, assaults, riots, vandalism, and sexual offenses.

3. Juvenile delinquency is more common among boys than among girls. Only 11% of prosecuted offenders in both Germany and Sweden are girls (Atzesberger, 1978; Nelson, 1981). Violent offenses, in particular, are typical of boys (Kreuzer, 1982).

4. Younger and younger age groups are becoming involved in crimes. In France, for instance, offenses committed by children under 13 years old have increased (Léauté, 1981). Although offenses committed by children under 15 years of age and cleared by the police have not increased in Finland from 1960 to 1978 in proportion to the population in the same age group, it has been considered probable that the proportion of hidden crime is especially high among children (Joutsen 1980). Children commit offenses, such as shoplifting and malicious damage, which are often difficult to detect and not worth the time and energy needed to track down the offender.

5. In several countries, offenses committed by young people are mainly larceny/thefts. According to Kreuzer (1983), this category represents about 80% of all offenses committed by children under 14 years old in the Federal Republic of Germany. By the age of 18 to 20, its proportion decreases to 43%, because the proportion of other offenses increases. In Finland, especially typical of young offenders (under 20 years old) compared with older citizens, is the unauthorized use or theft of a motor vehicle; in 1981 young offenders committed 69.2% of all offenses in this category (see Table 13.1). Other thefts was next highest (54.3% of total offenses). In 1981 young offenders committed 28.7% of all assaults, just higher than the percentage (26.2%) of youth's offenses in the total (Official Statistics of Finland, 1982). In single categories, there are differences between countries. For example, arson committed by young offenders is relatively more common in the Federal Republic of Germany than in France or Finland (67%, 25%, and 26% of total offenses, respectively). (Kreuzer, 1983; Léauté, 1981; Official Statistics of Finland, 1982).

For various reasons crime statistics in different countries are not always comparable. Therefore, some criminologists have given up their use (Joutsen, 1980). In addition, offenses leading to arrests are only the tip of the iceberg. Shapland (1978) states that there are many more crimes committed than lead to convictions or even come to the attention of the police. According to a study in Finland (Sipilä, 1982), 63% of 16-year-old boys ($N =$ 567) had committed an offense, but only 9% had been apprehended by the police. The

Table 13.1. Some types of offenses committed by young offenders in Finland 1981

	Age			Portion of total	
	≤ 14 yrs	15-17 yrs	18-20 yrs		
Type of offense	%	%	%	%	n
All offenses	3.3	9.8	13.1	26.2	133,257
Offenses listed in the penal code:					
Total	7.5	12.7	14.2	34.4	74,597
Manslaughter, murder	0.8	2.8	9.2	12.8	32
Assault	2.9	10.8	15.0	28.7	4,032
Rape	0.9	6.8	7.7	15.4	64
Robbery	9.6	16.8	13.6	40.0	731
Theft, petty theft	14.3	18.7	21.3	54.3	57,452
Aggravated theft	5.8	12.8	12.0	30.6	966
Unauthorized use or theft of a motor vehicle	18.9	35.1	15.2	69.2	5,623
Fraud, embezzlement	1.2	3.4	8.6	13.2	2,248
Drunken driving	0.4	5.9	9.8	16.1	3,704

more offenses committed, the higher the probability of being caught by the police. In spite of the problems in self-reported criminality as presented by Kreuzer (1983) — for example, quantitative self-reports on offenses ignore qualitative aspects in criminality — self-reports call attention to the high frequency of norm-breaking in adolescence, as well as the influence of the control policy on crime statistics.

Dealing with Juvenile Delinquency

The minimum age for criminal responsibility varies from country to country. It is 18 years in Belgium, 15 years in the Scandinavian countries, 14 years in the Federal Republic of Germany, 13 years in France, 10 years in Great Britain, and 7 years in Switzerland (Kaiser, 1983). The traditional procedures in dealing with offenses committed by children and young persons can be roughly divided into two systems: (a) the juvenile court system which has been adopted in England, the United States, and most European countries; and (b) the Scandinavian system as applied in Northern Europe. The latter has no juvenile courts (Joutsen, 1976).

Children below 15 years are dealt with solely by the local social welfare board in Finland. Offenders between 15 and 17 can be dealt with by both the courts and boards. Norway was the first Scandinavian country to pass a special child welfare act (1896), establishing local child welfare boards as the authority in charge of dealing with neglected and delinquent children (Joutsen, 1980). Sweden followed suit in 1902, Denmark in 1905, and Finland in 1936. The punishment of children was abandoned in theory and replaced by educational measures. The main purpose of the reform was to halt the criminal development of children at as early an age as possible.

A criminal career develops gradually, as Farrington (in press) showed in his longitudinal study. The best predictor of criminality is antisocial behavior at an earlier age. Aggressive behavior even at the age of 8 is a significant predictor of criminality — more for alcohol abuse and violent offenses than thefts — in late adolescence (Pulkkinen, 1983; Pulkkinen & Hurme, 1984). The need to interrupt the development of a criminal career is obvious, but it is not easy to find effective means to do so.

The concept of intervention emphasizes the intent to influence the development of an offender, while the concept of punishment is more directed to the severity of an offense. At the beginning of clinically oriented intervention, a medical, psychological and social study of an offender is made for an individual treatment plan; it takes into consideration the individual's personality, past history, needs, and life situation (Joutsen, 1976; Pinatel, 1981). Pinatel maintains that findings on imprisonment show how the shock of jail causes a desire to avoid a corresponding experience in the future in some offenders, but some offenders feel that they have fallen outside the society and start to enjoy rebelliousness. In many cases imprisonment does not prevent criminal behavior, but increases recidivism (Eerikäinen, 1979).

Burns (1982) regards self-concept as an important factor in juvenile delinquency. Labeling affects the child's self-esteem and social identity even more in the case of criminality than psychic disorders. Low self-esteem in the child's conventional environment may drive him to anti-social achievements, as a result of which a juvenile gang may become an important reference group which regulates his self-esteem. Self-esteem should be taken into account in setting the aims for treatment and choosing the method of intervention, Burns (1982) maintains. An increase in self-esteem, for example, is not sufficient; it may only increase criminality. Instead, it is essential to improve the child's feelings about his or her noncriminal behavior and offer him or her opportunities to achieve success with socially desirable behavior. Burns states that if interventions consider an individual's self-concept, behavior, and interaction with the environment, and produce adequate feedback, they may improve self-esteem and reduce juvenile delinquency.

The results of Eitzen (1976) with boys in a community-based home showed that boys' self-concepts could be modified by reinforcing socially approved behavior. When a boy found that his important people (the mother, friends, teachers) had improved conceptions of him, his own self-concept changed in the same direction. In the framework of the theories of cognitive consistency (e.g., Festinger, 1957), it can be expected that self-concept and the quality of behavior are related to each other. An individual fulfills his image of himself in his behavior, and, on the other hand, feedback on his behavior modifies his self-concept.

Makarenko (1975) tells a story about a 16-year-old boy who committed thefts in a Soviet collective. The administrative body of the collective, a general meeting, discussed his case. He was not punished. It was only stated that he would steal two more times. This treatment insulted the boy's feelings and he decided not to steal. He did, however, commit two thefts later, without being punished, and hereafter stopped stealing. The same method also proved successful in other cases of thefts in the collective.

Kaiser (1983) discusses extensively the possibilities of decriminalizing juvenile offenses in Germany, along the lines suggested by the Council of Europe in the early 1980s. In 25 years, the number of imprisoned young persons has doubled. In several European countries, for example, Great Britain, Switzerland, and Austria, measures toward the decriminalization of juvenile offenses and the replacement of punishment by educational aims had already been taken by the late 1960s. Sexual offenses, especially homosexuality and pornography, traffic violations, drug abuse, and minor property crimes are among those whose criminal status has changed in several countries. Kaiser (1983) notes that German juvenile court law offers an individualistic way of sentencing young persons for minor offenses, so that restraint in sending juvenile delinquents to prison and an expansion of the variety of "soft" sanctions are possible. Kaiser remarks, however, that the expansion of "soft" sanctions is not necessarily appropriate; the legal limits can not be unduly extended.

Kaiser (1983) calls for qualitatively enriched alternatives to a punitive approach to juvenile delinquency. Alternatives to prison are, for instance, supervision combined with work and the use of restitution. The victim is too often the neglected party in an offense. An immediate contact between the offender and the victim and a personal compensation of the consequences of an offense might develop the offender's sense of responsibility more than imprisonment or fines paid to the state. On the other hand, decriminalization via raising the age limit of criminal responsibility from 14 to 16 years as proposed in Germany has not yet been sufficiently clarified in regard to consequences (Kaiser, 1983).

Other methods available as alternatives to prison are admonition and "social training courses." The latter have been arranged in at least 20 locations in Germany since 1980. The point of departure is the young person's own interests and conflicts. The length of courses vary from a weekend to 10 days, depending on the needs of a group. There is also a 3-month follow-up period with repeated sessions during weekends. The relative inefficacy of traditional juridical interventions in juvenile delinquency, Kaiser (1983) suggests, is partly due to the fact that young people are generally vulnerable to conflicts between people and institutions and that conflicts have multiple causes in family, school, work, and friendships. Interventions are often late and irregular. From the preventive point of view, family policy, and especially the relationship between the mother and child, needs more attention. Adequate supervision of young people's activities has been shown to be most important (Levkovich, 1983; McCord, 1984).

CHARACTERISTICS OF SCHOOL MISBEHAVIOR AND VIOLENCE

First conflicts between the youth and society do not occur in relation to remote, formal institutions, but appear in connection with socialization (Kaiser, 1981). Adjustment problems at home and in school predict later problems, such as criminality, as shown, for example, in the longitudinal study by Pulkkinen (1983).

Violence at school manifests children's problems in adjustment — and possibly the role and values of aggression in the culture. Goldstein et al. (1984) estimate that "approximately 270,000 physical assaults occur annually in primary and secondary schools in the United States, and approximately 500 million dollars in damage from vandalism, arson, and theft are visited upon school property each year" (p.viii). Büscher (1979) mentions that the number of children's conduct disorders including aggression have rapidly increased also in German schools. Pupils in German special schools are often guilty of sexual offenses, robberies, and blackmailing, while the pupils of the junior high and high schools commit more frauds and embezzlements (Atzesberger, 1978). In Finland, truants especially commit many offenses (Sipilä, 1982). Misconduct in Finnish schools increased alarmingly in the late 1970s. In Sweden too, increasing group aggression in schools aroused wide attention in the 1970s (Olweus, 1978; Pikas, 1975). Unfortunately, no statistics of school violence were available to compare the situation in Europe and the United States.

It is generally believed that violence in European schools has not reached the level of American schools; for example, assaults on teachers are rarely reported. In Finland, for instance, there are no statistics or investigations regarding violence toward teachers. However, in an informal survey made by the Teachers' Trade Union (OAJ) (Personal information, 1984), mild corporal violence, such as kicking, biting, and slapping, was astonishingly frequent in 1981, even at the primary levels of the comprehensive school. In 7% of cases, visible injuries, such as bruises, were reported. In the United States, the number of assaults on teachers was 110,000 in 1979 (18,000 in 1955). In a few years during the 1970s, homicides increased in American schools by 18.5%, rapes by 40.1%, assaults on students by 85.3%, and assaults on teachers by 77.4% (Goldstein et al., 1984, p. 5).

Though nowadays, for example, in Scandinavian and German schools, there is more violence than 10 years ago, the problems seem to be more related to discipline than to interpersonal violence. Nevertheless, over 90% of pupils in Finnish secondary schools had seen mild violence (mockery, seizing the goods of others, and pushing) in their classes during an academic year (Huvila & Tilli, 1977). About 16% had sometimes been targets of more severe violence (threats, hitting, blackmailing). Around 40% of pupils said that violence hindered their schooling, but only 3% said that troubles were severe. The more violent friends the pupil had, the more he or she teased the others.

Winkel (1976) refers to the findings of teachers confronting a conflict situation on an average every 2.6 minutes. Because of continual conduct disorders, attention deficit disorders, and aggression, teaching is sometimes impossible (Lipp, 1980). This kind of school misbehavior has been the central topic in discussions of educational policy in the Federal Republic of Germany during the past decade (Ulich, 1980). Finnish school authorities have also displayed concern for classroom order. Kari, Remes, and Väänänen (1980) maintain that school misbehavior is different at different ages. For example, teasing is more common at the primary (1–6) than at the secondary (7–9) level. The most typical of both levels, however, is the disruption of teaching. In research series of Aho (1976, 1977, 1978), discipline seemed to differ from lesson to lesson, obviously depending on the teacher's and the pupils' attitudes toward the subject matter.

According to research from different European countries, about 5% of school children are openly aggressive and injure themselves, others, or their environment (Meichenbaum & Goodman, 1971; Olweus, 1978; Petermann & Petermann, 1979); in Finland, this is reported as only 1%. (Kari et al., 1980). Very often these numbers are, however, based on observations and ratings of the teachers, and they may ignore some violence. For example, when 12- and 14-year-old Finnish pupils were asked, about 8% claimed they had been severely violent against other pupils (Huvila & Tilli, 1977). Correspondingly, 8% of the boys and 3.2% of the girls were involved in bullying behavior — physical and verbal group aggression repeatedly directed towards the same individuals (Lagerspetz, Björkqvist, Berts, & King, 1982). Therefore, different violence statistics may depend on different conceptual classifications.

Conduct disorders vary greatly in nature. Ratings of all of them indicated high incidences, up to 20 to 40% of school children for more severe or intermediate disorders (Atzesberger & Frey, 1978; Ellmann, Koch, Meyer-Plath, & Butollo 1980). Only about 20% of children have been rated as not having any problems. Günther (1980) lists 30 problem behaviors in the school, ranging from gabbling to mocking, and from threats to assaults on students and teachers. He did not try to classify the problem like Huber (1979) who isolated four subcategories: (a) aggression, (b) unsatisfactory behavior during lessons, (c) disruptive verbal behavior, and (d) problems unrelated to the teaching.

Kulka, Klingel, and Mann (1980) attempted to conceptualize and measure the most critical dimensions of subjective person-environment fit in high school. They ended up with three dimensions: (a) School crime, (b) school avoidance, and (c) class misbehavior. The frequencies of the latter acts were low where opportunities for support from teachers met the need and increased for boys who wanted either more or less opportunity for such support than they had.

In Finland, teachers regard aggression as a more severe problem than do psychologists, who are more worried about depression and the neglect of others (Aho, 1975). Kivistö (1977) distinguished group violence from other types of conflicts. In group violence, differences of opinions are not essential; teasing occurs for its own sake, as a kind of amusement.

It is typical of bullies that they can not give any reason for their violence. In a Finnish study, the teachers regarded the bully boys stronger than their peers, dominant and tough. In the classroom they had difficulties concentrating. The bully girls were described as unbalanced, extremely talkative, rude, and domineering (Lagerspetz, Björkqvist, Berts, & King, 1982). Victims of the bullies, so-called whipping boys, are, according to Olweus (1978), somewhat sensitive and passive boys, whose dispositions and the character of their early close parental relationships have made them insecure and vulnerable in a peer group. Attacks from the peers augment their anxiousness and increase the psychological distance from their peers. Lagerspetz et al. (1982) did not find the victims to be significantly more anxious than bullies or well-adjusted pupils. The victims, however, had slightly lower self-esteem than others, somewhat higher subjective maladjustment, and negative peer relations. They were physically weaker than their well adjusted peers and more often obese and handicapped. The well-adjusted pupils were significantly more popular than bullies or victims.

The Finnish pupils and teachers seem to be rather resigned to school violence. About 25% ignored bullying or even accepted it (Kivistö, 1977). Lagerspetz et al. (1982) found that the bullies had a more positive attitude towards violence than the victims or the well adjusted pupils. In Britain, the bullying increases with the age, and it is about twice as common among boys as among girls. Girls, however, are more likely to use verbal bullying behavior while the boys would rather attack physically (Lowenstein, 1977).

Farrington, Berkowitz, and West (1982) also draw a distinction between individual and group fights. In individual fights, the young people were usually provoked, got angry, and started the fight, while group fights were more likely to involve weapons, produce injuries, and bring police intervention. Group fights were associated with frequent fighting and aggressive attitudes.

Olweus (1978) argues against the claim that serious whipping boy/bully problems in Swedish schools are limited to schools and classes of a certain size. Nor are they restricted to boys of a particular social class or to those with special external deviations. In general, however, school misbehavior seems to be related to the size of the school. In big schools with large class sizes, problems are more pronounced (Goldstein et al., 1984; Kari et al., 1980; Ulich, 1980). Frequent teacher changes also increase problems (Ulich, 1980). In Alikoski's view (1980), misbehavior at school is a significant manifestation of the school's inability to meet the challange caused by social changes. Olweus (1978) maintains that traditional pedagogical methods have a minimal effect on aggressive behavior.

PREVENTION OF SCHOOL MISBEHAVIOR

Primary and Secondary Prevention

It is common to distinguish between primary and secondary prevention of disorders. Primary prevention aims at the reduction of disturbances in the whole society. It may be either system- or individual-oriented (Ellmann et al., 1980). Characteristic of primary prevention is prophylaxis, taking measures before problems become apparent. Parental programs for child-rearing are examples of endeavors to advance children's normal social development. An increasing interest in these programs is obvious. The participation in the programs is voluntary, however, and those parents who are in special need of more information about child-rearing never attend them. One means of improving child-rearing and family life nationwide might be so-called "family education" in compulsory school. Nevertheless, at least in Finland, it has not yet been given sufficient time in the curriculum, in spite of 9th grade pupils' interest in the matter (Pulkkinen, in press).

There are also many kinds of more specific programs for children's positive social development, especially at the preschool level. In a program developed by the senior author (Pulkkinen, Heikkinen, Markkanen, & Ranta, 1977) the goal was to improve the children's self-control. Kalliopuska (1983) refers to the meaning of empathy, positive self-concept, and impulse control in the prevention of aggressive behavior. The immediate effects of the programs are normally found to be positive, but long-term follow-up data are often lacking, as they are for many other programs. Specific programs can be expected to be effective especially if parents, care-takers, or teachers absorb their ideas in their daily interaction with children. It again emphasizes the importance of parental education as well as teacher training.

The goal of secondary prevention is to eliminate the first indicators of later problems. Early measures are directed toward a selected "risk" group (Eisert & Barkey, 1979; Ellmann et al., 1980). According to Ellmann et al. (1980), indicators of school misbehavior can be seen early, already at the age of 2.5 years. Therefore, they have developed four prevention programs for 5-year-old impulsive-hyperactive and passive-withdrawn children and their mothers (parents). Their goal was to optimize the child's development by decreasing risk behavior and promoting more positive new behavior.

A homogeneous group, based on the risk diagnosis, consisted of 5 to 6 children whose basic program lasted eight 2-hour sessions. A corresponding group of the mothers was also formed. The goals of the mothers' program were to help them to diagnose their children's as well as their own behavior, to transmit functionally suitable alternative models of behavior, and to learn to define their children's need for help. To gain the optimal effect, the programs for children and mothers were parallel. Both children and mothers had specific learning tasks concerning social contacts, independence, activity, and coping with anxiety. It proved to be very important to focus the interest of the mothers on the risk behavior of their children, not on any kind of risk behavior. As in all preventive programs, the motivation of the subjects is a problem. Since the children's behavior is not yet clearly deviant, it may be difficult to motivate the parents to collaborate.

Ellmann et al. (1980) emphasize the need to operationalize the problems as accurately as possible and to analyze their causes carefully in any preventive program. It is also important to decide what is the most appropriate time for prevention, i.e., when it will be most effective. Further decisions concern the object of the prevention: a child, parents, care-takers, teachers, or external environment (e.g., housing or curriculum). Custodial care can often be considered a secondary prevention of a child's disorders. There are findings (Pulkkinen, 1984) that confirm the positive impact of custodial care on children's further development.

A large preventive campaign against harassment and bullying was started in Norwegian primary schools (grades 1–9) in 1983. The focus of the campaign is on situations in which one or more children repeatedly inflict injury and discomfort upon another child (Olweus, 1984). Research estimates suggest that about 5% of the children in a school population are fairly regular victims of such harassment and that about the same percentage can be described as bullies. According to Olweus (1984), several suicides among children and adolescents have been reported in Norway, in which bullying is likely to have been one important causal factor.

The campaign consists of the following measures:

1. A 32-page booklet for teachers and school managers giving an overview of existing research and a number of practical suggestions;

2. A 4-page brochure designed to inform and help parents of both victims, aggressors, and ordinary children, the goal of which was to reach the parents of children in primary schools;

3. A 25-minute video cassette showing episodes from the lives of two bullied children aged 10 (boy) and 14 years (girl), which also gave suggestions about how to handle the problems; and

4. A short inventory designed to obtain measurement of various aspects of the phenomenon, including frequency, and of the readiness of the particular unit (school, class) to interfere with the problems; the inventory is answered by the students individually and anonymously.

In connection with the campaign, research on the frequency of harassment in different school forms is being conducted by Olweus. A follow-up study of the effects of the campaign will also be carried out.

Different play techniques are recommended in Germany as a preventive means of school violence (Atzesberger & Frey, 1978; Petermann & Petermann, 1979; Uttendorf-Marek, 1976). For instance, (Atzesberger & Frey, 1978) describes a method in which groups of 5 to 6 pupils, including at most two pupils with a conduct disorder, are formed. The group meets at least once a week, at a time reserved for remedial teaching. A training period of 3 weeks is based on a theme, for example, "I don't have to hit others". The treatment of the theme consists of several stages including discussion, play, preparation for a real situation, action in a real situation, deepening discussion, perspective taking, and play from different perspectives practicing the new behavior.

As to violence toward teachers, causal factors may be related to teachers' provocative behavior, which they cannot themselves analyze or perceive. Teachers usually concentrate so closely on their teaching that they cannot observe their own behavior accurately. Kornmann (1980) states that many teachers find it difficult to describe pupils' behavior exactly. Therefore, some outside help is needed. Eisert and Barkey (1980) suggest video recording to help discern a teacher's positive and negative behaviors and their effects on pupils' behavior. This might be one of the methods to prevent school violence.

Teacher Training

Burns (1982) claims that teacher training emphasizes mainly the effective use of intelligence and academic skills in teaching, but ignores the problems of understanding one's self and others. High self-esteem is necessary for successful teaching, and its development should be encouraged in teacher training. Eisert and Barkey (1979) also maintain that, apart from didactic skills, a teacher should also be able to solve problems that arise in school. This presupposes supervised practice during which problem situations are both analyzed and solved. Teacher trainees should work out themes as follows to advance their definition and observation of behavioral categories and changes (Eisert & Barkey, 1979): (a) the comparison of different models of personality and behavior and their usefulness in interventions, (b) situational analyses by which precursory and consequent events in a teacher-pupil interaction are studied, (c) analysis of personal and professional skills and problems thorough enough to allow interpretation of pupil-teacher interaction, and (d) analysis of methodological problems involved in an intervention.

Finnish teachers and teacher-trainees differed in their conceptions of most problematic situations in a class (Gröhn 1979). Teacher-trainees found dealing with the discipline of the whole class most problematic, while experienced teachers considered the misbehavior of individual pupils the most problematic. Therefore, Gröhn (1980) suggests that supervised teacher training with gradually changing goals should continue from basic training to supplementary teacher education.

According to Mee's study (1983), there is a discrepancy between teachers' conceptions of proper methods in the control of pupils' behavior and the teachers' actual measures. Teachers pay more attention to negative than positive behavior and react negatively more than they think is appropriate. A negative reaction increases the probability of negative behavior in a pupil more than a neutral or positive reaction. Interaction with pupils may become stressful if adequate skills are lacking. In a joint Scandinavian study of teachers' work and well-being, (Mäkinen, 1982), Finnish teachers rated their relationships with the pupils and their parents more negatively than the teachers in the other Scandinavian countries. In the upper level of the comprehensive school, the relations between teachers and pupils were least satisfactory.

Teachers find social aspects of their work difficult. One of the main reasons for it may be teacher education, which in Western countries primarily focuses on didactic and curricular skills. Müller-Wolf (1978) maintains that teachers' awareness of their teaching skills and interaction with pupils develops much later than their actional skills and their concrete teaching behavior. Therefore, a training model for improving teacher-pupil interaction and communication was developed by Müller-Wolf at the University of Hamburg in collaboration with 12 psychologists. The model, which has been used since 1968, covers four main areas, diagrammed as four concentric circles in Figure 13.1. The innermost circle consists of the teacher as an individual, the outermost circle of his or her competencies to deal with the "educational environment". The four areas, their goals, and teaching methods to achieve them are discussed below (Müller-Wolf, 1978).

The Teacher as an Individual Person. Training aims at personal growth, development of individual abilities, and proper model behavior. The training methods include:

1. Participation in "basic encounter" groups;
2. Self-experience groups, assertive programs;
3. Sensitivity and relaxation training;
4. Basic courses in counseling and conflict solution;
5. Body awareness, meditation, participation in "Gestalt-groups";
6. Feedback on teaching behavior from colleagues, pupils, observing parents, experts, or teacher trainer; and
7. Basic courses in lecturing (clarity, structure, precision, organization of material).

Teacher-Pupil Interaction. This area involves social skills and is the focus of the model. Training aims at a nondirective teaching style, appreciation and emotional warmth, empathetic understanding, and self-congruence and genuineness. The training methods include:

1. Interactive skills training program (ISTP);
2. Training in the actual classroom situation (videotaping, interrupting the teaching process, replay and discussion of pupils, teacher, and teacher trainer); and
3. Class training, i.e., all pupils of a specific class and their teacher participate in a weekend or week-long training session, discuss their problems, and try to solve them.

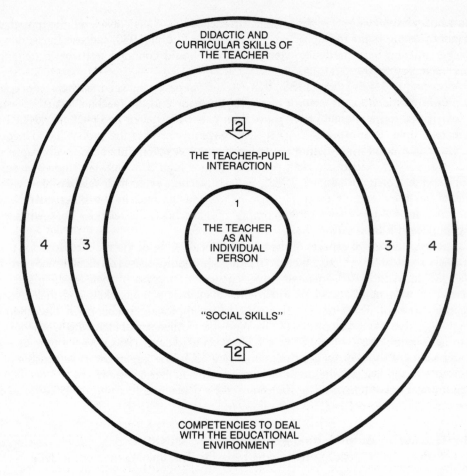

Figure 13.1. Basic Aspects of Teacher Training

Didactic and Curricular Skills. Training aims at curricular competence (knowledge of discipline, learning process, and teaching method), planning and organization of the teaching-learning process, communication skills (lecture skills, asking questions, etc.), and teaching techniques (visualization, small-group work, etc.). The training methods include

1. Training courses in project work and interdisciplinary projects, relating learning to the pupil and his every-day-life, basic principles of "action research" and their equivalents in school learning processes;
2. Training in complex lecture skills, group moderation, didactic techniques (visualization, hand-outs, structuring teaching contents, feedback techniques, etc.);
3. Basic training in curriculum development focusing upon social learning, intrinsic motivation of students, and student-centered "open" curricula, which are "action-oriented" and not merely academic; and
4. Planning and organizing the teaching-learning process—a problem-oriented course which starts with a problem assessment of the participating teachers and tries to give individualized help concerning the internal and external organization of the teaching-learning process.

Competencies to Deal with the "Educational Environment." This area, consists of the following goals

1. Dealing with the school administration, educational agencies, political educational bodies, teachers' union, the community, etc.;
2. Cooperation with teacher colleagues (e.g., team teaching, interdisciplinary project work, curriculum development with teacher colleagues, cooperative planning of teaching processes, how to resolve conflicts among teachers, etc.); and
3. Understanding the "life-situation" of those to be taught.

This wide program seeks to improve many important skills and attitudes needed in teaching. Included in teacher training, teachers become more competent in dealing with the class and also in the prevention of school misbehavior. Many aspects of this training model can also be used individually for self-training in the same or a similar form. Such a dynamic training course can be very valuable, argues Müller-Wolf (1978).

As was stated at the beginning of this chapter, teacher training in many countries is, however, more oriented toward academic than social skills. More cooperation between educators and psychologists is needed in teacher training to incorporate psychological knowledge of pupils and other social factors in teaching, and not only in specific therapeutic treatment or rehabilitation. Burns (1982) considers it indispensable to introduce and expose teachers to sensitive processes and complexities of personality structures. In many European countries, as well as in the United States, there seems to be an increasing tendency to concentrate on the counseling of teachers in interpersonal relationships, both in initial training and in-service courses. However, much is still to be done. In Finland, for instance, the counselling of teachers has started (Ojanen, 1982).

Collaboration Between School and Home

In the Scandinavian countries, more and more attention has been paid to the contacts between the school and the home and to their importance in the control of school misbehavior and violence. Goldinger and Magnusson (1978) state that school terrorism can only be avoided if children feel an association with the larger society. Children have to learn to know other children's parents, and the parents have to learn to know their child's peers and their parents. The teacher is considered the center of this social network.

In the discussion of what can be done with the whipping boy/bully problems in schools, Olweus (1978) also emphasizes the importance of the contact between the school and the home. He sets two types of goals for immediate action. The first goal is called the limiting goal, which entails a clear repudiation of repeated physical and mental maltreatment. Such an emphasis may come from the school authorities, the teachers, the classmates, and the parents. The second goal is called the integrative goal. Most important in achieving it is to intensify contacts between the school and home. "In order to achieve student care that is worthy of the name, there must be closer and more trusting relationships between the main teacher and the parents than is commonly the case" (Olweus, 1978, p. 187). Another point in an integrating program is that adults commit themselves to participating more actively in their children's lives. According to Nelson (1981), the best results in the treatment of school-age offenders have been achieved when the parents have collaborated with the school personnel.

Of course, it takes time away from both the teacher and the parents to intensify their mutual relationships and their contacts with children. The benefits, however, in the form of children's learning and adjustment, quite probably exceed the costs. Although lack of time is often referred to as an obstacle to contact between the teacher and the parents, there may be other hindrances as well, as some Finnish studies show.

In a study by Korpinen, Husso, and Korpinen (1980), the extent and forms of collaboration between home and school were mapped. The evenings arranged by the whole school were the most common form of collaboration, next were parents' evenings, discussions, exhibitions of pupils' work, and open houses. About 30% of teachers in lower grades had not arranged any kind of collaboration meeting in their own class. A study of the teachers' and parents' conceptions about the obstacles to collaboration revealed that the most essential obstacle in upper grades was the subject-teacher system. The pupils have no main teacher over several years. Even in lower grades, the teachers change often. The teachers also blamed big classes and schools, and parents think the teachers have not enough time and possibilities for collaboration (Korpinen, Korpinen, & Husso, 1980).

There were clear discrepancies between the expectations of teachers and parents on the topics to be discussed in collaboration meetings (Korpinen, Korpinen, & Husso, 1980). The most important topics for the teachers were the children's behavior disorders such as truancy, absence and school refusal, and problems of child upbringing, while the parents wanted most of all to get information about occupational choice and child development. In another study (Koivumäki & Pekkala, 1981), difficult topics to be discussed with the teacher were, in the parents' opinion, family problems, child-rearing, and the child's special problems. The parents expected a discussion of the child's learning difficulties and the choices to be made within the curriculum.

The results show that parents are more prepared to discuss academic problems than social problems with the teacher. Teachers have different expectations. Perhaps collaboration between school and home would be more successful if it were a regular part of schooling from the very beginning and if the child had a main teacher over several years. In the so-called Waldorf schools (Edmunds, 1979), developed according to Rudolf Steiner's philosophy, collaboration between home and school is at least more intensive than in the Finnish public schools.

In Sweden, Goldinger (1979) has worked intensively to enhance collaboration between home and school. She divides a class into four family groups of 5 to 6 children. These groups are formed before the child starts school at the age of 7, in cooperation with the teacher, the parents, and the day care staff. The groups are deliberately heterogeneous, and they remain unchanged until the fourth grade. The aim of family groups is to develop the children's self-confidence and their sense of responsibility and consideration. The groups of parents are formed to match the children's groups. The teacher meets the parents once a month.

According to Goldinger (1979), first graders are not yet ready for group work. In a small group the child may, however, feel a sense of security and learn to work with others. The teacher acts as a main director of the classroom work, to encourage free self-expression for everybody. Arising conflict situations can be solved reasonably when everyone has a chance to tell their wishes and an obligation to compromise their own demands and accept the final solution. This way, teasing and group violence can be reduced, the feeling of security increased, and self-confidence developed.

SPECIFIC INTERVENTIONS

An extensive review of the methods used in the control of school violence is presented in the recent book by Goldstein et al. (1984). They describe behavior-modification techniques, psychodynamic and humanistic interventions, teaching prosocial values and behaviors, school-modification programs, and community interventions. Corresponding approaches to school misbehavior can be found in Europe (see e.g., Atzesberger & Frey, 1978; Buchinger, 1979; Büscher, 1979; Eisert & Barkey, 1979; Huber, 1979; Kornmann, 1980; Nolting 1978; Petermann & Petermann, 1979; Sester, 1981; Uttendorfer-Marek, 1976).

There is a trend in Europe to emphasize the development of self-control as a solution to behavioral problems. For instance, Eisert and Barkey (1979) regard the development of self-control as one of the most important goals in therapeutic-pedagogic interventions. In the longitudinal study of the senior author (Pulkkinen, 1982), self-control proved to be a central explanatory concept for aggression and its alternatives.

Self-control is traditionally understood as a strong volition or internal strength by means of which an individual is able to monitor his or her own behavior and reinforce himself or herself. Self-control develops step by step when an individual learns to associate his or her behavior with situational factors and to find their functional relationships. Eisert and Barkey (1979) consider that the development of self-control in school demands guidance and supervision. Outer control can be gradually replaced by inner control.

Interventions for improving self-control are based on both learning theory and Soviet educational philosophy and studies (e.g., Luria, 1961; Vygotsky, 1962). By self-control, the present authors wish to emphasize an awareness of one's behavior and responsibilities in regard to others more than mere self-monitoring of behavior in strict learning-theoretical terms (Pulkkinen, 1984). On a high level, self-control brings freedom inward (capacity for choices of behavior) and outward (independence of external pressures).

Finnish teachers' opinions of the effectiveness of different methods in solving problems in schools were surveyed in a study by Gröhn (1980). She found that all kinds of suppressive means used by the teachers were the least successful and that pedagogic support and mental hygienic means were the most effective (see Figure 13.2). Ineffective suppressive means consisted of verbal suppression (from mild criticism to anger), psychic suppression (restrictions, sanctions, irony), and physical suppression (enforcement). Corporal punishment has been forbidden in Finnish schools for more than half a century.

Effective pedagogical support included increasing motivation and activation of the pupils, individualization of teaching, and supervision of the child's activities. These ideas are part of Montessori pedagogy, which is said to cause very little problems in school adjustment (Björksten, 1982; Sester, 1981). Analysis of the causes of a conflict was also considered effective (Gröhn, 1980). Referring a child to the school principal or counselor and restrictive behavior were almost as often a success as a failure.

As to the specific techniques, such as token reinforcement, model learning, role play, operant conditioning, and feedback techniques, the results have been inconsistent in reducing violence. It is likely that their effects depend at least partly on the teacher-pupil interaction; in a series of studies by Aho (1976, 1977, 1978), they seemed to decrease mainly verbal disturbances and negative attitudes towards authorities. Different reinforcement techniques should be involved with the prevailing situation of the child, argue Eisert and Barkey (1978), who consider a traditional analysis of behavioral problems insufficient for the planning of an intervention, because a researcher's orientation determines the target of and reasons for an experiment. Apart from the traditional microanalysis of problems, macroanalysis is also needed. It examines the need for interventions concerning larger systems, organizations, and institutions (e.g., parental education, teacher training). By analyzing the interests of different parties, the prerequisites for an intervention can be defined and an intervention technique chosen. The results of an intervention should also be evaluated on different levels. Eisert and Barkey criticize the literature on behavior modification for not describing the decision-making process used in choosing an intervention technique. It

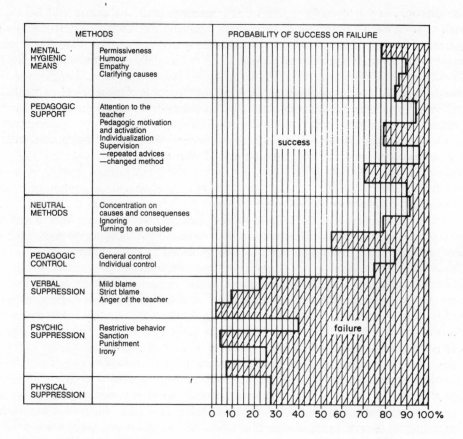

Figure 13.2. Methods Used by Finnish Teachers in Conflict Situations and Their Probability of Success or Failure

would be especially important to describe the role of the teacher and pupils in the decision making involved in determining the goals of an intervention, and the steps to those goals.

Democratic decision making has been a specific aim in so-called "collective" education, which is a modification of the method Makarenko used with Soviet school children. Makarenko (1975) emphasizes the child's responsibility for his behavior. Certain standards and requirements can be set for the child's behavior toward other people and the larger community. A collective is a group of individuals who aim at the same goal. Every member of the collective knows his place and obligations.

The decision-making body is a general meeting of the collective in which everybody is entitled to speak and vote. Common advantages take precedence over individual benefits, and they determine individual goals. Peer relationships are responsible interdependencies. In a collective, discipline guarantees an individual's rights and gives security concerning one's opportunities and responsibilities. An individual who breaks norms violates others' rights.

Makarenko's method was modified by Kaipio (1977) in a Finnish boarding school for anti-social boys under the title "education for cooperation and responsibility". Kaipio maintains that an overtly aggressive, anti-social boy benefits from this method, because his open anti-social behavior is a kind of struggle for just treatment. A passive anti-social boy is more difficult to socialize by this method, because he has submitted to the treatment which he feels unjust. It is important from the very beginning of the treatment that both have a chance to express their aggression and anger, but in a socially acceptable manner.

Education for cooperation and responsibility was experimented with in grades 3–6 in a Finnish school. (Olkinuora & Gorschelnik, 1982; Olkinuora & Tanner, 1983). The classes were divided into heterogeneous groups of 4 to 6 pupils. In each group a leader was appointed. The leaders formed the class council, which immediately dealt only with conduct disorders and met the norm-breaker in a special meeting. The proper penalty was decided by the teacher and by the general class meeting. Token reinforcement was combined with the method.

The great majority of the children's parents were not very interested in the experiment. Most teachers, however, considered that the program improved children's school adjustment. Although the method did not improve those children's behavior who were continually disruptive, it clarified the norms made together, especially at the primary level. Well socialized children caused social pressure on norm-breakers in class meetings.

The principles of education for cooperation and responsibility have also been applied in Sweden, for instance, in a class of difficult children (Havemose & Horn, 1978). The aim was to change aggressive behavior and negative norms by meetings in which disorders were dealt with analytically, critically, and constructively. At the beginning of the experiment, new working and action standards were clearly presented. Each small group had a new task to perform every week. Positive changes were found in aggressive children's behavior. Elmelind, Ivermark, and Söderlind (1978) report corresponding positive findings.

The sense of group may also be negative, Pikas maintains (1976), if it is limited to a group of bullies who tease others. He tries to break that feeling and clarify the victim's point of view to the bullies. Pikas also requires bullies to do the victim a concrete favor. An important advantage of this method, as well as of many other interventions, is that a teacher takes an action and tries to solve the problem.

Nolting (1978) recommends analysis of the situations that provoke aggression. Sources of aggression may be positive incentives for instrumental aggression, frustrations, or aggressive models. In the control of aggression, it is important to appraise cognitively the values that cause instrumental aggression. Thereafter, alternative behaviors should be sought. These include constructive means of solving conflicts. Solutions for the control of aggression are not, however, limited to an individual's behavior modification. They demand environmental psychological measures, control of the individual's exposure to filmed violence, guidance in child rearing, etc. Aggression is the whole society's problem.

DISCUSSION

It cannot be concluded that the amount of school violence was directly related to the amount of juvenile delinquency in Scandinavia. Instead, there are many other signs of maladjustment that all together are related to anti-social development. In addition to teasing other children, they include disrupting teaching, truancy and school avoidance, and underachievement and depression. Violence and other offenses are committed outside school, possibly combined with the use of alcohol. The small number of aggressive bullies do, however, cause many difficulties in schools for both classmates and teachers.

In order to control youth violence, measures on different levels are needed. Since the child's problems largely reflect problems at home, parental education and support is of primary importance. Although longstanding, its influences are slow and dependent on the parents' responsiveness. Collaboration between school and home is, in any case, essential, not only for the child's social adjustment in school, but also for his or her academic success. The parents' interest in and encouragement of the child's school work are related to the child's success and responsible behavior (Pulkkinen, 1982).

It is also important to emphasize social skills and pupil-oriented attitudes in teacher training. Teaching as a mere cognitive process does not take the child's whole personality into account. Education as a concept should not be limited to teaching, but should cover personality development as a whole. Conveying new facts and ideas should be seen as part of the socialization process. Such input can be utilized through a mature and responsible personality. Therapeutic attitudes toward a child who has difficulties in adjustment could be a kind of support that the society gives the child's development in spite of the problems at home. Homes do not exist for the school, schools exist for homes and especially for the children of a nation. Punishment-oriented treatment only increases children's difficulties.

Specific intervention programs may also be needed for the start of a remedial process if difficulties have intensified. Such programs should not, however, be separated from normal interaction for a long time; otherwise they cause satiation and remain unintegrated with the individual's goals. There are also serious ethical problems involved in all involuntary treatment programs, as Lehtimaja warns (1984). Predictions of future delinquent behavior tend to exaggerate the risks: Labelled people often respond to negative expectations and thus render the prophecies self-fulfilling. Lehtimaja maintains that there are also poor guarantees of the effectiveness of "special treatments". The good ideas of intervention programs should be incorporated into daily interaction; only then may they have lasting influences. It presupposes a closer collaboration between psychologists, social workers, and educators than what is nowadays often the case.

REFERENCES

Aho, S. (1975). *Opettajien käyttäytymisongelma-asenteet ja menettely-tavat ongelmien käsittelyssä. Liedon työrauhakokeiluprojekti: raportti 1.* (Report series A. Whole Nr. 36). Finland: Department of Education, University of Turku.

Aho, S. (1976). *Merkkivahvistamisen, mallioppimisen ja roolileikki-menetelmän soveltaminen koulun työrauhahäiriöiden korjaamiseen. Liedon työrauhakokeiluprojekti: raportti 2.* (Report series A. Whole Nr. 44). Finland: Department of Education, University of Turku.

Aho, S. (1977). *Operanttiehdollistamisen soveltaminen oppilailla esiintyvien työrauhahäiriöiden korjaamiseen. Liedon työrauhakokeiluprojekti: raportti 7.* (Report series A. Whole Nr. 53). Finland: Department of Education, University of Turku.

Aho, S. (1978). *Koulun työrauhahäiriöiden korjaantuminen annettaessa oppilaille palautetta omasta häiriökäyttäytymisestään. Liedon työrauhakokeiluprojekti: raportti 10.* (Report series A. Whole Nr. 57). Finland: Department of Education, University of Turku.

Alikoski, J. (1980). Koulun työtauhaongelmista ja niiden poistamis-mahdollisuuksista. *Kasvatus, 11,* 146–152.

Atzesberger, M. (1978). *Verhaltensstörungen in der Schule.* Stuttgart: Klett.

Atzesberger, M., & Frey, H. (1978). *Verhaltenstörungen in der Schule. Erscheinungsformen, Diagnostik, Behandlung.* Stuttgart: Klett.

Björksten, C. (1982). Skolen: Montessoriterapins preventiva aspekt. *Nordisk Psychologi, 34,* 153–159.

Buchinger, H. (1979). Die Verhaltensmodifikation in der Grundschule. *Ehrenwirth Grundschulmagazin, 6*(10), 9–12.

Burns, R.B. (1982). *Self-concept development and education.* London: Holt, Rinehart and Winston.

Büscher, P. (1979). Verhaltensmodifikation in der Schule. *Hörge-schädigtenpädagogik, 33,* 2–16.

Criminality in Finland 1981.(1982). Helsinki: Research Institute of Legal Policy.

Edmunds, F. (1979). *Rudolf Steiner education. The Waldorf Schools.* London: Rudolf Steiner Press.

Eerikäinen, K. (1979). Tämän päivän nuorisovangit–mistä, miksi, miten autetaan. *Mielenterveys, 19*(5), 22–27.

Eisert, H.G., & Barkey, P. (1980). *Verhaltensmodifikation im Unterricht - Interventionsstrategien in der Schule.* Bern: Hans Huber.

Eitzen, S. (1976). The self-concept of delinquents in a behavior modification treatment programme. *Journal of Social Psychology, 99,* 203–206.

Ellmann, R., Koch, H.J., Meyer-Plath, S., & Butollo, W. (1980). Im Schnittpunkt von Entwicklung-spsychologie und klinischer Psychologie. Entwicklungsverläufe und Prävention kindlicher Verhaltensstörungen. In U. Baumann, H. Berbalk, & G. Seidenstücker (Hrsg), *Klinische Psychologie (Bd. 3).* Bern: Hans Huber.

Elmelind, A.-C., Ivermark, I., & Söderlind, A. (1978). *Konfliktlösning och ansvarpedagogik.* Sweden: CD 1–uppsats Institutionen för tillämpad psykologi, Uppsala Universitet.

Farrington, D.P. (in press). Stepping stones to adult criminal careers. In D. Olweus, J. Block, & M. Radke-Yarrow (Eds.), *Development of antisocial and prosocial behavior: Theories, Research, and Issues.* New York: Academic Press.

Farrington, D.P., Berkowitz, L., & West, D.J. (1982). Differences between individual and group fights. *British Journal of Social Psychology, 21,* 323–333.

Festinger, L. (1957). A theory of cognitive dissonance. Stanford, CA: Stanford University Press.

Goldinger, B. (1979). *Familjegrupper i skolan.* Stockholm: Wahlström & Windstrand.

Goldinger, B., & Magnusson, G. (1978). *Lapsen tärkeät vuodet 7–12.* Helsinki: Otava. (Published originally in Swedish, 1977.)

Goldstein, A.P., Apter, S.J., & Harootunian, B. (1984). *School violence.* Englewood Cliffs, N.J.: Prentice-Hall.

Gröhn, T. (1979) *Opettajien ongelmallisina kokemat koulutilanteet ja heidän toimintansa näissä tilanteissa.* (Whole Nr. 72). Finland: Department of Education, University of Helsinki.

Gröhn, T. (1980). *Opettajan interaktiovalmiuksien parantaminen luokkaongelmien simulointia hyväksi käyttäen. Perusteita opettaja-koulutuksen harjoitusohjelman suunnittelua varten.* (Whole Nr. 80). Finland: Department of Education, University of Helsinki.

Günther, M. (1980). Disziplinierte Schüler durch Verhaltensmodifikation? In K. Ulich (Hrsg.), *Wenn Schüler stören.* München: Urban & Schwarzenberg.

Havemose, K., & Horne, M. (1978). *Ansvarpedagogik på lågstudiet, en förstudie.* Sweden: Institutionen för tillämpad psykologi. Uppsala Universitet.

Huber, H. von (1979). Über den Wert eines verhaltensmodifikatorischen Programms, durchgefürht in einer 4. Klasse einer Sonderschule E. *Praxis der Kinderpsychologie und Kinderpsychiatrie, 28,* 73–79.

Huvila, P., & Tilli, L. (1977). *Koululaisten keskinäinen väkivalta oppikoulussa.* (Report series A. Whole Nr. 52). Finland: Department of Education, University of Turku.

Joutsen, M. (1976). *Young offenders in the criminal justice system of Finland.* (Whole Nr. 14). Helsinki, Finland: Research Institute of Legal Policy.

Joutsen, M. (1980). *Dealing with child offenders in Finland.* (Whole Nr. 39). Helsinki, Finland: Research Institute of Legal Policy.

Kaipio, K. (1977). *Antakaa meille mahdollisuus, Johdatus nuorten yhteisökasvatukseen.* Jyväskylä, Finland: Gummerus.

Kaiser, G. (1981). Jugendkonflikte, Jugendpolitik and Jugendrecht.–Zur Kriminologischen Diskussion in der Bundesrepublik Deutschland. In J.M. Häussling, M. Brusten, & P. Malinowski (Hrsg.), *Jugendkonflikte. Kriminologische Forschungen und Analysen aus neun Ländern.* Stuttgart: Ferdinand Enke.

Kaiser, G. (1983). Möglichkeiten der Entkriminalisierung nach dem Jugendgerichtsgesetz im Vergleich zum Ausland. *Zeitschrift für Pädagogik, 29,* 31–48.

Kalliopuska, M. (1983). *Empatia—tie ihmisyyteer.* Helsinki, Finland: Kirjayhtymä.

Kari, J., Remes, P. & Väänänen, J. (1980). Disturbancies and disturbers — school discipline in the light of research. (Bulletin, Whole Nr. 160). Finland: Institute of Educational Research, University of Jyväskylä.

Kivistö, S. (1977). Miten ehkäistä kiusantekoa kouluissa. *Koulutyöntekijä, 5*(5–6), 2–3.

Koivumäki, S., & Pekkala, E. (1981). *Personal discussion as one form of collaboration between home and school. Part I. Parents' and pupils' opinions and comments about personal discussion.* (Bulletin, Whole Nr. 181). Finland; Institute for Educational Research, University of Jyväskylä.

Korpinen, E., Husso, M.-L., & Korpinen, R. (1980). *Collaboration between home and school. Part II. Collaboration at the lower level of the comprehensive school, teachers' and parents' conceptions of the functions of collaboration, parents' attitudes, and factors related to participation in collaboration.* (Bulletin, Whole Nr. 162). Finland: Institute for Educational Research, University of Jyväskylä.

Korpinen R., Korpinen E., & Husso, M.-L. (1980). *Collaboration between home and school. Part III. Teachers' and pupils' parents' conceptions about obstacles to collaboration and about the development of collaboration between home and school: practical arrangements, forms and contents of collaboration.* (Bulletin, Whole Nr. 163). Finland: Institute for Educational Research, University of Jyväskylä.

Kornmann, R. (1980). Verhaltensmodifikation in der Schulberatung. In K. Ulich (Hrsg.), *Wenn Schüler stören.* München: Urban & Schwarzenberg.

Kreuzer, A. (1983). Kinderdelinquenz und Jugendkriminalität. *Zeitschrift für Pädagogik, 29,* 49–70.

Kulka, R.A., Klingel, D.M., & Mann, D.W. (1980). School crime and disruption as a function of student-school fit: An empirical assessment. *Journal of Youth and Adolescence, 9,* 353–370.

Lagerspetz, K.M.J., Björkqvist, K., Berts, M., & King, E. (1982). Group aggression among school children in three schools. *Scandinavian Journal of Psychology, 23,* 45–52.

Léauté, J. (1981). Gewalttaten Jugendlicher – Analysen der Situation in Frankreich. In J.M. Häussling, M. Brusten, & P. Malinowski (Hrsg.), *Jugendkonflikte. Kriminologische Forschungen und Analysen aus neun Ländern.* Stuttgart: Ferdinal Enke.

Lehtimaja, L. (1984, July). *Roots of delinquency.* Paper presented at the sixth Biennial ISRA Meeting, Turku, Finland.

Levkovich, V.P. (1983). Family relations as a factor in the formation of the child's personality. In *Proceedings of the 2nd Finnish-Soviet Symposium of Personality. Tampere, Finland: (pp.39–50).* Publications of the Finnish-Soviet Committee on Scientific-Technological Co-operation.

Lipp, U. (1980). Der Lehrer als Berater. Möglichkeiten und Grenzen der Beratungstätigkeit in der Schule. In K. Ulich (Hrsg.), *Wenn Schüler stören.* München: Urban & Schwarzenberg.

Lowenstein, L.F. (1977). Who is the bully? *Home and School, 11,* 3–4.

Luria, A.R. (1961). *The role of speech in the regulation of normal and abnormal behavior.* New York: Leveright.

Makarenko, A. (1975). Neuvostoliittolaisen koulukasvatuksen ongelmia. Moskow: Edistys.

McClintock, F.H. (1981). Jugendkonflikte und Gewaltkriminalität in Grossbritannien. In J.M. Häussling, M. Brusten, & P. Malinowski (Hrsg.), *Jugendkonflikte. Kriminologische Forschungen und Analysen aus neun Ländern.* Stuttgart: Ferdinand Enke.

McCord, J. (1984, July). *Family sources of crime.* Paper presented at the sixth Biennial ISRA Meeting, Turku, Finland.

Meichenbaum, D., & Goodman, J. (1971). Training impulsive children to talk to themselves: A means of developing self-control. *Journal of Abnormal Psychology, 77,* 115–126.

Mees, U. (1983, September). *Consequences of aversive and non-aversive child-behavior.* Paper presented at the second European ISRA Conference, Zeist, The Netherlands.

Müller-Wolf, H.-M. (1978). The need for teacher training and a training model to promote democratic teaching behavior. *Scientia Paedagogica Experimentalis, 15,* 64–100.

Mäkinen, R. (1982). *Teacher's work, well-being, and health.* (Whole Nr. 46). Finland: Jyväskylä Studies in Education, Psychology and Social Research, University of Jyväskylä.

Nelson, A. (1981). Jugend unter sozialer Kontrolle — Analysen der Situation in Schweden. In J.M. Häussling, M. Brusten, & P. Malinowski (Hrsg.), *Jugendkonflikte. Kriminologische Forschungen und Analysen aus neun Ländern.* Stuttgart: Ferdinand Enke.

Nolting, H.-P. (1978). *Lernfall Aggression. Wie sie entsteht, wie sie zu vermindern ist. Theorie und Empire aggressiven Verhaltens und seiner Alternativen.* Reinbek: Rowohlt.

Official statistics of Finland (1982). *Criminality 1981. Criminality known to the police.* Helsinki: Tilastokeskus.

Ojanen, S. (1982). *Työohjaus — eräs keino opettajien henkisen kuormituksen keventämiseksi.* (Whole Nr. 1, 2–17). Finland: Department of Education. University of Oulu.

Olkinuora, E., & Gorschelnik, P. (1982). Yhteisökasvatuksen vaikutuksista oppilaiden normeihin peruskoulun ala-asteella. [Information about school experiment and research.] (Nr. 1, 4-16.) Finland: Experiment and research office, Administration of Education.

Olkinuora, E., & Tanner, K. (1982). Turun Aunelan koulun ala-asteen yhteisökasvatusmenetelmän prosessikuvaus. [Information about school experiment and research.] (Nr. 1, 2–17). Finland: Experiment and research office, Administration of Education.

Olweus D. (1978). *Aggression in the schools. Bullies and whipping boys.* New York: John Wiley & Sons.

Olweus, D. (1984). Description of the program: Bullying and harrassment among school children in Scandinavia: Research and a nationwide campaign in Norway.

Petermann, U. & Petermann, F. (1979). Gruppentraining in der Grundschule zum Abbau von Aggressionen. *Zeitschrift für Gruppenpädagogik, 5*(1), 25–36.

Pikas A. (1976). *Sovitaan pois.* Helsinki: Otava (Published originally in Swedish, 1975 as *Rationell konfliktlösning).*

Pinatel, J. (l981). Wissenschaftliche Erforschung von Jugendkonflikten Zur Begründung der klinischen Methode in der Kriminologie. In J.M. Häussling, M. Brusten, & P. Malinowski (Hrsg.), *Jugendkonflikte. Kriminologische Forschungen und Analysen aus neun Ländern.* Stuttgart: Ferdinand Enke.

Pulkkinen, L., (1982). Self-control and continuity from childhood to late adolescence. In P.B. Baltes & O.G. Brim, Jr.(Eds.), *Life-span development and behavior* (Vol. 4, pp. 389–417). New York: Academic Press.

Pulkkinen, L., (l983). Finland: The search for alternatives to aggression. In A.P. Goldstein & M.H. Segall (Eds.), *Aggression in global perspective* (pp.104–144). New York: Pergamon Press.

Pulkkinen, L. (in press). Nuoret ja kotikasvatus [Youth and home ecology]. Helsinki: Otava.

Pulkkinen, L., Heikkinen A., Markkanen, T., & Ranta, M.(1977). *Näin ohjaan lastani. Lasten itsehallinnan harjoitusohjelma.* Jyväskylä, Finland:Gummerus. (p. 624)

Pulkkinen, L., & Hurme, H. (1984). Aggression as a predictor of weak self-control. In L. Pulkkinen & P. Lyytinen (Eds.), *Human action and personality. Essays in honour of Martti Takala.* (Whole Nr. 54). Finland: Jyväskylä studies in Education, Psychology and Social Research. University of Jyväskylä.

Sester, H. (1981). Disciplin im Unterricht: Verbesserung durch indirekte Massnahmen. *Schulpraxis,* 1, 6–12.

Shapland, J.M. (1978). Self-reported delinquency in boys aged 11 to 14. *British Journal of Criminology, 18,* 255–266.

Sipilä, J. (1982). *Nuorten poikkeava käyttäytyminen ja yhteisön rakenne.* (Research Reports A. Whole Nr. 1). Finland: Institute of Social Policy, University of Jyväskylä.

Takala, H. (l981). Sukupolvet ja rikollisuus. *Sosiologia, 18,* 275–286.

Ulich, K. (l980, Ed.) *Wenn Schüler stören. Analyse und Therapie abweichenden Schülerverhaltens.* München: Urban & Schwarzenberg.

Uttendorfer-Marek, I. (1976). Unterricht über Unterricht (Unterrichtseinheiten). In A.C. Wagner (Hrsg.), *Schülerzentrierten Unterricht.* München: Urban & Schwarzenberg.

Winkel, R. (l976). *Der gestörte Unterricht. Diagnostische und therapeutische Möglichkeiten.* Bochum: Kamp.

Vygotsky, L.S. (l962). *Thought and language.* New York: Wiley & Sons.

Author Index

Achenbach, T. M., 6, 19, 169, 170, 172, 173, 174, 175
Adams, G., 155, 158
Adams, G. L., 108, 116
Adams, W. H., 10, 16, 17, 19
Adamson, G. W., 12, 21
Adkins, W. R., 96, 114
Agee, V., 76, 80, 87
Agras, W. S., 111, 114
Aho, S., 267, 275, 278
Aichhorn, A., 175
Albee, G. W., 157, 164, 166, 176
Albert, J. A., 213, 214
Alexander, J. F., 25, 34, 36, 37
Alexander, J. K., 215
Alexander, R. M., 36
Algozzine, B., 6, 10, 19, 22
Alikoski, J., 268, 278
Alioto, J. T., 182, 199, 214
Allenson, E. A., 109, 119
Alvord, J. R., 25, 34
Andison, F. S., 180, 185, 212, 214
Andrasik, F., 99, 117
Anthony, E. J., 163, 175
Appellof, E., 69, 70
Applefield, J. M., 181, 200, 218
Applegate, G., 112, 115
Apter, S. J., 1, 15, 20, 104, 115, 120, 122, 127, 129, 138, 141, 145, 157, 158, 262, 263, 266, 268, 274, 279
Argyle, M., 96, 114
Arthurs, R. G., 61, 70
Atkin, C. K., 185, 186, 190, 191, 195, 209, 213, 217
Atwater, J. D., 37
Atwater, S. K., 109, 114

Atzesberger, M., 262, 263, 266, 267, 270, 275, 278
Ausnew, H. R., 25, 36
Austin, J., 24, 35, 40, 55
Austin, P., 67, 71
Ausubel, D. P., 108, 114
Aversano, F. M., 122, 126, 137

Bachman, J. G., 185, 186, 217
Baer, D. J., 161, 176
Baker, K. E., 109, 115
Baker, R. K., 207, 214
Bakkestrom, E., 63, 73
Balfour, M. J., 12, 15, 19
Ball, H. E., Jr., 13, 22
Balla, D. A., 61, 67, 72, 247, 261
Ban, J. R., 121, 137
Bandler, R. J., 60, 70
Bandura, A., 39, 54, 90, 92, 114, 161, 175, 178, 179, 181, 185, 198, 199, 200, 214
Barchas, J. D., 62, 71
Bard, B., 247, 261
Barkey, P., 269, 270, 275, 279
Barkley, R., 247, 260
Barlow, D. H., 103, 116
Barnes, K., 199, 216
Baron, R. A., 56, 199, 215
Barrett, G., 199, 202, 215
Barth, R., 148, 155, 156, 157
Battle, C. C., 108, 116
Bayh, B., 122, 137
Beck, J. C., 247, 261
Becker, A., 108, 119
Becker, W. C., 117
Beilin, H., 6, 19
Bellack, A. S., 97, 104, 114

Belson, W. A., 186, 189, 190, 201, 209, 214
Benning, J. J., 122, 126, 137
Berck, P.L., 36, 56
Berger, D. E., 57
Berkowitz, L., 39, 54, 179, 182, 185, 199, 202,
    214, 215, 216, 217, 268, 279
Berleman, W., 155, 158
Berliner, D., 136, 137
Berman, A., 68, 70
Bernstein, B. B., 108, 115
Berry, R. S., 16, 19
Berstein, S., 161, 175
Berts, M., 267, 268, 280
Bettleheim, B., 162, 175
Bibace, R. M., 68, 71
Bielicki, R. J., 10, 16, 17, 19
Binder, A., 41, 42, 54
Birch, H., 145, 158
Björkqvist, K., 267, 268, 280
Björksten, C., 275, 278
Blake, G. F., 42, 54, 55
Blakely, C., 24, 26, 27, 35, 40, 54
Blanchard, K., 224, 225, 226, 236
Blanchard, S., 56
Blank, C. E., 63, 71
Blankenberg, W. B., 207, 215
Bliss, E., 63, 71
Blomberg, T. G., 42, 54
Bloom, R. B., 9, 19
Blum, F., 61, 73
Blumer, D. P., 61, 71
Boehm, R. G., 157, 158
Bohnstedt, M., 57
Bologna, N. C., 98, 116
Bornstein, M., 97, 114
Braaten, S., 11, 12, 13, 15, 19, 23
Brady, J. V., 60, 71
Braff, J., 151, 154, 158
Branch, M. N., 108, 117
Braukmann, C. J., 26, 35, 36, 37, 38, 57, 97,
    99, 114, 117
Breitrose, H., 215
Brentro, L. K., 80, 82, 88
Brethower, D. M., 17, 19
Brice, P., 213, 216
Brigham, T. A., 98, 116
Brinkerhoff, R. O., 17, 19
Broder, P. K., 25, 35
Brodie, H. K., 62, 72
Brodinsky, M., 124, 137
Bronner, A. F., 71
Brown, B. W., Jr., 215
Brown, G. B., 12, 19
Brown, W. A., 63, 72

Brown, W. K., 16, 19
Bry, B. H., 150, 158
Bryant, B., 96, 114
Buchinger, H., 275, 278
Buck, M. T., 8, 15, 16, 19
Buckley, N. K., 108, 119
Bucy, P. C., 60, 71
Buehler, R. E., 25–26, 35
Bullington, B., 42, 54
Bullock, L. M., 15, 20, 130, 137, 140, 158
Burchard, J. D., 27, 35
Burke, R. J., 158
Burns, R. B., 265, 270, 273, 278
Büscher, P., 266, 275, 278
Butollo, W., 267, 268, 269, 279

Cahoon, E. B., 61, 70
Calder, B. J., 203, 204, 205, 206, 211, 216
Callantine, M. F., 110, 114
Camino, L., 185, 217
Campbell, D. T., 137, 189, 203, 204, 215
Cantor, J. H., 109, 115
Cantwell, D. P., 67, 71
Caplan, G., 146, 158
Carpenter, W., 82, 88
Carr, R. A., 11, 20
Carr, E. G., 39, 55
Carter, R. M., 41, 42, 54
Casey, M. D., 63, 71
Catton, W. R., 207, 215
Cauce, I. M., 149, 150, 158
Chaffee, S. H., 178, 183, 185, 186, 189, 190,
    191, 195, 209, 213, 215, 217
Chess, S., 145, 158
Chi, C. C., 60, 70
Christiansen, K., 62, 63, 71, 73
Christiansen, S. O., 25, 35
Churchman, C. W., 223, 236
Ciminillo, L. M., 121, 137
Clark, D. G., 207, 215
Clarke, S. H., 41, 54
Cloward, R., 25, 35
Coates, R. B., 151, 158
Cobb, J. A., 89, 118
Cobb, S., 141, 149, 158
Cocozza, J., 151, 154, 158
Cohen, H. L., 25, 35
Coletti, R. F., 129, 137
Collingwood, T. R., 56
Comstock, G., 178, 179, 183, 185, 186, 189,
    198, 215, 217, 218
Conger, J. J., 91, 92, 114, 117
Conger, R. E., 91, 92, 118
Conn, G. T., 13, 22

Connolly, J., 122, 127, 138
Cook, T. D., 185, 189, 192, 194, 195, 196,
    197, 203, 204, 205, 206, 211, 215, 216
Cooper, M., 96, 115
Coopersmith, S., 169, 175
Corbett, T. F., 36
Cordray, D. S., 57
Corriveau, D. P., 63, 72
Cotler, S. B., 112, 115
Cotton, M., 56
Courtney, S. A., 98, 116
Cowen, E. L., 161, 165–166, 175
Craft, N., 2, 8, 14, 20
Crandall, V. C., 169, 175
Crandall, V. J., 169, 175
Cressey, D. R., 41, 52, 54, 55
Cronbach, L. J., 104, 115, 136, 137
Cullinan, D., 5, 13, 20

Dalton, K., 67, 71
Davidson, W. S., 24, 26, 27, 31, 35, 36, 37,
    39, 40, 41, 42, 44, 49, 54, 55, 56
Davies, P. D., 68, 69, 74
Dean, S. I., 106, 115
DeJames, P. L., 130, 137
De Lange, J. M., 97
DeLeon, J. L., 3
Del Rosario, M. L., 203, 204, 205, 206, 211,
    216
Deno, E., 2, 4, 7, 20, 22
DeRisi, W. J., 25, 35
Dermody, H. E., 24, 26, 35
DiGiuseppe, R., 9, 22
Dixon, M. S., 66, 68, 71
Dollard, J., 39, 55
Dollinger, S. L., 101, 119
Donahoe, C. P., 91, 115
Donnerstein, E., 199, 202, 215
Doob, L., 39, 55
Douds, A. F., 56
Dreikurs, R., 85, 87, 89, 110, 115
Drum, D. J., 108, 115
Duke, D. L., 124, 126, 137
Duncan, C. P., 108, 110, 115
Dundar, M., 56
Dunford, F. W., 42, 55, 56
Dunivant, N., 25, 35, 247, 248, 260
Dunn, L. M., 2, 20
Dunsmore, R. H., 61, 73

Edelbrock, C. S., 6, 19
Edelman, E., 106, 115
Edelstein, B. A., 97, 115
Edmunds, F., 274, 279

Eerikäinen, K., 265, 279
Egger, M. D., 60, 71
Ehrenkrantz, J., 63, 71
Eichelman, B., 62, 71
Eisenthal, S., 156, 158
Eisert, H. G., 269, 270, 275, 279
Eisner, E. W., 4, 20
Eitzen, D. S., 37, 57
Eitzen, S., 265, 279
Ekman, R., 199, 215
Elardo, P., 96, 115
Elder, J. P., 97, 115
Eller, B. F., 37
Elliot, D. S., 25, 35, 56, 121, 126, 137
Elliot, G. R., 62, 71
Ellis, D. P., 67, 71
Ellis, H., 109, 115
Ellmann, R., 267, 268, 269, 279
Elmelind, A.-C., 277, 279
Emery, R. E., 26, 27, 33, 35
Empey, L. T., 87, 88
Emshoff, J. G., 37
Epstein, M. C., 5, 6, 13, 20
Epstein, M. H., 5, 13, 20
Erikson, E., 7, 12, 13, 20
Erikson, J. A., 7, 12, 13, 21
Erlenmeyer-Kimling, L. A., 163, 175
Eron, L. D., 126, 138, 186, 188, 195, 197,
    202, 209, 213, 215, 216, 217
Ervin, F. R., 61, 65, 66, 72, 73
Essman, W. B., 60, 71
Esveldt-Dawson, K., 99, 117

Fagen, S. A., 15, 20
Falk, N., 129, 137
Fallis, A., 130, 139
Faretra, G., 151, 158, 248, 260
Farquhar, J. W., 198, 215
Farrington, D. P., 160, 175, 264, 268, 279
Fayol, H., 221, 236
Feeney, F., 56
Fein, D., 56
Feldhusen, J. F., 122, 126, 137
Felner, R. D., 149, 150, 158
Ferracuti, F., 63, 74
Feshbach, S., 39, 55, 179, 182, 185, 199, 202,
    216, 217
Festinger, L., 265, 279
Figler, H. E., 108, 115
Fink, A. H., 16, 20
Finnegan, T., 170, 177
Fischer, P., 213, 216
Fixsen, D. L., 13, 21, 35, 36, 37, 38, 57, 97,
    99, 102, 114, 117, 119

Fleming, D., 113, 115
Flores de Apodaca, R., 161, 175
Flynn, J. P., 60, 71
Fo, W. S., 26, 35
Ford, D. H., 108, 115
Fortis, J. G., 205–206, 216
Foster, H., 109, 115
Foster, H. L., 122, 124, 137
Foster, S., 100, 118
Frank, J. D., 108, 116
Frank, R., 110, 115
Fraser, M. W., 147, 156, 157, 158, 159
Frease, D. C., 161, 175
Frease, D. E., 121, 137
Freedman, B. J., 91, 115
Freemont, T. S., 127, 138
Frey, H., 267, 270, 275, 278
Friedman, T. T., 108, 119
Friesen, W. V., 199, 215
Fromm-Auch, D., 68, 69, 74
Fry, R. A., 101, 119
Fryrear, J. L., 56

Gable, R. A., 16, 20
Gadow, D., 85, 88
Gaffney, L. R., 25, 35
Gagne, R. M., 109, 115
Galbraith, J. K. 236
Ganzer, V. J., 37, 100, 118
Garber, J., 56
Garibaldi, A. M., 13, 20
Garmezy, N., 163, 164, 175
Gast, D. L., 13, 20
Gastaut, H., 61, 71
Geen, R. G., 182, 184, 199, 202, 214, 216
Gensheimer, L., 44, 49, 55
Genthner, R. W., 56
Gershaw, N. J., 12, 18, 20, 92, 105, 107, 114, 115, 117
Gerwitz, J., 92, 117
Gesten, E. L., 161, 175
Gewirtz, P., 238, 239, 260
Gibbons, D. C., 42, 54, 55
Gilbert, G. R., 56
Gillies, H., 63, 71
Glaser, D., 25, 35
Glaser, G. H., 66, 68, 71, 72
Glass, G. V., 25, 27, 29, 35, 40, 42, 43, 44, 55, 56, 136, 138, 180, 216
Glasser, W., 15, 20, 79, 83, 85, 88, 239, 247, 260
Glueck, E., 25, 35
Glueck, S., 25, 35

Gold M., 40, 55, 89, 115, 121, 138
Goldbeck, R. A., 108, 115
Golden, C., 69, 71
Goldinger, B., 273, 274, 279
Goldstein, A. P., 1, 10, 12, 15, 18, 20, 21, 39, 55, 91, 92, 93, 96, 104, 105, 106, 107, 108, 109, 110, 114, 115, 117, 120, 122, 124, 127, 129, 133, 136, 138, 141, 158, 262, 263, 266, 268, 274, 279
Gomez, A. G., 108, 116
Goodenough, D., 63, 73
Goodman, J., 267, 280
Gorney, R., 185, 217
Gorscheinik, P., 277, 281
Gottlieb, B. H., 147, 158
Gottschalk, R., 44, 49, 55
Gove, W. R., 161, 175
Gray, L. N., 205–206, 216
Green, D. R., 37, 98, 117
Greenleaf, D., 97, 116
Gresham, F. M., 15, 18, 20
Grey, A. L., 24, 26, 35
Grey, L., 85, 87
Griffin, W. H., 16, 20
Gröhn, T., 270, 271, 275, 279
Grosenick, J. K., 3, 4, 20
Gross, A. M., 98, 116
Gruber, R. P., 108, 111, 116
Grunwald, B. B., 89, 115
Guerney, B. G., Jr., 96, 116
Gullick, L. F., 221, 236
Gullion, M. F., 112, 118
Gulotta, T., 155, 158
Günther, M., 267, 279
Guttman, E. S., 89, 116
Guze, S. B., 63, 67, 71
Guzzetta, R., A., 110, 116

Haapanen, R., 57
Hall, J., 154, 159
Hallam, J., 199, 202, 215
Hanrahan, J., 199, 218
Haran, J., 13, 22
Hardy, T. W., 199, 218
Hare, M. A., 96, 116
Harlow, H. F., 116
Harootunian, B., 1, 15, 20, 104, 115, 116, 120, 122, 127, 129, 138, 141, 262, 263, 266, 268, 274, 279
Harper, T. N., 99, 117
Harris, D. B., 169, 176
Harris, J. W., 129, 138
Harris, L. H., 15, 19

Harris, T., 9, 20
Harrison, R., 199, 215
Harter, S., 166, 167, 168, 169, 172, 173, 174, 176
Hartig, P. T., 27, 35
Hartstone, E., 151, 154, 158
Hartup, W. W., 161, 176, 199, 218
Haskell, W. L., 215
Haug, M., 60, 72
Haussmann, S., 2, 8, 14, 20
Havemose, P., 277, 279
Hawkins, J. D., 147, 156, 157, 158, 159
Hawley, I. L., 96, 116
Hawley, R. C., 96, 116
Hays, J. R., 39, 55
Hayward, M. L., 110, 116
Hazell, J. S., 98
Head, S. W., 205, 216
Hearold, S. L., 180, 185, 211, 212, 216
Heath, L., 203, 204, 205, 206, 211, 216
Heck, E. T., 108, 116
Heckel, R. V., 37
Healy, W., 71
Heide, F., 87, 88
Heikkinen, A., 269, 281
Heiman, H., 96, 116
Heimberger, R. F., 61, 71
Heinemann, S. H., 109, 117
Heller, K., 106, 108, 110, 113, 115, 116
Hellix, W. A., 108, 115
Henderson, M., 98
Hendrix, C. E., 37
Henney, J., 154, 159
Hennigan, K. M., 203, 204, 205, 206, 211, 216
Henning, P., 122, 127, 138
Henry, C. E., 61, 73
Herring, J., 36
Hersen, M., 37, 99, 100, 103, 114, 116, 117
Hersey, P., 224, 225, 226, 236
Heston, L. L., 164, 176
Himmelweit, H. T., 202, 216
Hirschhorn, K., 63, 73
Hirschi, T., 154, 158
Hluchyji, T., 17, 19
Hobbs, N., 145, 158
Hobbs, T. R., 37
Hoehn-Saric, R., 108, 116
Hollbery, E. T., 117
Hollin, C. R., 98, 116
Hollon, S. D., 18, 21
Holmes, D. S., 110, 116
Holt, M. M., 37

Homskaya, E. D., 69, 72
Hopkins, B. L., 112, 116
Hopper, C., 98, 116
Horne, M., 277, 279
Howard, J. R., 38
Howitt, D., 188, 216
Hoyer, W. J., 109, 117
Hsu, J. J., 108, 109, 116
Huber, H. von, 267, 275, 279
Huesmann, L. R., 186, 188, 194, 195, 197, 202, 209, 213, 216, 217
Huey, W. C., 130, 138
Hull, C., 106, 116
Hummel, J. W., 98, 110, 116
Hunt, D. E., 104, 116, 123, 136, 138
Hunter, J., 25, 27, 32, 35, 40, 42, 44, 55
Huntze, S. L., 3, 4, 20
Hurley, R., 199, 218
Hurme, H., 264, 281
Hurwitz, I., 68, 71, 73
Husain, A., 247, 261
Hussard, H., 117
Husso, M.-L., 274, 279
Hutzler, J., 170, 176
Huvila, P., 267, 279
Hyman, I. A., 122, 138

Imber, S. D., 108, 116
Isralowitz, R. E., 87, 88
Ivermark, I., 277, 279

Jackson, G., 25, 27, 32, 35, 40, 42, 44, 55
Jackson, R., 13, 22
Jacob, T., 161, 176
Jacobs, D., 247, 261
Jacobsen, B., 163, 176
Jaffe, Y., 202, 217
Jens, K., 56
Jesness, C. F., 25, 35, 231, 236
Jessor, R. J., 127, 138
Jessor, S. L., 127, 138
Johnson, C. A., 112, 116
Johnson, M. E., 109, 119
Johnson, N., 67, 72
Johnson, R. C., 199, 218
Jones, M., 80, 88
Jones, M. C., 109, 116
Jones, N. F., 109, 116
Jones, R. R., 38, 91, 92, 118
Jones, V., 12, 20
Jones, V. F., 137
Joutsen, M., 262, 263, 264, 265, 279
Julian, V., 12, 13, 20

Kagan, J., 92, 117
Kahn, A. J., 24, 35
Kahn, M. W., 109, 116
Kaipio, K., 276, 279
Kaiser, G., 262, 264, 265, 266, 279
Kale, R. J., 112, 116
Kalliopuska, M., 269, 279
Kalsbeck, J. E., 61, 71
Kanfer, F. H., 108, 113, 116, 117
Kaplan, R. M., 216
Kari, J., 267, 268, 279
Karoly, P., 113, 117
Kashani, J. H., 247, 261
Katkin, D., 42, 54
Katkousky, W., 169, 175
Katz, R. C., 112, 116
Katzman, N., 178, 183, 185, 186, 215
Kauffman, J. M., 3, 20, 21
Kaufman, K. F., 13, 21
Kay, H., 216
Kaye, J. H., 112, 116
Kazdin, A. E., 13, 21, 103, 108, 110, 111,
    112, 117
Keller, H. R., 124, 136, 138
Kellner, R., 63, 73
Kelly, D. H., 121, 138
Kelly, F. J., 161, 176
Kempf, E., 60, 72
Kendall, P. C., 18, 21
Kendzierski, D. A., 185, 192, 194, 195, 196,
    197, 215
Kennedy, J., 8, 11, 15, 16, 21
Kenney, E., 75, 88
Kenny, D. A., 194, 216
Kent, R., 100, 118
Kessler, M., 164, 166, 176
Kessler, P., 186, 191, 193, 208, 210, 217
Kety, S., 163, 176
Kifer, R. E., 37, 98, 117
King, E., 267, 268, 280
King, L. W., 112, 115
Kirigin, K. A., 37, 38, 57
Kivistö, S., 267, 268, 280
Klassen, D., 148, 149, 159
Klein, M. W., 41, 42, 54, 55
Klein, N., 37
Klein, P., 12, 18, 20, 92, 107, 114, 115
Klein, R., 213, 216
Klerman, L. V., 8, 11, 15, 16, 21
Klingel, D. M., 267, 280
Kluver, H., 60, 71
Knoblock, P., 10, 21
Knopp, F. H., 79, 86

Knott, J. R., 61, 72
Koch, H. J., 267, 268, 269, 279
Koch, J. R., 41, 42, 55, 56
Kohlberg, L., 104, 117, 161, 176
Koivumäki, S., 274, 280
Kokaska, C. J., 16, 20
Kolb, B., 61, 62, 72
Kornmann, R., 270, 275, 280
Korpinen, E., 274, 279
Korpinen, R., 274, 279
Kovel, J., 108, 117
Krasner, L., 39, 55
Krattenmaker, T. G., 213, 216
Kreuzer, A., 262, 263, 280
Krisberg, B., 24, 35, 40, 55
Kristal, S., 112, 115
Kroth, R. L., 17, 21
Krynicki, V. E., 68, 69, 72
Kulka, R., A., 267, 280

Ladd, G. W., 104, 106, 113, 117
Lagerspetz, K. M. J., 186, 195, 197, 216, 267,
    268, 280
Lane, B. A., 69, 72
Lane, S., 86, 88
Larsen, E. D., 15, 21
Larsen, O. N., 205–206, 216
Larsen, R. D., 157, 158
Laub, J. H., 40, 55
Lawrenson, G. M., 10, 21
Laws, D. R., 63, 73
Lazarus, A. A., 109, 117
Learch, A. N., 16, 19
Léauté, J., 263, 280
Lee, D. Y., 99, 117
Lefcourt, H. M., 199, 216
Lefkotitz, M. M., 126, 138, 186, 188, 191,
    192, 195, 197, 202, 209, 215, 216, 217
Lehtimaja, L., 278, 280
Lemert, E. M., 41, 42, 55
Leventhal, B. L., 62, 72
Levitt, E. L., 26, 35
Levkovich, V. P., 266, 280
Lewis, B., 129, 138
Lewis, D. O., 61, 66, 67, 68, 72, 247, 261
Lewis, M. A., 37, 98, 117
Lewis, R. G., 56, 57
Lewis, W. W., 144, 158
Leyens, J. P., 185, 217
Liberman, R. P., 38
Liberson, W. T., 61, 73
Lieberman Research, 199, 217
Liebert, R. M., 199, 215

Lipp, U., 267, 280
Lipsey, M. W., 57
Lipton, D., 24, 35
Lishner, D., 156, 159
Litwack, S. W., 99, 113, 117
Logan, C. H., 42, 56
Long, N. J., 15, 20, 99
Lopez, M. A., 109, 117
Loughmiller, C., 16, 21
Love, C., 57
Low, H., 67, 72, 73
Lowenstein, L. F., 268, 280
Loye, D., 185, 217
Lundman, R. J., 39, 55
Lundstein, D., 63, 73
Luria, A. R., 69, 72, 275, 280

Maccoby, N., 215
MacDonald, M. L., 26, 35
Mack, G., 60, 72
Madden, N. A., 2, 21
Madsen, A., 61, 73
Maeroff, G., 239, 261
Magaro, P. A., 104, 117
Magnusson, G., 273, 279
Maher, C. A., 10, 11, 21, 22
Mahoney, M. J., 108, 117
Makarenko, A., 265, 276, 280
Mäkinen, P., 271, 280
Malamuth, N. M., 202, 217
Malcolm, P., 157, 158
Malone, T. P., 110, 119
Maloney, D. M., 99, 117
Malstrom, E. J., 199, 215
Mancuso, W. A., 138
Mandel, P., 60, 72
Mandler, G., 109, 117
Mann, C. R., 67, 72
Mann, D. W., 267, 280
Marholin, D., 26, 27, 33, 35, 113, 117
Mark, V. H., 61, 65, 66, 71, 72, 73
Markson, H. J., 8, 15, 16, 19
Marston, A. R., 108, 116
Martinson, R., 24, 35
Marvin, M., 122, 127, 138
Marx, M.H., 108, 115
Marzillier, J. S., 37, 101, 119
Masters, J. C., 18, 21, 108, 117
Matson, J. L., 99, 117
Mattsson, A., 67, 72, 73
Mattsson, D., 67

Matza, D., 25, 35
Mayer, J., 44, 49, 55
McAlister, A. L., 215
McCann, R., 122, 127, 138
McCauley, R. W., 3, 7, 13, 18, 21
McClintock, F. H., 263, 280
McCombs, M., 178, 183, 185, 186, 215
McCord, J., 266, 280
McCord, W., 141, 152, 158
McCormack, S., 130, 138
McCraft, P. J., 63, 71
McDermott, M. S., 121, 138
McDermott, R. A., 41, 42, 54, 55
McDill, E. L., 120, 122, 123, 125, 126, 138,
    145, 158
McDougall, J. H., 63, 71
McDowell, R. L., 12, 19, 21
McFall, R. M., 25, 35, 91, 115
McGaw, B., 180, 216
McGaw, G., 40, 42, 44, 55
McGrath, E., 19, 21
McGraw, G., 25, 27, 29, 35
McIntyre, J. J., 185, 186, 217
McKibbon, J., 85, 88
McKinnon, A. J., 10, 21
McLeod, J. M., 185, 186, 190, 191, 195, 209,
    213, 217
McPartland, J. M., 120, 122, 123, 125, 126,
    138, 145, 158
McWilliams, B., 80, 87
Medick, J., 130, 138
Mednick, S. A., 25, 35, 63, 73, 163, 176
Mees, U., 271, 280
Meichenbaum, D. M., 18, 21, 267, 280
Mendelson, W., 67, 72
Mennel, R. M., 24, 35
Merring, J., 56
Meyer, A. J., 215
Meyer, T. P., 199, 217
Meyer-Plath, S., 267, 268, 269, 279
Mezzich, A., 58, 72
Michelson, L., 104, 117
Milavsky, J. R., 186, 191, 193, 195, 208, 210,
    217
Milgram, S., 185, 217
Miller, A. D., 151, 158
Miller, N., 39, 55
Miller, R. B., 75, 88
Miller, S. R., 6, 22
Miller, T. I., 43, 56
Miller, W. C., 91, 114
Minkin, B. L., 99, 102, 117, 119
Minkin, N. M., 38, 99, 102, 117

Mitchell, J. B., 8, 11, 15, 16, 21
Mitchell, R., 149, 159
Mittelman, B., 162, 176
Mitzel, H. E., 124, 138
Mize, J., 104, 106, 113, 117
Monahan, J., 148, 149, 159
Monroe, R. R., 61, 72
Monti, P. M., 63, 72
Moriarity, A. E., 161, 176
Morse, W. C., 146, 159
Mosak, H., 110, 115
Mower, O., 39, 55
Moyer, K. E., 59, 60, 72
Müller-Wolf, H.-M., 271, 273, 280
Mulvihill, D. J., 64, 72
Murphy, L. B., 161, 165, 176
Murray, A., 8, 11, 15, 16, 21
Murray, C. A., 69, 72
Murray, J. P., 179, 180, 215, 218
Mussen, P. H., 92, 117

Narabayashi, H., 61, 67, 73
Narick, N. N., 97, 115
Nash, E. H., 108, 116
Nash, J. D., 215
Nauta, W. J. H., 60, 71
Neale, J. M., 217
Nejelski, P., 41, 54, 55
Nelson, A., 262, 263, 273, 280
Nelson, C. M., 13, 20, 21, 22
Nesdal, A. R., 39, 56
Nietzel, M. T., 26, 35
Nolting, H. P., 275, 277, 281
Novaco, R. W., 39, 55
Nowakowski, J. R., 17, 19
Nuell, L. R., 56

Ochberg, F. M., 64, 73
O'Dell, S., 112, 117
O'Donnell, C. R., 26, 35, 37
Offord, D. R., 161, 176
Ohanian, S., 130, 138
Ohlin, L. E., 25, 35, 151, 158
Oja, S. N., 136, 139
Ojanen, S., 273, 281
O'Leary, D., 100, 112, 118
O'Leary, K. D., 13, 21
O'Leary, O. D., 89, 117
O'Leary, S., 89, 117
Olkinuora, E., 277, 281
Ollendick, T. H., 37, 100, 117
Olweus, D., 67, 72, 73, 266, 267, 268, 269, 273, 281

Oppenheim, A. N., 202, 216
Orne, M. I., 108, 118
Osgood, C. E., 109, 118
Osgood, D. W., 42, 55, 56
Ossorio, P., 125, 139
Ounsted, C., 65, 67, 73
Owen, D., 63, 73

Palmer, T., 57
Papp, N. A., 36
Parke, R. D., 145, 159, 185, 199, 216, 217
Parsons, B. V., 25, 34, 36, 37
Patterson, G. R., 25, 35, 37, 89, 91, 92, 111, 112, 118
Paul, S. C., 101, 119
Pekkala, E., 274, 279
Penner, M. J., 73
Pentz, M. A., 100, 118, 127, 138
Pepe, A., 61, 73
Pepper, F. C., 89, 115
Petermann, F., 267, 270, 275, 281
Petermann, U., 267, 270, 275, 281
Peters, J. J., 110, 116
Peters, J. J., 110, 116
Petti, T., 99, 117
Phillip, J., 63, 73
Phillips, C. L., 36
Phillips, E. L., 13, 21, 26, 35, 37, 38, 57, 98, 102, 117, 119
Phillips, M., 42, 54
Piers, E. V., 169, 176
Pikas, A., 266, 277, 281
Pinatel, J., 265, 281
Pincus, J. H., 66, 68, 72
Polak, P. R., 152, 159
Polk, K., 25, 36, 121, 139
Polsgrove, L., 9, 13, 14, 21
Polster, R., 112, 117
Polyani, M., 136, 139
Pontius, A. A., 69, 73
Powe, L. A., Jr., 213, 216
Prentice, N. M., 25, 36
Price, R. H., 113, 118
Pries, R., 247, 261
Primavera, J., 149, 150, 158
Prinz, R., 100, 118
Puglisi-Allegra, S., 60, 72
Pulkkinen, L., 264, 266, 269, 275, 278, 281

Quay, H. C., 6, 21, 57

Rada, R. T., 63, 73
Rains, M., 161, 175

Ralph, J. L., 37
Ramsey, D., 9, 22
Ranta, M., 269, 281
Rapp, N. A., 56
Rappaport, J., 36, 56
Rascon, A., Jr., 129, 139
Rausch, S. P., 42, 55
Rawlings, E., 179, 182, 199, 202, 214
Ray, R. S., 89, 118
Redd, W. H., 37
Redl, F., 258, 261
Redl, R., 89, 106, 118
Redner, R., 24, 26, 31, 36
Reeves, A. G., 61, 73
Reid, J. B., 37, 112, 118
Reid, J. C., 247, 261
Reid, J. G., 91, 92, 118
Reilly, T. F., 15, 20, 140, 158
Reitan, R. M., 68, 73
Reith, H. S., 9, 21
Remes, P., 267, 268, 279
Remmers, H. H., 205, 217
Reppucci, N. D., 136, 139
Resnick, H. S., 156, 159
Rhodes, W. C., 36, 56, 145, 159
Richette, L. A., 25, 36
Ridley, S. D., 56
Rimm, D. C., 18, 21
Robbins, D. M., 247, 261
Roberts, D., 178, 183, 185, 186, 215
Roberts, T. K., 39, 55
Robin, A. L., 100, 118
Robins, A. J., 247, 261
Robins, L. N., 161, 176
Robinson, J. P., 185, 186, 217
Robinson, M. R., 36
Rodin, E. A., 61, 73
Roeser, T. D., 122, 126, 137
Rogers, C. R., 89, 118
Rogosa, D., 189, 217
Romig, D. A., 42, 56
Romig, V. A., 24, 36
Rose, T. L., 13, 20
Rosekrans, M. A., 199, 218
Rosemier, R. A., 5, 20
Rosenthal, D., 63, 73, 163, 176
Rosenthal, R., 27, 36, 91, 115
Ross, D., 179, 181, 199, 200, 214
Ross, S. A., 179, 181, 199, 200, 214
Roth, R., 6, 21
Rotter, J. R., 108, 118
Rowbotham, B. M., 68, 71
Rubel, R. J., 121, 139

Rubens, W. S., 186, 191, 193, 208, 210, 217
Rubin, D., 63, 73
Rubinstein, E. A., 179, 215, 217, 218
Rudisill, D., 57
Ruesch, J., 108, 118
Rule, B. G., 39, 56
Rulo, J. H., 161, 175
Rushton, J. P., 198, 218
Rutherford, R. B., Jr., 13, 15, 22
Rutter, M., 145, 158, 161, 176, 247, 261
Ruttiger, K. F., 69, 73
Rychiak, J. F., 199, 218

Sabatino, D. A., 5, 7, 10, 13, 22
Sacks, M., 82, 88
Sagan, C., 59, 73
Samenow, S., 75, 79, 85, 88
Sanchez, J., 141, 152
Sandler, I. N., 148, 159
Sarason, B. R., 100, 118
Sarason, I. G., 37, 100, 118
Sarason, S. B., 137, 139
Sarri, R. C., 5, 7, 9, 10, 13, 22
Saul, J., 26, 36
Saunders, J. T., 136, 139
Scarpitti, F., 24, 36, 39, 55
Schaefer, W. K., 25, 36
Schafer, W. E., 121, 139
Schalling, D., 67, 72, 73
Schbundy, D. G., 91, 115
Schinke, S. P., 107, 118
Schloss, P. J., 6, 9, 22
Schmid, R., 10, 22
Schmidt, F., 25, 27, 32, 35, 40, 42, 44, 55
Schulman, B. H., 110, 115
Schulsinger, F., 63, 73, 163, 176
Schulsinger, R., 163, 176
Schultz, J. L., 24, 36
Schultz, J. L., 24, 36
Schur, E., 41, 56
Schure, M. B., 25, 36
Schwartz, F., 199, 216
Schwartz, S. L., 15, 22
Schwitzgebel, R. L., 106, 118
Scoville, W. B., 61, 73
Sears, R., 39, 55
Sechrest, L. B., 24, 31, 36, 106, 108, 110, 115, 118
Sedlak, R. A., 6, 9, 22
Segall, L. J., 63, 71
Seidman, E., 26, 31, 35, 36, 56
Selderstrom, J., 154, 159
Selz, M., 68, 73

Serafetinides, E. A., 61, 65, 73
Sester, H., 275, 281
Severy, L. J., 57
Shah, S. A., 63, 73
Shanok, H. P. H., 66, 72
Shanok, S. S., 68, 72, 247, 261
Shapland, J. M., 263, 281
Sheard, M. H., 63, 71
Shoemaker, M. E., 101, 118
Shore, E., 110, 118
Shotland, R. L., 185, 217
Shure, M. B., 161, 176
Siegal, A. W., 68, 70
Sigel, I. E., 161, 176
Silber, D. E., 75, 88
Simpson, B. F., 16, 19
Sindelar, P. T., 4, 22
Singer, R. D., 185, 216
Sipilä, J., 263, 266, 281
Sizer, T. R., 19, 22
Skinner, J. C., 63, 71
Slack, C. W., 106, 118
Slavin, D. R., 110, 118
Slavin, R. E., 2, 21
Slavson, D. R., 89, 118
Slife, B. C., 199, 218
Sloane, H. N., 37
Smigel, J., 36
Smith, C., 129, 139, 247, 261
Smith, E. C., 25, 35
Smith, J., 12, 19
Smith, M. L., 25, 27, 29, 35, 40, 42, 43, 44,
    55, 56, 180, 216
Smith, P. M., 25, 36
Smith, R., 181, 200, 218
Smythe, D. W., 205, 218
Snellman, K., 41, 42, 55
Snellman, L., 26, 36
Snyder, H. N., 160, 170, 177
Söderlind, A., 277, 279
Solomon, E., 113, 118
Solway, K. S., 39, 55
Spatz-Norton, C., 103, 118
Spellacy, F., 68, 73
Spence, A. J., 96, 101, 119
Spence, S. H., 37, 91, 101, 118, 119
Spivack, G., 25, 36, 161, 176
Sprafkin, R. J., 117
Sprafkin, R. P., 12, 18, 20, 92, 105, 107, 115
Sprinthall, N. A., 6, 7, 22
Sprinthall, R. C., 6, 7, 22
Sprowls, J., 42, 54

Steele, G., 185, 217
Stein, E. M., 13, 22
Stein, L. I., 153, 159
Stein, N., 104, 115
Steketee, J. P., 26, 36
Stephens, T. M., 96, 119
Stephenson, R. M., 24, 36
Stern, G. G., 104, 119
Stern, M. P., 215
Steuer, F. B., 181, 200, 218
Stevenson, I., 109, 119
Steward, M. A., 67, 72
Stipp, H. H., 186, 191, 193, 208, 210, 217
Stoking, M., 63, 73
Stone, A. R., 108, 116
Stone, J., 37
Stonner, D., 182, 184, 199, 216
Street, D. R. R., 63, 71
Strizver, C. L., 13, 22
Stuart, R. B., 25, 36, 37, 39, 56, 57
Stumphauser, J., 25, 26, 27, 33, 36
Sturge, C., 161, 177
Sutton, L. P., 25, 35
Svensson, J., 67, 72
Swap, S. M., 145, 159
Sweet, W. H., 61, 73

Takala, H., 262, 281
Tannenbaum, P. H., 179, 218
Tanner, K., 277, 281
Tapp, J. T., 56
Taylor, B., 221, 236
Taylor, J. E., 110, 116
Teevan, J. J., Jr., 185, 186, 217
Temkin, S., 122, 127, 138
Tennenbaum, D. J., 76, 88
Test, M. A., 153, 159
Tharp, R. G., 26, 36, 111, 119
Thaw, R. F., 124, 139
Thelen, M. A., 101, 119
Thomas, A., 145, 158
Thomas, M. A., 5, 7, 13, 22
Thomas, S. V., 185, 192, 194, 195, 196, 197,
    215
Thorndike, E. L., 109, 119
Thurston, J. R., 122, 126, 137
Tilli, L., 267, 279
Tinklenberg, J. R., 64, 73
Toby, J., 257, 261
Tomalesky, M., 13, 22
Topping, K. J., 3, 4, 5, 22

Touchette, P. E., 113, 117
Tramontana, M. G., 112, 119
Trief, P., 102, 119
Tringo, J. L., 2, 22
Trower, P., 96, 114
Tulkin, S., 56
Tumin, M. M., 64, 72

Udin, H., 156, 158
Ulich, K., 267, 268, 281
Underwood, B. J., 109, 119
Urban, H. B., 108, 115
Urwick, L. F., 221, 236
Uttendorfer-Marek, I., 270, 275, 281

Väänänen, J., 267, 268, 279
Vaernet, K., 61, 73
Van Avery, D., 130, 139
Vaughan, G. M., 120, 124, 132, 135, 136
Venezia, P. S., 57
Vince, P., 202, 216
Voorhees, J., 68, 69, 73
Vorrath, H., 15, 22, 80, 82, 88
Voss, H. L., 25, 35, 121, 126, 137
Vygotsky, L. S., 275, 281

Wahler, R. G., 112, 129
Walberg, H. J., 145, 159
Walder, L., 126, 138, 186, 188, 202, 209, 215, 216, 217
Walen, S. R., 9, 22
Walker, H. M., 89, 108, 119
Walker, R., 109, 119
Wall, J., 156, 159
Wall, S. A., 15, 22
Wallbrown, F. H., 127, 138
Walsmith, C. R., 91, 114
Warkentin, J., 110, 119
Warren, J. M., 110, 114
Warren, M., 85, 88
Warren, M. Q., 231, 236
Watkins, B. R., 119
Weathers, L., 38
Weeks, H. A., 80, 88
Wehr, P., 39, 55
Weichselbaum, H. F., 42, 55, 56
Weiner, L., 108, 119
Weir, T., 158
Weis, J., 154, 159
Weissberg, R. P., 161, 175
Wells, D., 10, 22
Wells, W. D., 185, 218

Wender, P. H., 108, 118, 163, 176
Wenk, E. A., 122, 139
Wenrott, M. R., 38
Werner, J. S., 38, 102, 119
Wessler, R. L., 9, 22
West, D. J., 268, 279
Wetzel, R., 26, 36, 111, 119
Whalan, P. A., 112, 116
Whalen, C., 108, 119
Wharton, J. D., 203, 204, 205, 206, 211, 216
Whitaker, C. A., 110, 119
Whitaker, J. M., 57
White, J., 130, 139
White, M., 6, 22
White, R. W., 161, 162, 163, 166, 167, 177
Whitlock, C. C., 61, 71
Wickman, E. K., 6, 22
Wietzner, R. P., 12, 13, 20
Wiggins, S. E., 9, 22
Wilks, J., 24, 35
William, J., 40, 55
Williams, D., 61, 73
Williams, H. W., 56, 61, 71
Willner, A. G., 38, 57
Wineman, D., 89, 106, 118, 258, 261
Winett, R., A., 26, 35, 36
Winkel, R., 267, 281
Winkler, R. C., 26, 36
Wishaw, I. Q., 61, 62, 72
Witkin, H. A., 63, 73
Wolberg, L. R., 108, 119
Wolcott, O., 109, 116
Wolf, M. M., 13, 21, 26, 35, 36, 37, 38, 57, 99, 117
Wolf, N. N., 102, 119
Wolfensberger, W., 248, 261
Wolff, P. H., 68, 71, 73
Wolfgang, M. E., 63, 64, 74, 160, 177
Wolfred, T. R., 37
Wood, F. H., 1, 3, 8, 11, 12, 13, 21, 22, 23
Wood, M., 110, 119
Wood, P. D., 215
Wood, R., 104, 117
Wooderson, P. C., 247, 261
Woodward, C. V., 238, 261
Woodworth, R. S., 109, 119
Worchel, S., 199, 218
Worsley, K., 154, 159
Wresinski, M. D., 56

Yeudall, L. T., 68, 69, 74
Yochelson, S., 75, 79, 85, 88

Young, I., 157
Yule, W., 161, 176

Zamora, P., 86, 88
Zax, M., 165–166, 175
Zeiss, C., 154

Zigler, D., 166, 167, 176
Zillmann, D., 179, 199, 218
Zimmerman, D., 103, 119
Zimring, F., 40, 56
Zionts, P., 15, 23
Zlatchin, C., 199, 215
Zwier, G., 120, 124, 132, 135, 136, 139

Subject Index

Achenbach Child Behavior Checklist, 169
Aggression, 39
  animal studies, 59–60
  neurological correlates of youth violence,
    63–70
  neurophysiological correlates in humans,
    61–63
  See also Violence
Alcohol, effects on aggression, 61, 62
Antiandrogen, as aggression intervention, 62
Anticonvulsants, as aggression intervention,
  62
Antidepressants, as aggression intervention, 62
Antipsychotic medication, as aggression
  intervention, 62
Austria, and youth violence, 265
AWARE: Activities for Social Development,
  96

Behavior
  and school violence, 123–124
  social, 12–15
Brain lesions, effects on aggression, 61–63

Caseworkers, role in treatment, 26
Chain-of-Command theory, 222
Character Education Movement, 90
Child Welfare Reform Act, 221
Children, as underachievers, 43–44
Children's Social Desirability Scale, 169
Closed Adolescent Treatment Center, 76, 78–
  79
Combined Social Competence Inventory, 170,
  171
Community
  and developmental theory, 222–224

programs as a formal support service, 152–
  154
  as a therapeutic concept, 80–82
Community Mental Health movement, 147–
  148
Competence, measurement, 169–170
Coopersmith scale, 169
Coping, 160–177
Correctional system, 76
Counseling, 15
  See also Therapy, Treatment

Delinquent behavior
  etiology, 161–166
  See also Juvenile delinquents
Developing Human Potential, 96
Directive Teaching, 96
Discipline, 85–86
Diversion, 41–57
Down syndrome, 63

Ecology
  perspective, 141–144
  of youth violence, 140–159
Education
  academic training, 15–16
  future of, 18–19
  and the handicapped student, 248–253
  program evaluation, 17–18
  program goals and objectives, 10–12
  race issue in the schools, 238–240
  research of special programs, 3–4
  role of the school, 1–2
  special, education program options, 7–9
  special, for disturbed adolescents, 1–23
  special, nature of, 2–3

Education (continued)
  staffing needs, 9–10
  student needs, 5–7
  students' rights, 240–247
  vocational training, 15–16
Education for All Handicapped Children Act,
    251–254
Electroencephalogram (EEG), abnormalities in
    delinquent populations, 61
England, and youth violence, 263, 264
Epilepsy, and aggression, 61
Expulsion, 14
  See also Suspension

Family, as an informal support service, 155
Federal Republic of Germany, and youth
    violence, 262, 263, 264, 266
Finland, and youth violence, 262, 263, 264,
    267, 268, 270, 275, 276, 277
France, and youth violence, 263, 264

Genetics, as neurological basis of violence,
    62–63
Goal Attainment Scaling (GAS), 11–12

Home, and school relationship, 273–274
Hormones
  effects on aggression, 60
  imbalance of among delinquent youth, 67
Hospital, mental, 75
House of Refuge, 40

Institutional treatment programs, 75–88
  characteristics of for violent juvenile
    offenders, 80–87
Intensive Change Sex Offenders' Program, 79
Interpersonal Communication, 96

Juvenile delinquents, 264–266
  characteristics, 263–264
  demographics, 28–33
  intervention efficacy of juvenile justice
    system, 39–57
  programs for, 219–236
Juvenile Justice System, 24–38
  administrative planning, 234
  advocacy, 233–234
  budgeting and financial aspects, 229–230
  and community developmental theory, 222–
    224
  evolution, 40–41
  information systems management, 232–233
  intervention efficacy, 39–57

personnel, 230–231
professional development, 235–236
program development, 231–232
role of Supreme Court, 24

Learning, structured, 92–102
Learning disabilities
  and legal rights, 247–248
  relationship to youth violence, 69
Life Skills Education, 96
Lithium carbonate, as aggression intervention,
    62
Lookout Mountain Treatment Center, 77–78

Michigan Association of Children's Agencies,
    227–229
Modeling, 92
Moral Education and Values Clarification
    program, 90

National Center for Juvenile Justice, 170
Neurophysiology, as basis for youth violence,
    58–74
Neurotransmitters, effects on aggression, 60

Parents, 16–17
  and child management theory, 222
  as an informal support service, 155–156
  role in treatment, 26
Peers, as an informal support service, 156–
    157
Perceived Competence Scale for Children, 169
Performance feedback, 93
Pharmacologic interventions, 62
Piers-Harris self-concept scale, 169
President's Commission on Law Enforcement
    and Administration of Justice (1967), 41–
    42
Programmed reinforcement, 111–113
Psychiatry, as a formal support service, 151–
    152
Psychological skill training, 89–119, 103–104
Psychosocial support, 146–150
Psychostimulants, as aggression intervention, 62
Public Law 94–142, 2

Reality Therapy, 85
Reform school
  as a formal support service, 152
Relationship behavior, 225–227
Relationship Enhancement, 96
Research, psychological skills training, 103–
    104

Rewards, 13
Role playing, 92–93

School
  as an informal support service, 156–157
  misbehavior and violence, 266–268
  prevention of misbehavior, 268–270
School violence, 120–139
  background, 121
  causes, 130–134
  environment of, 127–130
  identity of the person, 125–127
  overview of the literature, 123–130
  relationship between school and aggression,
    121–123
  research, 134–137
Scotland, and youth violence, 263
Security, with treatment, 86–87
Situational leadership, 224–227
Skills, 93–95
Social competence, 160–177
  history, 162–163
  intervention, 166–170
  invulnerability, 164
  and primary prevention, 164–166
  research, 166–170
  vulnerability research, 163
Social Skill Training, 96
Social worker, and juvenile justice system,
  49–50
Staff, team management approach, 84–85
Stimulus variability, 110
Structured Learning Skills, 107
Student, handicapped, 248–251
Support
  pyschosocial, 146–150
  services, 151–157
Supreme Court, 251–254
Suspension, 13–14, 254–259
  See also Expulsion
Sweden, and youth violence, 262, 264, 268,
  273, 274, 277
Switzerland, and youth violence, 265

Task behavior, 225–227
Teacher
  role in treatment, 26
  training, 270–273

Teaching Conflict Resolution, 96
Team management, 84–85
Television and film violence, 178–218
  effects, 203–213
  effects on adolescents and young adults,
    182–198
  effects on young children, 181–182
  evolution, 179–180
  experimental implications, 198–203
  implications, 213
Therapy, 15
  See also Counseling, Treatment
Thistletown Regional Centre, 76–77
Trainer, 106–108
Trainer-trainee relationship, 106
Training, transfer and maintenance, 93
Tranquilizers, as aggression intervention, 62
Turner syndrome, 63
Transfer, 108–110
Treatment
  behavioral approach, 25–27
  institutional programs, 75–88
  sample of studies, 27–33
  security during, 86–87
  specialized, 86
  structured programs, 82–84
  See also Counseling, Therapy

Vandalism, 120–139
Violence, 39
  characteristics, 266–268
  definition, 58
  See also Aggression, Youth Violence

Youth
  antisocial, 43–44
  maladjusted, 43–44
  troubled, 43–44
Youth Correction Authorities, 220
Youth violence
  cross-cultural perspectives, 262-281
  legal issues, 237–261
  neurological bases, 58–74
  and psychosocial support, 146–150
  types of, 64–65
  See also Aggression, Violence

About the Editors and Contributors

Vicki L. Agee, PhD, is director of the Closed Adolescent Treatment Center (CATC) in Denver, Colorado. This unit is a long-term, intensive treatment center for violent adolescents. Dr. Agee wrote the grant that started the unit in 1972. She has written a book and a number of articles and has given many addresses, workshops, and seminars on the treatment of violent adolescents. Her current focus is on such areas as: the use of the therapeutic community; treatment of the sex offender and juvenile murderer; the use of victim awareness in treatment; staff management (including staff victimization problems with assaultive youths); limit setting with violent adolescents; and staff training. Her PhD is from the University of Texas at Austin.

Steven J. Apter, PhD (Syracuse University), was Professor of Special Education in the Division of Special Education and Rehabilitation at Syracuse University. He was the author of *Troubled Children/Troubled System;* and (with J. Conoley) *Working with Troubled Children: An Introduction to Childhood Emotional Disturbance and Behavior Disorders.*

George Comstock is the S.I. Newhouse Professor of Public Communications at Syracuse University. He was science adviser and senior research coordinator for the Surgeon General's Scientific Advisory Committee on Television and Social Behavior. For several years, Comstock was a senior social psychologist at the Rand Corporation, Santa Monica, California. He is senior author of *Television and Human Behavior* (Columbia University Press) and editor of *Public Communication and Behavior,* an annual serial volume to be published by Academic Press. His research interests include the social influence of the mass media and models for synthesizing and integrating findings from diverse studies. He holds a PhD and MA from Stanford University and a BA from the University of Washington.

William S. Davidson II received his MA and PhD degrees from the University of Illinois at Urbana-Champaign. He is Professor of Psychology and Chair of the Ecological Psychology Graduate Training Program at Michigan State University. He has also directed the Kentfields Rehabilitation Project and the Adolescent Diversion Project. His research interests are in crime and delinquency, social innovation, and research methodology.

Richard A. Ellison is Associate Professor of Law at Syracuse University College of Law. In addition to his research and teaching interests in the areas of conflict resolution, and family law, he is the author of articles in the family law area.

Barbara Forsstrom-Cohen, MS (Syracuse University), is a doctoral student in the Department of Psychology, Syracuse University and is a school psychologist for the Syracuse school system. She has been involved in various research projects concerned with aggression and marital violence.

Richard J. Gable joined the National Center for Juvenile Justice staff as an Associate Fellow in May of 1976. His work experience is varied, ranging from 12 months on an Indian reservation as a VISTA volunteer to teaching at the Clinical Psychology Center, a clinic operated by the Department of Psychology at the University of Pittsburgh. In addition, Mr. Gable was a supervisor at the Pittsburgh Mental Health/Mental Retardation Center where he founded and directed an adolescent drug treatment center. Mr. Gable has collaborated on numerous Center projects and has conducted the "Pittsburgh-Buffalo Study," an investigation of judicial proceedings involving 16- and 17-year-old youth in those cities; he was also co-author of the "Positive Outcomes Study", a study of delinquency from a more positive perspective, and was director of the Social Competence Project, a study of the coping skills in a delinquent population. He was involved as a principal researcher in developing a master plan for juvenile corrections in Alaska, a comprehensive evaluation of the Michigan Office of Children and Youth Services, and a multi-county detention planning study in Arkansas.

Leah K. Gensheimer completed her Bachelor of Science in criminal justice in 1979, after which she worked as a counselor for a diversion program in New Haven, CT. In 1982 she received a Master of Arts from Adelphi University in Applied Behavioral Psychology. Currently she is pursuing a doctorate degree at Michigan State University and is employed as a training supervisor for the MSU Adolescent Diversion Project. Her areas of interests include community-behavioral interventions, prevention of juvenile delinquency, social skills training of adolescents, and child care issues.

Barry Glick received his PhD from Syracuse University in 1972. Trained as a Counseling Psychologist, Dr. Glick has devoted his professional career to the development of policies, programs, and services for adolescents. His specialization is in Juvenile Delinquency as well as the emotionally disturbed adolescent. Dr. Glick has worked both in private child care agencies and in state government. He has held positions as child care worker, psychologist, administrator, and manager. He currently directs a facility for Juvenile Delinquent boys where he continues his research activities, publishing of journal articles, staff training and program development. Dr. Glick is certified by the National Board of Certified Counselors and holds membership in a number of professional organizations.

Arnold P. Goldstein, PhD (Pennsylvania State University, 1959), joined the Clinical Psychology section of Syracuse University's Psychology Department in 1963, and both taught there and directed its Psychotherapy Center until 1980. In 1981, he founded the Center for Research on Aggression, which he currently directs, and in 1985 moved to Syracuse University's Division of Special Education. Professor Goldstein has a career-long interest, as both researcher and practitioner, in difficult-to-reach clients. Since 1980, his main research and psychoeducational focus has been incarcerated juvenile offenders and child abusing parents. He is the developer of Structured Learning, a psychoeducational program and curriculum designed to teach prosocial behaviors to chronically antisocial persons. Professor Goldstein's books included *Structured Learning Therapy: Toward a Psychotherapy for the Poor, Skill Training for Community Living, Skillstreaming the Adolescent, School Violence, Aggress-Less, Police Crisis Intervention, Hostage, Prevention and Control of Aggression, Aggression in Global Perspective,* and *In Response to Aggression.*

Rand Gottschalk was born in New York City in 1955. He graduated from Southern Connecticut State University in 1978 with a major in psychology. He received a MA degree from Michigan State University in 1982 in Industrial/Organizational Psychology. Currently he is working on his PhD in Industrial/Organizational Psychology at Michigan State University. His research interests include methodological problems with meta-analysis, organizational innovational processes, and implicit leadership theory.

Berj Harootunian, PhD (University of Pennsylvania), is Professor of Education and Director of the Division for the Study of Teaching at Syracuse University. Among his publications are *The Structure of Teaching, Differences Between Good and Poor Problem Solvers; and Teachers' Conceptions of Their Own Success.*

Lawrence J. Lewandowski, PhD (University of Michigan), has been on the faculty in the Department of Psychology, Syracuse University since 1980. Dr. Lewandowski has written extensively about the neuropsychological functioning of various types of children and youths. He runs a clinical neuropsychology lab and teaches graduate courses on neuropsychology.

Jeffrey P. Mayer was born in New York City in 1955. He received the MA degree in psychology from Michigan State University, East Lansing, Michigan, in 1983. From 1979 to 1981, he was director of the Community Energy Conservation Education Project. From 1981 to 1983, he was a Research Associate at the Center for Innovation Research at MSU. Currently, he is a doctoral candidate in psychology at MSU. His current research interests concern program evaluation application and methods in public health, criminal justice, and organizational change.

Cathy A. Propper, MA in School Psychology, Syracuse University. She currently is pursuing her doctorate in School Psychology while working as a school psychologist in the Syracuse City School District. Ms. Propper completed her undergraduate work at Wellesley College and assumed a variety of positions in the mental health system of Boston before embarking on her graduate studies.

Lea Pulkkinen, Professor of psychology, Head of the Department of Psychology, University of Jyväskylä, Finland. She has recently completed a longitudinal study of social development from the age of 8 to 20. Publications based on this material include two books in Finnish (1977, 1984), two monographs (1969, 1982), and several articles in, for example, *Aggression and Behavior Change* (1977, edited by Feshbach and Fraczek), *Multidisciplinary Approaches to Aggression Research* (1981, edited by Brain and Denton), *Lifespan Development and Behavior,* vol. 4 (1982, edited by Baltes and Brim), *Aggression in Global Perspective* (1983, edited by Goldstein and Segall), *Journal of Youth and Adolescence,* 1983, and *Aggressive Behavior,* 1984. Her recent research interests are oriented toward an interdisciplinary approach to the development of youthful life styles in different ecological settings in collaboration with Soviet (Estonian) researchers.

Marketta Saastamoinen, MA, a research assistant at the University of Jyväskylä. At present she works as a clinical psychologist in Finland.

Frank H. Wood is Professor, Special Education Program, Department of Psychoeducational Studies, University of Minnesota, Minneapolis. From 1975 to 1979, he directed the Advanced Institute for Trainers of Teachers for Seriously Emotionally Disturbed Children and Youth. He is the author of numerous journal articles, monographs, and (with R. McDowell and G. Adamson) *Teaching Emotionally Disturbed Children.*

Pergamon General Psychology Series

Editors: Arnold P. Goldstein, Syracuse University
Leonard Krasner, SUNY at Stony Brook

Vol. 1.   WOLPE—*The Practice of Behavior Therapy, Third Edition*
Vol. 2.   MAGOON et al.—*Mental Health Counselors at Work*
Vol. 3.   McDANIEL—*Physical Disability and Human Behavior, Second Edition*
Vol. 4.   KAPLAN et al.—*The Structural Approach in Psychological Testing*
Vol. 5.   LaFAUCI & RICHTER—*Team Teaching at the College Level*
Vol. 6.   PEPINSKY et al.—*People and Information*
Vol. 7.   SIEGMAN & POPE—*Studies in Dyadic Communication*
Vol. 8.   JOHNSON—*Existential Man: The Challenge of Psychotherapy*
Vol. 9.   TAYLOR—*Climate for Creativity*
Vol. 10. RICKARD—*Behavioral Intervention in Human Problems*
Vol. 14. GOLDSTEIN—*Psychotherapeutic Attraction*
Vol. 15. HALPERN—*Survival: Black/White*
Vol. 16. SALZINGER & FELDMAN—*Studies in Verbal Behavior: An Empirical Approach*
Vol. 17. ADAMS & BOARDMAN—*Advances in Experimental Clinical Psychology*
Vol. 18. ZILLER—*The Social Self*
Vol. 19. LIBERMAN—*A Guide to Behavioral Analysis and Therapy*
Vol. 22. PEPINSKY & PATTON—*The Psychological Experiment: A Practical Accomplishment*
Vol. 23. YOUNG—*New Sources of Self*
Vol. 24. WATSON—*Child Behavior Modification: A Manual for Teachers, Nurses and Parents*
Vol. 25. NEWBOLD—*The Psychiatric Programming of People: Neo-Behavioral Orthomolecular Psychiatry*
Vol. 26. ROSSI—*Dreams and the Growth of Personality: Expanding Awareness in Psychotherapy*
Vol. 27. O'LEARY & O'LEARY—*Classroom Management: The Successful Use of Behavior Modification, Second Edition*
Vol. 28. FELDMAN—*College and Student: Selected Readings in the Social Psychology of Higher Education*
Vol. 29. ASHEM & POSER—*Adaptive Learning: Behavior Modification with Children*
Vol. 30. BURCK et al.—*Counseling and Accountability: Methods and Critique*
Vol. 31. FREDERIKSEN et al.—*Prediction of Organizational Behavior*
Vol. 32. CATTELL—*A New Morality from Science: Beyondism*
Vol. 33. WEINER—*Personality: The Human Potential*
Vol. 34. LIEBERT, SPRAFKIN & DAVIDSON—*The Early Window: Effects of Television on Children and Youth, Second Edition*
Vol. 35. COHEN et al.—*Psych City: A Simulated Community*
Vol. 36. GRAZIANO—*Child Without Tomorrow*
Vol. 37. MORRIS—*Perspectives in Abnormal Behavior*
Vol. 38. BALLER—*Bed Wetting: Origins and Treatment*
Vol. 40. KAHN, CAMERON & GIFFEN—*Methods and Evaluation in Clinical and Counseling Psychology*
Vol. 41. SEGALL—*Human Behavior and Public Policy: A Political Psychology*
Vol. 42. FAIRWEATHER et al.—*Creating Change in Mental Health Organizations*

Vol. 43. KATZ & ZLUTNICK—*Behavior Therapy and Health Care: Principles and Applications*

Vol. 44. EVANS & CLAIBORN—*Mental Health Issues and the Urban Poor*

Vol. 46. BARBER, SPANOS & CHAVES—*Hypnosis, Imagination and Human Potentialities*

Vol. 47. POPE—*The Mental Health Interview: Research and Application*

Vol. 48. PELTON—*The Psychology of Nonviolence*

Vol. 49. COLBY—*Artificial Paranoia—A Computer Simulation of Paranoid Processes*

Vol. 50. GELFAND & HARTMANN—*Child Behavior Analysis and Therapy, Second Edition*

Vol. 51. WOLPE—*Theme and Variations: A Behavior Therapy Casebook*

Vol. 52. KANFER & GOLDSTEIN—*Helping People Change: A Textbook of Methods, Third Edition*

Vol. 53. DANZIGER—*Interpersonal Communication*

Vol. 54. KATZ—*Towards the Elimination of Racism*

Vol. 55. GOLDSTEIN & STEIN—*Prescriptive Psychotherapies*

Vol. 56. BARLOW & HERSEN—*Single-Case Experimental Designs: Strategies for Studying Behavior Changes, Second Edition*

Vol. 57. MONAHAN—*Community Mental Health and the Criminal Justice System*

Vol. 58. WAHLER, HOUSE & STAMBAUGH—*Ecological Assessment of Child Problem Behavior: A Clinical Package for Home, School and Institutional Settings*

Vol. 59. MAGARO—*The Construction of Madness: Emerging Conceptions and Interventions into the Psychotic Process*

Vol. 60. MILLER—*Behavioral Treatment of Alcoholism*

Vol. 61. FOREYT—*Behavioral Treatments of Obesity*

Vol. 62. WANDERSMAN, POPPEN & RICKS—*Humanism and Behaviorism: Dialogue and Growth*

Vol. 63. NIETZEL, WINETT, MACDONALD & DAVIDSON—*Behavioral Approaches to Community Psychology*

Vol. 64. FISHER & GOCHROS--*Handbook of Behavior Therapy with Sexual Problems. Vol. I: General Procedures. Vol. II: Approaches to Specific Problems*

Vol. 65. HERSEN & BELLACK—*Behavioral Assessment: A Practical Handbook, Second Edition*

Vol. 66. LEFKOWITZ, ERON, WALDER & HUESMANN—*Growing Up To Be Violent: A Longitudinal Study of the Development of Aggression*

Vol. 67. BARBER—*Pitfalls in Human Research: Ten Pivotal Points*

Vol. 68. SILVERMAN—*The Human Subject in the Psychological Laboratory*

Vol. 69. FAIRWEATHER & TORNATZKY—*Experimental Methods for Social Policy Research*

Vol. 70. GURMAN & RAZIN—*Effective Psychotherapy: A Handbook of Research*

Vol. 71. MOSES & BYHAM—*Applying the Assessment Center Method*

Vol. 72. GOLDSTEIN—*Prescriptions for Child Mental Health and Education*

Vol. 73. KEAT—*Multimodal Therapy with Children*

Vol. 74. SHERMAN—*Personality: Inquiry & Application*

Vol. 75. GATCHEL & PRICE—*Clinical Applications of Biofeedback: Appraisal and Status*

Vol. 76. CATALANO—*Health, Behavior and the Community: An Ecological Perspective*

Vol. 77. NIETZEL—*Crime and Its Modification: A Social Learning Perspective*

Vol. 78.   GOLDSTEIN, HOYER & MONTI—*Police and the Elderly*
Vol. 79.   MIRON & GOLDSTEIN—*Hostage*
Vol. 80.   GOLDSTEIN et al.—*Police Crisis Intervention*
Vol. 81.   UPPER & CAUTELA—*Covert Conditioning*
Vol. 82.   MORELL—*Program Evaluation in Social Research*
Vol. 83.   TEGER—*Too Much Invested to Quit*
Vol. 84.   MONJAN & GASSNER—*Critical Issues in Competency-Based Education*
Vol. 85.   KRASNER—*Environmental Design and Human Behavior: A Psychology of the Individual in Society*
Vol. 86.   TAMIR—*Communication and the Aging Process: Interaction Throughout the Life Cycle*
Vol. 87.   WEBSTER, KONSTANTAREAS, OXMAN & MACK—*Autism: New Directions in Research and Education*
Vol. 88.   TRIESCHMANN—*Spinal Cord Injuries: Psychological, Social and Vocational Adjustment*
Vol. 89.   CARTLEDGE & MILBURN—*Teaching Social Skills to Children: Innovative Approaches, Second Edition*
Vol. 90.   SARBIN & MANCUSO—*Schizophrenia—Medical Diagnosis or Moral Verdict?*
Vol. 91.   RATHJEN & FOREYT—*Social Competence: Interventions for Children and Adults*
Vol. 92.   VAN DE RIET, KORB & GORRELL—*Gestalt Therapy: An Introduction*
Vol. 93.   MARSELLA & PEDERSEN—*Cross-Cultural Counseling and Psychotherapy*
Vol. 94.   BRISLIN—*Cross-Cultural Encounters: Face-to-Face Interaction*
Vol. 95.   SCHWARTZ & JOHNSON—*Psychopathology of Childhood: A Clinical-Experimental Approach, Second Edition*
Vol. 96.   HEILBRUN—*Human Sex-Role Behavior*
Vol. 97.   DAVIDSON, KOCH, LEWIS, WRESINSKI—*Evaluation Strategies in Criminal Justice*
Vol. 98.   GOLDSTEIN, CARR, DAVIDSON, WEHR—*In Response to Aggression: Methods of Control and Prosocial Alternatives*
Vol. 99.   GOLDSTEIN—*Psychological Skill Training: The Structured Learning Technique*
Vol. 100. WALKER—*Clinical Practice of Psychology: A Guide for Mental Health Professionals*
Vol. 101. ANCHIN & KIESLER—*Handbook of Interpersonal Psychotherapy*
Vol. 102. GELLER, WINETT EVERETT—*Preserving the Environment: New Strategies for Behavior Change*
Vol. 103. JENKINS—*The Psychology of the Afro-American: A Humanistic Approach*
Vol. 104. APTER—*Troubled Children/Troubled Systems*
Vol. 105. BRENNER—*The Effective Psychotherapist: Conclusions from Practice and Research*
Vol. 106. KAROLY & KANFER—*Self-Management and Behavior Change: From Theory to Practice*
Vol. 107. O'BRIEN, DICKINSON, ROSOW—*Industrial Behavior Modification: A Management Handbook*
Vol. 108. AMABILE & STUBBS—*Psychological Research in the Classroom: Issues for Educators and Researchers*
Vol. 109. WARREN—*Auditory Perception: A New Synthesis*

Vol. 110. DiMATTEO & DiNICOLA—*Achieving Patient Compliance: the Psychology of the Medical Practitioner's Role*

Vol. 111. CONOLEY & CONOLEY—*School Consultation: A Guide to Practice and Training*

Vol. 112. PAPAJOHN—*Intensive Behavior Therapy: The Behavioral Treatment of Complex Emotional Disorders*

Vol. 113. KAROLY, STEFFEN, O'GRADY—*Child Health Psychology: Concepts and Issues*

Vol. 114. MORRIS & KRATOCHWILL—*Treating Children's Fears and Phobias: A Behavioral Approach*

Vol. 115. GOLDSTEIN & SEGALL—*Aggression in Global Perspective*

Vol. 116. LANDIS & BRISLIN—*Handbook of Intercultural Training*

Vol. 117. FARBER—*Stress and Burnout in the Human Service Professions*

Vol. 118. BEUTLER—*Eclectic Psychotherapy: A Systematic Approach*

Vol. 119. HARRIS—*Families of the Developmentally Disabled: A Guide to Behavioral Interventions*

Vol. 120. HERSEN, KAZDIN, BELLACK—*The Clinical Psychology Handbook*

Vol. 121. MATSON & MULICK—*Handbook of Mental Retardation*

Vol. 122. FELNER, JASON, MORITSUGU, FARBER—*Preventive Psychology: Theory Research and Practice*

Vol. 123. CENTER FOR RESEARCH ON AGGRESSION—*Prevention and Control of Aggression*

Vol. 124. MORRIS & KRATOCHWILL—*The Practice of Child Therapy*

Vol. 125. VARNI—*Clinical Behavioral Pediatrics: An Interdisciplinary Biobehavioral Approach*

Vol. 126. RAMIREZ—*Psychology of the Americas: Mestizo Perspectives on Personality and Mental Health*

Vol. 127. LEWINSOHN & TERI—*Clinical Geropsychology: New Directions in Assessment and Treatment*

Vol. 128. BARLOW, HAYES, NELSON—*The Scientist Practitioner: Research and Accountability in Clinical and Educational Settings*

Vol. 129. OLLENDICK & HERSEN—*Child Behavioral Assessment: Principles and Procedures*

Vol. 130. BELLACK & HERSEN—*Research Methods in Clinical Psychology*

Vol. 131. GOLDSTEIN & HERSEN—*Handbook of Psychological Assessment*

Vol. 132. BELLACK & HERSEN—*Dictionary of Behavior Therapy Techniques*

Vol. 133. COOK—*Psychological Androgyny*

Vol. 134. DREW & HARDMAN—*Designing and Conducting Behavioral Research*

Vol. 135. APTER & GOLDSTEIN—*Youth Violence: Programs and Prospects*

Vol. 136. HOLZMAN & TURK—*Pain Management: A Handbook of Psychological Treatment Approaches*

Vol. 137. MORRIS & BLATT—*Special Education: Research and Trends*

Vol. 138. JOHNSON, RASBURY, SIEGEL—*Approaches to Child Treatment: Introduction to Theory, Research and Practice*

Vol. 139. RYBASH, HOYER & ROODIN—*Adult Cognition and Aging: Developmental Changes in Processing, Thinking and Knowing*

Vol. 140. WIELKIEWICZ—*Behavior Management in the Schools: Principles and Procedures*